ARCHIVAL RETURNS

Indigenous Music of Australia

Myfany Turpin, Series Editor

The many forms of Australia's Indigenous music have ancient roots, huge diversity and global reach. The Indigenous Music of Australia series aims to stimulate discussion and development of the field of Australian Indigenous music (including Aboriginal and Torres Strait Islander music) in both subject matter and approach.

Archival Returns: Central Australia and Beyond
Edited by Linda Barwick, Jennifer Green, and Petronella Vaarzon-Morel

For the Sake of a Song: Wangga Songmen and Their Repertories
Allan Marett, Linda Barwick, and Lysbeth Ford

Reflections and Voices: Exploring the Music of Yothu Yindi with Mandawuy Yunupingu
Aaron Corn

Songs from the Stations: Wajarra as Sung by Ronnie Wavehill Wirrpnga, Topsy Dodd Ngarnjal and Dandy Danbayarri at Kalkaringi
Myfany Turpin and Felicity Meakins

Wurrurrumi Kun-Borrk: Songs from Western Arnhem Land
Kevin Djimar

ARCHIVAL RETURNS

Central Australia and Beyond

Edited by Linda Barwick, Jennifer Green, and Petronella Vaarzon-Morel

SYDNEY UNIVERSITY PRESS

Print edition published 2020 by Sydney University Press
Fisher Library F03, University of Sydney NSW 2006, Australia
Email: sup.info@sydney.edu.au
sydneyuniversitypress.com.au

Published online 2019 as Special Publication No. 18 of *Language Documentation & Conservation*
Language Documentation & Conservation, Department of Linguistics
University of Hawai'i at Mānoa
Moore Hall 569
1890 East-West Road Honolulu, Hawai'i 96822 USA
http://nflrc.hawaii.edu/ldc

University of Hawai'i Press
2840 Kolowalu Street Honolulu,
Hawai'i 96822-1888 USA

Cover design based on a painting © April Campbell Pengart,
Ti Tree, March 2019, acrylic on canvas, 30 cm x 40 cm

Text accompanying cover painting:

Painting nhenh panth-akert thang mpwarek. Panth nhenh anem tyeperr impen anwantherr-henh arnang maparl arntwerrkem. Angkwey tyerrty mapel angernetyart arnang map panthelayel. Angkwey inang intey-warn akwernetyart arnang anantherr-henh map arntar-iletyek. Panth nhenh rlterrk anem, arnang map arntar-ilenhilenh, archive-el arntwerrkem-artek arnang map anantherr-henh. Arlkeny panthelayel anem amer map-akert thwen angkety map-akert. Merarrp merarrpel angetyam inehenh arnang map panth angerr nhenh-warn arntwerrketyek.

I made this painting of a coolamon. This coolamon holds our important knowledge. In the old days Indigenous people used to carry things around in coolamons. They used to store their important things in caves to look after them and keep them safe. This coolamon is strong and is used for looking after things, just like archives hold our knowledge. The designs on the coolamon represent the landscape of the land and the languages. The circles represent all the communities that bring their cultural materials to the 'big coolamon' for safekeeping.

April Campbell Pengart

A catalogue record for this book is available from the National Library of Australia.

ISBN (print): 9781743326725
ISBN (PDF): 9780997329575
http://hdl.handle.net/10125/24898

Contents

Figures

Tables

Foreword

David Ross
Central Land Council

I have worked for land rights and promoted the opportunities they afford since I joined the Central Land Council in 1979. What stands out about the men and women who fought for these rights is their unwavering commitment to land, language, and culture, in the face of generations of brutalising control over people's lives and the related domination of traditional lands. The desire of these senior cultural authorities to keep language and culture strong never wavered. They maintained culture out bush and by working with non-Aboriginal people to record songs, stories, ceremonies, and other cultural practices for future generations.

We have lost so many of our senior people. A young and fast-growing demographic combined with the stresses and forces of modern life put pressure on the reproduction of intergenerational knowledge and on cultural maintenance. Digital learning environments are becoming more prominent.

The reintegration of cultural heritage through the use of archival materials is part of a historical process of change, modification, and adaptation across the generations. More than ever before, future generations will turn to accessible digital archives (such as Ara Irititja and the Central Land Council's digital archive it spawned), which contain our tangible and intangible cultural heritage. Our heritage includes information about culturally significant places, Dreamings and people affiliated with them, songlines, ceremonies, and oral histories. Access to ethnographic material stored in archives, including photos, video, and audio recordings, is also fundamental to this.

Digital archives offer something positive for future generations. But we have to get it right. This volume offers insights into the future use and reimagining of archival materials. It looks at many aspects of cultural life: who manages digital archives, where material is stored, who looks after it, who can access it, and why access is needed are all critical questions Aboriginal people and institutions need to face and answer.

The challenges raised by distance from archives and the lack of technological infrastructure in communities, along with the complexities that come with diverse stakeholders and competing interests, demand flexible and creative solutions. Such matters, which are of concern to the Central Land Council and other representative bodies, have no easy answers.

Digital media and databases are increasingly becoming part of social and cultural learning processes. Like any archives, they need to be used to enliven place-based experiences, processes, and practices that form identities and maintain knowledge. Archival materials need to be reintegrated in communities according to cultural protocols and local contexts. Cultural knowledge is learned and earned and access to digital material should be done in the proper way.

Digital doesn't mean open and easy access. Those involved in the return and use of archival material must observe cultural protocols. People with rights to speak and make decisions about cultural heritage and property must be consulted and listened to. Levels of access and restrictions may need to be put in place so families and traditional owners can make decisions and have control. People have rights to knowledge. Bringing knowledge and archival material together is critical. Who controls them and how, who sets the conditions, and who makes decisions are all important considerations that need to be dealt with early. But let's not put up brick walls.

The essays in this book discuss these and other challenges involved in returning archival material in Central Australian and other contexts. I commend this volume and the efforts of all the authors and editors to engage with important concerns that affect current and future generations.

David Ross joined the Central Land Council in 1979, during the height of the land rights struggle. He led the CLC from 1999 until his retirement in 2019.

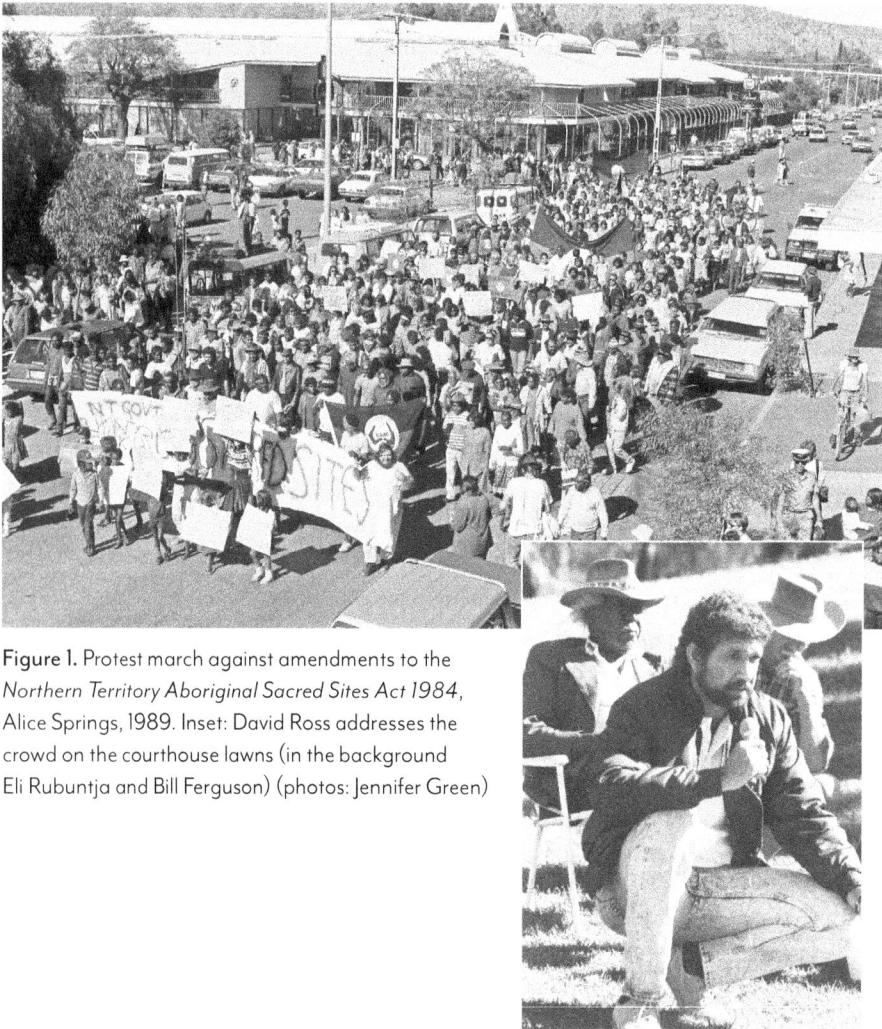

Figure 1. Protest march against amendments to the *Northern Territory Aboriginal Sacred Sites Act 1984*, Alice Springs, 1989. Inset: David Ross addresses the crowd on the courthouse lawns (in the background Eli Rubuntja and Bill Ferguson) (photos: Jennifer Green)

Editors' preface

Place-based cultural knowledge – of ceremonies, songs, stories, language, kinship, and ecology – is the thread that binds Australian Indigenous societies together. Over the last 100 years or so, records of this knowledge in many different formats – audiocassettes, photographs, films, written texts, maps, and, increasingly, digital audiovisual recordings – have been accumulating at an ever-increasing rate. Yet many recognise and lament the fact that this extensive documentary heritage of Australian Indigenous peoples is dispersed. In many cases Indigenous people who participated in the creation of the records, or their descendants, have little idea of where to find such records or how to get access to them. In addition to collections held by lands councils, native title representative bodies, and other Indigenous organisations, collections are found in a variety of university and government institutions and archives, both within Australia and outside of it. Some materials are held precariously in *ad hoc* collections, and their caretakers may be perplexed as to the best ways to ensure that the records are looked after for perpetuity. The future relevance of these documentation efforts depends on several interrelated factors: how sustainable the collections are, how well documented and described they are, and how accessible they are to the communities who own them or have rights to them. This volume focuses on strategies and practices that enable the return and circulation of documentary records of cultural heritage back to their communities of origin. While archival return may be undertaken to provide measures of social equity and justice to Indigenous Australians, the issues raised in enabling return are complex. There is no one-size-fits-all solution.

This volume presents a collection of chapters that address these issues from a variety of viewpoints. While languages and music constitute key themes in some chapters, we have taken a broad interdisciplinary view of the scope of this volume, which is co-published as a Special Publication of the open access journal *Language Documentation & Conservation* (University of Hawai'i Press) and within the Indigenous Music of Australia series of Sydney University Press. The contributors include linguists, musicologists, anthropologists, artists, lawyers, archivists, Indigenous cultural practitioners, and activists. Each brings to the volume particular disciplinary perspectives that, when taken together, give nuanced and varied views of the issues at stake. Some are primarily concerned with intercultural relations that emerge in the processes of returns; some with changing attitudes to records of the past; some with designing and testing new technologies on the ground in communities; some with how to mobilise old records of language and song to enrich language revitalisation projects; and some with ways to transform old records into other forms, including books and pedagogical materials for use in school classrooms. It is significant that several of the chapters in the volume are written by Indigenous people who are multiply engaged as both contributors to, and end users of, archives. They have firsthand experience of the conundrums and complexities that arise in trying to access archives, but also a clear vision of the benefits to their communities in doing so.

The volume grew out of an Australian Research Council Linkage project designed to reinvigorate the latent social power of research collections of Central Australian cultural knowledge by reintegrating them within the places and communities from which they originally emanated. As discussed in many of the contributions to this volume, such reintegration involves much more than simply obtaining copies of collections and lodging them in local repositories or returning materials to individuals on USB sticks. Navigating this complex terrain requires attention not only to the variable capacities of communities in terms of infrastructure and digital access, but also to the fact that attitudes to cultural knowledge and its transmission are constantly in flux.

Initially the focus of the volume was on Central Australia, and in particular the Central Land Council area, but the scope has broadened to include several contributions from beyond this region. The chapters are ordered roughly in an arc that begins in Arrernte country in Mparntwe (Alice Springs), where the main office of the Central Land Council is located, heads north through the Northern Territory as far as the Daly River region, back through parts of the Western Australian deserts and finally to Noongar country in the southwest corner of Western Australia (see Figure 1).

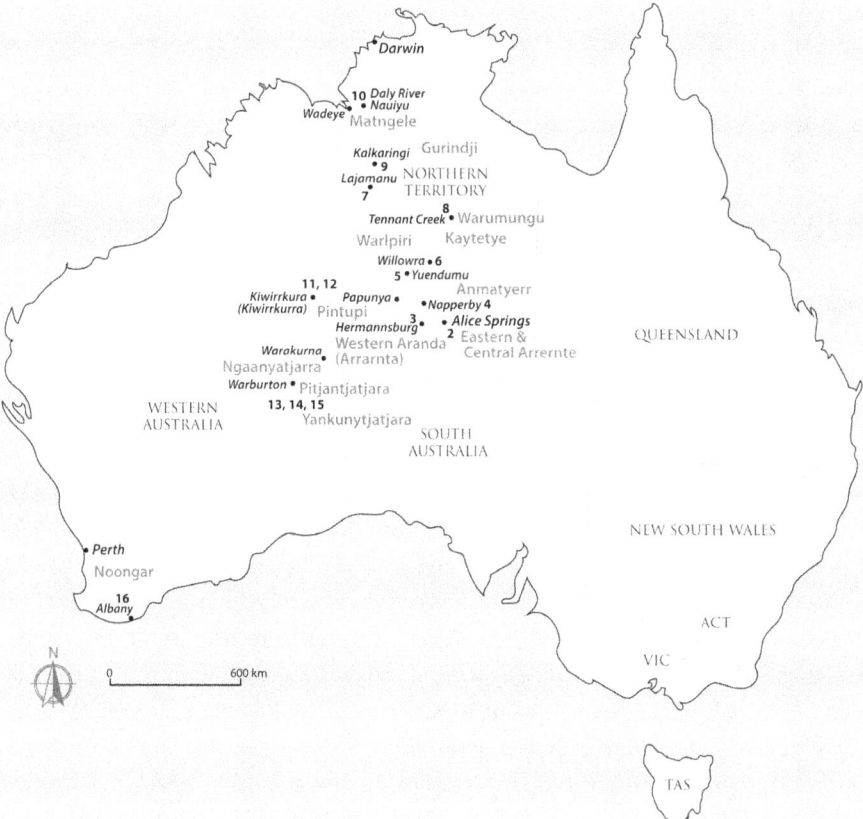

Figure 1. Map showing some languages – and the ordering of chapters in this volume (numbered) (map: Jennifer Green)

The chapters

Chapter 1, *Conundrums and consequences: Doing digital archival returns in Australia* (Barwick, Green, Vaarzon-Morel & Zissermann), takes a broad view of the social, political, and technical issues involved in negotiating returns. These questions are perforce framed by ethical and legal questions about access, competing ideas of ownership, and shifting community protocols surrounding rights of access to and the dissemination of cultural information. While accepting that the issues raised are seldom neutral and often complex, the chapter also argues for the power that culturally appropriate mobilisation of archival materials can have for inheritors of the knowledge they embody.

Chapter 2, *Deciphering Arrernte archives: The intermingling of textual and living knowledge* (Gibson, Angeles & Liddle), is an edited interview with two Arrernte men, Shaun Angeles and Joel Liddle, who discuss their deep and varied interests in records and the archives that contain them. Both are interested in harnessing the potential of archival material as a means of assisting in Arrernte language and cultural transmission. They explore some of the issues they encounter as they work through archives, the challenges of variant orthographies, the limitations of conventional cataloguing requirements, and the importance of reading archival texts in ways that see them emplaced and tested against the knowledge of elders. The chapter concludes with a discussion about the role of digital technologies in the future dissemination of cultural materials.

Orthography as a particular site of cultural contestation or as the pivot of a 'predicament' is also centre stage in Chapter 3, *Reflections on the preparation and delivery of Carl Strehlow's heritage dictionary (1909) to the Western Aranda people* (Kenny). Kenny discusses the difficulties she encountered when bringing into the public domain the Aranda, German, Loritja [Luritja], and Dieri dictionary manuscript compiled by Lutheran missionary Carl Strehlow in 1909, and the associated politics of knowledge and ownership involved in the process.

In Chapter 4, *Returning recordings of songs that persist: The Anmatyerr traditions of* akiw *and* anmanty, Gibson reflects upon the fieldwork experience of returning archival song recordings to Anmatyerr-speaking communities. Digitisation has made the return of recordings made by researchers in the past far more achievable than ever before. This technological advance, combined with the ethical and political imperative towards decolonising methodologies in Indigenous research, has resulted in considerable interest in ensuring that recordings of cultural value be returned to Indigenous communities. The account highlights the relational properties of song and its connections to people and place, and provides important insights into how these communities perceive the archiving and preservation of this material.

Three chapters deal with issues of archival access and return in Warlpiri country. Chapter 5, *Incorporating archival cultural heritage materials into contemporary Warlpiri women's* yawulyu *spaces* (Curran), looks at women's ceremonial practice of *yawulyu*, and the ways in which Warlpiri women engage with archival cultural heritage materials and incorporate them into present-day performance contexts. Case studies, including the production of songbooks, dance camps, and a community arts performance, illustrate that where there is engagement with legacy materials knowledgeable Indigenous people must take the lead, and they must be properly supported as part of the repatriation process.

Chapter 6, *Enlivening people and country: The Lander Warlpiri cultural mapping project* (Vaarzon-Morel & Kelly), presents a case study of a cultural mapping project directed by Lander Warlpiri people in Central Australia with the support of the Central Land Council. The project arose from concern over aspects of the changing lifeworld of younger people, and the increasingly circumscribed opportunities for them to acquire the embodied place-based knowledge and experiences that are regarded as foundational to local identity, social interrelationships, and cultural continuity. The project aimed to revitalise cultural knowledge through the intergenerational engagement of family groups in country visits and mapping activities, in concert with the performance of stories, song, and rituals. This process was augmented by ethnographic information derived from archival and other sources.

Chapter 7, the final Warlpiri contribution, *(Re)turning research into pedagogical practice: A case study of translational language research in Warlpiri* (O'Shannessy, Disbray, Martin & Macdonald), describes a process whereby methods and materials collected for language documentation research have been returned to speakers in communities through the implementation of professional development activities for Warlpiri educators in bilingual education programs. The focus is on the documentation of children's speech that took place in four Warlpiri communities in 2010. The materials were returned to the Warlpiri community and utilised in an active cycle of locally focused professional learning activities.

Chapter 8, *"The songline is alive in Mukurtu": Return, reuse, and respect* (Christen), examines the return, reuse, and repositioning of Indigenous archival materials, specifically within the Warumungu community in Central Australia. These practices of return have been spurred by decolonisation and reconciliation movements globally, and at the same time catalysed by new technologies. Cultural materials in new digital formats are not just returned, but through the process are reinvented, reused, and reimagined in kin-based and place-based networks. Examining the creation, use, and development of Mukurtu CMS, this article examines the implications for digital return as a decolonising strategy.

Chapter 9, *"For the children ...": Aboriginal Australia, cultural access, and archival obligation* (Croft, Toussaint, Meakins & McConvell) details two interrelated stories. The first is a moving personal account by Brenda L Croft about constructive archival management and access and her discovery of images of her grandmother. The second, contrasting example is about the consequences of restrictions on access to the Berndt Field Note Archive. This chapter raises crucial ethical and epistemological questions: for whom are archives created and conserved, who is obliged to care for and authorise access to them, and to whom do they belong?

Chapter 10, *Working at the interface: The Daly Languages Project* (Nordlinger, Green & Hurst), discusses the goals and outcomes of the Daly Languages Project, which has developed website landing pages for all of the languages of the Daly region of northern Australia. The chapter discusses each step in the design of the website landing pages and advises readers on how they can access and adapt the open-source framework for their own purposes.

Five chapters deal with different aspects of archival processes in the Western Desert. The first, Chapter 11, *"We never had any photos of my family": Archival return, film, and a personal history* (Myers & Stefanoff), is a conversation about processes behind the scenes of the acclaimed film *Remembering Yayayi*, which emerged from a project to return raw film footage filmmaker Ian Dunlop shot at the early Pintupi outstation of Yayayi in 1974. In 2006,

Myers and Stefanoff took this material back to Kintore and Kiwirrkura. One of Myers' long-term Pintupi friends, Marlene Spencer Nampitjinpa, provided a moving personal commentary on the footage, and this is included in the documentary. Stefanoff and Myers reflect on how the repatriation project catalysed memory and produced new Pintupi community historical knowledge, particularly about outstation life, early local forms of self-determination and the transformation of lives over a 40-year period.

In Chapter 12, *Return of a travelling song:* Wanji-wanji *in the Pintupi region of Central Australia*, Turpin discusses responses to the return of recordings of Pintupi song made in 1976, with particular focus on one song, *Wanji-wanji*, which featured on the recordings. *Wanji-wanji* was once a popular song performed for entertainment across the western half of Australia. For many who heard the recordings, it was an emotional experience. Those who knew the song recalled the place and time in which they had heard it long ago. The confidence of people's responses varied depending on factors such as whether the individual knew the song, whether they had experience in using archival recordings, and whether they perceived there was community interest and support for classical Aboriginal singing practices.

Chapter 13, *Never giving up: Negotiating, culture-making, and the infinity of the archive* (Thorner, Rive, Dallwitz & Inyika), looks in detail at Ara Irititja, an archive built to manage collections of photographs and other media in remote communities in the Ngaanyatjarra, Pitjantjatjara, and Yankunytjatjara lands. The chapter focuses on specific examples of what happens when photographs enter the archive, and what emerges when photographs become available for a variety of uses that are integral to Anangu cultural reproduction and cultural futures. In particular it discusses a case study of how the archive manages instructions about what to do with representations of a person after their death.

Chapter 14, *Nura's vision: Nura's voice* (Bryce, Burke & Rive), details the processes of collaboration that brought to fruition the autobiography of Pitjantjatjara woman Nura Nungalka Ward (1942–2013). The autobiography gives an extensive ethnography of daily life for Pitjantjatjara and Yankunytjatjara families still living on their traditional lands amid the profound changes brought by the arrival of white settlers, doggers, missionaries, and the atomic bomb tests. This chapter details Nura's processes, including her use of Ara Irititja to record her knowledge and then as a source for her book, which is the most significant publication to date to be sourced through the Ara Irititja project.

Chapter 15, *i*-Tjuma: *The journey of a collection – from documentation to delivery* (Ellis, Green & Kral), follows the iterative cycle of documentation, archiving, and return of a verbal arts collection resulting from a documentation project in the Ngaanyatjarra Lands of the Western Desert. The chapter discusses cultural, ethical, and technical issues negotiated in the process, including the workflow from the archived collection in PARADISEC (Pacific and Regional Archive for Digital Sources in Endangered Cultures) to LibraryBox, a portable digital file distribution tool designed to enable local delivery of media via the LibraryBox wi-fi hotspot. The research team also held a series of community film festivals in Western Desert communities as part of their strategy of consultation and return. Their study demonstrates that delivery solutions for archival media need to be tailored to the technological capacities of particular communities. They also argue for the value of long-term engagement between research teams and the communities they work with.

The final chapter in the volume, Chapter 16, *Ever-widening circles: Consolidating and enhancing Wirlomin Noongar archival material in the community* (Bracknell & Scott), details how senior Noongar of the Wirlomin clan in the south coast region of Western Australia established an organisation to facilitate cultural and linguistic revitalisation by combining community-held knowledge with documentation and recordings repatriated from archives. This process inspired the collaborative production of six illustrated bilingual books. They faced challenges due to issues of orthography and legibility in written records; the poor quality of audio recordings; and the incomplete documentation of elicitation sessions. Because the archive is so fragmentary, community knowledge is vital in making sense of its contents. Returning archival documentation of endangered Indigenous languages to the community of origin can provide empowering opportunities for Indigenous people to control, consolidate, enhance, and share their cultural heritage while also allowing time and space for communities to recover from disempowerment and dislocation.

Notes on terminology and spelling conventions

In Australian usage, the term 'Aboriginal' is generally used to cover the Indigenous nations of mainland Australia and Tasmania (not including the Torres Strait Islands). The term 'Indigenous' may be used as an umbrella term for all of Australia's first nations, covering both Aboriginal and Torres Strait Islander cultural domains. In this volume authors may prefer either term, or use them interchangeably. We have attempted to be consistent in the use of capitalisation for terms such as Aboriginal, Indigenous, and Dreaming (and equivalent terms in Indigenous languages), despite varying opinions. Other words – such as 'elder', 'country', 'law', 'traditional owner', and 'western' – are generally rendered in lower case unless individual authors have explicitly chosen to do otherwise. Where possible we have followed the conventions outlined in published dictionaries of Indigenous languages for the spellings of language words. However, this is not always straightforward as conventions vary between individuals, over time, and across regions.

Acknowledgements

We are grateful to all our contributors and peer reviewers, who have worked so closely with us to ensure the quality and relevance of the volume. The volume has benefitted immensely from the professionalism, sound judgement, and good humour of our wonderful research assistant, Katya Zissermann. Thank you so much, Katya. We really couldn't have done it without you! We are also indebted to our copy editor, Marg Bowman, for her attention to detail, patience, and encouragement. We thank April Pengart Campbell for the cover image and the story that accompanies it, Megan Ellis for book design, Brenda Thornley and Jennifer Green for the maps, and Chris Storey for the cover design. Individual photographers and artists are credited in the chapters. Thanks also go to LD&C editor Nick Thieberger for general advice and encouragement, and to Denise O'Dea, Agata Mrva-Montoya, and other staff at Sydney University Press for support with production of the volume.

Preparation and production of the volume has been supported by the Australian Research Council Linkage Project (LP140100806, with Chief Investigators Barwick, Green, Nordlinger, and Turpin), in partnership with the University of Sydney, the University of Melbourne, and the Central Land Council (Partner Investigator Brian Connelly). We also received in-kind support from CoEDL (the ARC Centre of Excellence for the Dynamics of Language) and PARADISEC (the Pacific and Regional Archive for Digital Sources in Endangered Cultures). Green's work in the final stages of production of this volume was supported by CoEDL and by RUIL (the Research Unit for Indigenous Language) at the University of Melbourne. See individual chapters for further acknowledgements of relevant funding.

The chapters in this volume have all been peer-reviewed and we are grateful to the anonymous reviewers who undertook this task and provided constructive and insightful comments on the content. The opinions expressed in individual chapters are not necessarily those of the editors.

Linda Barwick, Jennifer Green, Petronella Vaarzon-Morel

Contributors

Shaun Penangke Angeles is a Kungarakan and Arrernte man who grew up in the central desert lands of his mother in Mparntwe, Alice Springs. He belongs to a long lineage of *Kwatye-kenhe* "belonging to water" and *Yerrampe-kenhe* 'belonging to honeyant' families whose traditional country is centred on Apmere Ayampe and Apmere Alkwepetye to the north of Mparntwe. He is the Artwe-kenhe (Men's) Collection Researcher at the Strehlow Research Centre, Museum and Art Gallery of the Northern Territory, and is a member of the Indigenous Repatriation Program National Advisory Committee and the AIATSIS Return of Cultural Heritage's Project Advisory Committee.

Linda Barwick is a musicologist, and a professor at the University of Sydney's Sydney Conservatorium of Music. Her research centres on music's role in forming social identity, based on fieldwork (in Australia, Italy, and the Philippines) and collaboration with linguists, historians, and Indigenous researchers in community-based projects documenting song traditions. She is a Chief Investigator on the ARC Linkage Project LP1401000806, and participates in several other projects dealing with the revitalisation of song and languages. She is a Fellow of the Australian Academy of the Humanities and a member of the Australian Institute of Aboriginal and Torres Strait Islander Studies.

Clint Bracknell is a Wirlomin Noongar musician and researcher from the south coast of Western Australia and is Associate Professor at the Western Australian Academy of Performing Arts and Kurongkurl Katitjin Centre for Indigenous Australian Education and Research, Edith Cowan University. His research primarily focuses on the revitalisation of Noongar language and song. He serves on the Wirlomin Noongar Language and Stories Committee, the ARC Centre of Excellence for the Dynamics of Language Advisory Board, and the Australian Institute of Aboriginal and Torres Strait Islander Studies (AIATSIS) Council.

Suzanne Bryce has lived in Central Australia for more than 40 years, working with Anangu, the Pitjantjatjara people of northwest South Australia and southern Northern Territory. Her work is built on longstanding relationships, good language skills, and a strong commitment to the wellbeing of children and families. As a young woman living out bush, Suzanne began to record Anangu telling stories about their lives. Recording and translation have become a passion, developed while working in remote Aboriginal communities on various health-related projects. Over the last 10 years she has made regular contributions to the Ara Irititja digital archive and has worked on various publications and documentaries.

Julia Burke has worked for Central Australian Aboriginal organisations for more than 25 years in the fields of digital content development, social history, communications, and program development. Each role has held the challenge of articulating shared knowledge and manipulating information into accessible and meaningful content to empower local Indigenous groups. Cultural archiving projects include Ara Irititja and book projects include *Ninu grandmothers' law: The autobiography of Nura Nungalka Ward* and NPY Women's Council's *Ngangkari work Anangu way*. Currently Julia is the creative producer for the Central Land

Council's digital storybooks, which remake written English management plans into online and offline web applications using local languages. Julia is also the business and marketing manager for an Alice Springs–based camel tour company.

Kimberly Christen is the Director of Digital Initiatives for the College of Arts and Sciences and the Director of the Centre for Digital Scholarship and Curation at Washington State University, where she is a Professor in, and Director of, the Digital Technology and Culture Program. She is the founder of Mukurtu CMS, an open-source community access platform designed to meet the needs of Indigenous communities, Director of the Sustainable Heritage Network, and co-Director of the Local Contexts initiative, which provide educational resources for stewarding digital cultural heritage and supporting Indigenous communities in the management of intellectual property.

Brenda L Croft is from the Gurindji/Malngin/Mudburra peoples from the Victoria River region of the Northern Territory of Australia, and Anglo-Australian/German/Irish/Chinese heritage. She has been involved in the First Nations' and broader contemporary arts and culture for over three decades. Brenda's multidisciplinary practice-led research encompasses critical performative Indigenous auto-ethnography, representation, identity, re/memorying, Indigenous storying, and creative narratives. Her artwork is represented in major public and private collections in Australia and overseas. Her curatorial practice includes local, national, and international exhibitions. Based in Canberra, Brenda is Associate Professor, Indigenous Art History and Curatorship at the Australian National University.

Georgia Curran is an anthropologist with interests in Indigenous Australian music, languages, and performance. She lived in the Central Australian settlement of Yuendumu between 2005 and 2007 while undertaking her PhD fieldwork through the Australian National University. Since then, Georgia has continued to work on collaborative research projects with Warlpiri people, including two song book compilations of Warlpiri women's *yawulyu* songs with accompanying audiovisual materials. She is currently a research associate at the Sydney Conservatorium of Music.

John Dallwitz studied architecture and art teaching in Adelaide, before concentrating on photography and heritage conservation. Since 1986, he has worked exclusively on Aboriginal community heritage projects. In 1994, he was engaged by the Pitjantjatjara Council to work with Ngaanyatjarra, Pitjantjatjara, and Yankunytjatjara people to develop their acclaimed Ara Irititja project. Ara Irititja was presented with the 2015 Outstanding Project award by the Association of Tribal Archives Libraries and Museums in Washington, DC. He is now employed by the South Australian Museum as Manager of Ara Irititja and works to ensure that it is maintained for future generations of Anangu.

Samantha Disbray is Post-doctoral Research Fellow at the University of Queensland investigating languages in education and their socioeconomic value. Over the last decade, her involvement as a practitioner, researcher, and collaborator with Warlpiri colleagues and Warlpiri education has been extensive. From 2007 to 2012 she worked for the Northern Territory Department of Education supporting Indigenous language programs in schools. She has since undertaken research commissioned by the Warlpiri Education and Training Trust and has published works on Indigenous language policy and language in school programs in Australia. In 2017 she co-edited the *History of bilingual education in the Northern Territory*, with Brian and Nancy Devlin.

Elizabeth Marrkilyi Ellis is an Indigenous linguist and speaker of multiple Western Desert dialects. She has worked as a Ngaatjatjarra/Pitjantjatjara language teacher, interpreter, translator, and lexicographer over many decades. In 2015, she was awarded an ARC Discovery Indigenous Fellowship to document the verbal arts of her speech community. Between 2015 and 2019, she was affiliated with the ARC Centre of Excellence for the Dynamics of Language at the Australian National University. She recently published her autobiography (2016) *Pictures from my memory: My story as a Ngaatjatjarra woman* with Aboriginal Studies Press. Her honorary doctorate from the ANU was conferred in July 2019.

Jason Gibson is a Research Fellow with the Alfred Deakin Institute, Deakin University. He has close to two decades of experience in collaborative work with Central Australian people and a specific research interest in museum anthropology, cultural transmission, and cultural change. His first book, *Ceremony men: Making ethnography and the return of the Strehlow Collection* (SUNY Press), is in press.

Ian Green is a Visiting Research Fellow at the University of Adelaide, teaching and supervising research students in the Department of Linguistics and the School of Education. Ian's linguistic research is focused on the languages of the NT's Daly River region, an area in which he has undertaken extensive fieldwork, as documented in the Daly Languages website, and for which he has developed a range of grammatical descriptions and historical studies. He works closely with a number of Daly River communities on language education programs and pedagogies.

Jennifer Green is a Post-doctoral Fellow at the University of Melbourne. She is a key researcher in RUIL (the Research Unit for Indigenous Language) and is affiliated with CoEDL (the ARC Centre of Excellence for the Dynamics of Language). For more than four decades, Green has worked with Indigenous people in Central Australia documenting languages, cultural history, art, social organisation, and connections to country. Her doctoral research pioneered methods for the recording, annotation, and analysis of sand stories and other forms of multimodal verbal art. Currently she is researching Indigenous sign languages in a range of communities in Central and Northern Australia. She is a Chief Investigator on the ARC Linkage Project LP1401000806.

Peter Hurst is a teaching specialist in Linguistics at the University of Melbourne. As a member of the ARC Centre of Excellence for the Dynamics of Language, Peter created the database and webpages for the Daly Languages website. His PhD examined the syntax of reciprocal constructions in a variety of languages, and he is currently part of a team working on a project that examines how children learn polysynthetic languages (such as Murrinhpatha). He has previously examined the syntax of blended languages such as those spoken by children of the Tiwi Islands.

Janet Inyika was born in the Musgrave Ranges, and spoke Pitjantjatjara. She went to school in Ernabella, Amata, and Areyonga. She was an artist her whole life – a wood carver, painter, batik artist, and Tjanpi desert weaver. Janet was a strong supporter of, and consultant to, Aṟa Irititja. She worked tirelessly for many years with the NPY (Ngaanyatjarra, Pitjantjatjara, Yankunytjatjara) Women's Council as a staff member and also as a director. She was outspoken and passionate about mental health and drug and alcohol issues and was a leading advocate for reform. She passed away in 2016.

Luke Kelly is currently a consultant anthropologist based in Budapest, Hungary specialising in land tenure, cultural mapping, and survey work. He worked in the Tanami Desert as a regional anthropologist for the Central Land Council between 2009 and 2016. He has an MA in Social Anthropology and Sociology from the Central European University, Budapest.

Anna Kenny is a consultant anthropologist and was an ARC Postdoctoral Fellow at ANU (2012–2016). Since 1991 she has conducted field research with Indigenous people in Australia. She published a book called *The Aranda's pepa: An introduction to Carl Strehlow's masterpiece (1901–1909)* in 2013, co-edited with Nic Peterson a book called *German ethnography in Australia* in 2017, and in 2018 published *Carl Strehlow's 1909 comparative heritage dictionary: An Aranda, German, Loritja, and Dieri to English dictionary*. She is currently working on several native title claims and a book on TGH Strehlow's anthropology called *Shadows of a father*.

Inge Kral is a linguistic anthropologist affiliated with the ARC Centre of Excellence for the Dynamics of Language and the School of Literature, Language and Linguistics at the Australian National University. She draws on some 30 years' experience in Indigenous Australia as an educator and researcher. Her research interests include out-of-school learning and literacy; youth, digital media, and new literacies; Australian Indigenous languages; and verbal arts. She also researches youth media and literacy in an indigenous village in Peninsular Malaysia. Together with Ellis, Green, and Simpson she is a Co-Investigator on ARC-DI IN150100018 documenting and analysing the verbal arts of the Western Desert.

Joel Perrurle Liddle is an Arrernte man descended from *Untyeyampe* 'corkwood honey' from Apmere Uremerne (Ooraminna), *Aherrke* 'sun' from Apmere Irlpme (Bond Springs), and *Arenge* 'euro/hill kangaroo' from Apmere Tyuretye/Mparntwe (Alice Springs). His mother's family arrived in Victoria from Europe in 1853. Joel is employed as a researcher with the Baker Heart and Diabetes Institute. He has spent several years undertaking research of historical Arrernte archives to develop his knowledge of Arrernte language and culture. He is also a Research Affiliate with Charles Darwin University and the Strehlow Research Centre and is currently transitioning into a PhD to focus on Arrernte knowledges held in archives.

Gretel Macdonald has worked as a linguist for the Bilingual Resource Development Unit (BRDU) within Yuendumu School since 2016. In this role she works with Warlpiri educators in Yuendumu, Lajamanu, Willowra, and Nyirrpi to deliver a bilingual model of education, including building teacher capacity, documenting local curriculum, and developing resources. In 2018, she took on a co-project managing role alongside colleague Barbara Napanangka Martin to further develop and strengthen the Warlpiri Theme Cycle, the local Warlpiri language and culture curriculum. Prior to working with Warlpiri communities, Gretel was an intern linguist at Mirima Dawang Woorlab-gerring Language and Culture Centre in Kununurra.

Barbara Napanangka Martin has worked in Warlpiri education for more than 25 years. For many years she taught at Yuendumu School in both Warlpiri and English. Currently she is a senior literacy worker, and teacher mentor. In her role as senior literacy worker she makes Warlpiri books and other resources to support the teaching of Warlpiri language and culture. As a teacher mentor, she supports Indigenous and non-Indigenous teachers to develop their teaching practice. She is passionate about mentoring future leaders in Warlpiri education. Barbara is also the Deputy Chair of the Warlpiri Education and Training Trust, an advisory committee that funds projects which prioritise training and education, and promote lifelong learning for Warlpiri people.

Patrick McConvell is a linguistic anthropologist with special interests in kinship and linguistic prehistory. He has taught anthropology at Charles Darwin and Griffith universities, and is now an Adjunct Associate Professor at the Australian National University and Western Sydney University. He has worked with Australian Aboriginal people especially in the north-central region of the Northern Territory, and the Kimberley and Pilbara regions of Western Australia. He has been principal anthropologist and author of reports for 20 Aboriginal land and native title claims. A recent publication is *Southern anthropology – a history of Fison and Howitt's Kamilaroi and Kurnai* (Palgrave-MacMillan, 2015) with historian Helen Gardner.

Felicity Meakins is an ARC Future Fellow in Linguistics at the University of Queensland and a Chief Investigator in the ARC Centre of Excellence for the Dynamics of Language. She is a field linguist who specialises in the documentation of Australian Indigenous languages in the Victoria River District of the Northern Territory and the effect of English on Indigenous languages. She has worked as a community linguist as well as an academic over the past 19 years, facilitating language revitalisation programs, consulting on native title claims, and conducting research into Indigenous languages. She has compiled a number of dictionaries and grammars of traditional Indigenous languages and has written numerous papers on language change in Australia.

Fred Myers, Silver Professor of Anthropology at NYU, has been doing research with Pintupi-speaking Indigenous people on their art, their relationships to land, and other matters since 1973. Myers has published two books, *Pintupi country, Pintupi self: Sentiment, place and politics among Western Desert Aborigines* (1986) and *Painting culture: The making of an Aboriginal high art* (2002), several edited volumes, including *The traffic in culture: Refiguring anthropology and art* (with George Marcus, 1995), *The empire of things* (2001), and *The difference that identity makes* (with Tim Rowse and Laurie Bamblett, 2019), and the film *Remembering Yayayi* (with Pip Deveson and Ian Dunlop).

Rachel Nordlinger is Professor of Linguistics at the University of Melbourne, Director of the Research Unit for Indigenous Language, and a Chief Investigator in the ARC Centre of Excellence for the Dynamics of Language. Her research centres on the description and documentation of Australia's Indigenous languages and their implications for theories of language structure. She also works with Indigenous communities across Australia to support their efforts in maintaining and preserving their linguistic and cultural heritage.

Carmel O'Shannessy is a lecturer in the School of Literature, Languages and Linguistics at the Australian National University. Her research is in language contact and acquisition, including the emergence of Light Warlpiri, a new Australian mixed language, and children's development of Light Warlpiri and Warlpiri. She has been involved with languages and education in remote Indigenous communities in Australia since 1996, in the areas of bilingual education and in her current research.

Linda Rive has been a member of the Ara Irititja team for 12 years, and brings to it a passion for language and culture. Linda is an accredited interpreter and translator of Pitjantjatjara and Yankunytjatjara and has a very good knowledge of Ngaanyatjarra, as well as the numerous dialects that are represented in the Ara Irititja archive. She has worked with Anangu for 40 years and is a facilitator of communication between Anangu and the wider world. Her work focuses on recording oral histories and cultural knowledge in the central desert tri-state region of the Northern Territory, South Australia, and Western Australia.

Kim Scott is a multi-award winning novelist whose most recent novel is *Taboo* (Picador, 2017). Proud to be one among those who call themselves Noongar, Kim is also Chair of Wirlomin Noongar Language and Stories (www.wirlomin.com.au), which is responsible for a number of bilingual (Noongar and English) picture books and regional performances of story and song. Kim is currently Professor of Writing in the School of Media, Creative Arts and Social Inquiry at Curtin University.

Lisa Stefanoff is an ARC Research Fellow at the National Institute for Experimental Arts (NIEA), UNSW Art & Design, based in Mparntwe (Alice Springs), where she is undertaking an experimental media/arts practice-led story archival project with town camp women painters. A graduate of the NYU Department of Anthropology Program in Culture and Media, she has worked with desert and other Northern Territory communities and cultural organisations since 2002 as a researcher, creative producer of screen and radio works, public programmer, and curator.

Sabra Thorner is a cultural anthropologist who has worked with Indigenous Australians for almost 20 years, focusing on photography, digital media, and archiving as forms of cultural production and social activism. She is guided by collaborative and decolonising methodologies for co-producing knowledge. Her academic interests are, broadly, in visual/media anthropology, digital cultures, anthropology in/of museums, Indigenous Australia, and Indigenous art/media worlds. She has held fellowships from Fulbright, Wenner-Gren, the Smithsonian, and AIATSIS, and has published her work in the *Journal of Material Culture, Oceania*, and *Visual Anthropology Review*. She is an Assistant Professor at Mount Holyoke College.

Sandy Toussaint has worked with Kimberley Indigenous people since 1981. Focusing on collaborative, cross-disciplinary research, cultural ethics, visual storytelling, and epistemological inquiry, she was a senior researcher on the Royal Commission led by Pat Dodson, and the Aboriginal Land Inquiry. Sandy taught anthropology at the University of Western Australia for 20 years. Trustee of the Kaberry Kimberley Collection at AIATSIS, and member of UNESCO's Memory of the World Australian Committee, Sandy managed UWA's Berndt Museum between late 2013 and 2015. Honorary Professor in Arts/Science at UWA, and UNDA's Nulungu Research Institute, she is the author/editor of five books.

Myfany Turpin is a musicologist and linguist who works in Central Australia. She has written a dictionary, sketch grammar, and scholarly articles on the Aboriginal language Kaytetye. She has also documented traditional music of the Alyawarr, Anmatyerr, Arrernte, Warlpiri, and Gurindji peoples of the Northern Territory. She has published extensively on Aboriginal song-poetry including multimedia publications. She holds an ARC Future Fellowship at the University of Sydney to investigate the relationship between words and music in Aboriginal song, as well as a University of Sydney Fellowship to trace the origins of a ceremony once popular across Western Australia, South Australia, and the Northern Territory.

Petronella Vaarzon-Morel is an anthropologist with long-term experience working with Warlpiri and other Indigenous peoples in Central Australia. She has conducted research for Aboriginal land and native title claims and collaborated on interdisciplinary projects concerned with contemporary Indigenous land, livelihood, and social justice issues. For the past five years she has lectured in anthropology at New York University, Sydney and is currently also an Honorary Research Associate at PARADISEC, Sydney Conservatorium of Music, the University of Sydney. Her publications include peer-reviewed journal articles, reports, and monographs.

Katya Zissermann is a policy lawyer with 13 years' experience working for the Victorian Department of Justice and Victoria Legal Aid in the area of criminal law policy. In 2016 she completed postgraduate studies in linguistics at the University of Melbourne, focusing on Taemi, a language of Papua New Guinea. Since 2016, she has contributed to various projects in the University of Melbourne's School of Languages and Linguistics, including the Digital Daisy Bates project. She is currently engaged as a research assistant on the ARC Linkage Project LP1401000806.

Abbreviations used

ADSL	asymmetric digital subscriber line
AIAC	Ara Irititja Aboriginal Corporation
AIAS	Australian Institute of Aboriginal Studies
AIATSIS	Australian Institute of Aboriginal and Torres Strait Islander Studies
AIM	Aboriginal Inland Mission
ANU	Australian National University
APY	Anangu Pitjantjatjara Yankunytjatjara
ARC	Australian Research Council
CAAMA	Central Australian Aboriginal Media Association
CERG	Cultural Elders Reference Group
CLC	Central Land Council
CLR	Commonwealth Law Reports
CMS	content management system
FCA	Federal Court of Australia
GIS	geographic information system
GMAAAC	Granites Mines Affected Areas Aboriginal Corporation
GPS	global positioning system
IAD	Institute for Aboriginal Development
IPA	international phonetic alphabet
KMS	knowledge management system
LOTE	language other than English
MAGNT	Museum and Art Gallery of the Northern Territory
NFSA	National Film and Sound Archive of Australia
NPY	Ngaanyatjarra, Pitjantjatjara, and Yankunytjatjara
NT	Northern Territory
NTA	*Native Title Act 1993* (Commonwealth)
NTCF ILC	Northern Territory Curriculum Framework for Indigenous Languages and Cultures
NT DoE	Northern Territory Department of Education
NTRB	Native Title Representative Body
NYU	New York University
OLAC	Open Languages Archive Community
PARADISEC	Pacific and Regional Archive for Digital Sources in Endangered Cultures
PAW Media	Pintubi Anmatjere Warlpiri Media and Communications

PL	pastoral lease
SA	South Australia
SAM	South Australian Museum
SRC	Strehlow Research Centre
UWA	the University of Western Australia
WA	Western Australia
WDVA	Western Desert Verbal Arts
WETT	Warlpiri Education Training Trust
WLC	Wirliyajarrayi (Willowra) Learning Centre
WYDAC	Warlpiri Youth Development Aboriginal Corporation

For abbreviations used in linguistic glossing, please see footnotes in the relevant chapters.

Language Documentation & Conservation Special Publication No. 18
Archival returns: Central Australia and beyond
ed. by Linda Barwick, Jennifer Green & Petronella Vaarzon-Morel, pp. 1–27
http://nflrc.hawaii.edu/ldc/sp18
http://hdl.handle.net/10125/24875

Conundrums and consequences: Doing digital archival returns in Australia

Linda Barwick
The University of Sydney

Jennifer Green
The University of Melbourne, ARC Centre of Excellence for the Dynamics of Language

Petronella Vaarzon-Morel
The University of Sydney

Katya Zissermann
The University of Melbourne

Abstract

The practices of archival return may provide some measure of social equity to Indigenous Australians. Yet priceless cultural collections, amassed over many decades, are in danger of languishing without ever finding reconnection to the individuals and communities of their origin. The extensive documentary heritage of Australian Indigenous peoples is dispersed, and in many cases participants in the creation of archival records, or their descendants, have little idea of where to find these records. These processes of casting memories of the past into the future bring various conundrums of a social, political, and technical nature. They raise questions about the nature and dynamics of ongoing cultural transmission, the role of institutional and community archives in both protecting records of languages, song, and social history and disseminating them, and the responsibilities of researchers, organisations, and end users in this complex intercultural space. These questions are perforce framed by ethical and legal questions about access, competing ideas of ownership, and shifting community protocols surrounding rights of access to and the dissemination of cultural information. This paper arises from a project designed to reintegrate such research collections of Central Australian cultural knowledge with the places and communities from which they originally emanated. While we show that the issues raised are seldom neutral and often complex, we also argue for the power that culturally appropriate mobilisation of archival materials has for those that inherit the knowledge they embody.

Keywords: Indigenous archives, archival returns, intellectual property, cultural transmission, Central Australia

Introduction[1]

Returning archival photos or long-lost recordings of stories or songs to families and communities of origin can be the occasion of "happy tears," as recently reported by one of our collaborators. The phrase points to the complicated consequences that can flow when archival cultural records from the past are cast into the present. Archives, "the documentary by-product of human activity retained for their long-term value,"[2] exist in uneasy relationships with knowledge management systems that depend on face-to-face communication as the primary means of cultural transmission. To generalise, we can say that whereas face-to-face systems, which depend on human interaction, emphasise *process*, document-based systems such as institutional archives emphasise *products*, the traces of human activity encoded in material or electronic media (such as pen and paper, audiovisual media, images, and digital objects). Focusing on the Central Australian area, this chapter is about how archivists, end users, and intermediaries navigate this complex situation in doing archival returns.

For document-based systems, cultural transmission depends on norms and practices to select, preserve, and provide context for the archival objects and to enable future (unspecified) users the means to access, decode, and interpret them. Thus, contemporary institutional archives seek to apply principles-based international best practice to develop systematic procedures for the selection and preservation of the archival objects they hold, and to index them for an imagined future audience. Face-to-face knowledge systems, on the other hand, depend on the judgement and authority of custodians to guide and authorise performative systems of knowledge maintenance and transmission. The packaging of cultural knowledge in song, dance, and other performative modes, for specific audiences in particular contexts, affords a degree of flexibility and context-responsiveness that is impossible in the institutional archive.

For holders of Indigenous cultural knowledge in Australia, long-term abidingness (retention for "long-term value") is highly valued, but for many it is the process of enacting and transmitting knowledge, as well as the authorising context for the specific content, that needs protection. The Indigenous[3] world stresses interconnectedness, while at the same time knowledge is not available to all but rather to those with rights to know and hold the knowledge (Michaels 1986). This means that people are "keen to avoid being held responsible in any way for the management of, and particularly for the access to the resources of others" (Christie 2007: 33). Much Indigenous knowledge is localised, and it is important to know the reason it is being imparted, by whom, to whom, "and how the story fits into the wider networks of kinship, art, music, ceremonials and philosophy" (Christie 2005a: 62).

---

1   This research was funded by Australian Research Council Linkage Project LP140100806, with project partners the University of Sydney, the University of Melbourne and the Central Land Council. We also acknowledge support from LP160100743. We thank two anonymous reviewers, Myfany Turpin, David Parsons, David Avery, and Jane Lloyd for their feedback on an earlier version of this chapter.

2   International Council of Archives (https://www.ica.org/en/what-archive) (Accessed 15 March 2019.)

3   In Australian usage, the term 'Aboriginal' is generally used as an umbrella term to cover the Indigenous nations of mainland Australia and Tasmania (not including the Torres Strait Islands). In this chapter we use the broader term 'Indigenous' for all of Australia's first nations, covering both Aboriginal and Torres Strait Islander cultural domains.

Contemporary practices of archival return in Central Australia, the focus of the present volume (Barwick et al. 2019), thus bring into relief points of misfit between the unspecified imagined audience of the institutional archive and the specific interests held by those engaged in the transactions. Archivists may seek guidance from end users, often via intermediaries (such as researchers), on how to adapt archival systems and principles to maximise the future usefulness of the archival object. Knowledge holders, on the other hand, are more likely to be focused on finding appropriate channels to contain and transmit the performative power of the knowledge the archival objects encode, recruiting intermediaries and archivists as agents of proper process. From all three positions, conundrums, compromises, and unforeseen consequences are evident and inevitable.

We discuss and clarify some key terms used in our discussion below, and then turn to various aspects of return: planning considerations, legal constraints, and dissemination, and finally consider how practices of archival return are changing the contexts in which these practices occur.

'Return' or 'repatriation'?

There are competing views about the difference (if any) between 'archival return' and 'repatriation'. In this volume we generally prefer the more neutral term 'archival return', although we recognise that 'repatriation' can be an appropriate term in circumstances where the emphasis and motivation for return relate to making cultural knowledge available in its place of origin. Both terms invoke elaborate interwoven histories of communities, participants, collectors, and institutions, articulated in a complex space defined by larger social forces ranging from community politics to institutional mandates (Lancefield 1998: 49, 57–58). The term 'repatriation' stems from discussions focused on the return of collections of tangible objects, such as artworks, religious objects, and human remains, that have been amassed by museums and other institutions, sometimes in what may be regarded as "morally dubious circumstances" (Turnbull 2010: 8). Discussing sound recordings, Lancefield (1998: 48) defines repatriation (return)[4] as "any conveyance of copies of sound recordings made and deposited as scholarly documents from archives to people who feel that the sound is part of their heritage." For some, 'return' is synonymous with providing a copy of a recording or enabling access to a database (Christen 2011) (in the latter case, the term 'digital return' may be used), while for others it entails conveying (legal) ownership of an item (Anderson 2005b), or even returning original recordings to communities without retaining a copy at the source institution (Garrett 2014: 79).

Archives and archivists

In the broadest sense, any collection of material "retained for long-term value"[5] (such as a personal collection of photos) qualifies as an archive, but in this chapter we use the term

---

4   Lancefield uses both terms.

5   As noted in the first paragraph of this chapter, the wording is taken from the International Council on Archives' definition of archives as "the documentary by-product of human activity retained for their long-term value." See footnote 2.

'archive' to denote an infrastructure that enables systematic long-term preservation and use of cultural records. Archivists worldwide are currently undertaking an immense program to digitise analogue recordings to ensure ongoing access to information otherwise liable to be locked up in now-obsolete formats such as audio cassette or videotape. To stand the test of time, a robust digital preservation environment must seek as far as possible to avoid the risks inherent in fast-changing commercial digital technologies and platforms. To follow international best practice (IASA Technical Committee 2009), a digital archival system must incorporate such features as quality control on selection and accession (ingestion) of records to ensure that the records are verifiable and authentic. Archivists must apply unique identifiers, document measures for disaster recovery (such as regular checks on data integrity), and hold backups in multiple locations. To make holdings accessible to end users (the 'designated community'), archivists must make them easy to find and also available in formats that can easily be handled, providing them via user-friendly access points, with clear conditions of use that allow end users to reuse the information for their own purposes (Barwick & Thieberger 2018).

Digital preservation infrastructure is costly and out of reach for many small local archives. Collections that pre-date the digital era come with particular problems – carrier media may have deteriorated and require expensive solutions to repair and transfer the content to sustainable digital formats. In some cases, the window of opportunity for the rescue of technically fragile and near-obsolete objects may have closed already. Some local cultural centres with large digitised and born-digital collections may prefer to compromise on best-practice archival standards so as to retain local control, but many have entered into partnership agreements with larger institutional archives in order to outsource ongoing costs associated with digital preservation, while maintaining local control over access (Ormond-Parker & Sloggett 2012). Such partnerships are rarely straightforward: archivists may need to harmonise idiosyncratic or missing metadata for small collections, and the legal provenance of holdings may not be clear. In the long run, partnership agreements (and the future sustainability of collections) may come under question as organisational issues affecting the funding, governance, or staffing of local cultural centres may effectively orphan collections (Allard & Ferris 2015).

The complex issues involved in archiving raise the hackles of many players. Complaints may concern delays in the processing of deposits, difficulty in finding relevant materials within collections, or hurdles in access to materials. Some Indigenous researchers feel that they are disadvantaged, in terms of access to cultural materials, if they are not formally affiliated with research units or universities (Perrurle & Judd 2018: 110). For archivists, balancing the equation of curation, care, and distribution or access is a difficult task. Some archives are effectively 'frozen' and unable to deal with new collections because of a lack of capacity, and funding, to undertake what they and their constituents believe to be important work. Archivists may inherit impossible conundrums in their collections, with orphaned materials bereft of metadata or agreements to enable their connection to current generations of Indigenous peoples, or with legacy instructions for access to archival materials that no longer align with contemporary views of rights. The time and resources it would take to resolve all these problems is inestimable.

Communities

When discussing archival returns 'to the community', it is important to recognise that the term 'community' can be used in different ways. In its broadest sense, it is any group of people that have certain attitudes or interests in common (a community of interest); for example, 'the scientific community'. From an archival perspective, a 'Designated Community' is:

> An identified group of potential Consumers who should be able to understand a particular set of information. The Designated Community may be composed of multiple user communities. A Designated Community is defined by the Archive and this definition may change over time. (Consultative Committee for Space Data Systems [CCSDS] 2012: 1.11)

In this sense, the designated community of an archive could be, for example, the general public, and/or researchers in a specific disciplinary field, and/or descendants of those recorded. 'Community' in this sense is a very broad concept that seeks to generalise the likely knowledge base of its potential users in order to design appropriate packages of information for them. A more specific meaning of 'community' implies a focal place, the people of a district or country considered collectively. Thus in Australia, a 'community' commonly refers to a group of people living in a small town or settlement. For various reasons such a group of people might also form a community of interest.

For the purposes of archival returns, the 'community' might consist of descendants or heirs of those recorded, alongside others with expertise and interest in the content of a recording, such as speakers of a language, performers of song traditions, or senior landholders. With increased mobility and the ongoing history of disruptions to traditional lifestyles in remote Indigenous Australia, 'communities' may be widely dispersed (Burke 2018). Such diasporic communities set additional challenges when it comes to negotiating access to and the control of cultural records. An archival object may have significance for a large range of potential end users, many of whom may be difficult to locate and contact, and each of whom may have different interests, requirements, and capabilities to engage with returned materials. As Lancefield (1998: 47) comments, "The dynamic heterogeneity of most communities can render [the] pragmatic problem [of return] exquisitely complex."

Planning for archival return

Prompts for return

Some instances of return may be responses to direct requests from Indigenous people (Campbell 2014: 102) for use of archival materials in their work as teachers or rangers,[6] or for their own personal learning (some specific examples are discussed below). Such requests,

---

6   Under the Australian government's Indigenous Rangers program, teams of Indigenous rangers work to protect native plants and animals, control feral animals and invasive weeds, reduce dangerous wildfires, and maintain tourism and cultural sites. At the time of writing, 11 ranger groups are operating under the Central Land Council's Ranger program (https://www.clc.org.au/index.php?/articles/info/clc-rangers1). (Accessed 19 May 2019.)

which may involve records kept in *ad hoc* private collections, as well as those that have been properly archived in organisational or institutional repositories, are frequently enabled by the conduit of personal relationships with researchers. Without these active and enabling interpersonal relationships "even the most technologically capable or culturally responsive collections may remain silos" (Brown & Treloyn 2017: 59). Concern about the disparate locations of old records – potentially held in multiple personal collections as well as in the archives of a range of organisations – is widespread. As Arrernte elder and writer Veronica Dobson says, "It worries me that things have been collected and we don't know where they will end up. Young people don't know where to look. Information is sitting idle. It needs to be used by [Indigenous] rangers, for language work, and for research" (Central Land Council 2016).

Other instances of return are prompted by associated stakeholders (former community residents, academics, consultants, lawyers etc). What to do with priceless collections remains an urgent concern for the many Indigenous organisations that have been involved in the recording of language, song, oral histories, and other cultural materials as language documentation, as content for Indigenous radio and television, or for land claims and native title claims. Researchers and other visitors to communities may have long histories of acting as intermediaries, providing families or communities of origin with archival cassettes or photos as part of fieldwork. This practice has been especially common in disciplines such as ethnomusicology, where preparations for fieldwork often involved researchers sourcing archival materials, not only to familiarise themselves with musical styles they might later encounter, but also to contribute archival objects, where requested, as gifts of goodwill to establish and cement personal relationships (Seeger 1986).[7] While such gifts shielded the end user from the expense and inconvenience of travel to archives and payment for copies, they simultaneously positioned the researcher as an intermediary between the institution and the end user.

Archival returns are frequently framed in terms of cultural equity, social responsibility, respect for human dignity and the rights of Indigenous peoples, and for some, are motivated by a desire to redress inequities between institutions/researchers and originating communities (Treloyn & Emberly 2013: 160). Return can constitute, as Lancefield (1998: 49) writes, "some small, distinctly limited redress for certain acts of cultural appropriation enabled by colonial power" and facilitate critical reflection on colonial research legacies (Treloyn et al. 2016: 95). Although the custodianship of collections by academics is viewed by some as associated with their own professional gain (see Wright 2016), many are involved in trying to redress these problems and acknowledge that returning collections is "the right thing to do" (Campbell 2014: 102). As Haviland (2016: 472) writes, "My idea about 'repatriating' photographs and videos to Hopevale stemmed from the innocent notion that what the old men had tried to teach me belonged with their own descendants more than in the digital archives of institutional libraries."

Benefits and drawbacks of archival return

Those planning archival return projects are generally aware that the process has potential for both benefits and drawbacks, and usually aim to maximise the former and

---

7   Some researchers have chosen not to provide such copies.

mitigate the latter. They should also plan for the likelihood that complex processes can lead to unexpected consequences.

The reported benefits of connection to archival records are many, and returned materials may serve myriad purposes. Some benefits are framed in terms of preserving, reviving, and/ or sustaining knowledge. Communities may be empowered through ownership of their own histories, stories, and images and by being able to manage access to these materials (Lydon 2010; Ormond-Parker & Sloggett 2012: 191). With a paucity of personal records such as photo albums in some Indigenous communities, archival returns can enable people to fill in gaps in the family record and create memories for future generations (Campbell 2014; Thorner 2016: 11; Myers 2017: 117). Christen (2012) emphasises the revitalising role of archives in cultural preservation and production, arguing that through digital archives Indigenous people can "balance tradition and modernity on their own terms." Instances of return can be occasions of great local significance and have powerful emotional effects, with a sense of ancestors being returned home (Campbell 2014: 103; Treloyn et al. 2016: 97). Returned records may be regarded as a 'gift' from ancestors for current and future generations (Brown & Treloyn 2017: 55).

Reflecting senior people's desire to leave a cultural legacy, the reuse of archival materials for pedagogical purposes can constitute another potential benefit. For example, Christie describes how Yolngu people use digital technologies at school, bringing together groups of elders to tell stories of the land for children, making DVDs and other multimedia educational resources (Christie 2007: 31–32). Outside formal educational settings, archival records can be used to facilitate intergenerational transmission of knowledge, language, and culture (Christie & Verran 2013: 215; Treloyn et al. 2016: 95; van Gelderen & Guthadjaka 2017; Perrurle & Judd 2018). For example, archival records of songs can be used as primary resources for learning language and reinvigorating interest in song poetry and vocal techniques (Marett & Barwick 2003; Campbell 2014: 112; Thorner 2016: 11; Bracknell 2017). Legacy collections of visual arts may be accessed to provide inspiration to new generations of artists (Hinkson 2015).

To the extent that the return of archival materials can facilitate the transmission of cultural knowledge, returns may also be linked to personal healing and improved health and wellbeing (Anderson & Kowal 2012: 438; Thorner 2016: 11; see also Campbell 2014: 125). As one participant in our project commented:

> It is really important for us to pass on the knowledge from old people telling stories ... It makes us feel really happy and makes us feel strong inside. It's really important to pass on our culture and knowledge to our kids and these photos and stories can help.[8]

While old recordings may be of immense contemporary value to communities, they can also unavoidably reify otherwise evanescent verbal arts traditions and undermine those based on the value of improvisation (Treloyn & Emberly 2013; Campbell 2014: 103; Brown & Treloyn 2017). As Bialostocka writes, "Inventorying living heritage runs a risk of essentialising culture and 'fixing' cultural practices in time" (2017: 18). Brown & Treloyn note that:

---

8   Selina Napanangka, Willowra, pers. comm. to Petronella Vaarzon-Morel, 2018.

> while the intention of the repatriating researcher may be to contribute cultural materials
> that can be used to sustain a tradition, the form that they take may in fact threaten to harm
> the very systems of cultural property and authority that they seek to support and sustain.
> (2017: 163)

The acceptance of an archival record as authoritative can "interpose a factor in community adjustments which the researcher and the archivist did not intend and bear a responsibility for introducing" (Wild 1992: 13). From an artistic point of view, a negative impact may sometimes result from hearing old recordings if they demonstrate high quality linguistic and performance values that are hard to emulate, therefore confirming perceptions of cultural loss and presumably dispiriting current tradition-bearers (Campbell 2014: 103). When consulted about archival materials, people may also make decisions that are perhaps unexpected. In a case study, John Haviland (2016) returned to a community in Northern Queensland with a film he had made some 40 years earlier to find out what the descendants of those featuring in the film about traditional methods of preparing *gambarr*, a tar-like substance used for manufacturing spears and spear throwers, wanted to do with it. The community decided *not* to include the film in their local archive because of complex historical conflicts between family groups.

Strong traditional principles concerning rights and responsibilities govern the circulation of cultural knowledge, and may produce equally strong anxieties about inappropriate access to knowledge that may be restricted on the basis of gender, age, or for other reasons. Anxieties may be heightened in data management systems where information is pooled across family, clan, language, or country 'boundaries' (Christen 2005: 322; Christie 2007: 33). New kinds of tensions over rights in archival objects may arise as the result of state recognition and bureaucratisation of Indigenous property relations (see, for example, Glaskin 2007). What was once regarded as belonging to interrelated persons may be disputed if the group fragments, with individuals or branches of a family challenging each other's rights in property, including that of cultural property. We now discuss some legal issues raised in the practice of return.

Legal constraints on the practice of archival return

In any contemplation of the return of cultural heritage materials, a central question is: who can legally authorise return and any eventual reuse of returned materials? This question cannot be answered without first considering provenance: the circumstances in which, and the purpose(s) for which, the object was created in the first place. For example, a map created by a researcher to support a native title claim may have been commissioned by a land council or similar body, and may have been the subject of a contract which contemplated future ownership and uses. Similarly, language or song recordings produced during linguistic or anthropological fieldwork funded by an academic institution are likely to be subject to the policies and ethical frameworks of that institution. In such cases, these contracts and other legal instruments may provide an answer to the question of who can legally authorise return of materials to source communities.

However, in many situations, the provenance of an archival object may be difficult to establish – whether due to its age or the lack of associated documentation, or the lack of specific contractual agreements. In others, alternative uses of items created for one purpose (for example, use in a native title claim, or for a specific research project) may not have been contemplated, or may even have been specifically disallowed. In such cases, employees of government and institutional archives and universities, and holders of personal and community collections, cannot avoid grappling with the complexities of Australian intellectual property law. Even where provenance is relatively clear and the ownership of cultural materials is legally vested in institutions or in individuals, negotiations may be required to agree on and arrange for the return of those materials to their source communities. Future uses of the materials must also be negotiated and agreed. Such negotiations may not be straightforward. The following sections consider a number of the complexities arising from these issues.

Ambiguity in rights frameworks

Recent decades have seen a growing international movement towards the formal recognition and protection of Indigenous peoples' rights to and interests in their intangible cultural heritage, culminating in the United Nations *Declaration on the Rights of Indigenous Peoples* (2007).[9] Article 31 of this Declaration refers to the right of Indigenous people to "maintain, control, protect and develop their cultural heritage, traditional knowledge and traditional cultural expressions," including oral traditions and visual and performing arts. The Declaration requires states to take effective measures to recognise and protect the exercise of these rights. Some have argued that this requires the introduction of *sui generis*[10] legislation in Australia (Janke 1998; Stoianoff & Roy 2015). Despite indicating support for the Declaration in 2009, the Australian Commonwealth Government is yet to implement legislative measures to implement article 31.[11]

Incompatible concepts of property

Christie (2007: 36) notes that the western legal notion of 'property' "does not do justice to Aboriginal notions of relatedness, origins and identity." Myers questions the appropriateness of using the idea of 'cultural property' to describe "the fluid, relational and constantly changing ways in which Aboriginal ideas of protocol and custodianship continue to be negotiated in ongoing activity" (2017: 187). In the absence of specific equitable contractual arrangements, intellectual property laws and archival systems typically frame the Indigenous

---

9   See also the UNESCO *Convention for the Safeguarding of the Intangible Cultural Heritage* (2003). Australia is not a signatory to this convention. The World Intellectual Property Organisation Intergovernmental Committee on Intellectual Property and Genetic Resources, Traditional Knowledge, and Folklore is developing an international instrument for the effective protection of traditional knowledge, traditional cultural expressions, and genetic resources (http://www.wipo.int/tk/en/igc). (Accessed 19 March 2019.)

10 Unique, stand-alone.

11 In 2003, the Commonwealth Government circulated a draft Copyright Amendment (Indigenous Communal Moral Rights) Bill for comment. The Bill was criticised as placing unduly onerous requirements on Indigenous communities who wished to protect their intangible cultural heritage (Anderson 2004) and was not enacted. Interestingly, Victoria has recently introduced legislation to protect Indigenous intangible cultural heritage, including language, in Victoria (*Aboriginal Heritage Amendment Act 2016*).

contributor to research and its outputs as the 'subject', rather than as an 'author', thereby excluding them from copyright (Janke & Iacovino 2012; Anderson & Christen 2013) and inadvertently perpetuating problems of colonial exclusion (Anderson 2018). Some go so far as to say that these dynamics can operate to make Indigenous people feel "captives of the archives" (Fourmile 1989: 1).

Even where intellectual property rights can be said to be held by Indigenous contributors to research, such rights can only be held individually (not collectively). This does not properly reflect Indigenous law and practices regarding the custodianship and intergenerational transmission of knowledge (Christie 2008; Janke 2008). The expiry of statutory copyright periods for older material can solve immediate permission problems, but create other challenges – when materials enter the 'public domain' they can be accessed or used by anyone, regardless of cultural protocols protecting sacred, secret, or sensitive material (Anderson 2005b).

Complex questions of 'ownership'

Research and its products become 'property' regardless of the intentions of those involved (Anderson 2018). The creation of records automatically generates 'authors' and 'owners', whom Australian and international law deem – in the absence of specific contractual agreement to the contrary – to hold exclusive rights to control the movement, reproduction, publication, and dissemination of those records. To avoid infringing the rights of 'authors' and 'owners', permission must be sought by non-owners who wish to access and use the materials. Legal questions about 'authorship' and 'ownership' of cultural heritage materials, or the rights that these notions entail, may undermine or limit efforts to return materials.

For any single cultural record there are multiple possible rights holders (Hudson 2006: 9). These may include the researcher, any commissioning organisation or funding body, the Indigenous person or community whose image, voice, knowledge, or information is contained in the record, and any institution with which the record may have been deposited for archival purposes or to which it may have been bequeathed (Janke & Iacovino 2012). As noted above, the identity of rights holders may be determined by the provenance of the record; however, this may often not be the case. There may be a distinction between the ownership of the physical property (the photo, tape, digital recording, or transcript) and the ownership of the intellectual property (the copyright). There may be a further distinction between possession and ownership of the physical property. For example, an item may be in the possession of an archival institution but still be legally owned by an individual researcher or academic institution. Some Indigenous organisations require researchers and consultants to assign copyright and other property in project information to the organisation itself. The situation may be further complicated by the fact that many archival items are hybrid in form, containing, for example, fragments of song embedded in oral history narratives, and involving multiple participants. This makes the issue of rights even more complicated. A further practical challenge is that, in some cases, copyright holders may be unidentifiable or uncontactable (Anderson 2005b; Nakata et al. 2008), and succession rights may not be clear. For example, copyright may be held by a deceased estate.

It has been argued[12] that individuals who hold copyright in a work embodying Indigenous traditional cultural expression may have a fiduciary duty[13] to respect Indigenous customary law in reproducing, publishing, or otherwise dealing with that work (McClausland 1999; Janke 2009a, 2009b; Ritchie & Janke 2015). While the existence of such a duty on the part of the copyright holder may give rise to a *right* of custodians of traditional knowledge to ensure that this material is used by others in accordance with customary law, it does not make Indigenous people the legal *owners* of the records containing their knowledge or cultural expressions.

The nature of the archival object may have a bearing on the question of rights. For some sound recordings, Indigenous participants can be said to be 'performers' in a 'live performance' under the *Copyright Act 1968* (Cth) (Janke 2008) and, as such, have specific rights to protect against unauthorised use of their live performances. It is unclear whether a person who is recorded providing an oral history (see Hudson & Kenyon 2005: 122) or speaking an Indigenous language is giving a 'performance'.[14] For recently made recordings, performers are deemed to be co-owners of the sound recordings of their performances.[15] Performers' rights exist alongside copyright, and for old sound recordings do not displace the need to negotiate with the owners of copyright in those recordings. Hudson & Kenyon (2005: 127) argue that, for a recorded oral history interview, copyright in the words of the interview (as a 'literary work') may be jointly held by the interviewer and interviewee.[16]

Fair dealing, exceptions, and licences

Dilemmas of copyright ownership might be circumvented by relying on 'fair dealing' or other exceptions in the *Copyright Act*, which allow non-owners to use copyright materials for specific purposes (such as research or study, criticism or review, and private/domestic use) without infringement. However, these exceptions are narrow and do not authorise a range of uses such as the inclusion of copyright material in a database managed by an Indigenous community (Hudson 2006: 63). Other copyright exceptions exist for educational and cultural institutions, libraries, and archives, but it is not clear how these might operate in the context of archival return projects when the intentions of Indigenous communities are not defined (Anderson 2005b).

Where copyright licences are granted to communities, careful consideration must be given to the identity of those who will be authorised to use materials under the terms of the licence, how long the licence will remain in force, and the precise ways in which communities might wish to use returned materials in the future: digitisation, inclusion in a database, publication online, and annotation or alteration of the materials may each require special permissions. In the absence of such permissions, the use by Indigenous communities

---

12 On the basis of the Federal Court's decision in *Bulun Bulun & Anor v R & T Textiles Pty Ltd* (1998).

13 A duty involving a relationship of trust.

14 The definition of 'performance' excludes the "delivery of any item of news and information" (section 248A(2)(b) of the *Copyright Act*).

15 Section 22(3A) of the *Copyright Act*.

16 In contrast, spoken language data may not meet the test for 'originality' required for copyright to be held in the words of a sound recording (section 32 of the *Copyright Act*; see also Bell & Shier 2011).

of cultural heritage materials to "make new meanings" may contravene the copyright owners' rights (Anderson 2005a: 26).

Conundrums in navigating copyright

Historically, the distribution of intellectual property rights in the products of research was often simply not contemplated or understood (Myers 2017). Barwick (2004: 260) has discussed how the relationship between archives, contributors, owners, and users continues to be problematic due to "a lack of appropriate agreements and relationships rather than technical impediments." Balancing moral, commercial, and legal rights is complicated and not for the lay person. As Newman (2012: 453) points out, "(l)inguistic fieldworkers are not trained to know copyright law any more than copyright lawyers are trained to do phonetic transcription." Best practice for research projects in linguistics, musicology, and other related disciplines is to consult with people and document their instructions about long-term care of, and access to, their research materials, as well as to agree in writing on the sharing of intellectual property rights via co-authorship of research outputs. Ideally the principle of free and informed consent is an ongoing process, which may involve re-consultation if new purposes for old data arise (Janke & Iacovino 2012).

One of the problems with documenting consent for archiving is the ways that archives change over time – some questions that may have been asked in the past do not reflect current realities. Access to archived materials may no longer require a visit to the archival institution, but rather may be mediated online, with materials being directly downloadable. Some archives are moving towards open access, as an ethical and practical approach to the management of archival materials, and in some cases is a requirement of funding bodies and academic institutions. We have observed that there are shifting sensitivities, too, in Australian Indigenous communities about various types of access, particularly when it comes to viewing photos or films or listening to recordings of the deceased.

Legal considerations for native title claim materials

Huge quantities of material have been assembled in support of native title claims that have now been determined.[17] The question of ownership of copyright in these materials is not always straightforward (Ritchie & Janke 2015). As noted above, materials created to support native title claims may be subject to contractual agreement between a researcher and the commissioning organisation, which clearly sets out arrangements for ownership and the future management of the materials. Such materials are typically held by organisations, for example by land councils. As Koch (2008: iv) wrote:

---

17   Section 223 of Australia's *Native Title Act 1993* provides direction on what is required to establish native title, including the "existence of a system of traditional laws and customs and how these connect the people with the lands and waters claimed" (Bennett & Koch, Appendix 7 in Koch 2008: 46).

Many valuable and irreplaceable documents have been created during research for native title claims. Some Native Title Representative Bodies (NTRBs) have dedicated staff to manage these documents, but others are not able to care for them properly.

In this report, written now more than a decade ago, Koch recommended urgent action to assess the condition of records, to arrange for digitisation, to develop plans and protocols for access to materials, and to "ensure their preservation for posterity" (2008: iv). NTRBs also commonly hold similarly complex materials generated from externally funded land and sea management projects or deposited with them for safekeeping by clients. Conundrums for NTRBs in managing access to such materials range from legal issues concerning privilege, confidentiality, and copyright through to pragmatic problems such as how to obtain consent from clients who are widely dispersed and often living in remote communities (Twomey 2008).

As Indigenous representative bodies build their collections, many created without foresight for potential future reuse, they often need to re-engage with the stakeholders with whom the records were created, to obtain permissions, recreate missing metadata, and document instructions as to future handling and dissemination of the materials. Such a process requires careful judgement and expertise, and significant expenditure of time and resources, for which institutions do not have core funding. Enabling access to outside users is similarly unfunded under the original terms of establishment and ongoing operations of NTRBs (Koch 2008: 1, 50–51).

Indecision and uncertainty

The absence of an appropriate legal framework or an established process for dealing with Indigenous cultural materials can produce uncertainty and ambivalence for collecting institutions (Nakata et al. 2008) and individuals involved in the return of archival materials. On a smaller scale, disagreements among joint copyright owners about where cultural materials should be housed or how they should be used can also lead to indecision and paralysis. Where heritage materials have been deposited with cultural institutions, these practical difficulties can lead to significant uncertainty about how to share and allow access to those materials.[18] Holders of personal collections and autonomous archives confront the same challenges. Complex and unsatisfactory situations such as this in Australia and elsewhere have led some to observe that western intellectual property regimes do little to protect the rights of Indigenous peoples to control and protect their intangible cultural heritage (Janke 1998, 2008, 2009a). Alternative approaches are urgently required.

Practices of archival return

Platforms and formats for dissemination

For much of the 20th century, access to archival media such as recordings and photographs required individuals to visit the physical archive. Depending on any access and copying

---

18   Another issue for institutions to consider is whether the return of cultural heritage materials might breach their statutory information privacy obligations (Hudson 2006: 42–7; Bell & Shier 2011: 43–6).

restrictions (on the archival side) and on the receiver's technical and financial resources (such as funds to travel and pay for copies, as well as home access to playback machines), analogue copies of archival materials could be provided to the end user, typically in low-resolution analogue formats such as photocopies of photographs, or cassette tapes of sound recordings preserved on reel-to-reel tape. Further copying of these materials by the end user was discouraged, not only by archival access agreements, but also by the progressive deterioration in resolution over successive generations of analogue copies.

In an age where digital rather than analogue formats are the preferred medium for both recording and return, digital formats seemingly have many advantages: they better match the affordances of now widespread digital media playback devices such as mobile phones, they present the possibility of copying and sharing without loss of resolution, and they are frequently a means of intergenerational engagement, combining young peoples' typically greater digital literacy with older generations' wishes to support or revitalise traditional practices. Digital surrogates can enable ongoing access to old media that might otherwise become unplayable, thus allowing a new dynamic life for formerly hard-to-access physical objects (Christen 2011: 187). As pointed out by Newell (2012: 288), digital copies ("surrogates") have their own distinctive qualities that affect the ways in which users can connect with them. Geismar (2013) also draws attention to the "capacities and contradictions" of digital return. Digital return may be cyclical in ways that the repatriation of physical objects is not conventionally understood to be, since the same channels also permit a return from communities back to museums (Geismar 2013: 256). On the other hand, Geismar argues, "we need to pay attention to the implicit power relations that permit digital returns and to the hierarchies that 'keeping-while-giving' establishes" (Geismar 2013: 257; see also Bell et al. 2013).

Institutional archives are increasingly placing digital collections online, with a view to facilitating direct access by end users, usually with some form of authentication and agreement to conditions. Numerous constraints can impede end users from such apparently unmediated access. Typically text-centric and Anglo-centric archive interfaces may inhibit end users from discovering the existence of archival collections online in the first place (Barwick & Thieberger 2018). The ongoing 'digital divide' (Rennie et al. 2016) and other challenges associated with telecommunications in remote Indigenous communities are realities that any archivist planning online access must consider (Australian Communications and Media Authority 2008). Even where users can command such technical means, digital data costs for downloads may be prohibitive (van Deursen & van Dijk 2019). Not uncommonly, communities of speakers lack "the technical equipment and access to the Internet that would allow use of an archive in an active or autonomous way" (Treloyn & Emberly 2013: 173; Widlok 2013: 189) and there can be great disparity across a single region. Questions of long-term sustainable access to archival collections remain hard to answer in such circumstances.

Databases: structures, ontologies, and metadata

Christie (2004: 4) has argued that the way databases are constructed and their implicit ontologies reflect assumptions about "the nature of the world, and the nature of knowledge." As highlighted by Nakata & Langton (2005: 4), "Complex intersections between knowledge systems, in the context of political and cultural reassertion by Indigenous people, are what professionals now confront and must work through." Controlled by hierarchies and taxonomies that reproduce particular cultural assumptions about the ordered world, archives and databases may sequester objects into categories and classes that are unfamiliar to Indigenous end users (Christie & Verran 2013: 307–308; also Christie 2005b; Bow et al. 2015: 117). From an archival perspective, it is difficult to discover, search, and navigate the contents of a database or archive without good metadata, an integral aspect of databases that concerns the identification and description of information (Bow et al. 2015: 117). For example, working with Yolngu in northeast Arnhem Land, Christie found that the labels used to categorise metadata fields and to name files in many databases can prevent Yolngu researchers from discovering ideas, topics, and knowledge that are linked in Yolngu epistemology.

As non-Indigenous biases are typically inherent in databases, there is a risk that they may inhibit or undermine intergenerational knowledge transfer among Indigenous peoples by challenging traditional systems of ownership and authority (Christie 2005a; Treloyn & Emberly 2013: 174–175). Choosing what content to include in local databases can place onerous responsibility on individuals to make decisions that affect the whole community, and can give rise to inequities within the community based on who has access and who does not (Treloyn & Emberly 2013: 163). Brown & Treloyn (2017: 57) argue that we need "databases that aim to reflect and embed local Indigenous ontologies, cultural protocols and traditional knowledge in both the content and schema of the system." Such are the aspirations of the Ara Irititja (Hughes & Dallwitz 2007) and Mukurtu (Christen 2015) platforms, separately developed specifically for enabling community access and interaction with digital collections, and discussed elsewhere in this volume.

The act of inviting community members to participate in the collection and correction of the metadata of existing resources (Garrett 2014) is now regarded as an important form of engagement that assists in bringing an archive to life (Bow et al. 2015: 117). In 2017, Doris Stuart, an Arrernte elder from Mparntwe (Alice Springs), received digital copies of some photographs of herself taken in the 1980s (Figure 1). In this case, due to ongoing personal connections with the photographer, it had been relatively straightforward to connect her with her photographs. This experience prompted Doris to talk about how sad she was to see that, in some old archival photos from the Alice Springs area, Indigenous people were nameless.[19] "There has to be some recognition of who they are, how they looked, and what they stood for," she said. "Every photo tells a story isn't it? Stories are a record of the next generations" (Central Land Council 2016).

---

19   We have noted that it is very common for children not to be identified in historical photographs, even when the adults are. This has implications for people searching for individuals in images in later years.

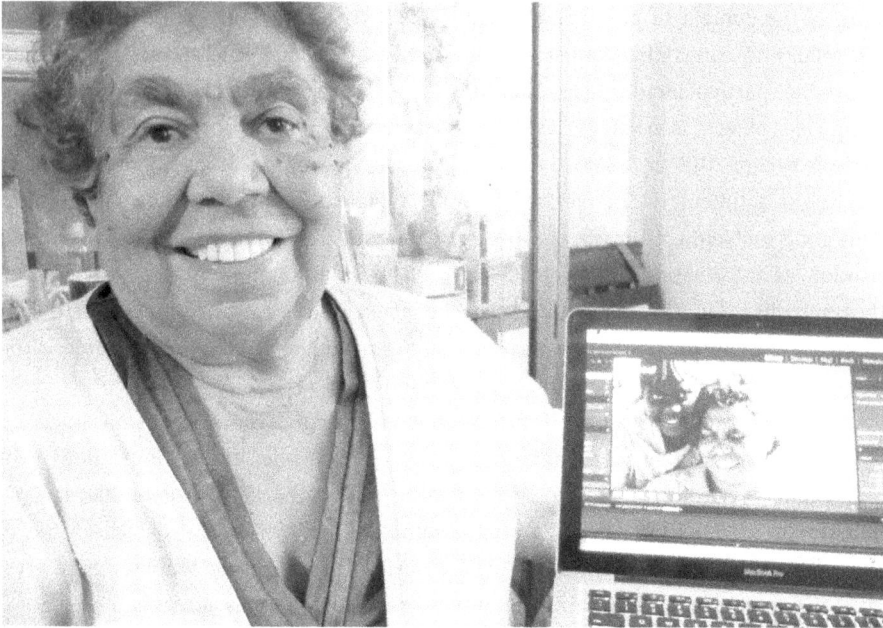

Figure 1. Doris Stuart is pleased to get a copy of some photos of herself taken near Alice Springs by Jennifer Green in the 1980s (photo: Jennifer Green)

McGrath (2010: ix) discusses how narratives offered in the 're-documentation' processes can "provide considerable insights into historical sociality and significance beyond the original moment in which the image was taken." This can be a form of "critical re-rendering" (Biddle 2016: 1; see also Hinkson 2015). Discussing the return of recordings to Yolngu communities, Toner (2003) proposed expanding the metadata to include commentaries by traditional owners about the contemporary significance of returned records, such as expressions of kinship to singers on recordings. The re-emplacing of records may be requested: Brown & Treloyn describe how one senior person "physically re-embedded … records into their place of origin by requesting a playback session at an old mission-era shed where he used to hear old people singing during his childhood" (2017: 56).

Describing the addition of "tribal metadata" to materials held by archival institutions as part of a "reciprocal curation" process in the creation of the Plateau Peoples' Web Portal, Christen (2011: 200) reports grappling with "the linguistic tension involved in using English terms to represent Native themes." She states that no "eloquent solution" could be found, although thoughtfully choosing English terms was regarded as the "best of the worst." Similar issues of language choice are highly relevant in Australia, where widespread multilingualism among older generations abuts with language shift to English, Kriol, and new languages created by younger generations (O'Shannessy & Meakins 2016). In many cases, the need to operate across multiple languages and low levels of vernacular literacy have tended to favour the use of English for metadata, and for access platform interface terminologies (as, for example, in the Central Land Council's Digital Archive, based on Keeping Culture KMS).[20]

---

20 https://clc.keepingculture.com/ (Accessed 16 April 2019.)

Materialities of archival media

Materials sourced from archives may be returned to individuals and to local institutions such as libraries, community organisations, or schools using various *ad hoc* modes of delivery. Content that is closely related to individuals and their families may be provided in person on DVDs, CDs, or flash media (USB sticks). Local delivery of larger collections to community hubs may be accomplished via media databases (Treloyn & Emberly 2013; see also Meakins et al. 2018), portable hard drives, or dedicated wi-fi hotspots.[21] Password-protected media databases hosted on community computers may allow people to search, sort, and shuffle various media and create their own cultural objects (Christen 2005: 326), though password-based rights management systems have been critiqued, since "information on a computer is never completely safe if the computer is shared in a public space" (Christie 2008). From these sources, recordings and photographs are downloaded and circulate in homes, cars, clinics, or social clubs, where they may become the inspiration for new creations, incorporating old recordings with the new (Campbell 2014: 111–112).

In the absence of (or in preference to) internet connectivity, users may "create a social network of digital exchange" (Mansfield 2014: 66) by sharing digital objects locally between mobile phones, tablets, and computers via local area wireless networks or peer-to-peer (Bluetooth) networks. The same technologies are used to share newly created digital resources recorded on mobile phones and distributed within family networks (Auld et al. 2012). USB storage devices containing video and audio recordings are also regularly exchanged and plugged into televisions or game consoles for viewing. Women may keep USBs (Figure 2), paper copies of archival access requests with snapshots of metadata, and images of their long-deceased relatives in their handbags – but lament the consequences of children rifling their contents. Hard drives and USBs fail; phones that hold fragments of archival collections get lost or broken. Even the collections of recognised Indigenous cultural production agencies and media organisations are not immune to such dangers – hard drive backup systems fail because of extreme climatic conditions and perhaps neglect and lack of foresight, and sometimes this results in the irreplaceable loss of material that has been entrusted to their care.

Materials returned to individuals might certainly be passed on in turn to others who are considered to have rights in the material (Campbell 2014: 111). But they might equally fall into the wrong hands or simply be lost. Clearly the easy portability of mobile devices can have both positive and negative implications: such modern digital objects may hold considerable power and new protocols are needed to deal with their potentials.[22] The solution adopted by several participants in our research was the individual purchase of small home safes, to provide security for the digital and technological ephemera of returns in home communities.

---

21 http://librarybox.us/whatis.php (Accessed 12 December 2018.) Note: The LibraryBox device is no longer available for purchase. For developments with RasberryPi, see http://www.language-archives.services/about/pi (Accessed 23 January 2019.)

22 Shaun Angeles Penangke. Old ways, new digitisation and the Strehlow Collection. Plenary talk. AMaGA (Australian Museums and Galleries Association) conference, Alice Springs, 15 May 2019.

Figure 2. A personal collection of USB drives, clearly indicating the various sources of the materials: the CLC Cultural Media Project, Batchelor Institute, and the University of Sydney (photo: Jennifer Green; reproduction courtesy April Campbell Pengart)

Changing contexts for archival returns

Planning for future reuse

What effect has their encounter with archival returns had on the opinions Indigenous people themselves express concerning the future of the cultural records they create in the present day? An analysis of a selection of consent documents relating mostly to recordings of Indigenous languages and song in the Central Australian region accrued over a three-decade period (Green et al. 2017) revealed that there was unanimity about the importance of retaining the data to pass on cultural knowledge to future generations. What varied were the strategies specified to enable this to happen. There was a slight trend over time towards a more open-access viewpoint. Yet the 'look but do not keep' viewpoint is also common – some participants didn't require permission for their data to be viewed in an archive but did want people to ask if they wanted a copy. A selection of these, sometimes contradictory, viewpoints are reflected in the verbatim comments below:

1. "Good to show kids what was really important to us. This is for kids today, and young people. It means a lot."
2. "It is OK to see these things without restriction – men, women, and non-Indigenous people can view. Can show to whitefellas from a long way."
3. "Is OK to use Anmatyerr language for making a dictionary and health books and to use in schools. But not for people to hear stories that may sound OK but may be very sacred to other people."

4. "We don't want the words mixed up. We [are] not happy if they use Dreamtime stories to make a cartoon book, or to make logos to put on T-shirts."
5. "You can put it on television – we want to see coloured people on TV."
6. "I would like to share my stories to the public so they can see how we share our stories to young children."

Comments concerning practices of restriction on accessing images or recordings of the deceased showed that the main concern was the potential effect on local populations and close family. What happened in far-off places beyond networks of kin and accountability was of lesser concern. Warumungu woman Ruby Frank reflects on the processes of reaching agreement with other members of her family group on access to archival cultural and ceremonial recordings. "People talked about how we wanted to run it, what is to be strict and what doesn't need to be strict. And what can be in the open," she said.[23]

The comments above reflect an overall respect for research materials, but also anxiety about their misappropriation or misuse. There is also much variation, not only between regions of Indigenous Australia, but also regarding different types of archival materials and what is at stake – whether these be photos of family, recordings of speech, oral histories, songs, or narratives, documentations of visits to country, and so on.

Participatory archiving

An increasing recognition of the inherent cultural bias in the structures and operations of archives, and of the colonising origins of many institutional archives dealing with Indigenous collections, has led to calls for 'participatory archiving' to allow users more say in structuring and managing collections (Huvila 2008). Numerous initiatives have established 'autonomous archives' that exist outside of government (Moore & Pell 2010). Many initiatives have sought to take advantage of the affordances of digital technologies to reimagine the relationship between people and collections (Christen 2005; Christie 2008; Nakata et al. 2008; Thorner 2010). In addition to the Ara Irititja and Mukurtu databases already mentioned, Australian community facilities designed with such factors in mind have been developed in many places, including in the Pilbara (Brown & Treloyn 2017: 57), in the Kimberley (Treloyn et al. 2016: 96), in northeast Arnhem Land (De Largy Healy 2014: 30; see also Anderson 2005b), and in Central Australia (for example, PAW Media and Communications based at Yuendumu, as well as the CLC's already mentioned Digital Archive). The Indigenous Remote Communications Association (IRCA) assists community organisations in planning and managing their collections (Indigenous Remote Communications Association 2010), while the Central Australian Youth Linkup Service supports workstations, some loaded with local collections, in multiple remote locations.[24]

Community language centres, often supported by the Australian government's Indigenous Languages and Arts funding scheme, provide another network of community-based infrastructure, coordinated by umbrella bodies such as First Languages Australia.[25] Such

---

23 Ruby Frank, pers. comm. to Jane Lloyd, 25 April 2019.

24 https://caylus.org.au/computerrooms/ (Accessed 16 April 2019.)

25 https://www.firstlanguages.org.au/ (Accessed 15 April 2019.)

centres commonly aspire to community-based language archiving (Linn 2014), in an emerging movement towards 'participatory delivery' of archival information that goes hand-in-hand with community-based language research. In a community-based language archive, "the archive actively engages with the relevant community in conducting all levels of documentation, describing and contextualising, maintenance, and dissemination of information"; community members are primary shapers and users of the archive (Linn 2014: 61).

Larger institutions are also part of this move. The Northern Territory Library established a network of local libraries and knowledge centres, and created the Community Stories platform, based on the Aṟa Irititja model, to provide facilities in numerous regional and remote libraries (Gibson 2009). AIATSIS (the Australian Institute of Aboriginal and Torres Strait Islander Studies), the primary national institution charged with the archiving and dissemination of Australian Indigenous information, provides copies of audio recordings, video recordings, and photographs to Aboriginal and Torres Strait Islander peoples through the Return of Material to Indigenous Communities (ROMTIC) program. The operations of such programs are not without their issues (see, for example, Campbell 2014).

Positive experiences from archival return have prompted some Indigenous people to look to archives to assist in cultural continuity:

> We want to send our things to the archive so that they can look after our things – like photos, videos, and other recordings. We are happy that they look after them for us [in Canberra] so that the next generations of children can see these things, after we are gone. In the old days these things got lost, and people didn't know where to look for photos and recordings of their songs and Dreaming stories. The poor things didn't know where to look. So that is why we are depositing things in the archive.[26]

Conclusion

While participatory approaches to archiving do not provide a blanket solution, the culture of archiving has certainly been changed through engagement with a wide range of users. We have seen that engaging in returns is rarely a straightforward enterprise for anyone involved in the process. Archivists, researchers and other intermediaries, staff of local autonomous Indigenous organisations, and end users are all faced with dynamic situations that require careful judgement and expertise. Ethical and legal questions about access, competing ideas of ownership, and shifting community protocols and expectations can be hard to avoid. For some genres of archival material (for example, personal photos) the stakes may not be so high, but for others, the unexpected and unregulated insertion of digital recordings from the past into the socio-political ecologies of the present has the potential to disrupt as well as to give pleasure and provide resources for sustaining traditions and enriching lives.

As Christen comments, "there is ... [no] one-size-fits-all answer to the archival questions indigenous peoples bring to bear on the institutions that hold much of their cultural heritage." Digital technologies "cannot ensure that respectful and reciprocal curation processes follow;

---

26   April Campbell Pengart, pers. comm. to Jennifer Green, 10 October 2018.

that must happen face-to-face through sustained dialogue and a commitment to collaborative archival practice" (Christen 2011: 209). Such commitment to sustained dialogue is time consuming and sometimes has unexpected consequences. Those of us engaging in archival returns are constantly given cause to reflect on the conundrums and unexpected consequences generated by our own institutions, practices, and training.

Some of the issues raised in this chapter are relevant to broader global discussions in the emerging field of Indigenous data sovereignty (see Kukutai & Taylor 2016). As we have discussed, it can be difficult to grasp the nature and dynamics of ongoing cultural transmission, the roles of institutional and community archives in both protecting and disseminating records of languages, song, and social history, and the responsibilities of researchers, organisations, and end users in this complex intercultural space. These questions are perforce framed by ethical and legal questions about access, competing ideas of ownership, and shifting community protocols surrounding the rights of access to and the dissemination of cultural information. While we have shown that the issues raised are seldom neutral and often complex, we also argue for the power that culturally appropriate mobilisation of archival materials can have for those that inherit the knowledge they embody. But it is not only end users who are affected by the practice of archival returns. Since archivists, intermediaries, and end users are all involved, doing archival returns cannot help but change archival systems and research practices too. It is fair to say that all records are situated in what Myers has termed "circumstances of cultural flow" (2017: 187).

References

Allard, Danielle & Shawna Ferris. 2015. Antiviolence and marginalised communities: Knowledge creation, community mobilization and social justice through a participatory archiving approach. *Library Trends* 64(2). 360–383. (doi:10.1353/lib.2015.0043)

Anderson, Heather & Emma Kowal. 2012. Culture, history, and health in an Australian Aboriginal community: The case of Utopia. *Medical Anthropology* 31(5). 438–457. (doi:10.1080/01459740.2011.636411)

Anderson, Jane. 2004. The politics of Indigenous knowledge: Australia's proposed Communal Moral Rights Bill. *UNSW Law Journal* 27. 585–604.

Anderson, Jane. 2005a. Access and control of Indigenous knowledge in libraries and archives: Ownership and future use. *Correcting course: Rebalancing copyright for libraries in the national and international arena.* Conference proceedings, Columbia University, New York. American Library Association and the MacArthur Foundation.

Anderson, Jane. 2005b. Indigenous knowledge, intellectual property, libraries and archives: Crises of access, control and future utility. *Australian Academic & Research Libraries* 36(2). 83–94. (doi:10.1080/00048623.2005.10721250)

Anderson, Jane. 2018. Negotiating who "owns" Penobscot culture. *Anthropological Quarterly* 91(1). 267–305. (doi:10.1353/anq.2018.0008)

Anderson, Jane & Kimberly Christen. 2013. 'Chuck a copyright on it': Dilemmas of digital return and the possibilities for Traditional Knowledge Licenses and Labels. *Museum Anthropology Review* 7(1–2). 105–126.

Auld, Glenn, Ilana Snyder & Michael Henderson. 2012. Using mobile phones as placed resources for literacy learning in a remote Indigenous community in Australia. *Language and Education* 26(4). 279–296. (doi:10.1080/09500782.2012.691512)

Australian Communications and Media Authority. 2008. *Telecommunications in remote Indigenous communities.* (http://bitily/ACMA2008) (Accessed 3 October 2019.)

Barwick, Linda. 2004. Turning it all upside down … Imagining a distributed digital audiovisual archive. *Literary and Linguistic Computing* 19(3). 253–263. (doi:https://doi.org/10.1093/llc/19.3.253)

Barwick, Linda, Jennifer Green & Petronella Vaarzon-Morel (eds.). 2019. *Archival returns: Central Australia and beyond* (Language Documentation & Conservation Special Publication 18). Honolulu HI: University of Hawai'i Press. (http://hdl.handle.net/10125/24898)

Barwick, Linda & Nicholas Thieberger. 2018. Unlocking the archives. In Nicholas Ostler, Vera Ferreira & Chris Mosely (eds.), *Communities in control: Learning tools and strategies for multilingual endangered language communities. Proceedings of FEL XXI Alcanena 2017*, 135–139. Hungerford, UK: Foundation for Endangered Languages. (http://hdl.handle.net/2123/20395)

Bell, Catherine & Caeleigh Shier. 2011. Control of information originating from Aboriginal communities: Legal and ethical contexts. *Études/Inuit/Studies* 35(1–2). 35–36. (doi:10.7202/1012834ar)

Bell, Joshua A, Kimberly Christen & Mark Turin. 2013. Introduction: After the return. *Museum Anthropology Review* 7(1–2). 1–21.

Biddle, Jennifer Loueride. 2016. Sentience and sentimentality in *Remembering Yayayi*. *The Cine-Files* 10 (Spring). (http://www.thecine-files.com/biddle2016/) (Accessed 13 February 2018.)

Bow, Catherine, Michael Christie & Brian Devlin. 2015. Shoehorning complex metadata in the Living Archive of Aboriginal Languages. In Amanda Harris, Nicholas Thieberger & Linda Barwick (eds.), *Research, records and responsibility: Ten years of PARADISEC*, 115–131. Sydney: Sydney University Press. (https://ses.library.usyd.edu.au/handle/2123/16671) (Accessed 20 February 2018.)

Bracknell, Clint. 2017. Maaya waabiny (playing with sound): Nyungar song language and spoken language. In Jim Wafer & Myfany Turpin (eds.), *Recirculating songs: Revitalising the singing practices of Indigenous Australia*, 45–57. Canberra: Pacific Linguistics.

Brown, Reuben & Sally Treloyn. 2017. Relational returns: Relationships and the repatriation of legacy song recordings in Australia. *University of Melbourne Collections* 20. 50–61.

Burke, Paul. 2018. *An Australian Indigenous diaspora: Warlpiri matriarchs and the refashioning of tradition.* New York, Oxford: Berghahn Books.

Campbell, Genevieve. 2014. Song as artefact: The reclaiming of song recordings empowering Indigenous stakeholders – and the recordings themselves. In Amanda Harris (ed.), *Circulating cultures: Exchanges of Australian Indigenous music, dance and media*, 101–127. Canberra: ANU Press.

Central Land Council. 2016. Keeping track of old memories. *Land Rights News Central Australia* 6(3). 21.

Christen, Kimberly. 2005. Gone digital: Aboriginal remix and the cultural commons. *International Journal of Cultural Property* 12(3). 315–345. (doi:10.1017/ S0940739105050186)

Christen, Kimberly. 2011. Opening archives: Respectful repatriation. *American Archivist* 74(1). 185–210. (doi.org/10.17723/aarc.74.1.4233nv6nv6428521)

Christen, Kimberly. 2012. Balancing act: The creation and circulation of Indigenous knowledge and culture inside and outside the legal frame. In Sean A Pager & Adam Candeub (eds.), *Transnational culture in the internet age*, 316–345. Cheltenham, UK: Edward Elgar Publishing.

Christen, Kimberly. 2015. A safe keeping place: Mukurtu CMS innovating museum collaborations. In Juilee Decker (ed.), *Technology and digital initiatives: Innovative approaches for museums*, 61–68. London: Rowman & Littlefield.

Christie, Michael. 2004. Computer databases and Aboriginal knowledge. *Learning Communities: International Journal of Learning in Social Contexts* 1. 4–12.

Christie, Michael. 2005a. Aboriginal knowledge traditions in digital environments. *The Australian Journal of Indigenous Education* 34. 61–66. (doi:10.1017/S1326011100003975)

Christie, Michael. 2005b. Words, ontologies and Aboriginal databases. *Media International Australia Incorporating Culture and Policy* 116(1). 52–63. (doi:10.1177/13298 78X0511600107)

Christie, Michael. 2007. Fracturing the skeleton of principle: Australian law, Aboriginal law, and digital technology. *Learning Communities: International Journal of Learning in Social Contexts* (November). 30–39.

Christie, Michael. 2008. Digital tools and the management of Australian Desert Aboriginal Knowledge. In Pamela Wilson & Michelle Stewart (eds.), *Global Indigenous media: Cultures, poetics, and politics*, 270–286. Atlanta: Duke University Press. (doi:10.1215/9780822388692-019)

Christie, Michael & Helen Verran. 2013. Digital lives in postcolonial Aboriginal Australia. *Journal of Material Culture* 18(3). 299–317. (doi:10.1177/1359183513492081)

Consultative Committee for Space Data Systems (CCSDS). 2012. *Recommendation for space data systems practices: Reference model for an open archival information system (OAIS), issue 2.* Washington DC: CCSDS Secretariat.

De Largy Healy, Jessica. 2014. Remediating sacred imagery on screens: Yolngu experiments with new media technology. *Australian Aboriginal anthropology today: Critical perspectives from Europe.* Paris. (http://actesbranly.revues.org/577) (Accessed 14 February 2018.)

Fourmile, Henrietta. 1989. Who owns the past?: Aborigines as captives of the archives. *Aboriginal History* 13(1/2). 1–8.

Garrett, Edward. 2014. Participant-driven language archiving. *Language Documentation and Description* 12. 68–84.

Geismar, Haidy. 2013. Defining the digital. *Museum Anthropology Review* 7(1–2). 254–263.

Gibson, Jason. 2009. *Managing Indigenous digital data: An exploration of the Our Story database in Indigenous libraries and knowledge centres of the Northern Territory.* Broadway, NSW: UTS ePress. (https://opus.lib.uts.edu.au/handle/10453/19485) (Accessed 26 February 2018.)

Glaskin, Katie. 2007. Outstation incorporation as precursor to a Prescribed Body Corporate. In James F Weiner & Katie Glaskin (eds.), *Customary land tenure and registration in Australia and Papua New Guinea: Anthropological perspectives*, 199–221. Canberra: ANU E-Press.

Green, Jennifer, Myfany Turpin & Carly Pettiona. 2017. *Trends in consent forms from Central Australian people: Report to CLC–CMP project management board.*

Haviland, John B. 2016. Making *gambarr*: It belongs to me, I belong to it. In Jean-Christophe Verstraete & Diane Hafner (eds.), *Culture and language use* 18. 455–480. Amsterdam: John Benjamins Publishing Company.

Hinkson, Melinda. 2015. *Remembering the future: Warlpiri life through the prism of drawing.* Canberra: Aboriginal Studies Press.

Hudson, Emily. 2006. *Cultural institutions, law and Indigenous knowledge: A legal primer on the management of Australian Indigenous collections.* Melbourne: Intellectual Property Research Institute of Australia.

Hudson, Emily & Andrew T Kenyon. 2005. *Copyright and cultural institutions: Guidelines for digitisation.* Melbourne: University of Melbourne.

Hughes, Martin & John Dallwitz. 2007. Ara Irititja: Towards culturally appropriate IT best practice in remote Indigenous Australia. In Laurel E Dyson, Max Hendriks & Stephen Grant (eds.), *Information technology and Indigenous people*, 146–158. Hershey, PA: Information Science Publishing. (doi:10.4018/978-1-59904-298-5.ch020)

Huvila, Isto. 2008. Participatory archive: Towards decentralised curation, radical user orientation, and broader contextualisation of records management. *Archival Science* 8(1). 15–36. (doi:10.1007/s10502-008-9071-0)

IASA Technical Committee. 2009. *Guidelines on the production and preservation of digital audio objects: Standards, recommended practices and strategies, IASA-TC 04.* 2nd edn (web version). (Ed. Kevin Bradley.) Aarhus, Denmark: International Association of Sound and Audiovisual Archives. (www.iasa-web.org/tc04/audio-preservation) (Accessed 19 October 2019.)

Indigenous Remote Communications Association. 2010. *Joining the dots: Dreaming a digital future for remote Indigenous media. IRCA submission to the Indigenous Broadcasting and Media Sector Review.* (https://www.yumpu.com/en/document/view/34120845/joining-the-dots-dreaming-a-digital-future-for-office-for-the-arts) (Accessed 19 October 2019.)

Janke, Terri. 1998. *Our culture: Our future: Report on Australian Indigenous cultural and intellectual property rights.* Michael Frankel & Company.

Janke, Terri. 2008. Indigenous knowledge & intellectual property: Negotiating the spaces. *The Australian Journal of Indigenous Education* 37(S1). 14–24. (doi:10.1375/S1326011100000338)

Janke, Terri. 2009a. *Beyond guarding ground: A vision for a National Indigenous Cultural Authority.* Rosebery, NSW: Terri Janke and Co.

Janke, Terri. 2009b. *Writing up Indigenous research: Authorship, copyright and Indigenous knowledge systems.* Terri Janke and Co. (http://docs.wixstatic.com/ugd/7bf9b4_a05f0ce9808346daa4601f975b652f0b.pdf) (Accessed 8 June 2018.)

Janke, Terri & Livia Iacovino. 2012. Keeping cultures alive: Archives and Indigenous cultural and intellectual property rights. *Archival Science* 12(2). 151–171. (doi:10.1007/s10502-011-9163-0)

Koch, Grace. 2008. *The future of connection material held by Native Title Representative Bodies: Final report* (Native Title Research Report), vol. 1. Canberra: Native Title Research Unit, AIATSIS.

Kukutai, Tahu & John Taylor (eds.). 2016. *Indigenous data sovereignty* (Centre for Aboriginal Economic Policy Research Research Monograph 38). Acton, ACT: ANU Press. (doi:10.22459/CAEPR38.11.2016)

Lancefield, Robert C. 1998. Musical traces' retraceable paths: The repatriation of recorded sound. *Journal of Folklore Research* 35(1). 47–68.

Linn, Mary S. 2014. Living archives: A community-based language archive model. *Language Documentation and Description* 12. 53–67.

Lydon, Jane. 2010. Return: The photographic archive and technologies of Indigenous memory. *Photographies* 3(2). 173–187.

Mansfield, John. 2014. Listening to heavy metal in Wadeye. In Amanda Harris (ed.), *Circulating cultures: Exchanges of Australian Indigenous music, dance and media*, 239–268. Canberra: ANU E-Press.

Marett, Allan & Linda Barwick. 2003. Endangered songs and endangered languages. In Joe Blythe & Robert McKenna Brown (eds.), *Maintaining the links: Language, identity and the land*, 144–151. Bath, UK: Foundation for Endangered Languages. (http://hdl.handle.net/2123/1314) (Accessed 19 October 2019.)

McClausland, Sally. 1999. Protecting communal interests in Indigenous artworks after the *Bulun Bulun* case. *Indigenous Law Bulletin* 4(22). 4–6.

McGrath, Pamela Faye. 2010. *Hard looking: A historical ethnography of photographic encounters with Aboriginal families in the Ngaanyatjarra Lands, Western Australia.* Australian National University. (PhD.)

Meakins, Felicity, Jennifer Green & Myfany Turpin. 2018. *Understanding linguistic fieldwork.* London: Routledge.

Michaels, Eric. 1986. *The Aboriginal invention of television in Central Australia 1982–1986* (Institute Report Series). Canberra: Australian Institute of Aboriginal Studies.

Moore, Shaunna & Susan Pell. 2010. Autonomous archives. *International Journal of Heritage Studies* 16(4–5). 255–268.

Myers, Fred. 2017. Whose story is this? Complexities and complicities of using archival footage. In Jane Anderson & Haidy Geismar (eds.), *The Routledge companion to cultural property*, 168–193. Routledge Handbooks Online.

Nakata, Martin N & Marcia Langton (eds.). 2005. *Australian Indigenous knowledge and libraries.* Broadway, NSW: UTS ePress.

Nakata, Martin N, Vicky Nakata, Alex Byrne, Jill McKeough, Gabrielle Gardiner & Jason Gibson. 2008. *Australian Indigenous digital collections: First generation issues.* Broadway, NSW: UTSeScholarship.

Newell, Jennifer. 2012. Old objects, new media: Historical collections, digitization and affect. *Journal of Material Culture* 17(3). 287–306.

Newman, Paul. 2012. Copyright and other legal concerns. In Nicholas Thieberger (ed.), *The Oxford handbook of linguistic fieldwork*, 430–556. Oxford: Oxford University Press.

Ormond-Parker, Lyndon & Robyn Sloggett. 2012. Local archives and community collecting in the digital age. *Archival Science* 12(2). 191–212. (doi:10.1007/s10502-011-9154-1)

O'Shannessy, Carmel & Felicity Meakins. 2016. Australian language contact in historical and synchronic perspective. In Felicity Meakins & Carmel O'Shannessy (eds.), *Loss and renewal: Australian languages since colonisation* (Language Contact and Bilingualism 13), 3–26. Berlin: De Gruyter.

Perrurle, Joel Liddle & Barry Judd. 2018. Altyerre NOW: Arrernte dreams for national reconstruction in the 21st century. *Learning Communities: International Journal of Learning in Social Contexts*, 23. 106–115. (doi:10.18793/lcj2018.23.09)

Rennie, Ellie, Eleanor Hogan, Robin Gregory, Andrew Crouch, Alyson Wright & Julian Thomas. 2016. *Internet on the outstation: The digital divide and remote Aboriginal communities* (Theory on Demand 19). Amsterdam: Institute of Network Cultures.

Ritchie, Eamon & Terri Janke. 2015. Who owns copyright in native title connection reports? *Indigenous Law Bulletin* 8(20). 8–11.

Seeger, Anthony. 1986. The role of sound archives in ethnomusicology today. *Ethnomusicology* 30. 261–276.

Stoianoff, Natalie P & Alpana Roy. 2015. Indigenous knowledge and culture in Australia – The case for sui generis legislation. *Monash University Law Review* 41(3). 745–784.

Thorner, Sabra. 2010. Imagining an Indigital interface: Aṟa Irititja indigenises the technologies of knowledge management. *Collections: A Journal for Museum and Archives Professionals* 6(3). 125–146.

Thorner, Sabra. 2016. Visual economies and digital materialities of Koorie kinship and community: Photographs as currency and substance. *Anthropology and Photography* 6. (http://www.therai.org.uk/images/stories/photography/AnthandPhotoVol6.pdf) (Accessed 20 October 2019.)

Toner, Peter G. 2003. History, memory and music: The repatriation of digital audio to Yolngu communities, or, memory as metadata. In Linda Barwick, Allan Marett, Jane Simpson & Amanda Harris (eds.), *Researchers, communities, institutions, sound recordings.* Sydney: University of Sydney. (https://ses.library.usyd.edu.au/bitstream/2123/1518/1/Toner%20 rev1.pdf) (Accessed 21 November 2018.)

Treloyn, Sally & Andrea Emberly. 2013. Sustaining traditions: Ethnomusicological collections, access and sustainability in Australia. *Musicology Australia* 35(2). 159–177. (doi:10.1080/08145857.2013.844473)

Treloyn, Sally, Matthew Dembal Martin & Rona Googninda Charles. 2016. Cultural precedents for the repatriation of legacy song records to communities of origin. *Australian Aboriginal Studies* 2. 94–103.

Turnbull, Paul. 2010. Introduction. In Paul Turnbull & Michael Pickering (eds.), *The long way home: The meaning and values of repatriation*, 1–11. New York: Berghahn Books.

Twomey, Justine. 2008. Legal and practical considerations in managing access to materials held by NTRBs and Land Councils. Appendix 6. In Grace Koch (ed.), *The future of connection material held by Native Title Representative Bodies: Final report* (Native Title Research Report 4), 39–45. Canberra: Native Title Research Unit, AIATSIS.

van Deursen, Alexander JAM & Jan AGM van Dijk. 2019. The first-level digital divide shifts from inequalities in physical access to inequalities in material access. *New Media & Society* 21. 354–375. (doi:10.1177/1461444818797082) van Gelderen, Ben & Kathy Guthadjaka. 2017. The Warramiri website: Applying an alternative Yolŋu epistemology to digital development. *Research and Practice in Technology Enhanced Learning* 12(14). 1–19. (doi:10.1186/s41039-017-0052-x)

Widlok, Thomas. 2013. Analogical problems with digital data. *The Asia Pacific Journal of Anthropology* 14(2). 183–194. (doi:10.1080/14442213.2013.768694)

Wild, Stephen A. 1992. Issues in the collection, preservation and dissemination of traditional music: The case of Aboriginal Australia. In Alice M Moyle (ed.), *Music and dance of Aboriginal Australia and the South Pacific: The effects of documentation on the living tradition* (Oceania Monograph 41), 7–22. Sydney: Oceania Publications.

Wright, Alexis. 2016. What happens when you tell somebody else's story? *Meanjin,* Summer.

Language Documentation & Conservation Special Publication No. 18
Archival returns: Central Australia and beyond
ed. by Linda Barwick, Jennifer Green & Petronella Vaarzon-Morel, pp. 29–45
http://nflrc.hawaii.edu/ldc/sp18
http://hdl.handle.net/10125/24876

2

Deciphering Arrernte archives: The intermingling of textual and living knowledge

Jason Gibson
Deakin University

Shaun Penangke Angeles
Artwe-kenhe Collection, Strehlow Research Centre

Joel Perrurle Liddle
Charles Darwin University

Abstract

Arrernte people are arguably the most documented Aboriginal group in Australia. Their language was studiously documented by Lutheran scholars, their ceremonies were subject to some of the most intensive ethnographic documentation and many of their songs were meticulously recorded. In addition, genealogical and historical archives are full of Arrernte social histories, and museum stores contain thousands of Arrernte-made artefacts. This chapter contains a condensed and edited transcript of interviews with two Arrernte men, Shaun Angeles and Joel Liddle, who discuss their deep and varied interests in these records and the archives that contain them. Both Joel and Shaun are of a younger cohort of Arrernte men living in the Alice Springs region who are increasingly interested in utilising the potential of archival material as a means of assisting Arrernte language and cultural transmission. These interviews explore some of the issues Arrernte peoples confront as they work through archives. We discuss the challenges of variant orthographies in the 19th and 20th century records, the limitations of conventional cataloguing requirements and the importance of reading archival texts in a way that sees them emplaced and tested against the knowledge of elders. Archival records are explained as being necessarily embedded within Arrernte social memory and orality and framed by local socio-cultural practices. Reflecting upon their own experiences, Joel and Shaun are able to provide advice to future generations in their dealings with collecting institutions and make recommendations to current and future researchers (ethnographic and linguistic) who are documenting Arandic material. The chapter concludes with a discussion about the role of digital technologies in the future dissemination of cultural materials.

Keywords: Arrernte, orality, Indigenous knowledge, anthropology, Aboriginal history

Introduction

Arrernte people are in the relatively fortunate position of having access to an extraordinarily detailed archive of linguistic and ethnographic information. Amassed over 130 years of assiduous documentation and observation by missionary and anthropological scholars, this archive now constitutes a treasure trove of linguistic detail, song texts, detailed descriptions of ceremony, and Indigenous toponymy. The following is a condensed and edited transcript of interviews with two Arrernte men, Shaun Angeles and Joel Liddle, who discuss their deep and varied interests in these records and some of the archives that contain them.[1] While much of the early linguistic work in the Arrernte region was carried out by Lutheran missionaries in the Western Arrernte region (Kempe 1891; Kenny 2018), my conversations with Shaun and Joel concentrate upon materials more relevant to their own ancestral ties to people of the Central and Eastern Arrernte area. Returning to these archives as passionate and engaged independent scholars, both reveal their commitment to seeing archival collections returned to communities for the benefit of Arrernte people. Both exhibit a desire to use the archive in a way that retains vulnerable aspects of the vivid, poetic, and empirically well-known local worlds of Arrernte people: place names, Dreaming stories, songs, and rituals.

Historical familiarity with literacy via Christian missions (Kral 2000) and greater access to education services via the Alice Springs township has enabled some Arrernte people to gain the necessary skills to engage with ethnohistorical sources (Malbunka 2004; Angeles 2016; Perkins 2016). Growing numbers of Arrernte people are now increasingly drawn to an archival body of material that is unmatched in size or scope anywhere in Australia. The plethora of Arrernte song recordings, texts, maps, stories, and genealogies present enormous opportunities for people to reconstruct cultural and individual identities, but at the same time they may be seen to impinge upon traditional forms of cultural transmission (Kenny 2013: 242). While the tensions between oral and literate forms of knowledge acquisition have been subject to considerable theoretical debate (Goody 1987; Ong 1988; Walsh 1995), Shaun and Joel accept the inevitable intermingling of archival and social memory. At the same time, they are also acutely aware of the need to carefully interpret, translate, and re-contextualise archival texts in social contexts and in dialogue with senior Arrernte people.

I first came to know Shaun as a friend in 2002 and our professional relationship developed further when we both serendipitously became involved in ethnographic collections. I was working in a curatorial capacity at the Melbourne Museum in 2013 when Shaun and a group of Arrernte men inspected the collections on pioneering anthropologists Baldwin Spencer and Francis Gillen (Morphy 1997; Jones 2005). Shaun later took on a role with the Strehlow Research Centre, the institution holding the manuscripts, artefacts, audio and film recordings of the linguist/ethnographer TGH Strehlow (Hill 2003; Gibson in press). Originally established by the Northern Territory Government in 1991 as a relatively autonomous government organisation, the centre has in recent years been transformed into an arm of the Museum and Art Gallery of the Northern Territory. Shaun's work on the collection over the last six

---

1   Due to various complicating factors I (JG) was unable to conduct this interview with both men present. Instead it was agreed that very similar questions would be put to each person and then their responses edited together. Both Shaun and Joel assisted with the selection and final editing of the transcript.

years has become critical to the centre's work of reconnecting Arrernte people (particularly men) with this dense corpus. I came to know Joel more recently, also via his interest in the Spencer and Gillen collection at the Melbourne Museum. In the discussion that follows, Joel describes his process of unearthing Arrernte language materials, deciphering their contents and navigating the politics and parameters of cultural knowledge.

What both men stress is the difficult work that is often required to make archival resources useful to contemporary communities. Coming to terms with inconsistent renderings of Arrernte, becoming familiar with multiple orthographies, negotiating access with institutions, and ensuring that one has a degree of local, cultural authority to work with significant recordings or texts are just a few of the challenges they face. While one of the principal ways of dealing with these documents is to return them to elders who possess detailed knowledge of Arrernte language and culture, the number of senior people with the required expertise needed to explain them is diminishing. Despite being sympathetic to the challenges institutions face, be they government-run museums and/or Aboriginal organisations such as the Central Land Council, to ensure that the use of cultural materials is managed sensitively, both men express a degree of frustration with access. Both Shaun and Joel express the sense of urgency that motivates them to identify and retrieve archival sources, transcribe and translate Arrernte texts, and extend upon the work of past ethnographers and linguists by further interrogating material with present-day elders. It is in this frisson between archives, orality, and sociality that they find both the pragmatic and existential value of these materials.

The interviews

JG: Each of you uses archival materials on a daily basis, either in your work or for personal edification. Can you give us some background to when you first started developing a curiosity about research materials that existed on Arrernte people?

SA: I've been curious since I was young, really. My grandmother spoke Arrernte, not fluently, but enough to teach us a little bit, a good sort of base, and I loved school and I loved learning. But I guess the point where I got really curious was after I was initiated and became a 'young man' according to Arrernte Law. After going through that ceremony, I had many, many questions. I guess I was very ignorant of the history of Arrernte people and the history of colonisation here in Alice Springs and Central Australia. I had learnt a little bit through school but learnt much more through conversations with my family. After I was initiated at age 19, I spent time with some really, really beautiful old men and it really opened up my eyes and made me ask, 'Who the bloody hell am I?' Then, when I was about 20 years old, I saw a film called *Mr Strehlow's film* by Hart Cohen, on SBS Television. That really triggered more of my curiosity and made me ask questions about my Arrernte culture. I wondered who was this fellow TGH Strehlow? And, more importantly, who were all these old men that he worked with and recorded so much of our song, ceremony, and language?

You see, we had a lot of questions about our own Arrernte identity, too, growing up. My nanna, Maureen Trindle (nee Stokes), was really close with her brothers, all the *Ayampe-arenye mape* 'all the people belonging to the Ayampe estate', so we knew who our family was.

But for me, as a young man growing up in Alice Springs, I had a lot of questions about how I fit into the Arrernte cultural system. I started to buy my own books and put my own little library together, in an attempt to understand who I was, and where I fitted into that whole *anpernirrentye* 'system of kin relationships'. So, in that time, I did a lot of my own research from home or just in my own time, as well as becoming familiar with anthropological and linguistic records.

JL: I started looking at archival Arrernte material probably in 2007–2008. I had lived with my family interstate in Victoria and in Canberra, but through my father we had these strong linkages back here to our Arrernte families. So, I had that exposure to people like my *aperle*, my 'father's mother', Emily Liddle (nee Perkins), too. She was a good pidgin English speaker but she also spoke Arrernte fluently. She was revered by my aunties and uncles as a sort of knowledgeable matriarch. I remember her saying a few things to … me in language just when we would visit Alice Springs. I'd hear her say things like *kele mwerre* 'okay, good', *nthakenhe* 'what's happening?', or *werte* 'hello'. I think she probably swore at us a couple of times too [laughs], so that sort of stuck with me. When we'd go back to live in Victoria, in the area we were living, it was kind of isolating. You just wouldn't see Aboriginal people around, and my dad is a visibly Aboriginal person, so you'd stick out in the street. It was kind of challenging because I knew I had this identity up here but I didn't know anything about it. I had a lot of questions about my Arrernte heritage and I became more curious about it as I grew up.

JG: Can you name some of the key resources that each of you accessed in order to further explore and learn about Arrernte culture and language?

JL: Our family had *The Eastern and Central Arrernte to English Dictionary* by Henderson and Dobson (1994) and I would have a look through that every now and then. It got sent to us by family when it came out and we always had it in the house. That was my first exposure to Arrernte language in detail, really, aside from hearing Nana talk and Dad reeling off a few words. I had also heard of the anthropologists Spencer and Gillen, and we knew there were other researchers who had done work with Arrernte people in the early times. But I didn't know that Spencer and Gillen had compiled these huge books, *The native tribes of Central Australia* (1899) and *The Arunta* (1927). They also left behind a huge archive of objects, notes, diaries, photographs, song recordings etc. When I did finally hear of their books I just went and bought them [laughs] and later I searched their archive using the Spencer and Gillen website. I also ended up visiting the collection at the Melbourne Museum. They've been the key resources I've used, but along the way I just started buying books or downloading any resource I could have access to. Sometimes they were academic papers written about Arrernte culture, people, land, and language, but other books like *Listen deeply* by Kathleen Kemarre Wallace and Judy Lovell (2009), or *Iwenhe Tyerrtye* by MK Turner and Veronica Dobson (2010) have helped me a lot. My nanna had some involvement with the botanist Peter Latz and wrote the foreword for his book *Bushfires and bushtucker* (1995), which is a brilliant resource. I think at one stage I bought every Arrernte book sold through IAD [the Institute for Aboriginal Development] publishing too!

SA: The Eastern and Central Arrernte Dictionary has been my number one companion over the last 17 years! I'm just fascinated with the amount of depth in our language and a lot of it has been recorded in there. That's where it really started for me. It was my entrance into my own world of being a young Arrernte man. Also, *The town grew up dancing* (2002) by Wenten Rubuntja and Jenny Green was really important.

JG: Publications are, of course, available to most, but few take that next step of digging further into the archives, into the historical, linguistic, and anthropological details. When did you go beyond the published work and begin to delve into the 'raw data' of archival collections?

SA: That's only been a recent thing with me, since I started working here at the Strehlow Research Centre really, about six years ago, and what I have found has just blown me away. Before beginning at the Strehlow Centre I had coordinated an Arrernte male elders' group at the Institute for Aboriginal Development and my first real sort of introduction into archives was when we were invited by yourself and Philip Batty to take a delegation of senior Arrernte and Anmatyerr men to Museum Victoria in 2013. I began to look at object documentation, access recordings of Arrernte song and realise the potential of this material. That was the start for me in terms of interacting and engaging with Indigenous archival material. It was such an exciting time. It was as if the world that I had been introduced to over the ten years leading up to this, with my own initiation and cultural work with elders, was also there in the archive ... It was a discovery of, 'Did people really record all this?' I had no idea. 'Were people collecting and documenting all of our sacred artefacts?' 'Did they really record all of this cultural information?' Well, actually, in some cases they didn't document them very well. I knew a little bit about archives and museums before that, but it was just very surface level stuff. I knew that some of these collections existed, but there was no way for me to know that they held such vast knowledge of our people. That trip to the Melbourne Museum started my process of discovery and a year later I started working with the Strehlow archive. Well, that has changed my life, it has totally changed my life.

JL: I started with all the publicly available books and resources anyone can buy from IAD or bookshops, but when I went back to uni in 2013 and was having to research, it just became a natural thing that I would look at Arrernte and relevant desert materials in published journals. I haven't really accessed anything that's like 'raw data' so to speak, as I haven't been employed as a researcher and until only recently didn't have any research affiliation. I'm finalising my PhD application so it is my hope that the raw data in archives will inform the bulk of that work. That journey is only beginning for me. I have just tried to develop resources from materials I have used and look for how they complement each other. I also do mapping projects (Figure 1). I'm always searching for information on place names in Central Australia. I usually take the maps made by Spencer and Gillen and Strehlow, and later ones produced by Arrernte people of the Alice Springs region. When I find a new place name in historic materials I'll try and work out how they sound and what they might mean, using my knowledge of the contemporary Arrernte orthography. I'll look at this Spencer and Gillen orthography and then at Strehlow's orthography and then try and put it into the Henderson and Dobson orthography. This helps me extract the place name in a form that we can read and pronounce more accurately. Potentially from there you could go and talk to, for example, *utnerrengatye* 'emu bush caterpillar' people that belong to a certain site and its associated *Altyerre* 'Dreaming'. There is the potential, with these archives, for people to reconnect with something very meaningful.

Figure 1. Joel Liddle examining Spencer and Gillen's maps of Arrernte place names and their Dreaming associations (photo: Jessie Bartlett)

SA: I have also used maps that were made by the anthropologist Olive Pink in the 1930s, maps that you actually helped us find in the AIATSIS collection. I showed these maps to senior men and we're still in a process of organising field trips to locate some of the sites on her maps. There's one man in particular that could help identify a couple of those sites in Olive Pink maps that relate to Ayampe country. I guess my experiences around that kind of stuff is that it is important not to rely on archives but to go to the primary source, straight to grandfathers and recording material that is still remembered and lived. And then using those recordings to empower myself, which then empowers my sons and my whole family, I guess.

JG: So, you're taking old records and interpreting them via a process of linguistic analysis so that they can be returned to contemporary Arrernte people?

JL: *Yewe alakenhe* ['Yes, that's how it's done']. The problem was, a lot of the stories recorded by Spencer and Gillen are sacred, and I had to be really vigilant to ensure that I didn't look into anything I shouldn't. You have to be careful when you uncover archival records. I didn't want to know about anything that belonged to men until I had been initiated. I didn't want to spoil that process. After going through Law[2] I've become a little more comfortable with looking more deeply into things, but you have to remain diligent. For the most part what I do is update

---

2   Participating in Arrernte men's ceremonial life.

the early work ... What I have done is change the Spencer and Gillen Arrernte into today's Arrernte for place names or for people's names. By doing this, if a similar word pops up again in the future I can identify the markers and will know what it says. It helps with pronunciation and also extracting a meaning from what was written down. You can then find the different components of the word that make up the place name. They're really interesting processes, so not only do you have a map but then you have a story that could be used to discuss with those knowledgeable elders later.

Spencer and Gillen were really inconsistent in their spelling. I have learnt Arrernte from the Henderson and Dobson orthography and, unlike Spencer and Gillen, I have found that it is really consistent and it's actually not that hard to learn. This orthography has been around for a long time too and elders were part of the process in developing it. But I also want to follow the rules that have been developed in this orthography. I'm not sort of advocating for linguistics or this really strict linguistic process, but I think in this day and age we need a spelling process, and we have one, and we should just stick with it. It's bizarre to look around town and see all these bastardised attempts at using Arrernte language on street signs, buildings, or workplaces. Henderson and Dobson's Arrernte was developed for people like me who are English speakers and are able to transfer our knowledge of English into utilising Arrernte, learning Arrernte, so that's why it's there. Arrernte has very distinct sounds, and they're tongue-twisting and tiring. You can't learn those sounds from Spencer and Gillen's orthography, you can't learn it from a phonetic orthography. Why use an inaccurate phonetic spelling for people (tourists and whitefellas) that have no interest in learning our language anyway? A language doesn't exist so it's easier for other people to say it who don't have the interest in actually learning it. When, really, you look at language representations throughout the world: they're symbolised differently for a reason, and often they're hard. Just put up our orthography and people can learn it. Once you actually learn that it's totally different, that's how you start to look at the world through the eyes of Arrernte people. That's the whole idea of learning another language.

Understanding Spencer and Gillen's writing of Arrernte is almost impossible unless you have some knowledge of Arrernte and can speak it a bit. Using their work is kind of like a process of extracting or decoding. And you also have to work with linguists, like Jenny Green, David Moore, Myfany Turpin and Gavan Breen, who have all helped me out in the past. Once you get a few of Spencer and Gillen's words identified you start to recognise them in the new orthography. You can then transfer this to the other Arrernte words they have written down. You will see something they've written, and then be like, "Oh I know what they're saying here!" And when you actually discover a word, or when you unlock one of their words, it's a real celebration. It is significant because within what is written can be a lot of secrets that reveal themselves. I use their books and their unpublished notes, which are on the Spencer and Gillen website, to work things out. When I do, it's like, "Ah, that's what that means, wow!"

It's changed my mind in the way I look at things. When I drive around out bush now, as opposed to what I would have done before I started learning about Arrernte language or about *apmere*, 'country', I don't think, "Oh, that's a nice hill" or "This is good country," I think, "I know that that's this story" and "I know that that's that place name." It's a different lens that you look through. You're looking at country with a new set of eyes. It's really hard to explain but it kind of boggles your mind a little bit. You want to make sure that's looked after, so you're nurturing that to carry on that *Altyerre* 'Dreaming'. It's huge, it's multilayered.

JG: Given these differences, is it hard to work with Strehlow's orthography when you are conducting research? Do you also have to go through a process of translating or decoding his Arrernte to try to make sense of what he's written?

SA: Initially it was hard, but then you work out his rules around his orthography, you can work it out. Because of my grounding in the contemporary orthography you can then make those distinctions between the two orthographies. But there are challenges with the Strehlow Collection, the Strehlow archive as a whole. For example, when he writes down an hour-long Arrernte story from a particular site and it fills 10 or 15 pages in his orthography, that's when it gets tricky. I found that with how he recorded site names you can generally work them out, but with everyday language and terms and even the 'old Arrernte', that more 'pure Arrernte', that's when it gets tricky. Or you come across words and you can sound them out but there's always this wondering, I guess. You wonder, "Am I saying this word properly?", "Can I find that equivalent in the contemporary Arrernte dictionary?", "What does it mean?" You really need to work closely with the old speakers. You really need to work closely with them to work out what was being recorded.

JG: I imagine it would be hard for anyone to begin unlocking the potential of these archives, and it must be doubly hard for people located in remote areas and who might not have significant English literacy skills. What do you think are some of the biggest obstacles for Arrernte people wanting to access archives?

SA: Yes, absolutely, there's thousands of challenges. I was, however, lucky to have a good base of literacy and numeracy, that was one skill that allowed me to float through archives with ease because I could understand the English (that's what most of our archives are primarily written in, but also German) and I used my knowledge of Arrernte to work with the language material. I am very thankful that I have those literacy and language skills. As Joel says, there are multiple orthographies for Arrernte, and this can make things challenging at times. TGH Strehlow, for example, created his own orthography and it's significantly different to our contemporary orthography, which was created by fluent Arrernte speakers with the help of linguists. That's the orthography that I grew up with, I learnt to read Arrernte in that orthography and I can write a little bit in Arrernte. Although I can read and understand Strehlow's Arrernte, I am often having to reimagine it in the new orthography, so that I can get the sounds right. If you don't do that, in some cases, you'd be lost as to what a word might be.

JL: I really want to use these archives so that I can develop new resources that are useable for today's generation. I've been able to learn from these archives, but they're very hard to decipher. To actually be able to go in to them you need to have that level of intellect where you can extract this information, and for a lot of our mob if you can't read and write, how are you going to benefit from these archives? You can't go deeper. I've benefitted being educated. It's like me and Shaun can do that, we're educated. Now, I guess, what I've learnt through the process is, there's so much work I have to do, I kind of feel responsible, in a way, to take what I have learnt through my research and put it in a format for more people to access.

I think, in general, the archive is very difficult for people to access and understand anyway, so I think even if people are using it there are issues of interpretation. I remember a time where you could go and get your genealogy from the Strehlow Research Centre, it was easy to access and all that, but that doesn't happen anymore because people don't understand how to interpret them properly. Unfortunately, in our community, people have lost knowledge of *anpernirrentye*, that kinship system. So, for example, you might see an ancestor name on a family tree or your grandfather on there and it'll say their conception site, but most people don't understand what a conception site means anymore. They'll say, "What's a conception site?" I've had a lot of people say this to me and I've had to explain it, and Shaun and I have discussed it; Shaun explained it to me really early on. So, I can see how genealogies, as one example, can be misused or misinterpreted. I think that some archival resources need keys or legends to help people understand them. They need to be decoded by someone who can do that work. I'm happy to do that work so that our community can benefit from it.

JG: Have you ever had problems accessing archives or archival material?

JL: I've had plenty [laughs]. I'm not the only Arrernte person that's faced this – it is difficult. I still struggle today with it. How can I access this information? What will they [museum staff] think when I go to this museum? Will they allow me to look at this stuff? That's been the hardest thing for me, actually. I don't have an anthropology degree, I'm not a linguist, I'm just a person who has Arrernte heritage and I am interested. I don't fall into the sphere of being a museum employee, or a trainee, or someone that writes about this stuff. I have definitely found it hard to access archives at the Central Land Council.[3] They have a closed-door policy. The Strehlow Collection has enormous potential but it is not easily accessed because it is under-resourced. Archives have a lot of information – not all of this stuff is sacred or even sensitive, but unfortunately processes for access have found themselves at a standstill. For example, I knew that my nanna recorded her *Untyeyampe ayeye* 'corkwood story' with an anthropologist at the land council before she passed on. I think it was a written document, like maybe a transcribed document. But I have been denied access to it many times. The problem also is that this research work is always underfunded and there are such limited opportunities for Aboriginal researchers to actually get in and do this work that would have such a huge benefit to the community and people's wellbeing.

It's sometimes been hurtful, too, you know, because my research has never been about learning anything that's not appropriate or that I'm not qualified to learn – given the opportunity my nan would say, "Yes, give that to Joel." She'd be really happy that I'm interested in all this sort of stuff. But with some archives you feel like you never get the full story. People don't know how to deal with you and I think I have had a lot of suspicion along the way, like they are suspicious. "What's this guy's intentions?", "Who's this guy, he just wants to learn everything and what's he going to use this knowledge for?"

---

3   The primary representative body for Aboriginal people in the southern half of the Northern Territory of Australia.

JG: Do you think there is a certain kind of wariness of Aboriginal people using archives because they might be taking 'shortcuts' or not engaging with oral histories or the memories of older people as a priority? This is certainly seen as being a more 'authentically' Indigenous mode of discovery. Do you think collecting institutions expect you to rely more on orality than the archive?

JL: It could be. I mean I have been directed to 'go and speak to this person or that person', and I have done that. But mostly that's a palm-off. It is frustrating because there are important cultural leaders around but our systems of learning have had to change a bit. We no longer spend every day out in the bush learning and practising that knowledge, or showing our worth like in times past. Now we have to balance our religion with a lot of other day-to-day challenges in this modern world. Unfortunately, knowledge is actually in a vulnerable state where we really need to work to protect it for future generations. That's what I want to do. I think we need to be working as hard as we can to make sure that we have everything in order, so that our future generations still have our religion, culture, and language. I've wanted to learn for myself because it's been a healing process, but then it's morphed into: okay, I see a lot of chaos in our communities, and I know what these archival collections have done for me, so I want to help it have that impact on other people's lives. I think a lot of the social issues we see are a direct result of people losing their cultural and linguistic identity.

It is difficult, it is hard. I don't know whether these institutions have dealt with this before or whether they've actually had an Arrernte person that's going to come in and access the records – I guess it is kind of new. I think having those processes in place, it's a professional relationship, and the institution is benefitting from the work that we will do, so being able to feed that back in to the archive. It was easy at the Melbourne Museum because the curator knew the work I was doing with Spencer and Gillen. But I think if it was someone strange coming off the street, maybe they wouldn't have been given the same treatment. We need people managing and working with this material who know the people – the families – and understand what the cultural sensitivities are. I think museums and other institutions get caught up in looking at this stuff as a historic collection. It's not, this collection is our religion, this is for us today. Look at the bible, for example; imagine if that had all these restrictions on access to their basic interpretations and rules for life? If that had been the case, that religion would have been finished long ago. Our community can benefit from the non-sacred stuff and, on the other hand, *akngerrapate* 'senior people' and qualified cultural people are the custodians of secret/sacred materials. We need to enrich it, like I said, to the point that we're totally satisfied and that the next generation inherits this house that is in order.

SA: What I really want to say about this kind of work, using archive material in a positive way, is that this stuff can change lives. Indigenous archives can change people's lives. We've seen a couple of examples of it here where a particular family group, a young family group that lacked strong leadership and strong cultural knowledge for their particular estate – we have been approached by them to conduct research into the Strehlow Collection. After six months of research, full-on intimate research, they found that their great-grandfather had worked with Strehlow in the 1930s. The way I see it is that their great-grandfather had left them, his descendants, 27 artefacts, an hour-long recording of ceremonial songs, multiple maps documenting significant sites in their country, genealogies, and this whole collection of archival documentation around their heritage. This was a group of young men who came into the building with their heads down and they were searching for cultural knowledge for their land. This process of researching, going through the archive with a fine-tooth comb, but knowing what we're actually looking for, and then finding all this material that they never grew up learning.

We then did a couple of field trips with an important elder, Alan Drover, who holds a lot of that deep memory for country, their country. We visited six or seven really significant sites; we took copies of archival material out of the building – photographs, some recordings, film footage, and maps – out into the field, got it dirty with red dust, used it in a way that empowered people, empowered their family. I see these men now here in the community, a couple of them are just changed men. That's no exaggeration. Those materials and that process of discovery changed the trajectory of their lives basically.

JG: How do you blend archival knowledge with the knowledge of senior men, Shaun? Have you taken Strehlow's Arrernte language text and taken it to older people to try and work through it?

SA: We've done that with small parts of the collection. An example is Strehlow's 1935 field diary, where he spent three months doing fieldwork in the Eastern Arrernte region. I went through a process of reading that diary out, word for word, to John Cavanagh, a senior East Arrernte man, with the objective of basically passing this information on to him. But it quickly evolved into something more interactive, where we were trying to articulate field maps that Strehlow had created which were primarily written in Arrernte, and certain paragraphs where he'd write fully in Arrernte. That process of going through approximately 150 individual pages took four to five months of reading word for word. But the thing that stood out to me the most was just how much of this language and cultural knowledge was still alive – how much of the Arrernte language was known to John Cavanagh. He was actually enriching Strehlow's archive by going through that process. For example, there were sentences, old Arrernte phrases, that these old men were using which couldn't have been interpreted or translated by anybody else but those old Arrernte speakers because much of it hadn't been documented in the dictionaries. By going through that process, we learnt a lot about previously unknown parts of that field diary. My goal is to do that for all of the 44 field diaries Strehlow wrote because people deserve the right to have this record, this entire archive, shared with them.

JG: Arrernte people are lucky in that this fascinating material exists, and much of it was written in Arrernte. Groups elsewhere in Australia are not as fortunate. The work required to return material in a format that is digestible, especially when it is text that requires translation and interpretation, must be enormous.

SA: That's right. And that was only one field diary and it took about four or five months. The field diaries are very different in nature to what Strehlow calls his 'Myth Books'. While the field diaries are, I'd say – just a rough estimation – 90 per cent English and 10 per cent Arrernte, the Myth Books are primarily written in Arrernte; 90–95 per cent is written in Arrernte and 5 per cent in English. These books have long transcriptions of song texts and ancestral stories, and in some cases translations, which makes our job a little bit easier. But the key thing is that these books correlate to the sound recordings. You have the audio record of the myth, and audio recordings also contain the *akngerrapate* 'senior men' speaking to Strehlow, telling him the story of a particular site, and that story can go for, like – in some cases those old men are explaining in fine detail the stories of these Arrernte sites – some of them can go for an hour. And then they will go straight into the song verses.

The thing with those sound recordings is that because the *akngerrapate* were speaking in a pure Arrernte, if we don't do work with these sound recordings to translate what these old men are saying, potentially in another 10 or 15–20 years down the track, nobody is going to know what these old men are saying, because the Arrernte that they're using is very, very different to the contemporary Arrernte that is being used. So, if nothing is done in this 10 to 15–year window, we run the risk of potentially not knowing large chunks of what this archive holds. It is urgent that we try to find some sort of funding, whether we have a dedicated person or persons working with the old speakers of Arrernte, and all the other languages of Central Australia, to just purely focus their time and energy into translating all this audio recording.

JG: Do you work on returning recordings of Arrernte song?

Figure 2. Shaun Angeles playing back song recordings from a laptop computer during a consultation session with senior men (photo: Ben Deacon)

SA: Yes, song is absolutely critical in knowing what our *apmere* 'land' is all about. But where song is not well understood, where particular songs are not known anymore, we need translations of their meaning. That is why getting translations of what these men told Strehlow, men telling their stories of the landscape, is so important. What I have found is that there's only a few old men – and I say old men because that's who I work with primarily, as the songs recorded by Strehlow were sung by men only – who can retell these stories with the amount of intimate knowledge that is contained in these song recordings. These old men talked for over an hour about a particular site and the stories associated with it. Today, however, it seems that men aged in the 40 to 45 (maybe even the 50-year-old) age bracket, in some pockets of Arrernte country, that level of information just isn't there.

JG: In your experience, how do you think Arrernte men generally feel about using returned song recordings to learn songs? Is this a growing trend?

SA: People love it – that's what people want, in my experience. The song recordings, the sound recordings of the stories and the verses associated with that site, people ask for those more than what they do for other assets in the collection. People are also making song recordings of their own. What I'm seeing is that people are holding these recordings to themselves, which I think is totally up to them. If they're recording something from their grandfather or their father or their uncles, it's their property, it's their intellectual property; they have the right to do what they want with it. There's been a couple of occasions where men have brought in old tapes that record their grandfathers in the '80s and the '90s and they're wanting to use this facility here to deposit them and, in some cases, digitise them. I think they do that because there is a sense of security in doing that. Also, there is a bit of status that goes along with it. It must be 'important' if it is in a museum or archive. The Strehlow Centre is an important institution, people know about it, they know what we do; we've got our bit of cultural heritage, we've got our song, we've got our ceremony or whatever, film, let's store it here. But I think the main factor is the security that these kinds of places offer people. I mean, that's only happened a few times in my six years here; I don't know if it's happening much in other institutions around the country.

We need to think about how do we treat a USB or a hard drive or a laptop if it holds sacred material? Does that object then become sacred because of its contents? And what are some of the security measures that we should place around these particular objects? I know like with me I've done exactly that: I've recorded some of my grandfathers singing songs. Personally, I treat that hard drive like it's a sacred object. I've gone out and bought my own safe and bolted it to the ground. I don't know if it's progress, if you can call it progression? But, it's definitely a type of responsibility that people are now taking on. Now that we're totally embedded in this new world – I mean we're never going to go back walking the country naked – we need to take measures to secure sacred material.

JG: In this environment of ubiquitous digital technology, sedentary living, and so on, is it desirable for people to access their cultural heritage via online tools? Trying to decode this material is an intellectual and research-intensive exercise but I would have thought that 'living archives' like those relating to Arrernte language need to be examined within social context and under advice from knowledgeable people.

JL: Absolutely. That was where I found myself; I wanted to learn a lot and I wanted to use these materials and that, but there's no point in just learning it yourself or trying to gain knowledge yourself and not actually utilising it within that social cultural context. What I have found is that a lot of the stuff I'm learning, some old people will remember these things and we'll discuss certain points. Discussions come up and they're like "oh yeah," or I might mention someone and they're like, "Oh I remember that old man," or "I thought that was that Dreaming, that place, but a lot of people have forgotten that one." People reconnect with that stuff. It's not just a personal, intellectual process, like going to university and studying something, it has to be open to our community. But a lot of people haven't had the opportunity to grow up knowing their culture and language – that's not the experience for a lot of our mob, a lot of them are stolen generation people, or they have grown up under assimilation policies and haven't had the access to that learning. I'd like to see basic learning materials they can access to get them up to speed so they can help maintain our language and culture.

Before I moved back to Alice and found out I could start learning I was like, "I'm going to start doing it!" It took a few years, but I made sure that I learnt as much as I could from these resources so I wasn't coming back real fresh and green. I knew I'd have to go and talk to old people, my relations, and I didn't want to be too 'green' for them.

JG: Can you think of any recommendation for getting archival records back to people in Central Australia? What advice could you give to researchers and institutions about what's the best way of giving their documentation or recordings back to Arrernte people?

SA: We wonder about this at the Strehlow Research Centre as well. I guess the first step is to identify the correct *apmere-kartweye* 'owners' and *kwertengerle* 'managers'. That's the first step, you really need to identify the right people, and this takes time. And then there needs to be extensive consultations around all this stuff because it can be highly significant material. And I guess that's the sort of work that we do on a daily basis here. Then there's the issues around digital repatriation of material, it has a lot of issues around it. Originally all this information was stored in people's brains, in their hearts, in their whole bodies, and their whole lives revolved around song, ceremony, place, story. Because of a whole lot of historical factors, there's been a lot of knowledge that has now been lost and we now use these sorts of vehicles of transmission, like USBs and hard drives, all this kind of new technology. One of my biggest concerns around digital repatriation is losing control of the content. We're potentially facing a situation where if we continue to repatriate footage and audio digitally, we could be in a situation in 10 to 20 years' time where there's thousands of copies out there.

People are loading stuff up to the cloud and on to their phones. Well, people lose phones all the time! So how do we work with that potentiality, how do we work with the issues, the dangers around that? Potentially history could repeat itself again, where you have this piece of technology that's holding important material and then you lose it again.

JL: There is that sense of urgency, and there are a lot of people in our community that want to learn this stuff. We need Arrernte researchers working with these materials and these opportunities need to exist. Opportunities to engage and work with our *akngerrapate mape* 'all the elders' need to be made, too.

We need to develop everyday open knowledges into basic digital mediums so everyone can learn from them now. Our people who don't speak need real opportunities and pathways to learn Arrernte language and they need to see that dual place naming exists within our community, and it's done in the Eastern/Central Arrernte orthography. So far, digital media, it's an untapped opportunity. But we're seeing it being used to support language revitalisation in other parts of the country. I've thought many times about a lot of my research, "Do I create a website and just publish my own regurgitated material?" I am working on projects that I will publish, that will be publishable, so at some stage that will happen.

The sacred material in these archives should not ever be for public viewing and, throughout publications over the years, things have been published that should never be viewed by anyone today. That belongs to that environment, that sacred area. With regard to non-sacred material, it's an urgent thing to actually go through what is out there so that then we can get that information and say, "Look this is what we as an organisation are going to publish or make available for people to learn from." At the end of the day, the old people [aka informants] who told the early researchers this stuff are often listed, and this just needs to be communicated so people today understand where this knowledge comes from. Republishing could exist with the oversight of senior people. It is impossible to please everyone in this space, but we've got to do this work and it takes a bit of courage. A lot of people will be very happy to learn more about their country. Archives and museums need to realise that more and more Aboriginal people will be wanting to access this stuff as time goes on.

JG: There are quite serious conditions around who can access what, so when something is deposited in an archival collection, what sort of information should go with it? How could we all improve the accessibility of archival collections?

SA: As much information as possible! You have to be thorough. We need information on exactly who the people were, including their skin names, their *arrenge* 'father's father's' country, who they were *kwertengerle* for. For example, with songs, we need to know the singers' names, their skin names, their countries, what the song is about, what country it belongs to, what *anyenhenge* (father/son clan group) is associated with that song. When people in the film industry say like, when you're taking footage of something, 'shoot the shit out of it,' well I think you have to 'record the shit out of it'. Record absolutely everything that you can. Because contemporary-day Arrernte people are faced with this legacy issue of going through archives where there's hardly any prominent information whatsoever, and we're in a situation now where we could potentially be facing thousands and thousands of objects, as well as many song recordings, that we don't know where they belong. This is all because of the lack of documentation around recordings or collecting. We deal with this every day, all the time, and if we can't relate an item to a person, family group, or country, it makes returning material very hard. This poses big questions for us around governance, around who cares for an object? How do we care for it? Where does it go?

What people have to understand is that Arrernte cultural knowledge is a really localised knowledge, even to the point where it's an estate-based knowledge set. I mean, you could go further and further and further down on the ground with it. It's just the nature of the culture and the *akngerrapate* 'senior' ancestors' knowledge, it's just the nature of it. People working with this material need to understand this. Collections lacking important cultural information don't do the community any favours. Institutions and researchers need to reflect back on themselves and have a look at their own internal requirements, processes and systems.

In the end, I'd love to see every community in Central Australia have their own repository of their own cultural heritage, because that's where it belongs, it belongs with the people. And the people can make the most use out of their own cultural heritage, obviously. Look, I don't know, that's a big question. I definitely think that we should be doing all that we can to empower local communities. We need more access, I mean that's what we try to provide as best we can here at the Strehlow Centre, so I understand that there are a lot of issues around doing that as well. Ideally, I would love to see archives with their custodians, with the families that are responsible for that particular song, documentation, or whatever. That's what we want, in an idealistic world that's what we want. I think it is happening, but it's happening slowly.

References

Angeles, Shaun. 2016. This beautiful body of knowledge at the Strehlow Centre. *Alice Springs News Online.* (http://www.alicespringsnews.com.au/2016/09/30/working-with-this-beautiful-body-of-knowledge-at-the-strehlow-centre) (Accessed 22 January 2019.)

Dobson, Veronica & John Henderson. 1994. *Eastern and Central Arrernte to English Dictionary.* Alice Springs: IAD Press.

Gibson, Jason. In press. Ceremony men: Making ethnography and the return of the Strehlow Collection. Albany: State University of New York Press.

Goody, Jack. 1987. *The interface between the written and the oral.* Cambridge: Cambridge University Press.

Hill, Barry. 2003. *Broken song: TGH Strehlow and Aboriginal possession.* Sydney: Random House.

Jones, Philip. 2005. 'Indispensable to each other': Spencer and Gillen or Gillen and Spencer? *Strehlow Research Centre Occasional Paper* 4. 6–25.

Kempe, H. 1891. A grammar and vocabulary of the language spoken by the Aborigines of the MacDonnell Ranges, South Australia. *Transactions of the Royal Society of South Australia* 14(1). 1–54.

Kenny, Anna. 2013. *The Aranda's pepa: An introduction to Carl Strehlow's masterpiece Die Aranda- und Loritja-Stämme in Zentral-Australien (1907–1920).* Canberra: ANU E-Press.

Kenny, Anna. (ed.). 2018. *Carl Strehlow's 1909 comparative heritage dictionary: An Aranda, German, Loritja and Dieri to English dictionary with introductory essays.* Canberra: ANU Press.

Kral, Inge. 2000. *The socio-historical development of literacy in Arrernte: A case study of the introduction of writing in an Aboriginal language and the implications for current vernacular literacy practices.* Melbourne: University of Melbourne. (Masters thesis.)

Latz, Peter. 1995. *Bushfires & bushtucker: Aboriginal plant use in Central Australia.* Alice Springs: IAD Press.

Malbunka, Mavis. 2004. Accessing family information at the Strehlow Research Centre. In Michael Cawthorn (ed.), *Traditions in the midst of change: Communities, cultures and the Strehlow legacy in Central Australia*, 13–15. Conference Proceedings. Alice Springs: Strehlow Research Centre.

Morphy, Howard. 1997. Gillen – man of science. In John Mulvaney, Howard Morphy & Alison Petch (eds.), *My dear Spencer: The letters of FJ Gillen to Baldwin Spencer*, 23–50. Melbourne: Hyland House Publishing.

Ong, Walter. 1988. *Orality and literacy: The technologising of the word*. London: Routledge.

Perkins, Rachel. 2016. Songs to live by: The Arrernte women's project is preserving vital songs and culture. *The Monthly*, July issue. (https://www.themonthly.com.au/issue/2016/july/1467295200/rachel-perkins/songs-live) (Accessed 19 January 2019.)

Rubuntja, Wenten with Jenny Green. 2002. *The town grew up dancing: The life and art of Wenten Rubuntja*. Alice Springs: Jukurrpa Books.

Spencer, Baldwin & Francis Gillen. [1899] 1968. *The native tribes of Central Australia*. New York: Dover Publications.

Spencer, Baldwin & Francis Gillen. 1927. *The Arunta*. London: Macmillan and Company.

Turner, Margaret Kemarre. 2010. *Iwenhe Tyerrtye: What it means to be an Aboriginal person*. Translated by Veronica Dobson. Alice Springs: IAD Press.

Wallace, Kathleen & Judy Lovell. 2009. *Listen deeply, let these stories in*. Alice Springs: IAD Press.

Walsh, Michael. 1995. 'Tainted evidence': Literacy and traditional knowledge in an Aboriginal land claim. In Diana Eades (ed.), *Language in evidence: Issues confronting Aboriginal and multicultural Australia*, 97–124. Sydney: UNSW Press.

Language Documentation & Conservation Special Publication No. 18
Archival returns: Central Australia and beyond
ed. by Linda Barwick, Jennifer Green & Petronella Vaarzon-Morel, pp. 47–63
http://nflrc.hawaii.edu/ldc/sp18
http://hdl.handle.net/10125/24877

Reflections on the preparation and delivery of Carl Strehlow's heritage dictionary (1909) to the Western Aranda people

Anna Kenny
Australian National University

Abstract

This chapter reflects on the predicaments encountered while bringing ethnographic and linguistic archival materials, and in particular an Aranda, German, Loritja [Luritja], and Dieri dictionary manuscript compiled by Carl Strehlow and with more than 7600 entries, into the public domain. This manuscript, as well as other unique documents held at the Strehlow Research Centre in Alice Springs and elsewhere in Australia, is surrounded by competing views about ownership and control. In this case study I discuss my research and work with Western Aranda people concerning the transcription and translation into English of the dictionary manuscript. I also discuss the immense difficulties I faced in seeing the dictionary through to final publication. I encountered vested interests in this ethno-linguistic treasure that I had not been aware of and ownership claims that I had not taken into account. They arose from diverse quarters – from academia, from individuals in the Lutheran church, from Indigenous organisations, and from the Northern Territory Government. One such intervention almost derailed the dictionary work by actions that forced the suspension of the project for over 12 months. In this chapter I track the complex history of this manuscript, canvas the views of various stakeholders, and detail interpretations and reactions of Aranda people to the issues involved.

Keywords: Aranda, Loritja (Luritja), Dieri, Strehlow, dictionary

Introduction[1]

This chapter is a case study of the repatriation of archival knowledge. It discusses some difficulties encountered while bringing ethnographic and linguistic archival materials into the public domain, in particular an Aranda, German, Loritja (Luritja), and Dieri dictionary manuscript compiled by Lutheran missionary Carl Strehlow in 1909, and looks at the associated politics of knowledge and ownership involved in that process. This manuscript – the original of which is held at the Strehlow Research Centre (SRC) in Alice Springs – is surrounded by competing views in relation to its dissemination and the control of its contents. For the Aboriginal[2] community, it is their cultural heritage and of great socio-symbolic importance, to which they assert ownership rights. For others, such as scholars, it is a body of knowledge that is perceived to be general patrimony, and others again (e.g. the Lutheran community) believe that they too have ownership rights that are based on historical associations.

The predicament in relation to the publishing of Carl Strehlow's dictionary manuscript and the issues that were raised were sparked by complaints about orthography. However, the complaints about orthography disguised the underlying issues, namely the desire of different interest groups to assert control over the representation of language and Western Aranda literacy, and by extension over people, and the ownership of history and knowledge. In the process of unravelling and considering the multiple audiences for this cultural representation with their oftentimes conflicting vested interests, it became clear that Strehlow's ethnolinguistic work effectively embodied different identities and histories. The various views about orthography, the community politics, and the agendas of the various interest groups can be understood in the context of Clifford's proposition in relation to cultural representations in a post-colonial context, to the effect that an ethnographer's audience is multiple, and ethnography is a negotiation between at least two but usually more "conscious, politically significant subjects" (Clifford 1988: 41).

1   An ARC postdoctoral fellowship at the ANU has made it possible to write this chapter. It is part of ARC Linkage grant LP110200803, 2011–2014 Rescuing Carl Strehlow's Indigenous cultural heritage legacy: the neglected German tradition of Arandic ethnography. A version of this chapter was given at the ESfO conference in Munich in June 2017. I thank Nic Peterson, Rainer Buschmann, Helen Wilmot, Brian Connelly, Felicity Green, Shaun Angeles Penangke, Adam Macfie, Wendy Stuart, Diana Romano, Sally Babidge, and John Morton for their support and suggestions to improve this chapter. I am also very thankful for the comments of my anonymous reviewers.

2   I use in this chapter 'Aboriginal' rather than 'Indigenous' when referring to people in Central Australia because they have a preference for the word 'Aboriginal'.

Figure 1. Map of Carl Strehlow's study area in Central Australia showing some place names in his spelling system (source: Kenny 2018: xi)

Ethnographic and linguistic materials in Australian archives

Over the past four decades, the interest in early unpublished Australian ethnographic and linguistic materials held in archives has increased significantly. This surge in interest is due substantially to land and native title claims made respectively under the *Aboriginal Land Rights (Northern Territory) Act 1976* (Cth) and the *Native Title Act 1993* (Cth) (NTA). Since the High Court judgement in *Mabo v Queensland [No. 2]* (1992) 175 CLR 1, which entitled the Meriam people "as against the whole world to possession, occupation, use and enjoyment of the island of Mer" (Brennan J 1992: [97]), Australia recognises that native title (i.e. traditional rights and interest in land) of Aboriginal peoples has not been extinguished by the declaration of British sovereignty. This allows them to make claims to their traditional lands under the NTA. Among other things, these processes have led anthropologists preparing claims to turn to the earliest ethnographic sources across the Australian continent in order to establish what the original situation was likely to have been in a region and to demonstrate that elements of these pre-colonial systems show some sort of continuity to the present systems (Peterson & Kenny 2017: 3).

Consequently, the interest and awareness among Aboriginal people (and many others) about the value, power, and significance of early ethnographic and linguistic materials held in archives in Australia and overseas has increased notably. While these documentary records support land and native title claims and cultural maintenance and revitalisation projects, they have, in some instances, nevertheless become a contributing factor in various conflicts and aggravated disputes in relation to the ownership and economy of knowledge in Aboriginal communities, particularly in contexts with actual or perceived economic implications (e.g. mining developments or tourist ventures). In such cases, archival records have often become more authoritative than orally transmitted ecological or ontological knowledge. It is therefore necessary to acknowledge the fundamental reality that, for increasing numbers of Aboriginal people, archival materials have also become highly politicised, disputed, and even misused.

Genealogical data such as those contained in the Strehlows' family trees (c. 1900–1960s), Tindale's genealogical data (c. 1920s–1960s), Daisy Bates' records (c. 1901–1909), and Phyllis Kaberry's fieldnotes (1930s), held respectively at the Strehlow Research Centre, the South Australian Museum, the National Library of Australia, and at the Australian Institute of Aboriginal and Torres Strait Islander Studies, are often at the centre of these politics of knowledge in contemporary remote Australia. For the Western Aranda[3] the material Carl and TGH Strehlow collected is particularly important and highly sensitive, especially information about place and Aboriginal systems relating to land and its ownership that are glossed in English 'the Dreaming' or 'the Law'. Olive Pink (1884–1975), who also worked with the Aranda and collected material about land ownership, wrote in the 1930s that songs relating to segments of Northern Aranda mythology "definitely establish a man's title, to use legal phraseology," and that "to inherit the song is to inherit the estate" (Pink 1936: 286). She showed that knowledge about segments of myth is owned by clearly defined individuals or groups of people. Morgan & Wilmot (2010) have written about the misuse of genealogical data from the Strehlow Collection. Such observations illustrate how archived knowledge is fraught with difficulties due to its contemporary relevance to land ownership, identity, community politics, and the interpretation and perception of history by different interest groups.

While it has been possible, despite great difficulties, to repatriate material culture (e.g. sacred objects) and human remains for decades now, archived information about Aboriginal cultures still remains highly problematic. Many institutions in Australia, including archives, museums, libraries, Native Title Representative Bodies (NTRBs), and other government bodies, grapple with the issues of 'Who has the rights to these knowledges?' and 'Who may access them?' Several reports identifying the issues and problems surrounding the protection and possible return of these often culturally sensitive materials have been written (e.g. Koch 2008; McGrath, Dinkler & Andriolo 2015; McGrath 2018), but none of them provide any general guidance or policies on how to return material into the public domain or to groups of Aboriginal people (Dunn et al. 2018).

The desire to return intellectual property and further repatriate material culture to Australian Aboriginal people has become important for many institutions, because they have had to realise that these materials are of great significance to Indigenous Australians. The Strehlow Research Centre[4] is such an institution that recognises that its collection is of paramount importance to the Aranda people.

---

3   In this chapter the spelling 'Aranda' is used when speaking about the Arandic group who identifies as 'Western Aranda' or when used in a particular ethnographic source. Other spellings include 'Arrernte', which is now used by most other Arandic groups in the regions, such as the Northern Arrernte, and 'Arrarnta', which is mainly used by people at Hermannsburg.

4   The SRC is part of the Museum of Central Australia, which sits under MAGNT (Museum and Art Gallery of the Northern Territory).

The Strehlow Research Centre

The SRC (see Figure 2) was opened in Alice Springs in 1991 by the Northern Territory Government and is regulated by its own legislation, the *Strehlow Research Centre Act 2005* (NT). Its history has been conflict-ridden due to many different ownership claims over one of the most valuable ethnographic collections of Central Australian material in the world.[5] The recordings of sacred songs, ceremonies, and mythology held in the Strehlow Collection include materials of both Carl and TGH Strehlow (respectively father and son) and are understood by the traditional owners as cultural assets and capital.

The SRC holds 44 field diaries, 17 other diaries, more than 150 genealogies, countless site maps with thousands of site names, approximately 100 unpublished manuscripts (dictionaries, ethnography, novels, papers, and lectures), thousands of letters dating back to the late 1800s (in German, Aranda, and English), as well as more than 20 kilometres of film, more than 170 hours of sound recordings, more than 10,000 photographs and slides, and circa 1200 sacred objects held on behalf of the traditional owners in a special vault in the basement of the Strehlow Research Centre. It also houses the professional library of TGH Strehlow and many rare books about Aboriginal Australia.

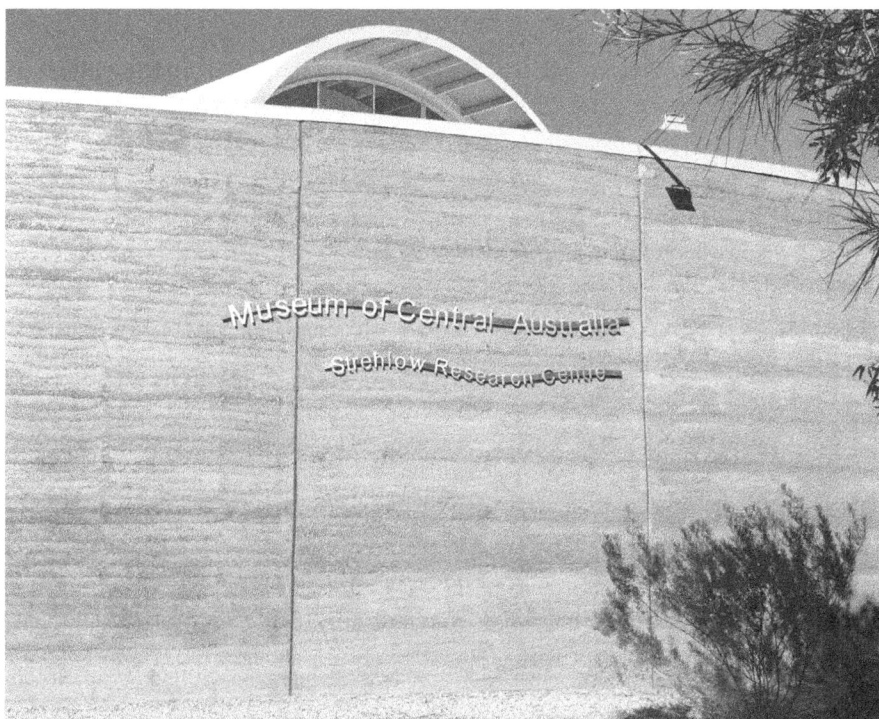

Figure 2. The Strehlow Research Centre in Alice Springs, Central Australia (source: Anna Kenny)

---

5   https://www.clc.org.au/index.php?/articles/info/strehlow/ (Accessed 10 April 2019.)

The Strehlow Collection was the focus of possibly the most bitter fight in Australia about the ownership and return of sacred objects to their rightful owners. While the collection of these original materials by Carl and TGH Strehlow and the creation of the SRC itself has been extremely problematic at both ethical and political levels (see for details McNally 1981; Hugo 1997: 127–136; Kaiser 2004), the SRC is nonetheless an institution that courts and attracts the attention of Central Australian Aboriginal people (and particularly Aranda people), whose cultural heritage is stored in its archival facilities and vaults. Of its seven board members, four are Aboriginal and at the time of writing the centre employed two Aboriginal persons as staff members and others on a casual basis when funding permits.

Shaun Angeles Penangke, a Northern Arrernte man employed by the SRC, has remarked that "the archives are already acting as our elders today"[6] and that the senior knowledgeable men he works with comment with admiration on the materials that the Strehlows collected, because they show their ancestors as powerful holders of the Law, the Dreaming. It is not only the records of the sacred songs and ceremonies or the objects that Aboriginal people access and value, but also family trees that sometimes show the names of forbears they did not know, or photographs of their ancestors whom they had never met.

Carl Strehlow's dictionary manuscript

The Strehlow Collection includes Carl Strehlow's manuscripts, which for most of the 20th century were believed to have been housed in Germany and destroyed in World War II. His published work *Die Aranda- und Loritja-Stämme in Zentral-Australien* was based on three of these manuscripts entitled *Sagen* (myths/legends), *Cultus* (cults), and *Leben* (life). *Sagen* contains the Aranda and Luritja myth collections, *Cultus* details songs that were sung during ceremonies, and *Leben* describes aspects of social life. They were published in seven instalments between 1907 and 1920 and are the richest ethnographic texts written on Western Aranda and Luritja cultures of Central Australia at the beginning of the 20th century. The original manuscripts survived in Australia. Strehlow had in fact only sent copies of them in segments for comment and publication to his editor, Baron von Leonhardi, in Germany (Kenny 2013: 37). It was these copies that were destroyed at the Ethnological Museum of Frankfurt during Allied bombings in World War II.

The dictionary is the fourth manuscript (c. 1909) (see Figure 3) and remained unpublished until 10 August 2018. It contains more than 7600 entries in Aranda, 6800 in Loritja, and 1200 in Dieri with German glosses. It probably represents the most comprehensive collation of Indigenous words of Australian languages compiled around the turn of the 20th century, closely matched only by Reuther's work on the Aboriginal languages and cultures of the Lake Eyre Basin (Lucas & Fergie 2017).

The journey of this dictionary manuscript as well as the other three manuscripts is fascinating. They disappeared in the first part of the 20th century and appeared again many decades later at the turn of the 21st century. The dictionary's journey began mid-1910, just after Carl Strehlow had completed his ethnolinguistic work, and when he had departed with his family from Central Australia for Germany. At the request of his German editor, he took

---

6   Shaun Angeles Penangke, pers. comm. to Anna Kenny, 23 January 2018.

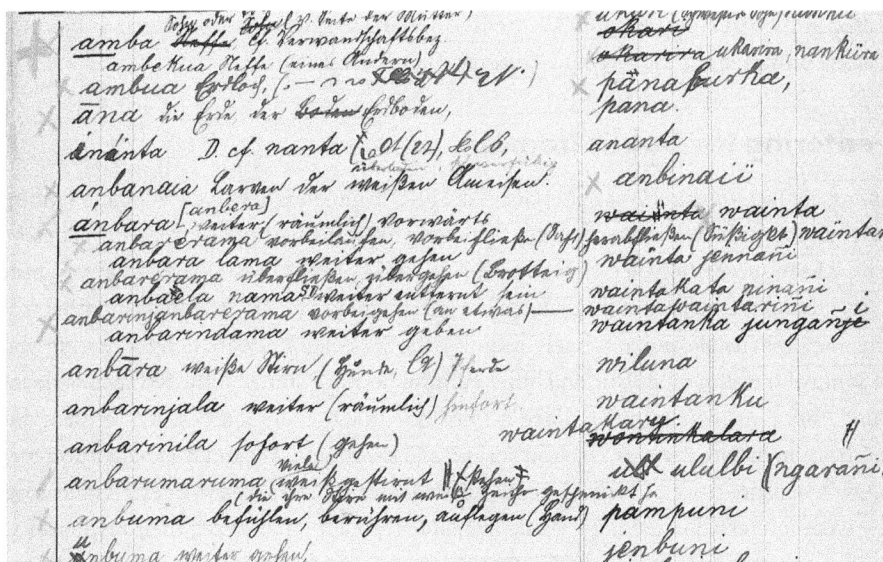

Figure 3. A page of Carl Strehlow's dictionary manuscript (c. 1900–1909) with 7600 entries in Aranda and German, 6800 in Loritja, and 1200 in Dieri (source: Anna Kenny)

many items with him in his luggage that were of anthropological interest, including the dictionary manuscript for publication. However, his editor died in Frankfurt from a stroke late in October 1910, only days before he was to meet Carl Strehlow and, as a consequence, the dictionary was never published. The dictionary as well as the other manuscripts returned with him back to the Hermannsburg Mission in Central Australia in 1912. Carl Strehlow and some Aranda men subsequently used the dictionary manuscript there to create a typed wordlist for an Aranda bible translation between 1913 and 1919. Three years later all manuscripts were taken on Carl's excruciating final journey to Horseshoe Bend in 1922, having been packed by his 14-year-old son, TGH Strehlow, in the fortnight before the family's departure from the Hermannsburg Mission (Strehlow 1969: 9).

Following Carl Strehlow's death at Horseshoe Bend on 20 October 1922, his wife, Frieda Strehlow, despite her ambivalence towards her husband's ethnographic work on Aboriginal religion and culture, gave the manuscripts to their youngest son, TGH Strehlow, when he started his language studies in the early 1930s at the University of Adelaide. The dictionary manuscript seems to have been a lifelong companion of TGH Strehlow, who later became one of Australia's most controversial anthropologists. Indeed, he took it with him when he returned in 1932 to Central Australia,[7] and when he died in 1978 it was found on his desk at the University of Adelaide. All manuscripts disappeared for some time thereafter, but surfaced again in the 1990s. They were among the items confiscated from the house of TGH Strehlow's second wife, Kathleen Strehlow, by Northern Territory Government order.[8] In exchange for a considerable sum of money, Kathleen Strehlow had previously agreed to make over all of her late husband's research materials and associated records to the Northern Territory Government. Following a protracted dispute over their ownership, they were ultimately

---

7   TGH Strehlow's Diary I (1932: 2); see also Kenny (2013: 153).

8   Schedule B of a draft of the *Strehlow Research Centre Act*, held at the SRC.

deposited at the Strehlow Research Centre in Alice Springs, where they remain, subject to the regulatory provisions of the *Strehlow Research Centre Act 2005*.

Re-entering the public domain

My initial contact with archival materials at the SRC began nearly two decades ago within the context of native title claims over country belonging to Western Aranda and Luritja peoples that have now been successfully determined by the Federal Court of Australia. As a native German-speaker, I found the earliest of these materials (as compiled by Carl Strehlow and others) to be readily comprehensible and extremely useful. After this claim research, my intention was to make some of the ethnolinguistic and other cultural heritage stored at the SRC available to the relevant Aboriginal communities, since it remained functionally inaccessible to them due to its codification in 19th century German scripts and shorthand. When I drew attention to Carl Strehlow's treasure trove of early ethnolinguistic material, and asked Western Aranda people if they were interested in having it made available through publication, their responses were enthusiastic, particularly in view of their concerns about language loss. The Strehlow Research Centre also endorsed this proposal. Based on the positive responses to the idea of publishing Carl Strehlow's dictionary manuscript, and believing that a dictionary was a harmless – that is, politically neutral – product that no one would oppose, I worked on its transcription and then its translation with Aboriginal people at various times between 2013 and 2016.

The initial difficulties I encountered in preparing the dictionary were mainly technical and required time and patience. Thus, in the first instance, the manuscript had to be painstakingly transcribed from the German script and shorthand annotations Carl Strehlow used (see Figure 4). After transcription and digitisation of the manuscript, the process of bringing it into the public domain involved many months of work with Western Aranda and Luritja speakers. Detailed collaboration with a small group of fluent Western Aranda speakers was essential for the purpose of checking Carl Strehlow's original translation into German and my own subsequent translation of the German into English.

It was often difficult to find an English gloss, because some words were not known to my informants. Other terms seemed familiar or related to known words, but the specific form of the word was unclear, or the spelling did not provide an accurate pronunciation guide and made the words unrecognisable.[9] It takes quite some work to interpret this resource, as senior Aranda woman Rhonda Inkamala remarked, but at the same time the very process of working through this type of material can enrich one's own understanding (Inkamala 2018: 17).

Other difficulties surrounding archived knowledge of Aboriginal cultures include gender restrictions, age restrictions, personal affiliations to information, uneven distribution of knowledge in a group, different versions of family histories, variations in traditional narratives and competing ownership claims to knowledge. Some of these aspects had to be considered in relation to Carl Strehlow's dictionary manuscript and required extensive consultation, because information relating to language is still highly valued as cultural capital and therefore important in the economy of knowledge.

---

9   This problem with Strehlow's original renderings would not, of course, have been solved by the use of any subsequent alternative orthographies.

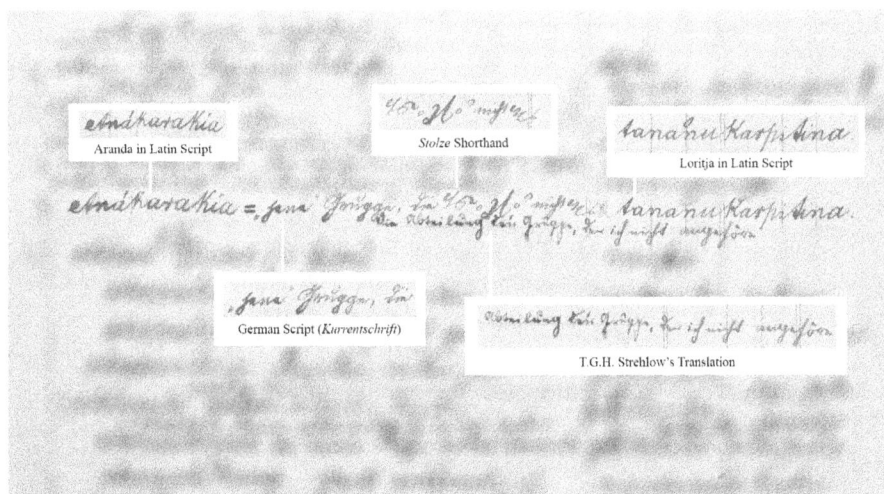

Figure 4. A page showing different scripts and shorthand used in Carl Strehlow's work (source: Kenny 2018: 51; image manipulation: Shane Mulcahy)

However, the main difficulties in publishing this dictionary manuscript only really surfaced in April 2016 when my work with fluent speakers of Aranda and Luritja had nearly been completed. There were several groupings whose vested interests in this ethnolinguistic material I had not previously been aware of, and whose views or ownership claims I had not taken into account. These interested parties included academics, non-Indigenous individuals within the Lutheran community, the Finke River Mission (FRM), different Western Aranda groups, and several government branches (including the SRC itself, which holds and legally owns the manuscript), the Central Land Council (CLC), IAD (Institute for Aboriginal Development) Press, and representatives of the Minister for Central Australia in the Northern Territory Government.

Problems with the dictionary project initially became evident when complaints about orthography were made by a non-Indigenous Lutheran source. This source (an amateur linguist) seemed to feel that the latest of a long, and ever-evolving, line of Lutheran-inspired orthographies should be employed rather than Carl Strehlow's original orthography, as was my intention. This would have done injustice to the pioneering ethnolinguistic work and defeated much of the purpose of the dictionary – namely to show what Strehlow recorded and *how* he recorded it.

The orthography issue in this post-colonial context is not simply about codifying language in a consistent, phonemic manner or about 'proper' spelling. It is, in fact, determined by localised historical, symbolic, and political factors. Western Aranda people have very strong views about the orthography of their language due to its symbolic meaning and the sense that language is owned regardless of whether one can speak it or not, as long as it is the language of one's ancestral lands. The elements that play a role are the formation of group and individual identity and autonomy, language ownership, and loyalties felt towards ancestors. It is important to many Western Aranda that they feel in control of the writing of their own language – free from the concerns of others, whom they fear may have more power, such as the state, academia, the Finke River Mission, non-Indigenous Lutherans, etc.

Because the Lutherans played a major role in developing Western Aranda literacy for overtly religious purposes, they too have very strong views about the proper orthography of Western Aranda. The Lutheran spelling system of the Finke River Mission has been taught over the past 130 years in at least seven different variations due to frequent revisions. Therefore, there are major competing views about orthography that at times are pursued with vigour and aggression.[10]

The complaints about orthography disguised the underlying issues, namely the desire of different interest groups to assert control over the representation of language and Western Aranda literacy, and by extension over people, and the ownership of history and knowledge. The scale and intensity of the complaints I received about the production of the dictionary surpassed anything I could have anticipated. These complaints arrived in a series of letters via the ethics committee of my university, the Northern Territory Government, the Central Land Council, and the Institute for Aboriginal Development.

These circumstances compelled the Central Land Council and, to a lesser extent, the Strehlow Research Centre, to become proactively involved in the process of bringing Carl Strehlow's dictionary into the public domain, since both organisations supported this aim. On the other hand, my university called its ethics committee together for meetings to discuss Arandic orthography, my field methodology, and my approach to consultations. I had to respond to their queries in several reports outlining dates, places, the persons I had consulted and so forth. The ethics problem was resolved within months, but the damage caused by the complaints of a non-Indigenous gatekeeper was by no means mended. With the generous assistance of mainly the Central Land Council, further information sessions and community consultations over a 12-month period between April 2016 and April 2017 were organised (see Figure 5). No less than 12 meetings were held in Central Australia to make sure that the Western Aranda at Hermannsburg and its surrounding outstations as well as in Alice Springs were informed about the dictionary's content in its published form. These consultations were conducted by an experienced CLC anthropologist and myself with small family groups and larger community groups. The consultations themselves variously involved formal discussions, informal interviews, the recording of diverging (and sometimes quite unexpected) opinions about orthography and archived materials, and several large-scale community meetings attended by additional staff members of the CLC and SRC.

Organising these meetings required considerable resources and logistical support, both of which the Central Land Council provided. The logistics included organising meeting spaces in remote areas, notifying people, picking up individuals from remote outstations, catering for lunches, and printing posters and other information brochures. Overall the costs were substantial, and the process as a whole was very time-consuming.

Even after the extended rounds of consultations, the different groups within the Aboriginal community were still divided on how the dictionary should look and what should or should not be added. Finally, a compromise was found that avoided conflict. It was decided

---

10   See Kenny (2017) for an extensive discussion of the many diverging views about the different orthographies employed in and around Hermannsburg. The different views about correct spelling have generated considerable dispute among the Western Aranda.

Figure 5. Auriel Swan, Christobel Swan, Helen Wilmot, Mildred Inkamala (left to right), and Anna Kenny presenting the dictionary work at Hermannsburg, mid 2016 (image courtesy of MAGNT, Adam Macfie)

to publish it as a 'Heritage Dictionary' (see Figure 6) – that is, as an exact transcription of the original handwritten manuscript[11] – because the Western Aranda understand its original form to reflect their history and identity as a particular Arandic group (Kenny 2017: 278), and to maintain its historical authenticity (Kenny 2018: 5). This compromise also avoided having to tackle the fraught politics of orthography, which were mainly the result of the colonial involvement of the Lutheran mission at Hermannsburg and caused some conflict in the community (Kenny 2018: 10).

CARL STREHLOW'S 1909 COMPARATIVE HERITAGE DICTIONARY

kĕtja *Leben (in Zusammensetzungen).* ◇ life (in word compounds).
ketjultakama *(Leben-abbrechen), erschlagen, erschießen.* ◇ (end life), slay, shoot. ⓛ aluru kátantánani
kĕuma *anfachen (Feuer).* ◇ fan (fire). ⓛ kurkaltunañi
kimbara *postp. zuerst, vorn.* ◇ (postposition) first, in front. ⓛ warika
  arakimbara laka *das rote Känguruh liefe vorn an.* ◇ the red kangaroo leads [?]. ⓛ malluwarika jennu
  erá kimbala *er zuerst.* ◇ he first. ⓛ paluru warika
kirbminjambaralama *alles Gebüsch niedertretend weiter laufen.* ◇ treading undergrowth down while pressing or running on. ⓛ multurkumulturku jennañi
kintja (kĕntja) *Blütenspitzen, Blüten.* ◇ blossom tips, blossoms. ⓛ akintji
kinjinta *in Zusammensetzungen: Haupt.* ◇ in word compounds: head.

knaïïninta *Halbgeschwister (Kinder von ein und demselben Vater).* ◇ half siblings (children from one father). ⓛ mamatungu
knaninja *ewig, rein, heilig (z.B. Sonnenlicht).* ◇ everlasting, pure, sacred (e.g. sunlight). ⓛ tukutita? ('?' added by CS)
knanakala *Totem-Platz.* ◇ totem place; dreaming, father's dreaming. ⓛ arata
knaritjilama *zu viel tun.* ◇ do too much. ⓛ puntutu
knãraɟ manna knara *groß (Gestalt), viel z.B. viel Brot.* ◇ big (posture), much (e.g. a lot of bread). ⓛ puntu ⓜ pirna
  knarerama *groß werden.* ◇ to grow up. ⓛ punturingañi
  knarilama *[groß machen] viel sammeln.* ◇ collect/gather much [make big]. ⓛ puntuni
  knarindora *sehr groß, sehr viel.* ◇ very big, very much. ⓛ puntulenku

Figure 6. Sample entries from *Carl Strehlow's 1909 comparative heritage dictionary: An Aranda, German, Loritja and Dieri to English dictionary with introductory essays* (source: Kenny 2018: 242)

---

11   The only addition to each entry was an English gloss.

On 9 October 2018 *Carl Strehlow's 1909 comparative heritage dictionary: An Aranda, German, Loritja and Dieri to English dictionary with introductory essays*[12] was launched by CLC Director David Ross at the SRC in Alice Springs (see Figure 7). This launch was mainly attended by Western Aranda people.

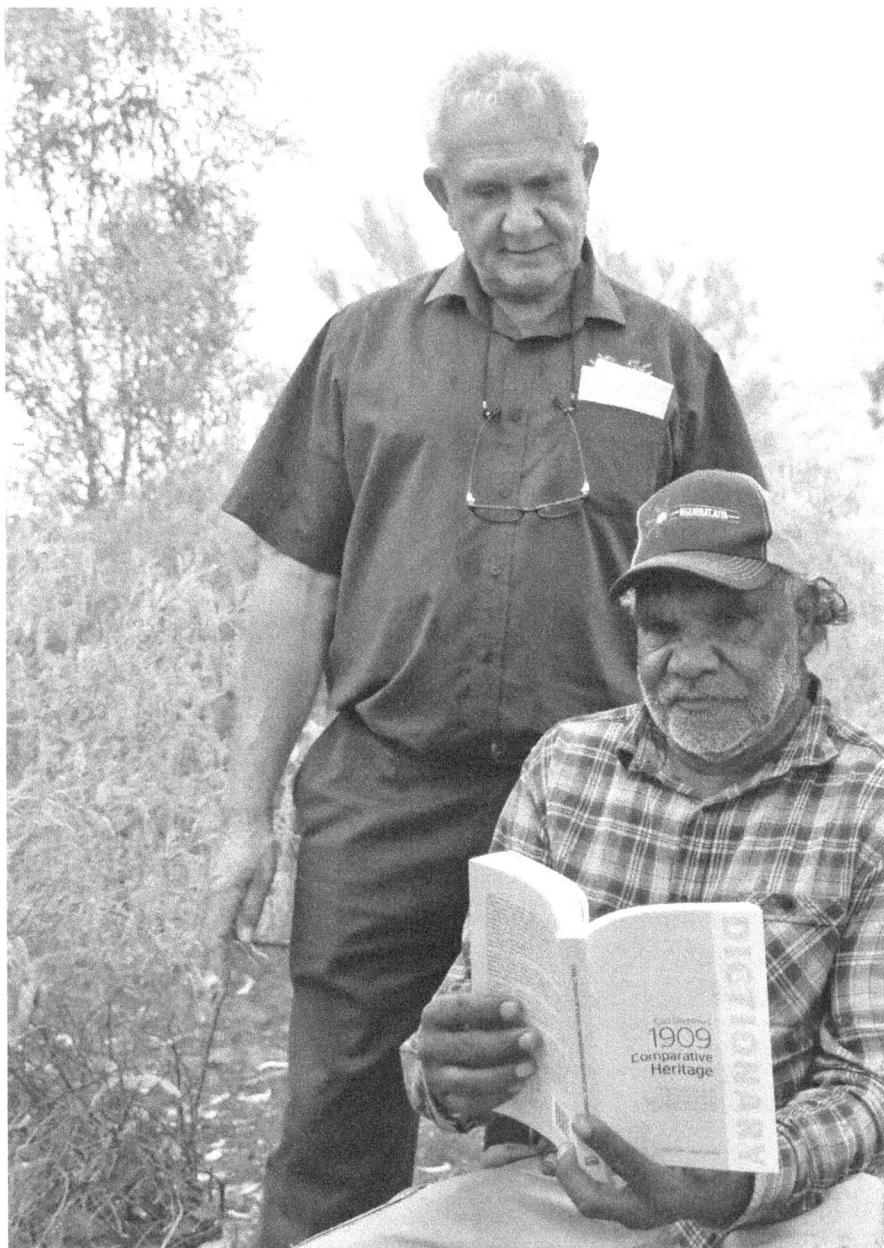

Figure 7. CLC Director David Ross (left) and Conrad Ratara (right) at the dictionary launch on 9 October 2018 at the Strehlow Research Centre in Alice Springs (source: Central Land Council, Alice Springs)

12   Access at: http://doi.org/10.22459/CSCHD.08.2018

The predicament

The situation described above relates directly to Clifford's post-colonial critique to the effect that an ethnographer's audience is multiple, and ethnography involves at least two but usually more "conscious, politically significant subjects" (Clifford 1988: 41). The groups and individuals involved in this predicament were not all active and some only became active – reluctantly – when others did.

In the process of unravelling and considering the multiple audiences for this cultural representation, with their oftentimes conflicting vested interests, it became clear that Strehlow's ethnolinguistic work effectively embodied different identities and histories. One of those identities was explicitly articulated when some Aboriginal people made clear to me the central fact that, for them, their language was not an abstract academic or linguistic resource, but was tied closely to their culture and identity. They said, for example, that "My language goes with my culture, my place, my dreaming. If you do not have language, you have no culture, you are nothing," "My language is who I am. It gives me power. My language makes other people respect me," and "Language is where we come from, what makes us, in our culture. It makes us who we are" (Kenny 2017: 277).

Aranda people refer both to the content of and the orthography used for the Aranda language in Carl Strehlow's unpublished manuscripts as *ankatja ingkwia*[13] 'old language' or *ankatja ekarlta* 'strong language', meaning the language of the 'old people' – their ancestors. They explicitly distinguish it from 'church language' and 'today's language' (Kenny 2017: 265). In some instances, these archived materials are even viewed as ancestral voices of the past. At other times, however, the realisation surfaced that it is not possible to reproduce knowledge as it was formerly. According to some senior informants who worked with me on the dictionary manuscript, one "cannot get that old language back – too far gone. The old people took that language with them when they passed away" (Kenny 2017: 276).

Codified and archived knowledge is always recontextualised (Strathern 1995: 3), interpreted, and reinterpreted and, as Jorgensen & McLean have shown in their edited volume *Indigenous Archives*, knowledges can be and are creatively constituted and reconstituted (Jorgensen & McLean 2017: viii). When these processes occur with manuscripts such as Carl Strehlow's dictionary or other archival materials, e.g. a genealogy, photograph, or sacred song, in politicised environments they become highly symbolic and stand for history and identity, which can generate conflict.

Although at the Hermannsburg Mission the missionaries mitigated some of the frontier violence against the Aranda, the missionaries remain an integral part of Australian colonial history (Monteath & Fitzpatrick 2017: 199).[14] The historical circumstances of the Lutheran involvement with Western Aranda people included a subtle yet violent appropriation of the Aranda language since the late 1870s (Kenny 2017). They appropriated parts of the Aranda language for bible translation, imposed on the Western Aranda people rigid non-Indigenous

---

13 In Carl Strehlow's dictionary: *ankatja* (Wort [word], Sprache [language] auch, 'Märchen, Fabel, Mythe' [also, fairytale, fable, myth]).

14 See also Ganter 2016. German missionaries in Australia: A web directory of intercultural encounters. http://missionaries.griffith.edu.au (Accessed 10 April 2019.)

social structures and suppressed important cultural practices relating to Aboriginal belief systems that they understood to be 'heathen'. This caused the reduction of vocabulary relating to the spirit world as well as ecology (Kenny 2018: 7) and some ontological shifts over the past century (Austin-Broos 2009, 2010). The Lutheran church and community still have a strong presence in some Central Australian Aboriginal communities, although these communities are now often located on Aboriginal land such as Ntaria (the former Hermannsburg Mission) or the former Jay Creek government settlement on the Iwupataka Aboriginal Land Trust.

Members of the Lutheran community connected to the Finke River Mission have a strong view about the ownership of Lutheran history in Central Australia that includes ownership claims over Aranda heritage and language as recorded by German missionaries. For many Lutherans, their history is embodied in items such as this dictionary manuscript created by one of their missionaries more than 100 years ago. In this case, ironically, the item relates to Aboriginal mythology. At that time, the Lutheran authorities were in fact highly critical of Strehlow's ethno-linguistic work and derided it, alleging that he was neglecting his missionary duties. Drawing upon little more than the institutional paternalism of their Church's past in Central Australia, the same present-day Lutherans appear to 'know' what is good for Aboriginal people,[15] which in their view allows them to take control of cultural representations.[16]

The Aboriginal versions of events sometimes do not mesh well with the view the local non-Indigenous Lutheran community has of their 'mutual history'. This 'history' is further manifest for the latter in their Finke River Mission archival holdings in Alice Springs and the Lutheran Archives in Adelaide. To some degree, attempts to return cultural heritage and decolonise history do not sit well with non-Indigenous views of identity and history as constituted from the same materials. Aboriginal people, too, see their history embodied in items such as this dictionary manuscript that a Lutheran missionary created more than 100 years ago. For many Western Aranda, for example, the language contained in Carl Strehlow's dictionary stands for their culture, in which their kin and specific ontological beliefs relating to land are embedded.

While some Lutherans have recently objected to projects of cultural representation, others have been protective of their legacy in such situations. Their objections to progressive post-colonial developments such as the Northern Territory Land Rights movement (Eames 1983) go back to the 1970s, or the 1990s, when a leading Lutheran in Anmatyerr country backed a breakaway 'Anmatjere Land Council' (Morton 1994). To illustrate further the conservative colonial legacy that continues to dog many (if not all) Lutheran interventions in Central Australia, it is worth considering Austin-Broos' work (2009: 25–101). She describes the conflicting narratives about the Lutheran founding of Hermannsburg and the bringing of Christianity to Central Australia.

---

15   A point made by a representative of one of the government offices who had to approach me after complaints had been made about my dictionary work (May 2016).

16   In addition to the orthography issue, this sense of entitlement was manifest in the way in which some non-Indigenous members of the Lutheran community reacted to and resisted two other separate projects being undertaken at the time of my research: the Jay Creek settlement cemetery restoration and the Strehlow Research Centre field repatriation project, both of which cast different (i.e. negative) perspectives on colonial events and the Lutheran past in Central Australia.

Concluding remarks

There are at least three sets of difficulties involved in bringing these archived cultural materials into the public domain. Firstly, the materials have to be decoded because they may be codified in scripts that only a few specialists now know, or they may use language that includes, for example, anthropological terms, concepts, and models that are not easily understood. Secondly, the cultural sensitivities and restrictions surrounding archived Indigenous knowledges must be discussed with relevant target groups (e.g. senior people, particular ethnic groups) and thirdly, the politics of knowledge and ownership – that is, the different interest groups that may think they have rights to a body of knowledge – have to be taken into account.

In hindsight, my view that a dictionary was a harmless choice for an intellectual repatriation project appears very naïve. And indeed, in the context of the Strehlow Collection, this dictionary manuscript belongs to the least restricted category of items. I had not considered the many views that different interest groups had about the ownership of Carl Strehlow's dictionary manuscript, nor its significance as a symbol of identity for both the Aboriginal community and the Lutheran non-Indigenous community. Although this manuscript is 'only' a dictionary – not a sacred object per se or a manuscript with restricted religious content – its symbolic meaning goes well beyond what one might think an ethnolinguistic manuscript might stand for. Not only is it a unique heritage item, it is also attached to weighty views about history constructed by diverse interest groups who believe that they own history and have the correct version of it.

These tensions that arise due to the diverse views of ownership of knowledge can result in scenarios that are costly, time-consuming, and painful, and cause some institutions to be overly fearful about sensitivities as well as protective of their archival materials. In Australia this sometimes makes it very difficult even to access knowledge that was originally public knowledge for both Indigenous and non-Indigenous people and which could have been expected to remain in the public domain, such as linguistic and certain ecological information.

Although there are enormous problems regarding sensitive information in early ethnography and native title records, they should not have a paralysing effect on attempts to make important information available. Among the archived materials are pieces that assist Aboriginal community groups to recover their cultural heritage and regain pride in it. Indeed, some records are of incommensurable richness and are unique treasures and, thus, of great value to Aboriginal people (Kenny 2018) who may want to celebrate them (McGrath 2018). This makes it worthwhile to overcome the 'risk, benefit, and aggravation equation'.

These archival records are an integral part of the creation and writing of Aboriginal history and have become relevant in the process of decolonising history and constituting identities. Many Indigenous Australians have undertaken the reinterpretation, recontextualisation, and reconstitution of archived knowledges, turning to the archives to access materials collected by colonial administrations and directly incorporating such materials within Aboriginal identities and expressions of Aboriginal histories.[17] Indeed, in the hands of Indigenous people,

---

17   See, for instance, Jorgensen & McLean (2017: xiv); Carroll (2017); Lydon (2017: 377–378).

such re-renderings of archived materials can become powerful tools to reclaim their history and autonomy.[18]

References

Austin-Broos, Diane. 2009. *Arrernte present, Arrernte past: Invasion, violence, and imagination in Indigenous Central Australia.* Chicago: Chicago University Press.

Austin-Broos, Diane. 2010. Translating Christianity. *The Australian Journal of Anthropology* 21(1). 14–32.

Carroll, Khadija von Zinnenburg. 2017. Anachronistic archive: Turning the time of the image in the Aboriginal avant-garde. In Darren Jorgensen & Ian McLean (eds.), *Indigenous archives: The making and unmaking of Aboriginal art*, 342–361. Perth: UWA Publishing.

Clifford, James. 1988. *The predicament of culture.* Cambridge, MA: Harvard University Press.

Dunn, Kara, Trinity Handley, Anna Kenny, Luke May & Hana McDonald. 2018. *Native title anthropology in a post-determination world.* (CNTA paper presented in Melbourne, 8 February 2018.)

Eames, Geoff. 1983. The Central Land Council: The politics of change. In Nicolas Peterson & Marcia Langton (eds.), *Aborigines, land and land rights*, 268–277. Canberra: Australian Institute of Aboriginal Studies.

Ganter, Regina. 2016. *German missionaries in Australia: A web directory of intercultural encounters.* (http://missionaries.griffith.edu.au) (Accessed 10 April 2019.)

Hugo, David. 1997. Acquisition of the Strehlow Collection by the Northern Territory Government: A chronology. In David Hugo (ed.), *Occasional paper (Strehlow Research Centre)* 1, 127–137. Alice Springs: Strehlow Research Centre.

Inkamala, Rhonda. 2018. Working on the dictionary. In Anna Kenny (ed.), *Carl Strehlow's 1909 comparitive heritage dictionary: An Aranda, German, Loritja and Dieri to English dictionary with introductory essays*, 15–22. Canberra: ANU Press.

Jorgensen, Darren & Ian McLean (eds.). 2017. *Indigenous archives: The making and unmaking of Aboriginal art.* Perth: UWA Publishing.

Kaiser, Simone. 2004. The Stern case. In Michael Cawthorn (ed.), *Traditions in the midst of change: Communities, cultures and the Strehlow legacy in Central Australia: Proceedings of the Strehlow Conference, Alice Springs, 18–20 September 2002*, 66–76. Alice Springs: Strehlow Research Centre.

Kenny, Anna. 2013. *The Aranda's pepa: An introduction to Carl Strehlow's masterpiece Die Aranda- und Loritja-Stämme in Zentral-Australien (1907–1920).* Canberra: ANU Press. (http://doi.org/10.22459/AP.12.2013)

Kenny, Anna. 2017. Aranda, Arrernte or Arrarnta? The politics of orthography and identity on the Upper Finke River. *Oceania* 87(3). 261–281.

18 Michael Arid's work on archival materials called *Transforming Tindale,* for example, threw a different light on archival photographs that had been taken to illustrate Tindale and Birdsell's physical anthropology data cards, which were based on information they had collected in Queensland in the 1930s and 1950s. The images were turned around to reconnect people with their ancestors and kin (see Lydon 2017: 374–377).

Kenny, Anna. (ed.). 2018. *Carl Strehlow's 1909 comparitive heritage dictionary: An Aranda, German, Loritja and Dieri to English dictionary with introductory essays.* Canberra: ANU Press. (http://doi.org/10.22459/CSCHD.08.2018)

Koch, Grace. 2008. *The future of connection materials in NTRBs.* Canberra: AIATSIS.

Lucas, Rodney & Deane Fergie. 2017. Pulcaracuranie: Losing and finding a cosmic centre with the help of JG Reuther and others. In Nicolas Peterson & Anna Kenny (eds.), *German ethnography in Australia*, 79–113. Canberra: ANU Press.

Lydon, Jane. 2017. Transformations of the photographic archive. In Darren Jorgensen & Ian McLean (eds.), *Indigenous archives: The making and unmaking of Aboriginal art*, 362–382. Perth: UWA Publishing.

McGrath, Pamela Faye, Ludger Dinkler & Alexandra Andriolo. 2015. *Managing information in Native Title (MINT).* Canberra: AIATSIS.

McGrath, Pamela Faye. 2018. Providing public access to native title records: Balancing the risks against the benefits. In Ann Genovese, Trish Luker & Kim Rubenstein (eds.), *The court as archive: Rethinking the institutional role of federal superior courts of record*, 213–238. Canberra: ANU Press.

McNally, Ward. 1981. *Aborigines, artefacts and anguish.* Adelaide: Lutheran Publishing House.

Monteath, Peter & Matthew P Fitzpatrick. 2017. German missionaries and Australian anthropology. *Anthropological Forum* 27(3). 197–208.

Morgan, Rebecca & Helen Wilmot. 2010. *Written proof: The appropriation of genealogical records in contemporary Arrernte society.* AIATSIS Native Title Research Unit Issue Paper vol. 4, no. 5. Canberra: AIATSIS.

Morton, John. 1994. *The proposed Anmatjere Land Council: Its historical antecedents and an estimation of levels of support.* Report to the Aboriginal and Torres Strait Islander Commission, Canberra.

Peterson, Nicolas & Anna Kenny (eds.). 2017. *German ethnography in Australia.* Canberra: ANU Press.

Pink, Olive. 1936. The landowners in the northern division of the Aranda tribe, Central Australia. *Oceania* 4(3). 275–305.

Strathern, Marilyn (ed.). 1995. *Shifting contexts: Transformations in anthropological knowledge.* London: Routledge.

Strehlow, Carl. 1907–1920. *Die Aranda- und Loritja-Stämme in Zentral-Australien.* 7 vols. Frankfurt am Main: Joseph Baer & Co.

Strehlow, TGH. 1969. *Journey to Horseshoe Bend.* Sydney: Angus and Robertson.

Language Documentation & Conservation Special Publication No. 18
Archival returns: Central Australia and beyond
ed. by Linda Barwick, Jennifer Green & Petronella Vaarzon-Morel, pp. 65–89
http://nflrc.hawaii.edu/ldc/sp18
http://hdl.handle.net/10125/24878

4

Returning recordings of songs that persist: The Anmatyerr traditions of *akiw* and *anmanty*

Jason Gibson
Deakin University

Abstract

Digitisation has made the return of recordings made by researchers in the past far more achievable than ever before. This technological advance, combined with the ethical and political imperative towards decolonising methodologies in Indigenous research, has resulted in considerable interest in ensuring that recordings of cultural value be returned to Indigenous communities. In this chapter, I reflect upon the fieldwork experience of returning archival song recordings concerning public aspects of male initiation ceremonies, known as *akiw* and *anmanty*, to Anmatyerr-speaking communities in the Northern Territory of Australia. Despite attenuation of song knowledge across the region, these songs continue to be sung at annual ritual events. Once these recordings were returned to these communities, Anmatyerr people quickly received them as important reiterations of their present-day socio-cultural expression. Evidently imbricated in a complex, ritually based form of complementary filiation and knowledge dissemination, these songs are shared and taught in a fragile and changing context of ceremonial practice. The account provided here offers insights into songs associated with arguably the most persistent and significant form of ceremonial practice in Central Australia, although sparsely documented in the Anmatyerr region. I also highlight the relational properties of song via their connections to place, *Anengkerr* 'Dreaming' and people and provide important insights into how these communities perceive the archiving and preservation of this material.

Keywords: Anmatyerr, ethnomusicology, ceremony, Aboriginal history, repatriation

Introduction[1]

A decade ago the Australian musicologist Allan Marett (2010: 253) ruminated on the future of Australian Aboriginal song traditions. He concluded that "what survives today, mainly in the remote northern and central parts of Australia, represents only a tiny fraction of what was, at the time of first European contact, a vast, rich and dynamic ceremonial complex that reached into every corner of the continent." But even these remaining traditions, he observed, are so critically endangered that they are unlikely to "survive for more than another generation or two" (Marett 2010: 253). Such gloomy predictions have been reinforced in recent state-ments from the International Council for Traditional Music estimating that approximately 98 per cent of Indigenous Australian musical traditions have been lost.[2] It is this record of cultural loss and decline that has inspired a range of initiatives to return archival recordings of song to Aboriginal communities (Treloyn & Emberly 2013; Treloyn, Martin & Charles 2016; Turpin 2017; Bracknell 2017). As with similar initiatives found across the globe (Gunderson, Lancefield & Woods 2018), these projects are often driven by a desire to see defunct songs revived or to have song performance as a form of community practice or tradition maintained and supported.

In this chapter, I discuss the return of archival recordings of song to remote communities in Central Australia where singing continues to play an important part in social and cultural life. This return was part of a much larger Australian Research Council funded project concerned with finding ways of improving Aboriginal access to cultural heritage collections either held by museums, Aboriginal organisations, or by individual researchers.[3] Specifically focused on the needs of Aboriginal people living in remote communities in the Northern Territory of Australia, where access to cultural heritage and information technology services is poor, the project aimed to find effective and 'culturally appropriate' ways of mobilising archival materials. While the scope of the project included attention to the infrastructure and resourcing needs of these communities, it was far more concerned with finding ways of enabling archival access without violating cultural protocols, eroding traditional rights, or upsetting local rules around the dissemination of cultural information. My own particular interest was in the ways in which recordings of song were currently being returned, how the arrival of this material was being managed at the local level and how these recordings were being reintegrated into people's lives. The repatriation of this 'sonic heritage' is now more achievable than ever before

1   I would like to acknowledge the following people for their generous participation in this research: Lindsay Bird Mpetyan, Harold Purvis/Payne, Herbie Bloomfield, Ken Tilmouth Penangk, Jack Cook Ngal, Malcolm Heffernan Pengart, Huckitta Lynch Penangk, Ronnie McNamara, Shaun Angeles, and Martin Hagan. I would also like to thank the Strehlow Research Centre, Jennifer Green, Margaret Carew, and Myfany Turpin for access to their recordings. Additional feedback from Jennifer Green and Myfany Turpin was invaluable, as were the comments from two anonymous reviewers.

2   http://www.ictmusic.org/sites/default/files/ICTM%20Statement%20on%20Indigenous%20Music%26Dance.pdf (Accessed 12 December 2018.)

3   The ARC Linkage Project 'Re-integrating Central Australian community cultural collections' (LP140100806) is a partnership between the Central Land Council (CLC), the peak Indigenous representative body covering the southern half of the Northern Territory, the University of Sydney, and the University of Melbourne. I was employed by the project to carry out this research.

(largely thanks to technologies of digitisation) but questions remain over the impact these archival returns are having on communities and cultural practices.

The account below describes the process of returning recordings of songs that are still in use among various Anmatyerr-speaking communities today. The content of these songs relates to the crucially important young men's initiation ceremonies that occur annually in most Anmatyerr communities and have an equivalence across many other Central Australian communities. The song and ceremonial traditions of Anmatyerr people have nonetheless received far less scholarly attention than that of their Warlpiri (Meggitt 1966; Peterson 1997; Curran 2010, 2011) and Arrernte neighbours (Strehlow 1971), and anthropological research into Central Australian ritual life has been on the wane for some time. The last in-depth ethnographic exposition of Arandic ceremonial practice was undertaken by Moyle (1986), although Turpin has produced some highly significant ethnomusicological research (for example, Turpin 2013; Turpin & Green 2018). As such, considerably more ethnographic work needs to be carried out before a more complete picture of these traditions can be ascertained. Among the repatriated materials discussed here are a suite of recordings made by contemporary researchers Jennifer Green, Myfany Turpin, and Margaret Carew and an earlier recording made by the pioneering Arandic ethnographer TGH Strehlow. Strehlow's recording was made in 1949 and the more recent recordings of Green and Turpin in 2007 and Green and Carew in 2012. The songs captured on these recordings are sung by Anmatyerr men and are used during two regionally distinct Anmatyerr ceremonies, *akiw* and *anmanty*. *Akiw/akew* refers to the 'bush camp' where male initiates reside during their initiation rites but also to the suite of songs sung while the young men are under instruction from their male elders. *Anmanty*, on the other hand, refers to the set of songs used by Western and Central Anmatyerr men during the public aspects of initiation ceremonies (known as *apwelh* elsewhere in the Arandic region). They sing *anmanty* as the women perform *anthep*, the distinctive women's dance used during these ceremonies.[4] Both the songs associated with *akiw* and *anmanty* continue to be regularly sung at these annual ritual events; however, as is shown below, they have suffered considerable attenuation in recent decades.

The recording and preservation of traditional Aboriginal song has its beginnings in early anthropological practice in Australia. Recordings were first made in the late 19th and early 20th centuries as a document of 'primitive' 'verse' or 'chants' and at this time Aboriginal singing was regarded as a relic of 'stone age' culture. Later in the 20th century, however, while the conception of Aboriginal people as 'primitive' weakened under new non-evolutionary anthropological models (Gray 2007), the desire to 'salvage' threatened traditions intensified (Gruber 1970). TGH Strehlow's recordings were, for example, made with the explicit intention of seeing that Central Australian songs would be 'preserved' for 'eternity' (Gibson 2017), and similar objectives continued to drive ethnographic work elsewhere in Australia, particularly among ethnomusicologists and linguists who are keenly aware of the decline of global linguistic diversity. Contemporary work in these fields maintains an urgent need to record, document, and archive threatened forms of linguistic and cultural expression. The aforementioned Green

---

4   Men at Napperby noted that they used *apwelh* to specifically refer to the cleared space utilised as a ceremonial ground and *anmanty* was used to refer to the songs sung by the men, as well as the ceremony in general.

and Turpin recordings were indeed funded under a Hans Rausing Endangered Languages Project with precisely these objectives in mind.[5]

Understanding what informants, singers, and community members make of these recordings, however, requires its own form of ethnographic and historical enquiry. Strehlow's informants, for example, participated in the documentation of their songs amid conditions of considerable inequity and an unusually lengthy and entangled relationship with TGH Strehlow, a highly singular and 'possessive' ethnographer (Hill 2003). His various performers and informants did nonetheless communicate their own interests in having their song expertise recorded and sought greater recognition of their complex and diverse ceremonial practices (Gibson in press). During the making of the more contemporary recordings Green, Turpin, and Carew produced, senior singer Jack Cook Ngal expressed similar aspirations. He wanted future generations of Anmatyerr people to have access to these recordings so that they might be used for revivification, but also so that others might come to understand the full importance of these repertoires as critical to Aboriginal identity.

> This song here *anwern impem* [we leave behind], *ilernakarl alyek anmanty* [the *anmanty* songs that we sang], so that they can carry [this tradition] on when we are gone ... They can teach them themselves ... That why we are here today, *inang ntwerrketyeh* [so they can hold on to this] Anmatyerr side. *Mer nhenh* [This country], this Australia here, this belongs to Aboriginal people. They've got to be strong, hold the country. (Jack Cook, pers. comm. to Jennifer Green, 7 June 2007)

The return of archival recordings of *akiw* and *anmanty* to Anmatyerr communities today has produced different responses. These recordings were revered less for their historical or heritage value and more for their capacity to reiterate and uphold present-day socio-cultural practices associated with the initiation ceremonies. As I explain below, *akiw* and *anmanty* continue to be known and sung by a small group of men who practise and teach these songs during ceremonial gatherings involving men across the generations. Despite a noticeable decline in the number of expert singers and an attenuation of song knowledge for other genres of traditional song, Anmatyerr people have maintained the importance of *akiw* and *anmanty*. Learnt entirely within an Anmatyerr domain of ceremonial practice, ritually based knowledge dissemination and the dictates of appropriate kin relations, these songs persist and remain crucial to the work of 'making men' (rites designed to mark entrance into the world of adulthood).

The growing influence of post-colonial politics and decolonising methodologies combined with the portability of digital objects in recent decades has meant that song recordings are now being returned to Indigenous communities with great regularity. Given the vulnerability of Aboriginal song traditions in Australia discussed earlier, it is understandable that this return is generally carried out with the intention of assisting revival, reconstruction, or reinvention. In communities where song persists, though, the return of recordings that still hold currency and are still performed produces different responses. These responses outlined below give us an indication of how Anmatyerr communities continue to manage, integrate, and deal with the return of recorded song.

---

5   Grant id: IPF0100, SG0048.

The return

I took the recordings of *akiw* and *anmanty* with me to the communities of Engawala (Alcoota) and Laramba (Napperby) on repeated field trips between 2015 and 2017. The more recent recordings had been made by female linguist/ethnomusicologists working with men, so it was considered appropriate that a male researcher should also investigate the significance and meaning of these songs. While women are permitted to listen to *anmanty* and *akiw* songs and have some understanding of their significance, they are only ever sung by men. Used to induct younger males into manhood, their full significance is the domain of men. As Michaels put it, women might know some of the details but they are generally not permitted to speak of these things in public or exchange them in any economic sense (Michaels 1985: 508). Thus, even though it was entirely permissible that female researchers could make these original recordings – in fact Green, Turpin, and Carew were urged to make these recordings – it was considered that further prompting about the contemporary significance of these archival materials might best be done by a male. Such discussions might also elicit new perspectives.

The other recording reviewed during the course of this research was made by the somewhat controversial ethnographer TGH Strehlow. Strehlow worked almost entirely with Aboriginal men throughout the course of his four-decade-long career and came under fire for his revelation of secret men's rituals (Morton 1995; Hill 2003). I had serendipitously discovered Strehlow's recording of *anmanty* during the course of my dissertation research. Strehlow had recorded a suite of songs with a Western Arrernte man (Nathanael Rauwiraka) whose conception site lay within the Anmatyerr territory of Ilewerr (Lake Lewis) and which he titled the *ahenenh* 'woma python' song of Ilewerr. It was while these songs were being played back to Anmatyerr men at Napperby that the men identified the *anmanty* song set among them, despite Strehlow having made no specific reference to *anmanty* in his documentation. Included in the Strehlow recordings were additional songs referring to other ancestral stories in the Ilewerr estate region, including many men-only, restricted songs relating to the *ahenenh* and other songs which the Napperby men had not learnt.

The methodology used to review the various song recordings involved playing these recorded materials to well-known song experts (many of them the original singers) and then inviting them to provide commentary. The men were also asked to advise on any cultural restrictions that might apply to the materials, discuss their status as cultural property and provide further instructions on how the recordings might be distributed and accessed in the future. This often involved consultations with senior men, in the presence of one or two younger men who oversaw discussions and provided support for their elders. Once the cultural status of the materials had been ascertained, however, subsequent listening sessions became more relaxed and the men would begin to call over others in the community to share in the songs, and engage in further deliberations. Participation in the listening sessions was also seen as a way of having Anmatyerr views documented, seeing the expertise of senior singers recognised and ensuring that the future use of the material would be based upon their specialist recommendations.

The *akiw* 'bush camp'

Very little has been written about the meaning or significance of *akiw*. Speakers of the mutually intelligible Arandic languages, Eastern and Central Arrernte and Anmatyerr, use the term to denote a men's ceremonial camp, also known in English as a 'bush camp' (Dobson & Henderson 1994: 68; Green 2010: 22; Turpin & Ross 2012: 55). *Akiw* is thus both a place and an event where men, specifically young male initiates, are exposed to various ceremonial traditions including songs, mythologies, body paint designs, and other ritual practices. First noted by Strehlow in his fieldwork notes with Arrernte speakers, the term evokes a male-only ceremonial camp where cultural and religious instruction takes place.[6] These 'bush camps' are still spoken of as less colonised spaces, often located on the edges of community settlements, where the full vitality and regenerative energies of traditional culture can be displayed and shared.

Akiw is not just a space or place, as it equally refers to the songs and stories recounted during these 'bush camp' events. What is remarkable, though, is that despite considerable work on Arrernte ritual, song, and mythology over many years (Spencer & Gillen 1899, 1904; Strehlow 1907; Strehlow 1947, 1971), there is no published ethnographic record of *akiw*. The Anmatyerr dictionary notes that the term *akiw* (or *akew*) is used for the camp where male initiates congregate during young men's initiation ceremonies and also refers to the songs sung at this gathering (Green 2010: 22). The recordings of *akiw* songs that Green and Turpin made at Mulga Bore in 2007 therefore add new information on a little-documented Arandic cultural practice. The recordings were made over two days and each session was filmed and audio recorded with the three expert singers of *akiw*: Harold Payne Mpetyan, Lindsay Bird Mpetyan, and Ken Tilmouth Penangk (Figure 1). Green and Turpin were camped at Mulga Bore for several days, recording women's *awely* songs and women's sand-drawing narratives. The *akiw* songs were recorded on the verandah of a house in the community and women and children were well within earshot.

Harold's son, Joseph Ngal, sat nearby to learn from the experience. After discussing these recordings with the three original singers, I came to realise that while *akiw* may be used as a generic term, the suite of songs was of particular local significance.

Singers of this particular suite of *akiw* primarily speak and identify with the Eastern Anmatyerr language. They and their families nonetheless possess close personal and cultural ties to the speakers of Eastern Arrernte and Alyawarr. Ceremonies will also often involve people from across the wider Arandic cultural-linguistic region and include speakers of Anmatyerr, Arrernte, and Alyawarr. The people that sing and use these *akiw* songs mostly reside in the communities of Engawala (Alcoota) and Mulga Bore. While the principal singers of *akiw* generally reside in Eastern Anmatyerr communities, they are also highly mobile and will often spend time in the township of Alice Springs and other Aboriginal communities in the region. I found it very difficult to meet up with Harold Payne, for example, due to his frequent movement between the communities of Mulga Bore, Engawala, Adelaide Bore, Arlparra (New Store), and Ti Tree.

---

6 Strehlow's Field Diary (1953: 50), Strehlow Research Centre, Alice Springs.

Figure 1. A young boy, Joseph Payne, sits with Lindsay Bird and Harold Payne as they listen back to their recording of *akiw*, with Myfany Turpin in the foreground (left–right), Mulga Bore, 7 June 2007 (photo: Jennifer Green)

Returning *akiw*

I began consultations with people at Engawala in September 2017. A decade had elapsed since the Turpin and Green recordings were made, and Ken Tilmouth, one of the most well-respected elders from the northeastern Arrernte and Anmatyerr regions, was eager to review them again. Green and Turpin had returned copies of these recordings on DVD soon after they were made, but being susceptible to damage (particularly in harsh desert climes and amid overcrowded dwellings) these copies were not dependable in the long term. Ken and I had already spent considerable time together discussing other recordings and artefacts Strehlow collected in the 1960s, so my interest in *akiw* – which, being a more open tradition, is less fiercely guarded than a person's own cultural inheritance is – was treated with a degree of ease. These songs, he explained, belonged to his country (father's father's estate) of Atwel but they were known widely by many men and could be sung by a larger cohort of people than his own sacred songs. Although *akiw* is still part of the general "revelatory regime of value" (Myers 2014: 80) in these desert societies – where the fundamental concern is to limit the dispersal of highly valued forms of cultural property and knowledge – it was less circumscribed. *Akiw* was not a form of cultural property governed by particularly high levels of exclusivity and secrecy, but something more liberally managed and shared among men.

How each of the original singers was personally responsible for *akiw* became a theme of our discussions. However, in the intervening years the three men had aged considerably and sadly Harold's son had passed away. The loss of this young man was a cruel reminder of the high mortality rates among impoverished Australian Aboriginal communities and the subsequent impacts that this has on cultural transmission. In small communities like these, where there are limited numbers of people to take on roles as active performers of particular ceremonial traditions, the death of one or two people can have serious consequences. One of my key inquiries became ascertaining just how vulnerable *akiw* was: did the reality of what Jackson (2007) refers to as "cultural endangerment" influence people's attitude towards these recordings or would they respond in other ways? As *akiw* had received so little attention in the previous literature, it would also be hard to assess cultural change or attenuation over time.

As soon as my consultations began in earnest, though, it was clear that *akiw* not only persists but remains critical to the education of young men. At Engawala, Harold Payne briefly listened to the first 10 seconds of the recording before shifting his focus to an explanation of the song. While the recording was the catalyst, his primary interest was in describing the various totemic sites and topography that featured in *akiw*. The songs principally referred to the estate of Atwel, a large area to the west of Alcoota Station which takes in parts of the Mount Riddock, Bushy Park Station, and Delny cattle station leases (Gray 2007: 138), and in particular the site of Awerr-pwenty (lit. *awerr* 'boy'; *pwenty* 'ceremony'), also known as Mount Bleechmore. While Tilmouth was repeatedly acknowledged as a senior *merek-artwey* 'owner', 'boss', or 'custodian' for this estate and therefore its associated song/ceremonial traditions, Harold and his classificatory brother Lindsay Bird (the other two singers on the recordings) were described as *kwertengerl* 'guardians', 'managers', or 'offsiders', who work with him in tandem. These men belonged to the neighbouring estate of Ilkewartn and thus shared the responsibility of maintaining *akiw* for the 'owners' from Atwel.[7]

The term *kwertengerl*, and its equivalent in other Australian Aboriginal languages, has been the subject of considerable attention in the anthropological literature for some time (Pink 1936). The idea of a *kwertengerl* denotes an important social role often found in many parts of Australia (Young 1981; Nash 1982, 1984; Morphy & Morphy 1984; Keen 1997).[8] For Sutton, the dual roles of the 'manager' and 'owner' are a "ritual based system of formalised complementary filiation" (Sutton 2003: 194) whereby (using the Arandic terminology) the *kwertengerl* – who are related to the *merek-artwey* via their mother's and their mother's brother's country – manage, advise, and protect the ritual knowledge and sites possessed by the *merek-artwey*. Anthropological sources from across Australia suggest that these types of rights and duties vary in character and intensity but were present among most Aboriginal groups (Morton 2017: 63). In the Anmatyerr context, the *kwertengerl* will, for example, play an important role in helping the *merek-artwey* maintain the integrity and long-term transmission of their estate-based

---

7   While there was an expectation that men from across the generations from both of these estates (Atwel and Ilkewartn) would respect and carry out these obligations, key individuals were often singled out as being 'number one' (foremost) *kwertengerl* or *merek-artwey* due to their inherited rights in the material as well as their seniority, social standing, and cultural expertise.

8   In other parts of Australia equivalent groups are known as *kirda* (Warlpiri), *mangaya* (Warumungu), *gidjan* (Jawoyn), *ngimirringki* (Yanyuwa), etc.

(place-based) rituals, songs, dances, and so on.[9] Likened to a 'governance structure' by some Warlpiri people (Pawu-Kurlpurlurnu, Holmes & Box 2008), these complementary tasks ensure that everyone within this network of relatedness has a role to play. As I have argued elsewhere (Gibson 2018), this system of complementary filiation could be better understood and incorporated into the management of Central Australian archival collections.

As *kwertengerl* for the *akiw* songs, both Harold Payne and Lindsay Bird were obliged to know the repertoire and the associated mythic traditions in fine detail. Evidencing deep intimacy with the material, both men described these songs as Apwert-urrperl-areny (songs belonging to the site of Apwert-urrperl 'black hill') and specifically referred to important associations with the sites of Kwepal and Awerr-pwenty (both within the larger Atwel estate region). It was at Kwepal that two ancestral women who permanently resided in this area (*mer akweteth*) observed the *awey-map*, a group of young boys, travelling from the far south (perhaps from as far away as Port Augusta in South Australia) and being led by a man known as Kwekaty through Alice Springs and further north. As we listened to the recordings, Harold would point out various aspects of the song's contents. For example, there were references to *alpeyt* 'the white tail tips of the bilby' (*Macrotis lagotis*) that were worn by the female ancestors, the 'smell' of *ahakey* 'native currants' (*Psydrax latifolia*), and other landscape features, such as *utnathat* 'mulga flowers' and a non-edible grass or a plant with 'red' seed heads.[10] Although extremely brief, the various explanations Harold and others gave suggest that translations of these song texts could be developed if sufficient time was allocated for in-depth linguistic and ethnomusicological analysis.

At the very heart of this song tradition was a Dreaming narrative involving travelling *awerr* 'boys' that has already been partially noted in the literature for the Alice Springs region (Spencer & Gillen 1899; Gunn 2000: 114–115; Gray 2007: 139; Kimber 2011: 29–30). In these particular *akiw* songs the narrative (songline) begins where these ancestral figures move northwards, beyond Arrernte territory and into the Anmatyerr-speaking area. Each of the three singers explained that the ancestral women of Atwel watched the group of boys as they arrived at a rockhole on the western side of Mueller Creek before the boys move through Atwel and to the next estate of Ilkewartn, Harold and Lindsay's patrilineal country. From this point on in the narrative, Harold, as an owner for the Ilkewartn estate, gave the names of the numerous geographical sites where the boys travelled across Ilkewartn country but it was only by working together that these three singers (one *merek-artwey* and two *kwertengerl*) were able to legitimately discuss and share their profound knowledge of the material.

Managing *akiw*

The complementary relationship referred to earlier underscored the importance of highly localised but also interpersonal processes of sharing knowledge of songs, not only as

---

9   *Kwertengerl* may also be recruited from classificatory kin from the opposite moiety with appropriate subsections *and* knowledge or seniority to fulfil these roles. For example, the *kwertengerl* for people of the Pwerrerl subsection are Ngwarray.

10   My audio recorder failed when recording this information and I have been unable to follow up the Anmatyerr name for this species of grass.

performance, but as markers of landscape, story, and social relations. These songs continue to be circulated among men according to these present and ongoing social relationships, and thus any present and future management of recordings of *akiw* needs to be handled in the same way. They were, as Bird explained it, *tywerreng anyent-areny* 'sacra from one area or region', and needed to be understood as bound to relationships that emanate from specific estates. As ceremonial knowledge is highly valued, and vital to socio-cultural reproduction in these communities, men seek to gain and be associated with its presentation and transmission. The norms of kinship, reciprocity, compassion, and the need to "always ask," as Myers (1982) notes in respect to the utilisation of material resources, equally apply to the use and dissemination of intangible cultural heritage.

For Anmatyerr people today, the recordings of *akiw* need to be managed with contemporary ceremonial and social lives in mind. *Akiw* continues to be sung in the ceremonial camps for young men and, as one man put it, the song series is used to "*angkety mpwarem*" – to raise speech bans or restrictions on the young men. At this juncture they are permitted to talk and socialise again after a period of seclusion. As noted above, senior men and women still know and understand the mythic content of these songs. But, even though many remain familiar with *akiw*, the fact that these songs refer to specific places and Dreamings, and belong to certain families, means that senior custodians should first give approval prior to their use or dissemination. Those with rights in the material therefore include 'owners' and 'managers' but also others with links via Dreaming. It was explained, for example, that one Eastern Arrernte man had rights in *akiw* because an ancestral *amwang* 'snake' had travelled through his country and then on to Atwel, and others were said to have responsibilities due to the fact that the song was used so widely in ceremonial gatherings. While primary ownership and rights in the material were underlined by the dyadic system of complementary filiation and the focus on estates, *akiw* was important to an expanded network of people via these relationships. The senior *merek-artwey* and *kwertengerl* were responsible for leading and instructing in these song traditions but others could know and perform them.

The return of these recordings thus sparked a deep sense of pride among those community members who had maintained their essential ceremonial practices. In every consultation, younger men were brought along to participate in the listening sessions. This was done not so that they could learn from the recorded material, but to hear the elders explaining the song content and its significance. They were encouraged to join in on the conservations with me and assist with explanations. The manner in which this was done left me with little doubt that comprehension and aptitude in ceremonial matters, although possessed by a small cohort, was present across the generations. Keenly aware that in other parts of Australia these traditions had waned, senior Anmatyerr men would often turn our conversations towards the issue of ongoing ceremonial practice. In demonstrating their knowledge of this material and their ability to 'sing along' with recordings, each of the men involved felt significant pride and enjoyed social prestige. Indeed, on other occasions where contemporary singers have not recognised songs from the archive, their responses have often been a mixture of sadness and shame (Gibson in press). Some of the songs associated with the Ilewerr estate that Strehlow recorded, for example, were completely unknown to the elders at Napperby. Upon listening to these recordings people looked to the ground, shook their heads in disbelief and explained that the socio-economic realities of stockwork and labouring on cattle stations when they were young men meant that they had missed the opportunity to learn 'everything'. The return of archival recordings can therefore produce uncomfortable responses. In this case it exposed previously unrecognised areas of cultural loss. Prior to the return of this material these men were unaware of what they did not know.

What was critical about these discussions though was the manner in which the recordings should be treated. They were not something to be relied upon or used in a way that might circumvent the interpersonal, oral, and observational basis of cultural exchange in these small communities. Quite different from the discourse of 'cultural transmission', where it is assumed that ideas, information, or skills might be 'transmitted' from person to person, for these Anmatyerr men the emphasis was on the importance of immersion in social action. Rather than understanding song knowledge as something that eventuates following directed instruction, careful listening, or persistent practice (although it does involve all of these things), their sentiment suggested something more holistic. The type of intergenerational 'transmission' of tacit knowledge that these Anmatyerr men discussed was more akin to the idea that capabilities and understandings are, as Ingold puts it, 'grown' and 'regrown' in each generation via personal interactions, social movement, and long-term exposure and participation (Ingold 2000: 356). To know how a song ought to be sung certainly requires observation and listening, but to know the various sites that a song refers to, its mythico-religious connotations, and the embodiment of these relations in contemporary and past generations of people requires lengthy germination. As Povinelli (2016: 157) has observed in northern Australian Aboriginal communities, the process of 'learning' involves a 'refashioning' of the self that cannot be separated from an entire host of relations and interactions with place, in-place beings, and kin. Intensely located cultural skills such as the singing of *akiw* are intertwined in this nexus and cannot simply be 'added on' to one's person. Such knowledges and skills are 'grown' within people via social interaction and interactions with country. This is precisely why these Anmatyerr men, although happy for recordings of song to act as a supportive resource, remained focused on song genres that were present and in use. The recordings of *akiw* were seen as useful as a form of cultural security, but secondary to the more immediate forms of interpersonal, oral, and observational learning within the contexts of social and ceremonial life.

While all were adamant that *akiw* was still being heard, learnt, and sung during the annual ceremonial gatherings, there was a recognition that these recordings might assist future generations. Fully aware of the history of song loss across much of Australia, some younger Anmatyerr men expressed a degree of anxiety about their cultural future and therefore were more open to the opportunities offered by recording technologies. For the moment, though, the pedagogical practices modelled by their fathers and grandfathers – careful observation, participation, listening, and deference to seniority and expertise – held precedence. The older men repeatedly shirked any offer of digital copies of the material, as they clearly did not need the resource themselves and did not see recordings as a required resource for the education of young men at this point in time. Some younger men, however, did see the potential in having access to recordings but appeared unsure about how to handle these resources among their generally low-tech, impoverished, and poorly serviced communities. Those who did ask for copies of *akiw* commented that they would be able to play the recordings via the USB input on their car stereos during the male activities such as hunting trips. The songs could then be played during recreation, used as a catalyst for further discussion and ensure a limited circulation among a local cohort of related families.

Anmanty as a regional tradition

In Anmatyerr communities to the west, including Laramba (Napperby), Yuelamu (Mount Allan), Ti Tree, and Aileron, a different song tradition, known as *anmanty*, is associated with male initiations. Apparently equivalent to what Anmatyerr speakers term *apwelh* (Green 2010: 117), this tradition concerns the public aspects of a young man's initiation and is sung by groups of men during these ceremonies. As indicated earlier, I first learnt of this tradition from its present-day 'owner', the senior Anmatyerr custodian of the Ilewerr region, Huckitta Lynch, in 2016 while working with him on the song recordings of TGH Strehlow. It is possible that certain *anmanty* songs can be used in multiple genres, and Lynch commented that some of these songs, in addition to being used during *anmanty* ceremonies, could be used to heal the sick. While the songs referring to the *ahenenh* were considered secret-sacred, the *anmanty* songs were identified as public repertories open for discussion. Soon other Anmatyerr men had gathered around to listen to the recording and quickly joined in with the singing. Collectively they explained how many of these songs were still performed at '*anmanty*-time', during the annual initiation gatherings.

While the terms *anmanty* and *apwelh* were used interchangeably by some of the men, it appears that *anmanty* is the specific name given to the earliest stage of the initiation ceremonies in the Western and Central Anmatyerr area. Men sing the *anmanty* songs as the women perform *anthep*, 'a women's dance', across the *apwelh* 'cleared ceremonial ground'. The *anmanty* songs are highly particular to the mythological activity of the Ilewerr estate. *Anmanty* is therefore related to, but not the same as, the *apwelh* ceremonies conducted elsewhere in the Arandic region, where different songs are apparently sung during these public aspects of the ceremony. Far greater ethnographic and ethnomusicological research is certainly required into the specific content of these ceremonies; however, *anmanty* was described as consisting of different 'parts'. The first 'part' of the *anmanty* performance was referred to as *mwerlkenty*. This is the first dance performed in the early morning when a man will stand at the edge of the *arnkenty* 'men's camp' on one side of an *apwelh* and signal over to the women's camp located at the other side of a cleared performance space. This man will hold aloft a *terekerr* 'corella' feather and twirl it in the air to signal to the women to begin dancing towards 'boys' who are to be initiated.

When I returned to Laramba with other recordings of *anmanty*, there was immediate interest. These songs had been recorded with Jack Cook Ngal and Benny Nolan Kemarr at Yuelamu (Mount Allan) in 2007 by Green and Turpin (Figure 2). Following a request from Cook, further recordings were made in 2012 by Green and Carew. Cook clearly possessed the cultural rights to sing *anmanty*; however, some important questions remained about how access and use of the recordings might be handled. As the songs related specifically to the single estate of Ilewerr, it was considered that the senior 'owner' for that country needed to be consulted. Green and Turpin thus made various attempts to include Lynch in this process and were ultimately able to play the Cook recordings to him. His response at the time was that the singing voices sounded as if they were "in a cave," and suggested that new recordings could be made with a large cohort of singers in situ. According to both Lynch and Cook, *anmanty* was a highly local affair, centred upon the happenings of ancestors within the margins of the Ilewerr estate and with significant yet tangential links to travelling dancing women ancestors from the west.

Figure 2. Jack Cook listening to playback of recordings of *anmanty* made by Jennifer Green and Myfany Turpin with Cook and Nolan in 2007 (photo: Jennifer Green)

Anmanty was identified as a distinctly Anmatyerr song set from and about Ilewerr and men from a range of different estates sang it. Most Anmatyerr songs are the personal heritage of family groups and the principal means by which people demonstrate their patrilineal clan identity, as belonging to a defined clan estate. These estate groups are responsible for tracts of land, associated *Anengkerr* 'Dreamings', and related ceremonial practices and it is up to the more senior and ritually expert members of the group to decide when, how, and where songs can be performed. This relationship to song is quite different to the popular conception of a 'songline' where people will sing of ancestors as they journey across multiple sites and estates and travel considerable distances. As a distinctly local song tradition, featuring local ancestors, *anmanty* fits with the previously observed Arandic stress on defined clan estates (Strehlow 1965), although admittedly this can be over-emphasised (Keen 1997; Morton 1997).

The return of these recordings, however, revealed an interesting ethnographic paradox of sorts. Even though *anmanty* is regarded as the personal heritage of large family groups, it appears to be quite distinctive in the manner in which it is shared. Quite unlike most other estate-based song repertoires in the Arandic region, *anmanty* is known by men from many different communities and the song is used in initiation ceremonies in multiple communities. Numerous men commented that *anmanty* was primarily sung in the Anmatyerr-speaking communities of Laramba (Napperby), Alyuen (Aileron), Aleyaw (Ti Tree), and Pmara Jutunta (6 Mile), but was also used in the communities of Willowra, Yuelamu (Mount Allan), and Yuendumu, where the use of the Warlpiri language is more predominant. Use of these songs was also spreading southwards into the Arrernte-speaking region, where a different young men's initiation song set used to be sung. In recent years, however, the decreasing number of senior male Arrernte singers had led to the enlistment of Anmatyerr elders to perform the necessary ceremonies for making young men. Close kin, and linguistically and culturally very similar, to the Arrernte, these ritual experts have stepped in to fill the breach.

There was little doubt, however, that *anmanty* was not only Ilewerr-centric but that it was considered distinctive to the Anmatyerr people. As one elder described it:

> *Anmanty* is really for Anmatyerr people, not for Luritja people, Pitjantjatjara, Pintupi, or Warlpiri people. They have their own culture. Their ceremony is 'self-again' [independent]. They don't know this *anmanty* law ... Some other people come in to learn. They want to learn with Anmatyerr people because they can't use their songs from somewhere else. They have to come here to learn. (Jack Cook, pers. comm. to J Green, 7 June 2007)

The regional variation in the song and ceremonial content of young men's initiation repertoires has been noted elsewhere in the literature (Strehlow 1968, 1978). Recent research by Georgia Curran (2010: 94) has revealed, for example, that the Warlpiri communities to the west of the Anmatyerr continue to sing a set of songs during their *Kurdiji* (initiation ceremonies) that reference sites across large swathes of Warlpiri territory before terminating at Nyepwat, a site within the Ilewerr estate region (Curran uses the Warlpiri cognates for these Anmatyerr site names: Yunyupardi for Nyepwat and Yuluwurru for Ilewerr). The dancing women songline referenced in Curran's thesis passes by Nyepwat and continues eastwards to Pwely, Alhanker and then into Alyawarr country. Among the Western and Central Anmatyerr, however, the *anmanty* song set references local ancestors that travelled between sites such as Nyepwat, Alparr, Tyelempelelemp, and Kwamparr, all within the Ilewerr estate.

Putting *anmanty* in place

The recordings made by Strehlow, Green and Turpin, and Green and Carew inspired the senior singers of *anmanty* not only to demonstrate their knowledge and use of the songs today, but to make the song's relationship to the landscape explicit. Lynch explained that it was necessary to travel to and see the sites referred to in the songs (Figure 3). At the site of Kwamparr (Claypan Bore), for example, *Anengkerr* ancestors had gathered for an initiation ceremony and made *arretyet* 'long dancing sticks/poles'. At Alparr (lit. 'coolamon') a sole female ancestor named Arlerl-arlerl Penangk had left her baby behind in a coolamon as she travelled along Artety Ulpay (Napperby Creek) and down towards the salt lake of Ilewerr in search of firewood and food. This ancestor had last *angan-irrek* 'been spiritually conceived' in Lynch's older sister, Mampey Penangk. According to family history, Mampey would listen closely to the singing of *anmanty* during these ceremonies and ensure that all the men correctly recited 'her' verses. And at Nyepwat, the site was marked by a complex stone arrangement representing the ancestors who had gathered for the first initiation ceremonies. The description of this site and the ceremony it represented had clear equivalences with the mythological origins of young men's initiation ceremonies that Spencer and Gillen (1899: 394–402) had recorded more than a century earlier. Nyepwat, the Laramba men claimed, was so significant to this initiation mythology that it was once well known to Arrernte and Anmatyerr men everywhere.

Figure 3. Approximate locations of some of the sites associated with *anmanty* in the Ilewerr estate

The response to this material highlighted not just the opportunities that collaborative research might offer scholarship, but just how important the performative aspects of people's engagement with sonic heritage can be. During a third visit to the community in October of 2016, Lynch and his *kwertengerl* insisted upon producing another recording of *anmanty* that could be archived alongside those made by Nathaniel Rauwiraka with Strehlow in 1949 and by Cook in the 2000s (Figure 4). In making these recordings Lynch was reaffirming his status as the *merek-artwey* for Ilewerr. While not discounting the rights of others, such as those spiritually conceived in the Ilewerr estate or related to it as *kwertengerl*, he and his cohort of senior singers at Laramba were keen to have their important links to this ceremony recognised. The point being made was that although others can sing *anmanty*, they would not necessarily have the right to visit these related sites within the Ilewerr estate without permissions from Lynch and his *kwertengerl*. Few others would have the intricate knowledge of these places and their related stories.

A journey to the site of Nyepwat in October 2016 with two younger men from the community in tow was a particularly vivid example of just how eager these men were to demonstrate their expertise. Wanting to emphasise the relationship of this tradition to the landscape of Ilewerr, we travelled to a number of sites where relevant small songs from the *anmanty* repertoire were sung in situ.[11] Upon arriving at Nyepwat, Lynch and three of his *kwertengerl* sang small songs from the *anmanty* series that related to specific natural features – a tree, two standing stones, and other geological formations – each representing the figures of various ancestors. In addition, we were taken to sites associated with the travelling dancing women songline that travels from the west and continues east.[12] One elder described the stone arrangement, and the story it represented, as being so integral to Anmatyerr people that it was "like a sacred site, but not a sacred site," meaning that the site and the *anmanty* performances were not exclusive to an audience of initiated men, as in the case of secret-sacred men's rituals, but something fundamentally important to all Anmatyerr people.[13] As Ronnie McNamara put it, "It is important for ceremony. The centre is there. It is the main one *for everybody*."[14] *Anmanty* is spoken of as a highly significant, community-held tradition, lacking the exclusivity, gender restrictions and, thus, dangers associated with other, more closely guarded religious ceremonies.

This was also an opportunity to reveal to the younger men present just how important it was to learn songs within the context of a totemic landscape. The only way that the full significance of these songs could be properly grasped would be via the careful tutelage of ceremonial experts who could point out particular trees, claypans, and rock formations. To do this required excellent geographical and cultural knowledge. In this case, the returned recordings served as a catalyst for senior men to take younger men with them to sites that had not been visited for decades. Lynch spoke of how he had been shown these places by the men who had also taught him to sing *anmanty* (past *merek-artwey* for Ilewerr, Dick Utyew and Charlie Artetyerwenguny) and he observed how only a handful of men now knew the locations and details of all of these sites.[15] During this same fieldwork trip, a group of Anmatyerr men consisting of two younger men and four elders camped in the bed of the Napperby Creek and spent each afternoon listening to archival recordings of *anmanty* and other Anmatyerr songs. In the early mornings and evenings, the senior men would spend their time clarifying songs and singing, while during the day we would visit sites and discuss the interconnectedness of song, place, mythology, and person.

As with the discussions of *akiw* in the east, what was clear from these discussions was just how secure *anmanty* was when compared with other genres of male song. The public male ceremonial genre, referred to as *althart*, and the more private and gender-restricted songs

---

11 In a song series, a 'small song' is defined as a sequence of songs that have the same verse (see Ellis & Barwick 1987).

12 This connection with the dancing women mythology in *anmanty* needs to be explored in later research.

13 Ronnie McNamara, pers. comm. to Jason Gibson at Laramba, 1 November 2016.

14 Ronnie McNamara, pers. comm. to Jason Gibson at Laramba, 1 November 2016.

15 Artetyerwenguny was an informant to TGH Strehlow during a fieldwork visit to Aileron in 1968.

associated with particular estates were far more vulnerable, for they were not used in these large initiation gatherings, and only a handful of men knew them. In some cases, entire song sets for particular estates had fallen out of usage. However, numerous men of middle and older generations from across the region knew *anmanty* and most felt confident that they could keep the tradition going. In fact, there is evidence among the Anmatyerr (Gibson in press), and further published evidence from the neighbouring Warlpiri, that participation in these types of young men's initiation ceremonies is growing (Peterson 2000; Curran 2011). So crucial are these ceremonies to the functioning of Central Australian Aboriginal cultural and social life that the very suggestion that *anmanty* (and the various other songs sung during the different open and closed aspects of these ceremonies) might cease to be known was an almost unbearable thought to all concerned. These ceremonies constitute entry into adulthood, ensure inclusion in local, cultural, and religious instruction, and act as a sign of wider Central Australian Aboriginal solidarity. Despite Cook's aforementioned consideration that the recordings of *anmanty* might one day be necessary for the continuation of this tradition, it was clear that all was being done to prevent this becoming a reality.

In the mid to late 20th century, initiation ceremonies were generally held at numerous locations and would feature only two or three initiates. In recent years, however, with a decrease in expert singers across the Anmatyerr and Arrernte regions, initiation ceremonies are taking place at fewer locations and the number of initiates attending ceremonies is growing. Many men describe the increase in the number of initiates (to as many as 19 in recent ceremonies) as being *mamety*, meaning socially unacceptable and likely to bring bad luck. There is also a growing feeling that considerable pressure is being put on a small number of singers to sustain these all-important ceremonies.[16] The aforementioned reliance on senior Anmatyerr to sing at Eastern Arrernte initiation ceremonies, for example, demonstrates this general trend towards cultural attenuation in the Arandic region. Yet, while the Arrernte have only partial recordings of their public initiation songs, the Anmatyerr are fortunate to have these numerous and detailed recordings of *anmanty*.[17] If required or desired, they will be able to turn to the archive to revive this distinct tradition.

---

16 There is also some concern about the time of year when these ceremonies are held. In the past, initiation ceremonies were reputedly held at any time of the year, but as people became more and more integral to the pastoral economy the European 'Christmas' or 'holiday' period became the only 'free' time available for extended ceremonies. With a warming climate, however, many are now wondering if it might be better to return to a flexible regime and provide some relief to elderly singers. This seems unlikely, though, as the association between these ceremonies and 'Christmas time' has become a key part of the tradition.

17 TGH Strehlow mostly concentrated on estate-based, restricted male songs; however, he did make recordings of what he labelled *ndapa* 'dancing women songs' that were sung in the Western Arrernte region (see Strehlow 1971: 393–417).

Figure 4. Huckitta Lynch in the foreground with Peter Cole (left) and Lesley Stafford (right) at Artety Ulpay (Napperby Creek) during an *anmanty* recording session on 3 November 2016 (photo: Ben Deacon)

Archives and access

At present these communities view all of the recordings, whether made in the mid 20th century or in recent decades, as confirmation of present and enduring cultural practices. They remind people of the presence of ancestors in the landscape as well as personal and kin ties to these ancestors and their *Anengkerr* stories. In this sense, the recordings of both *anmanty* and *akiw* are welcomed as sources of pride and yet at the same time they remind people of the need to grow and regrow song traditions across the generations. Rather than turning to issues of archival management and preservation, my discussions with Anmatyerr men almost always veered towards the importance of knowing song in its context. They emphasised the importance of hearing and singing songs as lived expressions, produced amid a complex milieu of reflection, sociality, and relationships, but also bolstered by a depth of knowledge in ritual and *Anengkerr* that makes them so traditionally affective.

The threat of cultural endangerment has not yet reached the threshold where archival recordings of *akiw* or *anmanty* are required for the purposes of revivification and reimagining. The relatively small cohort of men that knows *akiw*, and the larger group that knows *anmanty*, intend to rely upon their ongoing knowledge and use of these traditions rather than seek out clarification or authorisation from the archive. Younger men across the Anmatyerr region do nonetheless speak of an obvious decline in the number of senior men available to teach these fundamental ceremonies. The passing of each elder is often likened to the demise of entire 'libraries' or 'archives' of cultural knowledge, but men across the generations agree that, as fascinating and edifying as these recordings may be, their contents can never replace the performativity and tacit knowledge at the heart of song and ceremony. As John Bradley, an anthropologist working on Yanyuwa song in the Gulf of Carpentaria, has noted, recordings like these will only ever work as "aspirational motivators" towards song performance, and their potential will always be mediated by larger social factors (Bradley 2011: 9). The Anmatyerr emphasis on the grounded, personal, and experiential basis of ceremony thus acknowledges this perspective.

This is not to say that preserving and accessing these recordings is not a future concern. When it came to discussions of access and preservation copies, the men agreed that AIATSIS (Australian Institute of Aboriginal and Torres Strait Islander Studies) was a suitable repository, although only if Anmatyerr families had ready access. Suggestions for local archiving solutions in Central Australia were less forthcoming, however. While Cook and Lynch, for example, considered the *anmanty* recordings to be 'free' for anybody to hear and that they should be made available to anyone who was interested, they pointed out clearly that the relevant owners and managers of Ilewerr needed to oversee the provision of copies. The senior singers of *akiw* gave similar advice. The 2007 recordings were archived at the Endangered Languages Archive (ELAR) with instructions that Ilewerr families be consulted before the recordings are used in any way.[18] Subsequent recordings of *anmanty* made by Green and Carew with Cook in 2012 and then by Angeles, Deacon, and Gibson with Lynch during 2016 were to be lodged with the Strehlow Research Centre. As is explained below, although the Strehlow Research Centre may be deemed a suitable place for these recordings, as it contains an extensive collection of Arandic song, the reasons for archiving *anmanty* had more to do with personal relationships with staff at the centre.

Objects and relationships

A key observation made during this research was the importance that Anmatyerr men placed on their personal relationships with researchers, recordists, and collections staff. Anmatyerr people foregrounded these personal relationships as being inherently critical to the present and future management of archival recordings. Rather than wanting to replace personal ties and responsibilities of care with impartial, standardised, and institutional models of management, Anmatyerr men often looked for personal or kinship ties to ground the handling of their recordings. Researchers, on the other hand, although respectful of and keen to cultivate these relationships, were often focused on establishing distinct rules and guidelines for future access and dissemination. Those making recordings today are eager to ensure that there are processes and agreements in place for use of this material in the long term. Without such agreements, researchers/recordists will not only be open to accusations of 'gatekeeping' but will have to field access requests and play an ongoing role in management of the material. If they pass away, or are no longer active in the field, what happens then?

With these issues at the forefront of their minds, contemporary researchers are now often searching for technical, institutional, or non-personal solutions that might enable access without the requirement of their personal involvement. In a recent paper on the repatriation

---

18   https://elar.soas.ac.uk

of song recordings to Aboriginal communities in the Kimberley, for example, Treloyn, Martin & Charles (2016) discuss ways of using digital technologies to tag and archive recordings without the need for a researcher to act as a conduit to archival discovery and exploration. The ideal here is that Indigenous peoples will be able to do all this themselves and have uninhibited access to their cultural heritage. While the objective of improved access and greater Indigenous control over cultural and historical materials should be unquestioned, the collaborative nature of these recordings ought to receive greater consideration. Writing of ethnographic collections in North America, Aaron Glass (2015) has, for example, argued that this type of material is most often 'co-constructed' and emergent "from social encounter and interaction based on relations of consultation and complicity between scholars and research associates" (2015: 19–20). Factoring in the intercultural origins of this material, while elevating Indigenous control over these archives, may not always be a straightforward exercise.

Part of the issue here is that the practices, policies, and procedures of researchers and collecting institutions do not fit easily with cultural practice. In the museum domain, for example, performative aspects of local practice such as songs, dances, and rituals have come to be institutionalised as new categories of 'object' alongside more conventional museum pieces (Geismar & Tilley 2003: 170). Song recordings in the digital age therefore become ephemeral, intangible, and endlessly reproducible 'files'. The transformation of ephemeral events and practices into 'archival objects' has, in this context, profoundly changed the scope of what can be construed as a cultural object. From an Anmatyerr point of view, the creation of any archival object will entail relationships among and between people. There is now a growing body of literature demonstrating that Aboriginal people regard the act of sharing cultural knowledge, be it in the form of acrylic painting (Myers 2002), other forms of Indigenous art (Morphy 1992), or in the making of ethnographic collections (Gibson in press), as integral to the establishment of a significant relationship. If we accept that these relationships are also often essential to the co-production of an ethnographic record, in this case a song recording, then it would be imprudent to try and circumvent them. Any researcher interested in decolonising methodologies or wanting to acknowledge the intercultural nature of their work would do well to honour and respect these relationships. While the establishment of better systems of access, preservation, and use ought to be instituted, personal relationships need not be displaced. Many Indigenous communities will, for example, expect a long-term researcher to return to their communities, to provide copies of their materials, and, in some cases, to assist communities in reconnecting with failing or lost traditions.

When discussing archiving and preservation protocols, for example, most men pointed out that they were unaware of any of the archival institutions or their staff. They were, however, familiar with the relatively small number of researchers who had collaborated with them in the recording of their songs and felt comfortable simply contacting the relevant researchers for copies. While this of course does not solve issues of long-term accessibility and preservation, it should be noted that men like Cook place their trust not in institutions but in people.

> If these young fellas don't carry on the *anmanty* song, well they can get the story from you
> or Jenny Green. And they can go on and on, all the way then. When we're all gone, you

and Jenny can tell the story, "Well Jack Cook told me that if you fellas don't understand the *anmanty* song he told us, to tell you mob the story so you can carry on." *Alakenh* [just like that]. (Jack Cook, pers. comm. to Jason Gibson, 1 November 2016)

When asked where copies of the *anmanty* recordings should be kept, Lynch also quickly gestured towards his classificatory grandson, an Arrernte man who works at the Strehlow Research Centre in Alice Springs. This person could be trusted because he understood the ways in which song was tied to estates and Dreamings and, as he lived locally, could be called upon if copies were required. While we might critique Cook and Lynch's responses as deficient in regards to concerns about long-term management, on the other hand they also speak to an antagonism towards objectification, particularly as the song traditions in question continue to have existential and pragmatic value. These song collections constitute a modern genre of material culture, drawn out of traditional practice, mediated by interpersonal exchanges with researchers, and incorporated into collecting regimes and institutions. Without the type of local Indigenous-run collecting institutions that have emerged, for example, in parts of Melanesia (Geismar & Tilley 2003; Stanley 2007), Anmatyerr communities in Central Australia continue to emphasise the interpersonal and relational as a means of caring for intangible cultural heritage.

Conclusion

The return of these recordings triggered a range of responses from Anmatyerr men and brought up significant questions about cultural endangerment and the processes of cultural transmission. It is evident that considerably more research needs to be conducted before a better description of *anmanty* and *akiw*, in ethnomusicological, linguistic, and anthropological terms, can be developed. Comparative investigations into the similarities and differences of contemporary young men's initiation ceremonies across the Western and Central Anmatyerr, Warlpiri, and Arrernte communities could illuminate much about the processes of cultural transmission and change across cultural and linguistic blocs.[19] At any rate, the recordings discussed here provide us with an excellent starting point for future research into the public aspects of these ongoing ceremonies.

Any archival objects of cultural significance to Anmatyerr people circulate in ways that produce relationships among and between people. In the study presented above, the return of recordings of *akiw* and *anmanty* were received as reiterations of connections with eternal Dreamings, ongoing cultural performances, personal roles and responsibilities, and the systems of complementary filiation. Anmatyerr people looked to their own networks of relationship, and their own ongoing cultural gatherings and performances as the primary means through which traditions like *akiw* and *anmanty* will find future expression. In Anmatyerr society this type of cultural property is not self-made but extends outward from an identity derived from the pre-existing *Anengkerr*. This fundamentally spiritual or mythic grounding of ceremonial performance asserts a relationship between objects, places, and people. Rights to the cultural

---

19   For example, the absence of Warlpiri cognates for some of the key terms associated with these
      ceremonies – *akiw, apwelh, anthep,* and *anmanty* – suggests that there may be something distinctive about
      these ceremonies in the Arandic region.

heritage expressed in the recordings of *akiw* and *anmanty* are thus conceived as a bundle of socio-moral entitlements and obligations.

Archiving was thus not seen as a means of maintaining or sustaining *akiw* or *anmanty*, but as a last resort if cultural reproduction failed. The spectre of cultural endangerment has been with Anmatyerr people for decades and with significant social changes in the mid 20th century, ceremonial and religious practice has undergone significant change. People are nevertheless reluctant to treat traditions like these as thing-like entities or texts that can be repurposed or reimagined outside of, or even alien to, the nexus of the geographic, mythic, and relational. As expressions of Dreamings, these songs are regarded as embodying extremely potent properties that only ritual experts who stand in appropriate relationships to land and ancestors can deal with. For Anmatyerr and Arrernte people who have witnessed ceremonial practices disappear from their lives at a rapid pace – since the mid 20th century – archiving of this type of material is a secondary measure. What is foremost in people's minds is the safeguarding of song via the retention of cultural practice.

This does not mean, however, that where song knowledge persists, recordings become insignificant. As is shown here, the return of recordings can act as a catalyst to performativity and reiterate people's own pedagogies of orality and listening. Furthermore, the process of returning archival materials can enlighten the research community and collecting institutions about their own responsibilities – personal and institutional – and present opportunities for cultural change within these spheres (see Gibson 2018). While listening to the recordings the senior men would speak over the audio, make gestures to indicate the direction of particular sites, draw ceremonial designs in the sand, and discuss the location of ancestors in the local geography. Repatriation of sonic heritage, therefore, need not be predicated on the idea that it is most valuable when songs are severely threatened or defunct. These recordings can offer a great deal, even where song persists.

References

Bracknell, Clint. 2017. Maaya Waab (play with sound): Song language and spoken language in the southwest of Western Australia. In Jim Wafer & Myfany Turpin (eds.), *Recirculating songs: Revitalising the singing practices of Indigenous Australia*, 45–57. Hamilton, NSW: Hunter Press.

Bradley, John, Amanda Kearney, Leonard Norman & Graham Friday. 2011. 'These are the choices we make': Animating Saltwater Country. *Screening the Past* 31. 1–17. (http://www.screeningthepast.com/2011/08/these-are-the-choices-we-make-animating-saltwater-country/) (Accessed 24 December 2018.)

Bradley, John & Yanyuwa Families. 2010. *Singing Saltwater Country: Journey to the songlines of Carpentaria*. Sydney: Allen & Unwin.

Curran, Georgia. 2010. *Contemporary ritual practice in an Aboriginal settlement: The Warlpiri Kurdiji ceremony*. Canberra: Australian National University (Doctoral dissertation.)

Curran, Georgia. 2011. The 'expanding domain' of Warlpiri initiation rituals. In Yasmine Musharbash & Marcus Barber (eds.), *Ethnography & the production of anthropological knowledge: Essays in honour of Nicolas Peterson*, 39–50. Canberra: ANU Press.

Dobson, Veronica & John Henderson. 1994. *Eastern and Central Arrernte to English Dictionary*. Alice Springs: IAD Press.

Ellis, Catherine J & Linda Barwick. 1987. Musical syntax and the problem of meaning in a Central Australian songline. *Musicology Australia* 10(1). 41–57.

Geismar, Haidy & Christopher Tilley. 2003. Negotiating materiality: International and local museum practices at the Vanuatu Cultural Centre and National Museum. *Oceania* 73(3). 170–188.

Gibson, Jason. In press. *Ceremony men: Making ethnography and the return of the Strehlow Collection*. Albany: State University of New York Press.

Gibson, Jason. 2017. 'Only the best is good enough for eternity': Revisiting the ethnography of T.G.H. Strehlow. In Nicolas Peterson & Anna Kenny (eds.), *The German-language tradition of ethnography in Australia*, 243–271 (Monographs in Anthropology). Canberra: ANU Press.

Gibson, Jason. 2018. 'You're my kwertengerl': Transforming models of care for Central Australian Aboriginal museum collections. *Museum Management and Curatorship* November. 1–17.

Glass, Aaron. 2015. Indigenous ontologies, digital futures: Plural provenances and the Kwakwaka'wakw Collection in Berlin and beyond. In Raymond Silverman (ed.), *Museum as process: Translating local and global knowledge*, 19–44. London: Routledge.

Gray, Geoffrey. 2007. *A cautious silence: The politics of Australian anthropology*. Canberra: Aboriginal Studies Press.

Gray, Peter. 2007. *The Alcoota Land Claim: Report and recommendations*. Canberra: Office of the Aboriginal Land Commissioner.

Green, Jennifer. 2010. *Central and Eastern Anmatyerr to English Dictionary*. Alice Springs: IAD Press.

Gruber, Jacob W. 1970. Ethnographic salvage and the shaping of anthropology. *American Anthropologist* 72(6). 1289–1299.

Gunderson, Frank, Robert C Lancefield & Bret Woods (eds.). 2018. *The Oxford handbook of musical repatriation*. Oxford: Oxford University Press.

Gunn, RG. 2000. Central Australian rock art: A second report. *Rock Art Research: The Journal of the Australian Rock Art Research Association (Aura)* 17(2). 111–126.

Hill, Barry. 2003. *Broken song: T.G.H. Strehlow and Aboriginal possession*. Sydney: Random House.

Ingold, Tim. 2000. *The perception of the environment: Essays in livelihood, dwelling and skill*. London: Routledge.

Jackson, Jason Baird. 2007. The paradoxical power of endangerment: Traditional Native American dance and music in Eastern Oklahoma. *World Literature Today* 81(5). 37–41.

Keen, Ian. 1997. The Western Desert vs the rest: Rethinking the contrast. In Francesca Merlan, John Morton & Alan Rumsey (eds.), *Scholar and sceptic*, 65–93. Canberra: Aboriginal Studies Press.

Kimber, Richard G. 2011. *Cultural values associated with Alice Springs water*. Alice Springs: Commissioned by the Alice Springs Water Management Branch of the

Northern Territory Department of Natural Resources, Environment and Sport.
(http://www.territorystories.nt.gov.au/handle/10070/235032). (Accessed 9 June 2018.)

Marett, Allan. 2010. Vanishing songs: How musical extinctions threaten the planet.
Ethnomusicology Forum 19(2). 249–262.

Meggitt, Mervyn. 1966. Gadjari among the Walbiri Aborigines of Central Australia.
Oceania 36(4). 283–315.

Michaels, Eric. 1985. Constraints on knowledge in an economy of oral information.
Current Anthropology 26(4). 505–510.

Morphy, Howard. 1992. *Ancestral connections: Art and an Aboriginal system of knowledge.*
Chicago: University of Chicago Press.

Morton, John. 1995. 'Secrets of the Arandas': T.G.H. Strehlow and the course of revelation.
In Chris Anderson (ed.), *Politics of the secret*, 51–66 (Oceania Monograph 45). Sydney:
University of Sydney.

Morton, John. 1997. Arrernte (Aranda) land tenure: An evaluation of the Strehlow model.
Occasional paper (Strehlow Research Centre) 1. 107–126. Alice Springs: Strehlow
Research Centre.

Morton, John. 2017. 'Mother's blood, father's land': Native Title and comparative land tenure
modelling for claims in 'settled' Australia. *Oceania* 87(1). 58–77.

Moyle, Alice Marshall. 1966. *Handlist of field collections of recorded music in Australia and the
Torres Strait.* Canberra: Australian Institute of Aboriginal Studies.

Myers, Fred. 1982. Always ask: Resource use and land ownership among Pintupi Aborigines
of the Australian Western Desert. In Nancy M Williams & Eugene S Hunn (eds.),
Resource managers: North American and Australian hunter-gatherers, 173–195. Boulder:
Westview Press for the American Association for the Advancement of Science.

Myers, Fred. 2002. *Painting culture: The making of an Aboriginal high art.* Durham, NC:
Duke University Press.

Myers, Fred. 2014. Paintings, publics, and protocols: The early paintings from Papunya.
Material Culture Review 79 (March). 78–91.

Peterson, Nicolas. 2000. An expanding Aboriginal domain: Mobility and the initiation
journey. *Oceania* 70(3). 205–218.

Peterson, Nicolas. 2008. Just humming: The consequence of the decline of learning contexts
among the Warlpiri. In Jean Kommers & Eric Venbrux (eds.), *Cultural styles of
knowledge transmission: Essays in honour of Ad Borsboom*, 114–118. Amsterdam: Aksant
Academic Publishers.

Pink, Olive. 1936. The landowners in the Northern Division of the Aranda Tribe, Central
Australia. *Oceania* 6(3). 275–305.

Povinelli, Elizabeth A. 2016. *Geontologies: A requiem to late liberalism.* Durham, NC:
Duke University Press.

Spencer, Baldwin & Francis Gillen. 1968 [1899]. *The native tribes of Central Australia.*
New York: Dover Publications.

Spencer, Baldwin & Francis Gillen. 1904. *The northern tribes of Central Australia.* London:
MacMillan and Co.

Stanley, Nick (ed.). 2007. *The future of Indigenous museums: Perspectives from the Southwest Pacific*. New York: Berghahn Books.

Strehlow, Carl. 1907. *The Aranda and Loritja tribes of Central Australia part 1: Myths, legends and fables of the Aranda tribe*. Frankfurt am Main: Municipal Ethnological Museum.

Strehlow, TGH. 1947. *Aranda traditions*. 2nd edn. New York: Johnson Reprint.

Strehlow, TGH. 1965. Culture, social structure, and environment. In RM Berndt and CH Berndt (eds.), *Aboriginal man in Australia*, 122–145. Sydney: Angus & Robertson.

Strehlow, TGH. 1968. Spencer 1901 recordings. Alice Springs: Unpublished manuscript at the Strehlow Research Centre.

Strehlow, TGH. 1971. *Songs of Central Australia*. Sydney: Angus and Robertson.

Strehlow, TGH. 1978. Central Australian man-making ceremonies with special reference to Hermannsburg, Northern Territory. *The Lutheran* 12(7). 150–155.

Treloyn, Sally & Andrea Emberly. 2013. Sustaining traditions: Ethnomusicological collections, access and sustainability in Australia. *Musicology Australia* 35(2). 159–177.

Treloyn, Sally, Matthew Dembal Martin & Rona Googninda Charles. 2016. Cultural precedents for the repatriation of legacy song records to communities of origin. *Australian Aboriginal Studies* 2. 94–103.

Turpin, Myfany. 2013. *Antarrengeny awely: Alyawarr women's songs from Antarrengeny*. Alice Springs: Batchelor Press.

Turpin, Myfany. 2017. Finding Arrernte songs. In Jim Wafer & Myfany Turpin (eds.), *Recirculating songs: Revitalising the singing practices of Indigenous Australia*, 90–102. Hamilton, NSW: Hunter Press.

Turpin, Myfany & Alison Ross. 2012. *Kaytetye to English dictionary*. Alice Springs: Institute for Aboriginal Development Press.

Turpin, Myfany & Jennifer Green. 2018. Rapikwenty: 'A loner in the ashes' and other songs for sleeping. *Studia Metrica et Poetica* 5(1). 52–79.

Language Documentation & Conservation Special Publication No. 18
Archival returns: Central Australia and beyond
ed. by Linda Barwick, Jennifer Green & Petronella Vaarzon-Morel, pp. 91–110
http://nflrc.hawaii.edu/ldc/sp18
http://hdl.handle.net/10125/24879

Incorporating archival cultural heritage materials into contemporary Warlpiri women's *yawulyu* spaces

Georgia Curran
Sydney Conservatorium of Music, The University of Sydney

Abstract

National archives house a rich legacy of materials that document many intangible aspects of Indigenous cultural heritage. It is the moral right of Indigenous people to have access to these materials, but their reintroduction back into present-day worlds is not without impact. Here, I analyse contemporary spaces in which Warlpiri women have engaged with archival cultural heritage materials and incorporated them into present-day contexts for the performance of *yawulyu*. These include the production of song books, dance camps at bush locations, and broader community arts performances. These cases illustrate that for proper engagement with these legacy materials knowledgeable Indigenous people must lead activities which are supported as part of the repatriation process.

Keywords: Warlpiri, cultural heritage, performance, women's songs, community development

Introduction

Early in 2018, 13 Warlpiri women and I huddled together in a small listening room at the Australian Institute of Aboriginal and Torres Strait Islander Studies (AIATSIS), eagerly anticipating what we were about to hear. The group had travelled from the Tanami Desert settlement of Yuendumu to Canberra, along with three men, who sat in the room next door, presumably going through a similar process. We had contacted the access manager at the sound archive several weeks earlier, requesting that particular materials be available for the group's visit. Narrowing this down had been a daunting task – the broad array of Warlpiri materials in the archive seemed almost endless and details of each item were not readily displayed in the catalogue. Unable to identify individual recordings, we asked for access to several large collections made by prominent researchers whom Warlpiri people remembered, and some of whom were still in contact with Warlpiri people today. These ethnographers, anthropologists, musicologists, and linguists, who have lived in and travelled through Warlpiri country over the last century, had diligently archived their recordings here, and, content aside, they provide a fascinating overview of the breadth of intercultural interactions between Indigenous peoples and visitors to their country during this time.

As I clicked play on the computer screen, crackles of a recording from another era filled the room. Made by musicologist Stephen Wild, who had lived in the settlement of Lajamanu in the early 1970s, this recorded session of Warlpiri song was just one of many Wild had done. The unison voices of close female relatives of my companions filled the room. The thudding of feet hitting the earth as they danced was clearly audible. Looking up, I saw that Nampijinpa was crying. After listening to similar archival recordings with these women over many years, I had become used to this kind of emotive response to hearing the voices of dearly loved relatives who had passed away. I reached out to comfort her and asked if she wanted me to turn the recording off, something no one had ever desired but which I continued to offer nonetheless. She emphatically insisted that I keep it on, as she was crying "in a happy way."

"We don't do *yawulyu* like that anymore," Nampijinpa stated as explanation for her tears. "There were so many people dancing, now we just have a few." While Nampijinpa and others listened nostalgically, I was left with thoughts of the frailty of this genre of Warlpiri women's song in the contemporary world and the very different contexts in which it is held today. These recordings clearly had immense cultural heritage value, but were they also affecting present-day contexts? Was the richness evident in these legacy recordings resulting in the downplaying of the contexts in which Warlpiri women carry out performances today, working hard, in the face of many challenges, to hold on to their musical knowledge and practices? Or were they providing stimulation and inspiration for these contexts? Either way, present-day engagement with these legacy recordings was not without impact.

In this chapter, I address the issues surrounding the return of legacy cultural heritage materials to the generations of Warlpiri people living in Yuendumu, an Aboriginal community in the Tanami Desert region of Central Australia. I focus particularly on a broad genre of Warlpiri women's song, *yawulyu*. Today, Warlpiri women are actively engaged in new and creative ways of ensuring that *yawulyu* continue to be held into the future. In this chapter I describe several contemporary contexts that illustrate ways in which archival sound recordings and photographs have been reincorporated into present-day performances. The impact of returning legacy recordings into these contexts is the central topic of this chapter. I begin by delineating the Yuendumu-specific context within the Australia-wide effort of researchers to return materials of cultural heritage significance to their communities of origin. I then give an overview of the many recordings of Warlpiri women's *yawulyu* that are held in national and local archives and that for the most part are inaccessible in any real way to the current generation of Warlpiri women who carry this tradition forward. I then go on to describe some recent contexts in which Warlpiri women have utilised archival cultural materials in contemporary performance spaces.

Firstly I discuss the use of old recordings and photographs in a song documentation project that resulted in the book and CD collection *Yurntumu-wardingki juju-ngaliya-kurlangu yawulyu*: Warlpiri women's songs from Yuendumu (Warlpiri Women from Yuendumu 2017a & b). Secondly I discuss the biannual Southern Ngaliya girls' dance camps that have been held for the last 10 years at outstation sites around Yuendumu. And thirdly I reflect on Unbroken Land, a community arts event produced by Incite Arts that was held in Alice Springs in September

2018, at which a group of Warlpiri women from Yuendumu were invited to perform *yawulyu*, alongside a number of other theatrical contributions to a broader event. With reflection on these contemporary contexts, I argue that efforts to repatriate archival cultural materials must also include support for community-led activities that provide spaces for Indigenous people to engage with these legacy materials.

Repatriation and the return of Indigenous cultural heritage materials

Human remains and objects of significance stolen from Indigenous families in the past have become a focus of many repatriation efforts in Australia today. In some instances, although many more remain, these tangible, material components of Indigenous persons have been returned to the descendants of these families. The songs, dances, designs, stories, and photographs documented over the course of the 20th century are records of intangible components of Indigenous cultural heritage that powerfully connect Indigenous persons across generations. These recorded materials are thus also the owned cultural property of Indigenous groups, and present-day descendants have moral rights as well as responsibilities to pass on associated knowledge and practices to future generations (Curran et al. 2019). Within a Central Australian context, the intrinsic importance of song to Indigenous identity is paramount, with songs connecting people to their inherited country, cosmological beliefs, and kinship networks. Legacy sound recordings and other materials are thus of enormous cultural heritage value.

The repatriation of digitised versions of photographs and video and sound recordings to Indigenous communities is, without a doubt, the proper ethical path to follow.[1] As such, efforts by researchers to return materials from archives or individual collections back to communities are now widespread. As Treloyn & Charles observe:

> In Australia, the return and dissemination of audio and video recordings from archival and personal collections to cultural heritage communities has emerged as a primary, and almost ubiquitous, fieldwork method. (2015: 163)

These efforts, however, have multifaceted effects within present-day contexts and on the ways in which Aboriginal people remember and continue to maintain songs and associated knowledge. As Anderson reminds us with respect to the return of stolen objects of significance to Indigenous peoples:

> 'Repatriation' ... [is] strictly speaking an impossibility. An object of cultural significance, left long out of its original context, cannot be put back. The context changes, the significance of the object changes, original meanings are forgotten or transformed. (This is not to say that the objects become meaningless or unimportant.) (Anderson 1995: 9)

---

1   Many institutions, including AIATSIS, that hold these archives have undertaken large-scale efforts to digitise recordings made on older sound-recording technology. These efforts recognise the national significance of these materials.

Therefore 'repatriation', if this is to be done in its true sense, must be more than a simple return of material to a community archive or the provision of copied materials to interested individuals, although these are clearly important too.[2]

Later in this chapter, I discuss some examples of Yuendumu-centred activities that focus on developing community-led activities to reincorporate these materials responsibly within present-day contexts.

The body of documentation of Indigenous ceremonial practices and songs for archival purposes, although sometimes pejoratively labelled as the result of salvage ethnography,[3] must be acknowledged as producing a highly significant legacy of cultural heritage materials. In Yuendumu, and likely in other Warlpiri communities, people never tire of watching archival films of the spectacular conflict resolution ceremonies for which Warlpiri people are famous. One of the most popular films requested for group screenings in Yuendumu is the Australian Institute of Aboriginal Studies (AIAS) film of a 1967 *Ngajakula* ceremony (Sandall 1977), with spoken analytical commentary by much-loved anthropologist Nicolas Peterson. Also of immense interest is the Lander & Perkins (1993) film of the counterpart ceremony *Jardiwarnpa – a Warlpiri fire ceremony*, a brighter and more spectacular production. With the beginnings of Warlpiri Media Association in the 1980s, Yuendumu has been at the forefront of documenting many aspects of local cultural life and houses a large on-country archive of this material. Pintubi Anmatjere Warlpiri (PAW) Media and Communications (previously Warlpiri Media Association) has for several decades produced films that Warlpiri people owned and produced in collaboration with the many non-Indigenous media workers they have employed over the years.[4] In a recent film, *Yarripiri's journey* (Daw & Cadden 2017), made by young Warlpiri directors Simon Japanangka Fisher Jnr and Jason Japaljarri Woods, and produced by long-term community media workers Anna Cadden and Jonathan Daw, Warlpiri elders tell the ancestral Jardiwanpa story as it moves from south to north through Warlpiri country. The film incorporates ceremonial footage from the 1993 Lander & Perkins film, artistically embedding the latter within footage of landscape taken more recently during the current film's production. This use of archival footage echoes the ways that Indigenous peoples worldwide have incorporated historical photographs into their own media, asserting cultural identity in a modern world (see Ginsburg 1995 for examples).

2   As an anonymous reviewer pointed out, the word 'repatriation' is increasingly used to refer to objects or materials that are handed back permanently. As the materials discussed in this chapter are all recordings of intangible aspects of culture, 'repatriation' is used here to refer more to archival return, the re-incorporation of recorded materials into the cultural worlds where they were made, even though other copies and often original recordings may be housed permanently elsewhere.

3   'Salvage ethnography' refers to a form of early 20th century anthropology in which recordings of languages and ceremonial practices were made with the assumption that the documented traditions were 'disappearing' and would not survive in the future.

4   Hinkson (2002) has illustrated the "long and complex history of *intercultural* engagement at Yuendumu" (2002: 160), noting that it is "intercultural in terms of who was participating and driving the projects, intercultural in terms of the traditions being engaged, intercultural in terms of the meanings produced" (2002: 164–165). She argues that this was not acknowledged in Michaels' earlier works, though certainly it was a factor in the 1980s and is increasingly so as PAW workers engage with new forms of media in the present day.

In the 1980s, Eric Michaels (1986, 1987) examined Warlpiri people's engagement with then-new media (television and audiovisual recording technology), focusing in part on the impact of recording technology on forms of orally transmitted knowledge, and finding that Warlpiri knowledge transmission is negotiated in the moment, such that audiovisual recordings sat at odds with traditional 'face-to-face transmission'. Several decades later, however, Barwick et al. (2013) found that younger generations in other Central Australian communities preferred to supplement traditional teaching and learning modes with the use of writing and audiovisual media. Warlpiri people have embraced literacy over the last 50 years, and while this was not applied to the writing of ceremonial texts, there have been recent community publications of written ceremonial texts, one of which will be discussed later in this chapter (Warlpiri Women from Yuendumu 2017a & b). Warlpiri people are nowadays embracing all types of archival materials, incorporating not only audiovisual media and photographs but also written documentation into contemporary contexts for holding and nurturing valued musical traditions and associated cultural knowledge.

Yawulyu, the Warlpiri word for a genre of song performed by Aboriginal women across Central Australia, was originally sung by ancestors in a creational moment known in Warlpiri as *jukurrpa*. The songs follow ancestral travels across Warlpiri country and evoke the landscape features and activities of these ancestral beings. Song words are often esoteric or cryptic, requiring explanation from knowledgeable elders. Warlpiri women take a lifetime to learn to sing *yawulyu*, but participate in ceremonies from a young age, dancing and being painted up with ochred designs. Traditionally, *yawulyu* were held as part of larger ceremonial activities to nurture the identity of specific women who related to the focal *jukurrpa* and country. Today, *yawulyu* continue to nurture the patrilineally inherited connections of women to country, but do so in significantly changed performance contexts. Dussart has argued that:

> the modified functionality of Aboriginal ceremony, by virtue of its dramatic evolution both in purpose and structure, offers tremendous insight into the dynamic construction of indigenous social identity in a context of extended colonial pressures. (2004: 253)

Dussart's work (2000, 2004) illustrates some of the dramatic changes to ritual forms that took place in the 10-year period from 1990 to 2000. Opportunities to hold *yawulyu* have further declined in the decades since Dussart's analysis, yet the strength of a collective of senior Warlpiri women means that *yawulyu* finds a place in the contemporary world, often being held for openings of buildings, community programs and art exhibitions, as part of organised bush trips, and during school events and visits to country. In preparation for *yawulyu* events held today, it is common for women to request photographs and sound and video recordings as memory aids, often just to get the tune right or remember a body design. Fortunately for Warlpiri women in these contexts, a large body of such materials exists, but less fortunately these materials are unorganised and efforts to enhance accessibility take significant time.

A brief review of the archives of Warlpiri women's *yawulyu*

As outlined elsewhere (Curran et al. 2018), Warlpiri culture is one of the most widely researched and recorded among Aboriginal groups in Central Australia. While the musical lives of Warlpiri people have not received as much focused attention as other areas of Warlpiri culture, there are several key older works that include song texts and stories (see Wild 1987; R Moyle 1997; Morais [Dail-Jones] 1992), as well as some more recent publications (Gallagher et al. 2014; Laughren et al. 2010; Turpin & Laughren 2013; Warlpiri Women from Yuendumu 2017a & b). This research has been undertaken across Warlpiri communities that span a broad area of the central desert including the communities of Lajamanu, Alekerenge, Willowra, Nyirrpi, and Yuendumu. Since Warlpiri women frequently travel between these communities, and have intimate family connections across them, with many living in different communities over the course of their lifetime, many Warlpiri women have been and continue to be involved in *yawulyu* events right across this broad area of Central Australia. Recordings that researchers have made in other communities over the last five decades, and circulating CD and USB copies of these, also have significant impact on Warlpiri women's engagement with archives. Although I review here the materials that have been recorded across Warlpiri communities, due to these broad geographical and social interconnections the focus of this chapter is particularly on *yawulyu* performance contexts in Yuendumu.

Many researchers travelling through Warlpiri country in the earlier half of the 20th century made recordings with early forms of sound technology including wax cylinders (Basedow 1926; Tindale 1931, 1932) and cassette tape recorders (Elkin 1953a, 1953b, 1953c[5]; Barrett 1954, 1955, 1956, 1962, 1963, 1964; Holmes 1964; Lewis 1964; West 1961). These mostly focused on men's songs, due largely to the gendered positions of the predominantly male researchers but also due to widespread misunderstandings that dominated the early 20th century, whereby the ritual lives of Indigenous Australian women were understood to be simplistic and profane (Kaberry 1939).[6] There are a few rare early recordings of *yawulyu* and other women's song genres (see Table 1).

---

5   Elkin transferred these to discs with 12 inch (standard groove), 33⅓ RPM.

6   An exception to this is the female researcher Sandra Le Brun Holmes, who made recordings with both men and women from various Aboriginal groups (1964), although she only recorded Warlpiri men singing during her time at Lajamanu.

Table 1. Pre-1966 recordings of Warlpiri women's songs (taken from A Moyle 1966)

Place recorded	Year recorded	Recorder	Description in archive deposit, with my comments (in italics)
Phillip Creek	1953	AP Elkin	'Women's secret Yowalyu ceremony – Wailbri and Waramunga (Waramanga) tribes' *Linda Barwick has also documented further details from Elkin's sound recordings, fieldnotes, and photos (Barwick 2003).*
Yuendumu	1954	Murray Barrett	Sanba bui sanba (sung by women) *These songs have recently been identified as being an older style of* purlapa *(a genre of Warlpiri song sung by men and women) (Curran et al. 2018).* Rara rara – lullaby song (sung by women)
Yuendumu	1955	Murray Barrett	Curl curl (sung by girls) Widiwid dogulbana (by women) Bogul bogul (by women) *Also identified as being an older style of* purlapa *sung by both men and women in performance context, but here elicited by Barrett only from women.*

Large and comprehensive collections of sound recordings of *yawulyu* begin from the 1970s as increasing numbers of female researchers and workers began living in and travelling through Warlpiri communities. Table 2 outlines the collections of *yawulyu* currently housed at the sound archive at AIATSIS. Other collections of *yawulyu* also exist but have been archived elsewhere (notably those of Ros Peterson, Françoise Dussart, and Carmel O'Shannessy). AIATSIS and individuals who have worked in Warlpiri community organisations also hold significant video footage of Warlpiri women performing *yawulyu* for various community-based events over the last four decades. Much of this is also archived in the Warlpiri Media Archive at PAW Media and Communications, although details of its content is yet to be documented. It is therefore difficult to estimate the scale of the collections of audiovisual materials on Warlpiri women's *yawulyu*.

Table 2. Collections of Warlpiri women's *yawulyu* deposited in the AIATSIS sound archive (based on their catalogue)

Dates	Place	Recorder
1953	Phillip Creek	AP Elkin
1967	Yuendumu, Alice Springs, Ernabella	Alice Moyle
1969–1979	Lajamanu, Yuendumu	Stephen Wild
1973–1987	Yuendumu, Lajamanu	Mary Laughren
1976	Alekerenge	James Horne
1979	Lajamanu	Barbara Glowczewski
1981–1982	Willowra	Megan Dail-Jones (Morais), Petronella Vaarzon-Morel
1981–1982	Balgo, Fitzroy Crossing, Bililuna, Looma, Ngumpan, Wangkatjungka	Richard Moyle
1982, 1987, 1988	Balgo, Sturt Creek	Sylvie Poirier
1982–1992	Alekerenge, Lajamanu, Yuendumu, Willowra	Lee Cataldi, Peggy Rockman
1987–1988	Tennant Creek and Alekarenge	Gertrude Stotz
1989–1990	Lajamanu	Jennifer Biddle
1996–1997	Alekerenge	Linda Barwick
2000–2001	Balgo, Kununurra, Halls Creek	Lee Cataldi
2005–2008	Yuendumu	Georgia Curran

Most of these recordings have now been digitised and deposited at community organisations and archives, and are thus much more easily shared among Warlpiri people (via CDs and USBs). Recently, I have been involved in projects that have seen the return of many of these major collections to the Warlpiri Media Archive in Yuendumu. Significant engagement with these collections is, however, still to occur.

Contemporary *yawulyu* spaces and the use of archival materials

Although the contexts for holding *yawulyu* have declined in recent decades, nowadays there are a number of opportunities for women across the Central Australian region to hold and share their ceremonies (examples include annual week-long camps held separately by the Central Land Council and the NPY Women's Council). Due to the dedicated commitment and efforts of Warlpiri women, Yuendumu-based community organisations also provide support for *yawulyu* events, and there are now several locally based forums for holding and performing *yawulyu*. Significant among these are the Southern Ngaliya girls' dance camps that have been held twice a year since 2010.[7] Set-up and supported spaces such as these are the main contexts

---

7   Incite Arts sought funding and provided support for these camps from 2010 to 2017, partnering with Yuendumu-based Warlpiri Youth Development Aboriginal Corporation (WYDAC). For the last two years, WYDAC has obtained funding and run these camps without this external assistance.

today in which large groups of Warlpiri women come together to hold *yawulyu*, although some women may continue to sing *yawulyu* in groups within their family camps.[8] Here, I outline three recent projects explicitly focused on supporting the contemporary vitality of Warlpiri *yawulyu*. *Yawulyu* has considerable vibrancy compared to Warlpiri songs sung by men, which do not have the same level of support, mostly because no group of men exists of comparable numbers or collective strength.

Making *yawulyu* song books

Two *yawulyu* song books, together featuring five different sets of *yawulyu* songs, have been published in recent years. *Jardiwanpa yawulyu* (Gallagher et al. 2014) documents songs relating to an ancestral Inland Taipan snake, Yarripiri, in his travels northwards through Warlpiri country. *Yurntumu-wardingki juju-ngaliya-kurlangu yawulyu* (Warlpiri Women from Yuendumu 2017a & b) features four different song sets: *Minamina yawulyu* 'Songs of the travelling ancestral women', *Watiyawarnu yawulyu* 'Acacia seed Dreaming songs', *Warlukurlangu yawulyu* 'Songs of the place belonging to fire', and *Ngapa yawulyu* 'Rain Dreaming songs'. Both these books are based on recordings that I made with Warlpiri women between 2005 and 2008 while I was undertaking PhD fieldwork as part of the 'Warlpiri Songlines' project. Many different genres of Warlpiri song were recorded for this project, but due to the gendered segregation dominating Warlpiri ceremonial life and my own positioning as a woman, *yawulyu* is the most prominent genre in this collection.[9] This project was carried out in an era of digital recording where solid-state sound recording devices were easily transportable for fieldwork, and I was able to deposit these recordings regularly at the Warlpiri Media Archive, based at PAW Media and Communications in central Yuendumu. Here, I discuss a *yawulyu* book project in which some of these recordings are featured, through textual documentation of the songs' words and rhythms as well as through audio-links (sound pens and QR links). While Warlpiri women could have had access to these sound recordings through their community-based archive, and I regularly gave CD copies to individuals upon request, it was not until these books were being produced that Warlpiri women fully engaged with these archived recorded materials.

From 2013, I began to work with Warlpiri women to revisit these recordings. Many workshops have been held over the last five years, aimed at collectively listening to these recordings, writing down the words of the songs, and recording stories and reflections to

---

8   A notable exception to this are the *yawulyu* that are sung in the late afternoon surrounding *Kurdiji* ceremonies, held several times in Yuendumu and other Central Australian communities over the summer months. While nowadays the Warlpiri people utilise their royalty money from mining activities on their country to support these events, there is no support provided from community organisations, which are often closed at this time of year.

9   The project 'Warlpiri Songlines: Anthropological, linguistic and Indigenous perspectives' was a partnership between the Australian National University, the University of Queensland, the Central Land Council, and the Warlpiri Janganpa Association (Australian Research Council Linkage Project).

include in the book.[10] Following the enthusiasm generated around the first book, *Jardiwanpa yawulyu* (Gallagher et al. 2014), in 2016 we began community workshops to compile the second volume containing four *yawulyu* song sets. The group decided that they wanted this book to be dedicated to Warlpiri women from the past, present, and future, as it drew together the voices of women who had long passed away and present-day generations, and was a way to pass this on for the future. In this way, the book combined the voices of multiple generations of Warlpiri women, many of whom would have had little contemporaneous interaction with each other during their lives. Additionally, Mary Laughren, who worked as a linguist at the Yuendumu school during the 1970s and 1980s, contributed her photographs from this period in which large groups of women were captured dancing and singing *yawulyu* and being painted up near the Yuendumu Women's Museum when it was opened in 1981.[11] Interest in the use of these photographs in the books reflects shifting attitudes towards the use of photographic materials, which is also occurring elsewhere in Australia. In Jennifer Deger's eloquent reflection on the presence of photographs in Yolngu grieving rituals, she notes:

> the inseparability of such images from the potent affective charges they generate, and the ways such indelible, inhering images mark and transform our inner landscapes and thence our relationships with the world and others. (2008: 292)

The photographs make the printed *yawulyu* books cherished community resources and for some individuals these are the only photographs they have of family members who are now deceased.

In all the workshops held for the production of these *yawulyu* song books, there were opportunities for Warlpiri women to sing, dance, and paint up. Towards the end of the project, we hired a filmmaker to produce four short films of the *yawulyu*, which feature on a DVD insert in the 2017 book. This opportunity for filming resulted in another afternoon and evening of *yawulyu* dancing (see Figure 1). Two related book launch events, held off Warlpiri country in Alice Springs for the Northern Territory Writers Festival (May 2017) and at the Sydney Conservatorium of Music (August 2017), gave Warlpiri women an opportunity to perform *yawulyu* and share these songs outside the Warlpiri world. The *yawulyu* performances at all these events were directly influenced by the book content. At each event, *Minamina yawulyu* and *Ngapa yawulyu* were performed; these are owned respectively by Barbara Napanangka Martin and Enid Nangala Gallagher, two key women crucial to the documentary aspects of this project. These performances were a way for a generation of Warlpiri women, who had missed out on opportunities to learn *yawulyu* in more traditionalised contexts, to assert

---

10   The first book project, *Jardiwanpa yawulyu* (Gallagher et al. 2014), was undertaken with the support of Batchelor Institute's Centre for Aboriginal Languages and Linguistics, and the project was managed by Margaret Carew. Due to the enthusiasm shown by the core group of Warlpiri women involved in this project, I was able to obtain funding through the University of Sydney to support a Yuendumu-based project to make another book.

11   The Yuendumu Women's Museum has not been used for more than two decades but there are current plans to revamp this space.

their ownership, learn from more senior women, and utilise literacy skills to document the performance, while also engaging the generation below them.

These *yawulyu* song books and CD products have provided contemporary contexts for Warlpiri women to engage with archival sound recordings and photographic materials, and have created resources that Warlpiri people can genuinely use in educational contexts, including *yawulyu* events. Most importantly, however, these projects set up spaces in which Warlpiri women can reflect on, nurture, and hold *yawulyu*. Establishing such spaces is significant because fewer contexts for *yawulyu* exist in the contemporary Warlpiri world.

Figure 1. Katrina Nampijinpa Brown and Enid Nangala Gallagher dancing *Warlukurlangu yawulyu* at Mijilyparnta in July 2016 for inclusion in the DVD insert for the Warlpiri women's *yawulyu* book (photo: Anna Cadden)

Southern Ngaliya girls' dance camps

Until 2017, the Southern Ngaliya girls' dance camps were organised by Alice Springs-based community arts organisation Incite Arts, in collaboration with the Warlpiri Youth Development Aboriginal Corporation (WYDAC, the Yuendumu-based youth program previously named Mount Theo program) and a core group of senior Warlpiri women. The Incite Arts website describes the project objectives as:

> build[ing] a platform to collectively focus on: achieving stronger links with traditional song and dance; creating new generations fluent in the ceremonial and cultural knowledge of their parents/grandparents; strengthening of Warlpiri culture; showcasing within and beyond the region.[12]

---

12   https://incitearts.org.au/sn/

In 2017, WYDAC took over the organisation and funding of these events. The Southern Ngaliya dance camps are held twice yearly, in the first weekend of the school holidays in April and October. Large groups of women travel to outstations near Yuendumu where they camp for several days. These camps are strictly women-only: even though men may assist with transport, they must stop at a distance away from the camp as female drivers transfer the women to the site of the dance camp. Such strictness about gender segregation reflects the female-only contexts of the *yawulyu* associated with men's initiation events (these *yawulyu* often take place while women are not allowed to move from their camp, to avoid the risk of running into men en route for ceremonial business). At the Southern Ngaliya dance camps, groups of women often travel to nearby sites during the daytime and share stories about country. In the afternoons, the women paint up for several hours while singing *yawulyu* and then dance just prior to and after sunset. For Warlpiri women, the Southern Ngaliya dance camps have become an important time for nurturing *jukurrpa* and sharing songs and dances with younger women.[13] Often Warlpiri women from other communities such as Lajamanu, Willowra and Nyirrpi will travel to attend these camps, drawing in their own regionally focused *yawulyu*. These camps, held in remote bush locations, require enormous logistical support. All food, water, and bedding needs to be pre-organised, as does transport for the many women who attend. A significant commitment of funding is required for these events, as they also involve payments for Warlpiri women to attend, a practice now standard across Central Australia.

While these dance camps have now been held for eight years, it is only more recently that archival resources have been incorporated into these events. In April 2017, during a dance camp at Mirjirnparnta, and during the same period that the 2017 *yawulyu* book described above was being made, many women began to request copies of the photographs of *yawulyu* body designs for use during their painting-up sessions (see Figure 2). In more recent times there has been a trend for the designs used in these painting-up sessions to be less complex and for the same designs to be painted up on many women. Furthermore, while in past decades different *yawulyu* verses would have unique designs, more recently all women were painted with a standard design for each *jukurrpa*. In 2017, archival photographs were used as a way to break with this trend, so that women who had associations with particular country were painted with individualised designs to reflect this. Interestingly, children do not seem to be included in this practice, with all children being painted with the same design, perhaps because at that stage in life they do not have the maturity to hold their *yawulyu* properly.[14]

Additionally, the women expressed an interest in watching archival films during the late evening. At this particular camp they watched *Jardiwarnpa – a Warlpiri fire ceremony* (Lander & Perkins 1993). At the dance camp held the following October at Jurlpungu, a screen was not available, and the Warlpiri women instead chose as their evening entertainment to listen to sound recordings I had made in 2006, including some that had not been published with the 2017 book. By April 2018, at a dance camp at Yuwali (Bean Tree), PAW Media and

13   Interestingly, these events are regarded as being for 'fun' *yawulyu*, and are not used as an opportunity to hold very serious 'finishing up' *yawulyu* following the deaths of loved Warlpiri women. This may be due to the time and logistical restrictions put in place by the supporting organisations.

14   An anonymous reviewer noted that children have always had simpler designs and that it would be good to compare contemporary photographs with earlier ones to see the extent to which this has changed.

Figure 2. Cecily Napanangka Granites is painted by Lucky Nampijinpa Langton with the *jintiparnta yawulyu* design remembered from an archival photograph, April 2017 (photo: Georgia Curran). [Inset] Yarraya Napangardi painted with the *jintiparnta* design in the 1980s (photo: Mary Laughren)

Communications staff transported a large portable screen out to the bush site. Not all requests for viewings of archival footage at these events could be met. While this is by no means the first time that Warlpiri women have shown an interest in using archival materials within performance spaces, it was certainly the beginning of this being technologically possible, with portable screens and iPads with digitised photographs and audiovisual recordings available to support these performance contexts.

Unbroken Land, 2018

In September 2018, the community arts event Unbroken Land was held for the third time at the Alice Springs Desert Park (after previous events in 2015 and 2016). Although, through their connections with Warlpiri women's dance camps, Incite Arts had invited the Southern Ngaliya dancers from Yuendumu to participate in previous years, logistics and other personal circumstances had meant that 2018 was the first time they were able to travel into Alice Springs to participate. In the words of Jenine Mackay, Incite Arts' CEO and artistic director of Unbroken Land, as a community arts event it focused on "drawing together different sectors of the community which normally don't have a chance to interact." Within a western creative framework, elements drawn from Greek theatre (including a chorus leader and chorus in an epic narrative structure) formed the basis of a promenade performance through the Alice Springs Desert Park; the audience walked a kilometre through four stage spaces, each at a different location in the park. The various parts of the event were drawn together around the theme of water – a particularly poignant theme in this desert context. Part 3 of this broader production had a focus on 'traditional song', and the Southern Ngaliya dancers performed several verses of *Ngapa* 'Rain' *yawulyu*, followed by performances from a contemporary dance troupe, a Pitjantjatjara Arrernte woman, and a Western Arrernte woman. The audience then moved on to the next staged section of the performance. These performances were done twice a night over three consecutive nights.

Several months beforehand, in preparation for this event, Enid Nangala Gallagher had expressed an interest in centring the performance around a recording of a *Ngapa yawulyu* song set that I had made with senior women over a decade earlier and that had recently featured as part of the boxed set of four CDs (Warlpiri Women from Yuendumu 2017b). Many women in these recordings had since passed away, and Enid, although only in her 50s, is now a senior owner for these *yawulyu*. One track from the CD set, which centred on Jukajuka, a site close to Yuendumu and central to the westward travels of the *Ngapa jukurrpa*, was chosen for the performance.

For the performance a large photo of this site was projected onto several transparent muslin cloth panels as a background for the dancers. The panels had *ngapa* 'water' designs printed along the sides, and the Warlpiri women all wore skirts on which these designs had been digitally printed. While constraints of the westernised theatre context and timings made it difficult for the Warlpiri women to use the performance to hold *yawulyu* as they would in a more traditional setting, they embraced this new context in which to share the values of their musical traditions. For several hours each afternoon, prior to the performance, they were given a space and external support to paint up properly, rehearse songs, and chat with other groups of Aboriginal women. On each of the three evenings, the Warlpiri performers chose to perform different dances associated with the *Ngapa yawulyu* (see Figure 3). During the performance they did not play the actual recording, because there were senior women present to sing, but it was used to structure the performance such that it could be controlled within the tight requirements of the theatre context, and it allowed the Warlpiri women to plan flexibly and fit in with the technical aspects of the overall event.

Figure 3. Warlpiri women dance *Ngapa yawulyu* as part of Unbroken Land, September 2018, led by Pamela Nangala Sampson (front left) and Maisy Napurrurla Wayne (front right).

Figure 4. Katie Leslie leads contemporary dancers in her choreographed 'coolamon dance' to a recording made by Warlpiri women of *Ngapa yawulyu* in 2006 (photo: Incite Arts)

Following the Southern Ngaliya dancers, a group of contemporary dancers performed a 'coolamon dance' to the recording of *Ngapa yawulyu* (see Figure 4). This performance was choreographed by Katie Leslie, an Aboriginal dancer from NSW who knew the Warlpiri women through having previously assisted with the Southern Ngaliya dance camps. The Warlpiri women enjoyed watching this tastefully done performance and hearing the voices of their deceased relatives dominating the auditory component of the performance space. Enid reflected that it would be good for younger Warlpiri girls to do dances like this to older recordings, revealing a vision for a future where younger generations engage with *yawulyu* in new and creative ways while still being guided by the voices of knowledgeable elders.

Conclusion

In remote Indigenous communities across Central Australia, recent decades have seen large-scale shifts in the structures of Indigenous social lives. These factors have had enormous impacts on the contexts in which land-based genres of music like *yawulyu* are being performed. While *yawulyu* and other genres of song intrinsic to Aboriginal identities were once performed frequently and passed on orally through generations, today support is required from community organisations to set up the time and space, and to assist with logistical aspects. As has been demonstrated, in Yuendumu Warlpiri women actively seek out support for opportunities to perform *yawulyu* and more recently have expressed an increasing desire to incorporate the documentary efforts of previous generations into these performances. Nampijinpa has now asked me to bring her a CD copy of the *yawulyu* recordings that made her cry at AIATSIS in 2018. She wants to sit with a big group of women and listen to them all together, "just to feel happy." She also thinks that her granddaughters will come to sit down and listen to these songs if she has the recordings. These are precisely the kinds of contexts that can be set up for multiple generations to engage properly with legacy cultural materials.

I have argued in this chapter that the meaningful repatriation of archival materials must involve these kinds of community-led contexts for engagement. These do not have to be grand but must be sensitively led by knowledgeable Indigenous people who understand the value and power of these intangible aspects of Indigenous persons and can properly negotiate their impact on present-day contexts. Alongside this, as attitudes towards images and recordings of the deceased rapidly shift, these cultural heritage materials are more easily incorporated into public spaces, and many more contexts may open up for engagement with archival materials.

References

Anderson, Christopher. 1995. *Politics of the secret* (Oceania Monographs 45). Sydney: Sydney University Press.

Barwick, Linda. 2003. *Warlpiri and Warumungu materials in the Elkin Collection.* Report prepared for Julalikari Council Aboriginal Corporation, Tennant Creek, NT.

Barwick, Linda, Mary Laughren & Myfany Turpin. 2013. Sustaining women's yawulyu/awelye: Some practitioners' and learners' perspectives. *Musicology Australia* 35(2). 1–30.

Curran, Georgia, Barbara Martin & Margaret Carew. 2019. Representations of Indigenous cultural property in collaborative publishing projects: The Warlpiri women's *yawulyu* song books. *Journal of Intercultural Studies* 40(1). 68–84.

Curran, Georgia, Simon Fisher & Linda Barwick. 2018. Engaging with archived Warlpiri songs. In Nicholas Ostler, Vera Ferreira & Chris Moseley (eds.), *Communities in control: Learning tools and strategies for multilingual endangered language communities* (Proceedings of the 21st Foundation for Endangered Languages Conference). Alcanena, Portugal, 19–21 October 2017.

Daw, Jonathan & Anna Cadden (producers). 2017. *Yarripiri's journey* (film) (directed by Simon Japanangka Fisher & Jason Japaljarri Woods). Yuendumu, NT: PAW Media and Communications.

Deger, Jennifer. 2008. Imprinting on the heart: Photography and contemporary Yolngu mournings. *Visual Anthropology* 21(4). 292–309.

Dussart, Françoise. 2000. *The politics of ritual in an Aboriginal settlement: Kinship, gender, and the currency of knowledge.* London and Washington: Smithsonian Institution Press.

Dussart, Françoise. 2004. Shown but not shared, presented but not proffered. *The Australian Journal of Anthropology* 15(3). 253–266.

Gallagher, Coral, Peggy Brown, Georgia Curran & Barbara Martin. 2014. *Jardiwanpa yawulyu: Warlpiri women's songs from Yuendumu* (including CD). Batchelor, NT: Batchelor Press.

Ginsburg, Faye. 1995. The parallax effect: The impact of Aboriginal media on ethnographic film. *Visual Anthropology Review* 11(2). 64–76.

Hinkson, Melinda. 2002. New media projects at Yuendumu: Inter-cultural engagement and self-determination in an era of accelerated globalisation. *Continuum: Journal of Media and Cultural Studies* 16(2). 201–220.

Kaberry, Phyllis. 1939. *Aboriginal women, sacred and profane.* New York: Gordon Press.

Lander, Ned & Rachel Perkins. 1993. *Jardiwarnpa – A Warlpiri fire ceremony* (film). Sydney: Film Australia.

Laughren, Mary, Myfany Turpin & Helen Morton. 2010. *Yawulyu Wirliyajarrayi-wardingki: Ngatijirri, ngapa* (Willowra songlines: Budgerigar and rain). Willowra, NT: Willowra community.

Michaels, Eric. 1986. *The Aboriginal invention of television: Central Australia, 1982–86.* Canberra: Australian Institute of Aboriginal Studies.

Michaels, Eric. 1987. *For a cultural future: Francis Jupurrurla makes TV at Yuendumu.* Sydney: Art & Text.

Morais [Dail-Jones], Megan. 1992. Documenting dance: Benesh movement notation and the Warlpiri of Central Australia. In Alice M Moyle (ed.), *Music and dance of Aboriginal Australia and the South Pacific: The effects of documentation on the living tradition,* 130–144. Sydney: Oceania Publications.

Moyle, Alice M. 1966. *A handlist of field collections of recorded music in Australia and Torres Strait.* Canberra: Australian Institute of Aboriginal Studies.

Moyle, Richard. 1997. *Balgo: The musical life of a desert community.* Nedlands, WA: Callaway International Resource Centre for Music Education.

Sandall, Roger 1977 [1967]. *A Walbiri fire ceremony, Ngatjakula* (motion picture). Canberra: Australian Institute of Aboriginal Studies.

Treloyn, Sally & Rona Googninda Charles. 2015. Repatriation and innovation in and out of the field: The impact of legacy recordings on endangered dance-song traditions and ethnomusicological research. In Amanda Harris, Nick Thieberger & Linda Barwick (eds.), *Research, records & responsibility,* 187–205. Sydney: Sydney University Press.

Turpin, Myfany & Mary Laughren. 2013. Edge effects in Warlpiri yawulyu songs: Resyllabification, epenthesis and final vowel modification. *Australian Journal of Linguistics* 33(4). 399–425.

Warlpiri Women from Yuendumu (edited by G Curran). 2017a. *Yurntumu-wardingki juju-ngaliya-kurlangu yawulyu: Warlpiri women's songs from Yuendumu* (including DVD). Batchelor, NT: Batchelor Institute Press.

Warlpiri Women from Yuendumu (produced by G Curran). 2017b. *Yurntumu-wardingki juju-ngaliya-kurlangu yawulyu: Warlpiri women's songs from Yuendumu* (4 CD boxed set). Batchelor, NT: Batchelor Institute Press.

Wild, Stephen. 1987. Recreating the Jukurrpa: Adaptation and innovation of songs and ceremonies in Warlpiri society. In Margaret Clunies-Ross, Tamsin Donaldson & Stephen A Wild (eds.), *Songs of Aboriginal Australia,* 2nd edn, 97–120. Sydney: Oceania Publications.

Archival collections including recordings of Warlpiri songs, made pre-1966
(from Moyle [1966] and the AIATSIS online catalogue)

Barrett, Murray. 1954–1957, 1962–1965. Singing and interviews from Yuendumu, NT. [AIATSIS accession no: BARRETT_M01 (A000055–A000082)]. 26 hours, 18 minutes. Recorded at Yuendumu, NT and Rugiri, NT.

Basedow, Herbert. 1926. Arrernte, Kaytetye, Lurtija and Warlpiri ceremonial songs. [AIATSIS accession no: BASEDOW_H02 (A008758–A008759)]. Mackay Exploring Expedition in Central Australia. 1 hour. Recorded at Macdonnell Ranges, NT.

Elkin, AP. 1953a. Pidjindjara [i.e. Pitjantjatjara] secret totemic ceremony (III); Wailbri [i.e. Warlpiri] secret totemic ceremony: University of Sydney Northern Territory recordings. [AIATSIS accession no. A011086B]. 21 minutes. Recorded at Areyonga, SA.

Elkin, AP. 1953b. Wailbri [i.e. Warlpiri] secret totemic ceremony (II), (III): University of Sydney Northern Territory recordings. [AIATSIS accession no. A011087A & A011087B]. Total of 44 minutes. Recorded at Northern Territory.

Elkin, AP. 1953c. Wailbri [i.e. Warlpiri] women, (I), (II);Waramunga [i.e. Warumungu] women; secret Yowalyu (I), (II): University of Sydney Northern Territory recordings. [AIATSIS accession no. A011088A & A011088B]. 22 minutes. Recorded at Phillip Creek, NT.

Holmes, Sandra Lebrun. 1964. Music recorded at Beswick and Bagot. [AIATSIS accession no. HOLMES_S04 (A000325–A000328)]. 6 hours, 11 minutes. Recorded at Cape Don, NT, Gunbalanya, NT, Maningrida, NT, Beswick, NT, Djilkminggan, NT, Borroloola, NT, and Barkly Tablelands, NT. Recorded at Beswick and Bagot, NT.

Lewis, P. 1964. Warlpiri circumcision ceremony with spoken commentary; Christmas church service. [AIATSIS accession no. LEWIS_P01 (A004034A)]. 1 hour, 4 minutes. Recorded at Yuendumu, NT.

Tindale, Norman B. 1931–1932. Copies of tapes made originally by EH Davies, Norman B Tindale and others, of songs and cultural discussions. [AIATSIS accession no. SAM_01 (A009564–A009693; A019205)]. 74 hours, 29 minutes. Originally archived with South Australian Museum. Recorded at Cockatoo Creek, NT.

West, Lamont. 1961. Narratives, language elicitation, wailing, Bunggul (songs), texts on ritual and mythological subjects, Kunapipi ritual singing and explanations of ceremony. [AIATSIS accession no. WEST_L03 (A004630–A004639)]. 6 hours, 51 minutes. Recorded at Beswick, NT.

Archival collections held at AIATSIS that include *yawulyu*
(from the AIATSIS online catalogue. Additional sound recordings of *yawulyu* may also be held in individual collections and other archives)

Barwick, Linda. 1996–1997. Warlpiri and Warumungu Songs. [AIATSIS call no. BARWICK_ LO1]. 16 sound cassettes (ca. 90 minutes each). Recorded at Tennant Creek and Warrabri, NT.

Biddle, Jennifer. 1989–1990. Warlpiri songs. [AIATSIS accession no. BIDDLE_J02 (A025117–A025136)]. 8 hours, 42 minutes, 12 audiocassettes. Recorded at Lajamanu, NT.

Biddle, Jennifer. 1989. Women's Yawulyu preparation and performance. [AIATSIS accession no. BIDDLE_J01 (A025844–A025846)]. 2 audiocassettes, 60 minutes each. Recorded at Lajamanu, NT.

Cataldi, Lee & Peggy Rockman. 1982–1992. Yimkirli Project: Warlpiri narratives and song. [AIATSIS accession no. CATALDI-ROCKMAN_01 (A016173–A016256; A016425–A16480; A016482–A016508; A017111–A017140)]. 220 hours. Recorded at Warrabri, Lajamanu, Yuendumu, and Willowra, NT.

Cataldi, Lee. 2000. Lexical elicitation, narratives, conversation and songs. [AIATSIS accession no. CATALDI_L07 (A038104–A038133)]. 13 hours duration. Recorded at Balgo and Halls Creek, WA.

Cataldi, Lee. 2000–2001. Stories, songs, conversation and language elicitation from Balgo. [AIATSIS accession no. CATALDI_L08 (A037576–A037592)]. 10 audiocassettes, 60 minutes each. Recorded at Balgo, WA.

Cataldi, Lee. 2001. Tapes recorded at Balgo, WA in 2001 including singing and a women's law meeting. [AIATSIS accession no. CATALDI_L09 (A030989–A031011)]. 10 hours, 11 minutes. Recorded at Balgo and Kununurra, WA.

Curran, Georgia. 2005–2008. Warlpiri songlines project. [AIATSIS call no. PETERSON-CURRAN_01]. 110 hours. Recorded at Yuendumu, NT.

Dail-Jones [Morais], Megan. 1981–1982. Warlpiri women's yawulyu singing and an initiation ceremony at Willowra, NT. [Accession no. DAIL-JONES_M01 (A019516–A019555)]. 19 hours, 48 minutes. Recorded at Willowra, NT.

Dail-Jones [Morais], Megan. (and Petronella Vaarzon-Morel). 1981–1982. Warlpiri women's yawulyu singing and interviews at Willowra, NT. [AIATSIS accession no. DAIL-JONES_ M02 (A021587–A021599; A021700–A021736)]. 29 hours. Recorded at Willowra, NT.

Elkin, AP. 1953. Wailbri [i.e. Warlpiri] women, (I), (II);Waramunga [i.e. Warumungu] women; secret Yowalyu, (I), (II): University of Sydney Northern Territory recordings. [AIATSIS accession no. A011088A & A011088B]. 22 minutes. Recorded at Phillip Creek, NT.

Glowczewski, Barbara. 1979. Warlpiri women's songs recorded at Lajamanu, NT. [AIATSIS accession no. GLOWCZEWSKI_B01 (A018450–A018456)]. 3 hours, 29 minutes. Recorded at Lajamanu, NT and Gordon Downs, WA.

Glowczewski, Barbara & Stephen Wild. 1979. Warlpiri ceremonial singing. [AIATSIS accession no. GLOWCZEWSKI-WILD_01 (A009000)]. 32 minutes. Recorded at Gordon Downs, WA.

Horne, Jim. 1976. Women's songs and narratives from Warrabri, NT. [AIATSIS accession no. HORNE_J01 (A004417A–A004418B)]. 2 hours. Recorded at Warrabri, NT.

Laughren, Mary. 1973–1987. Oral history, stories and songs from Yuendumu and Lajamanu. [AIATSIS accession no. LAUGHREN_M02 (A015019–A015059; A015067–A015080; A015161–A015214; A015333–A015343)]. 120 hours. Recorded at Yuendumu and Lajamanu, NT.

Moyle, Alice M. 1967. Warlpiri and Pintupi song series, stories and some children's songs. [MOYLE_A09 (A002643–A002652)]. 19 hours, 35 minutes. Recorded at Yuendumu, Alice Springs, NT and Ernabella, SA.

Moyle, Richard. 1982. Ceremonial and other group singing from the Balgo area. [AIATSIS accession no. 033572-033599; 034700-034726]. 26 hours, 4 minutes. Recorded at Balgo, WA.

Moyle, Richard. 1982. Stories, songs and ceremonial singing. [AIATSIS call no. MOYLE_R26]. 17 hours. Recorded at Balgo, Fitzroy Crossing and Bililuna, WA.

Moyle, Richard. 1982. Initiation and other ceremonial singing, and discussion regarding men's business. [AIATSIS accession no. 029384–029399; 030000–030053]. 34 hours, 28 minutes. Recorded at Balgo, Looma, Ngumpan, Wangkatjungka, WA and Lajamanu and Yuendumu, NT.

Moyle, Richard. 1981. Men's and women's singing from Balgo area. [AIATSIS accession no. 029699; 029900–029929]. 14 hours, 23 minutes. Recorded at Balgo, WA.

Poirier, Sylvie. 1982, 1987, 1988. Song series, ceremonies and stories from Balgo, WA. [AIATSIS accession no. POIRIER_S01 (A018586–A018599; A019500–A019515). 14 hours, 8 minutes. Recorded at Balgo and Sturt Creek, WA.

Stotz, Gertrude. 1987–1988. Discussion of mother–daughter relations; Warlpiri women's songs, NT. [AIATSIS call no. STOTZ_G01]. 6 hours. Recorded at Tennant Creek and Warrabri, NT.

Wild, Stephen. 1979. Warlpiri Christmas and Easter Purlapa, circumcision singing, contemporary band songs, women's songs at Lajamanu and at Yuendumu, NT. Some singing with Pitjantjatjara women. [AIATSIS accession no. WILD_S02 (A006146–A006167)]. 11 hours, 35 minutes. Recorded at Yuendumu and Lajamanu, NT.

Wild, Stephen. 1970–1971. Warlpiri men's and women's songs, including circumcision and other ceremonial singing. [AIATSIS accession no. WILD_S04 (A002389–A002413)]. 49 hours, 14 minutes. Recorded at Lajamanu, NT.

Wild, Stephen. 1970–1971. Warlpiri songs recorded at Hooker Creek, NT. [AIATSIS Accession no. WILD_S06 (A002424–A002428)]. 4 hours, 52 minutes. Recorded at Lajamanu, NT.

Wild, Stephen. 1969. Warlpiri and Gurindji singing. [AIATSIS accession no. WILD_S03 (A002195–A002229)]. 38 hours, 1 minute. Recorded at Lajamanu, NT.

Language Documentation & Conservation Special Publication No. 18
Archival returns: Central Australia and beyond
ed. by Linda Barwick, Jennifer Green & Petronella Vaarzon-Morel, pp. 111–138
http://nflrc.hawaii.edu/ldc/sp18
http://hdl.handle.net/10125/24880

6

Enlivening people and country: The Lander Warlpiri cultural mapping project

Petronella Vaarzon-Morel
The University of Sydney

Luke Kelly
Consultant anthropologist

Abstract

This chapter discusses a cultural mapping project funded and directed by Lander Warlpiri Anmatyerr people in Central Australia with the collaboration of the authors and the support of the Central Land Council. The project arose from the concerns of elders over the changing lifeworld of Warlpiri people today and the reduced opportunities for younger people to acquire the embodied place-based knowledge and experiences regarded as foundational to local identity, social interrelationships, and cultural continuity. It aimed to revitalise cultural knowledge through engaging family groups in activities such as country visits and mapping, during which the teaching and recording of place names, Dreaming tracks, and countries occurred along with the performance of associated stories, song, and rituals. This process involved the sharing and negotiation of the knowledge of country elders hold, augmented by ethnographic information derived from archival and other sources; for example, land claim maps and digitised material, including photographs, audio and visual recordings of narratives, places, song, and geo-referenced data. Attending to the ways in which local Indigenous practices of representing and inscribing people's relations with space and place may differ from and interlace with dominant western spatial regimes, cartographic practices, and technologies, we explore outcomes and issues that have arisen during the process of re-animation and evocation of place-based knowledge and memories.

Keywords: Indigenous mapping, Warlpiri, place making, cultural heritage, archives

CC Licensed under Creative Commons
Attribution-NonCommercial 4.0 International

Introduction[1]

Many Indigenous people in Australia today voice concerns about their displacement from familial country. Linking social problems to the impacts of modernity and the settler state on their lives and cultures, they view engagement with kin and country as offering restorative promise (see Lempert 2018). Lander Warlpiri and others stress the need to understand the nature of cultural relationships to different places and persons affiliated with them, and view the opportunity to live in one's ancestral country as important for wellbeing. As Dwayne Ross Jupurrula stated, "young people need to learn about their country and how they are connected. Land teaches people who they are, their identity, and relationships. They need to know about these things because we are connected through different Dreamings."[2] This chapter discusses a cultural mapping project at Willowra in the Northern Territory (NT), undertaken with the aim of grounding people's identities and relationships to country and each other. It considers how digitised cultural material – photographs and recordings of songs, stories, histories, and interviews – and land claim maps are being repurposed or reused to strengthen people's sense of place and selves.

Like many Indigenous people, Warlpiri view ancestral land as the foundation of moral Law and identity, and stress the importance of gaining embodied knowledge of it. Munn (1996: 453) noted that "the Law's *visible signs* are topographic 'markings'" [emphasis in original]. These 'markings' or traces are not simply surface inscriptions on the landscape, but features created out of the bodies and substances of Jukurrpa (Dreaming) beings as they travelled throughout the land, singing about their interactions with other entities. In the course of their journeys they named significant places[3] and established the "lawful processes" which govern "order, meaning and obligation" (Meggitt 1972: 71) in the Warlpiri world. As discussed later, individuals hold country with which they are spiritually identified. Varying bases of identification give rise to different rights in and responsibilities for country and the Dreaming narratives, songs, sites, and sacred objects associated with them. More broadly, Dreaming tracks articulate relations of similarity and difference between persons and country, which traditionally structure ritual, marriage, and social relations.

The centrality of land to cultural identity, territoriality, and language (Rumsey 1993; Sutton 2003) has prompted some scholars to liken the land to an archive (Neale 2017). In this sense, a return to country is an archival return. But if the land is an archive, its contents

---

1   We are indebted to Teddy Long Jupurrula, George Ryder Jungarrayi, Julie Napaljarri Kitson, Dwayne Jupurrula, and Willowra families for generously sharing their knowledge and experiences with us during this mapping project. We are also grateful for the support of the members of the Willowra WETT and GMAAAC committees, and of Karina Menkhorst and members of the CD program at the CLC, Brian Connelly, and the anthropology and geospatial sections of the CLC. We especially thank the two anonymous reviewers for their thoughtful comments on an earlier draft of this article. Thanks also to Linda Barwick, Jennifer Green, Katya Zissermann, David Avery, Åse Ottosson, Nic Peterson, Fred Myers, and Jim Wafer for their feedback on drafts. Petronella originally presented the article in the Twelfth International Conference on Hunting and Gathering Societies (CHAGS XII), Penang, 2018, in the session entitled 'Cultural maps and hunter-gatherers' being in the world', convened by Ute Dieckmann.

2   Pers. comm. to P Vaarzon-Morel, 2016.

3   See Myers (1986) and Wilkins (2002) for a discussion of Aboriginal concepts of place.

and meanings are mediated by knowledgeable persons (Myers 2000) and ancestral spirits. With the passing of elders whose embodied knowledge of country was gained through long-term immersion, walking from sacred site to sacred site, and exchanging spiritual substance (Povinelli 1993; Myers 2013: 444; Peterson 2017), people are seeking new modes of learning about ancestral country. Although Indigenous peoples' histories, cultures, and situations vary, in recent decades the cultural mapping of country has become a key decolonising strategy aimed at reclaiming Indigenous places and enlivening peoples' language, cultures, and landed identities. Just how this is achieved and what is at stake in the process are important issues.

In the Australian context, Aboriginal people's knowledge of country in the forms of toponyms, Dreaming narratives, songs, design, ritual, language, and other cultural modes of expression form part of their intangible cultural heritage. To this end, language and song revitalisation projects have played an important role in "renewing and re-activating relationships with Country" (Wafer 2017: 28), as have visual media projects involving film, video, photography, and contemporary art.[4] Many such projects have drawn on archival materials and explored how information and recordings generated in the use of such material may be stored for future generations. Yet, although Aboriginal relations to the land are central to these discussions, outside the land and native title claims arena,[5] and with the exception of Peterson (2017) and Walsh & Mitchell (2002), surprisingly little attention has been paid to the potential role of and issues associated with maps and mapping in facilitating intergenerational learning about country.

There is, however, a robust and growing international literature concerned with the ways that maps may misrepresent Indigenous ways of conceptualising and dwelling in their lands. While there are various approaches to these issues, most recognise that cartography is not a neutral practice but is shaped within historical and cultural contexts and employed for political ends. It is widely accepted that western-style cartography has informed colonial spatial and property regimes which have resulted in the dispossession and displacement of Indigenous peoples (Carter 1987; Ryan 1996; Louis et al. 2012; Craib 2017). As Sletto (2009: 445) states "maps are representational objects intimately implicated in projects of place making, and therefore they are tools of power." To this end, there has been an explosion in what Peluso (1995) named "counter-mapping" and alternative ethno-cartography projects,[6] with Canada and USA leading the way (Chapin et al. 2005).[7] The objectives of such projects vary but include "putting people on the map," defending and claiming land, mapping customary use and occupancy, land management, and documenting history and culture for local people and the wider public (Chapin et al. 2005; Wainwright & Bryan 2009; Hirt 2012; Louis et al. 2012; Palmer 2012).

---

4 Acrylic desert paintings, regarded as simulacra of maps (Sutton 1998b), have motivated intergenerational learning about country (see Neale 2017).

5 See Koch (2008) for a discussion of issues associated with returns of material produced during native title hearings and held by the Federal Court of Australia.

6 Other names for Indigenous mapping projects include: 'cultural mapping', 'community-based mapping', 'critical Indigenous cartography', and 'participatory mapping'. It is beyond the scope of this chapter to address such matters.

7 Chapin et al. (2005) noted that details of many mapping projects are not publicly available. This remains the case.

Yet, as scholars (Chapin et al. 2005) have observed, counter-mapping projects are not without problems. While issues raised in the literature relate to the type of mapping undertaken (for example, a place names map versus a land utilisation map or a map to advance land claims), a criticism of mapping projects undertaken with, or on behalf of, Indigenous peoples is that the use of scientific cartographic tools and practices can replicate western ontologies and are another form of colonialism (see Hirt 2012). Commenting on contemporary maps employed in land claims, Wainwright & Bryan state:

> Indigenous maps work within the typical set of cartographic abstractions that treat the world as an object comprised of spaces – polygons manipulated in a GIS – that are universally definable in terms of a set of points, lines, and polygons defined by latitude and longitude, scale and projection. (2009: 155)

Sletto (2009) observes that maps can reify dynamic cultural practices by representing knowledge simply as marks on a map. In the context of land management in NSW, Byrne writes that the tendency to map natural and cultural values as separate layers is "at odds with holistic conceptions that local people have of their landscape" (2008: 259). In line with such observations, there is increasing interest in alternative ways of mapping that reflect Indigenous peoples' ways of *being in* country, and their "'more-than-abstract' spatial practices" (Roth 2009: 208; Dieckmann 2018).[8]

In addition to issues of representation, there are concerns about circulation and the failure to implement protocols to protect information contained on maps (Sletto 2009: 451).[9] Worried about the possibility of outside bodies gaining information which might work against Indigenous interests, on the instructions of custodians land councils in Australia have placed access restrictions on maps and related material produced for land claims (see Hercus & Simpson 2002: 2).[10] In discussing such issues in relation to the Central Australian context, Peterson notes that access to places may be restricted by gender and age,[11] and, because many important places are named in the published literature,[12] "once their location was known control over access would be lost, opening the way for further unauthorised visits and potential damage" (2017: 246). Furthermore, custodians of sites may be keen to safeguard place

---

8   This reflects a wider debate concerning 'representation' and 'dwelling' (Ingold 1996). As Myers (2013) notes, in Australia the debate has focused on Indigenous art. Myers argues for both "'representation' and 'dwelling' as co-existing frameworks of engagement with landscape" (2000, 2013: 458). This accords with our understanding of Warlpiri engagements with land.

9   Similar issues in relation to genealogies in Central Australia are discussed in Morgan & Wilmott (2010).

10   For a recent example of orders made by the High Court of Australia in response to Aboriginal custodians' request to restrict ethnographic materials produced for their native title claim see Northern Territory v. Griffiths et al. (2019).

11   Places consist of assemblages of topographic features, of which some may be restricted according to factors such as age and gender (Vaarzon-Morel 2016; see also Wilkins 2002). While putting names on a map need not violate protocols but serve to alert people to places to avoid, elders sometimes prefer not to specify such places (Elias 2007: 235).

12   The forthcoming Warlpiri Dictionary contains numerous entries for sites in the Warlpiri region. We also note linguist David Nash's (2010) interest in compiling an atlas of Indigenous place names in Central Australia.

names and locations lest distant others claim knowledge of the land and assert the right to make decisions about it.[13] As Peterson (2017) observes, this situation has produced quandaries for land councils and Indigenous constituents who want access to the maps.

The process of creation of maps can itself highlight power structures and inequalities and be a cause of concern. For example, GIS and digital mapping technologies require skills, infrastructural support, and access to the internet, which Indigenous people may not possess. In reference to Central Australia, Peterson observes that the use of digital maps can disrupt traditional structures of knowledge, by giving young people with computer skills "control of the same body of place location knowledge as much older people" (2017: 247; see also Chambers et al. 2004: 24). Arguing that maps are inherently neither good nor bad, Wainwright & Bryan emphasise the need to focus on "social processes through which maps are produced and read" (2009: 154). Surveying the various issues raised in the counter-mapping literature, what is clear is the need for those involved in mapping projects to be aware of cultural assumptions underlying mapping activities, the sociopolitical contexts in which maps are produced and employed, and how maps may implicate particular ways of perceiving, experiencing, and delimiting the world.

The cultural mapping project that is the subject of this chapter was funded and directed by Lander Warlpiri Anmatyerr[14] people from Willowra in collaboration with the authors (anthropologists) and the support of the Central Land Council (CLC), Alice Springs. Known in English as the Lander, the generally dry Yarlalinji River runs through Willowra, which is located in the southern Tanami Desert about 350 kilometres from Alice Springs. Like many communities in Central Australia, recent decades have seen the passing of members of the older generation who possessed an intimate knowledge of the land. Guided by elder Teddy Long Jupurrula and endorsed by the local community, the project aims at grounding young people's identities, relationships, and cultural futures in country. It is hoped in this way to refigure their sense of country, that is, its social, spiritual, and symbolic meanings. The Warlpiri concept of 'country' is central. It concerns ancestrally animated land, specific tracts of which people identify with and possess rights and interests in (see Sutton 2003, 1998a). While not yet completed, the project has involved visits to and documentation of sacred sites, while elders share their knowledge with family groups as they engage with their ancestral landscapes. In the last phase of the project, archival materials were employed in order to augment the intergenerational transmission of cultural knowledge and support the co-constitution of persons and places.[15] In what follows we discuss the mapping process and consider practical, ethical, and other matters it raises.

The chapter is divided into three sections. First, we provide a historical context for shifts in Lander Warlpiri engagements with country and consider what is at stake for people in the mapping project. We also describe how the project developed. In the second section we discuss

---

13 Peterson (2017: 247) notes that where there is more than one place name for a site, or different spellings in different languages, choosing just one may unduly advantage one group over another, given the relationship of language to landed identity and the significance of 'ownership' of land in the legal context (see Peterson 2017: 241–242; Weiner & Glaskin 2007). This is no small matter.

14 Hereafter Lander Warlpiri.

15 See also Wafer (2017: 26–27).

the methodology and resources employed in the project and provide a case study of a cultural mapping trip. In the third section we explore the outcomes and issues that have arisen during the process of re-animation and evocation of place-based knowledge and memories. Relatedly, we illuminate tensions that can result from the complex interplay of archival returns with contested understandings of territorialities, landholding, and differing social formations over time. Throughout we attend to the ways in which local people's practices of representing and inscribing place (see Wilkins 2002) may differ from, build upon, and/or exceed western spatial regimes, cartographic practices, and technologies.

Background to the project

Historical context

The project arose from the concerns of Willowra elders over the increasingly circumscribed opportunities for younger people to acquire the place-based knowledge and experiences that are regarded as foundational to local identity, social organisation, and cultural continuity. As is the case in many parts of Australia, the lifeworlds of Willowra people today are radically different to those of their forebears, whose social relations were anchored in the landscape. The elders acquired visceral knowledge of country during eras in which they travelled on foot, sometimes using horses and/or donkeys, then, post 1970s, motor vehicles. While Warlpiri continue to maintain religious and cultural practices, other domains of life have changed following European settlement of their land.

The process of colonisation of Lander Warlpiri country began in 1860 when John McDouall Stuart attempted to cross Australia from south to north.[16] In 1928, soon after settlers moved into the region with cattle, conflicts over water and Aboriginal women culminated in settlers killing many Warlpiri, Anmatyerr, and Kaytetye people along the Lander and Hansen Rivers.[17] This event became known as the Coniston Massacre. While many locals took refuge in hills, others fled the region, eventually to be settled in government settlements such as Yuendumu, Warrabri (Ali Curung), and Hooker Creek (Lajamanu). Those who remained in the Willowra region continued hunting and gathering on their traditional lands while avoiding encounters with settlers. However, this situation changed after 1948 when the Willowra pastoral lease (PL) was taken over by the Parkinson family, with whom local people established relatively good relations.

In 1973, the Commonwealth purchased Willowra station on behalf of the local residents. Concerned about the vulnerability of leasehold tenure, the traditional owners lodged a land claim to the pastoral lease under the *Aboriginal Land Rights (Northern Territory) Act 1976*. This was followed by a claim to the adjoining Mount Barkly station, which had been purchased by the Aboriginal owned Willowra Pastoral Company. Claims were also lodged to Kaytetye, Warlpiri, and Warlmanpa country adjoining Willowra to the east and to Yurrkuru, on unalienated Crown Land.[18] The claims, lodged by the CLC (involving Vaarzon-Morel), were

---

16   See Wafer & Wafer (1983: 35–44) for a description of Stuart's journey and his renaming of Warlpiri places.

17   See Vaarzon-Morel (1995).

18   These claims followed upon the first Warlpiri claim, the 1978 Warlpiri and Kartangarurru-Kurintji land claim.

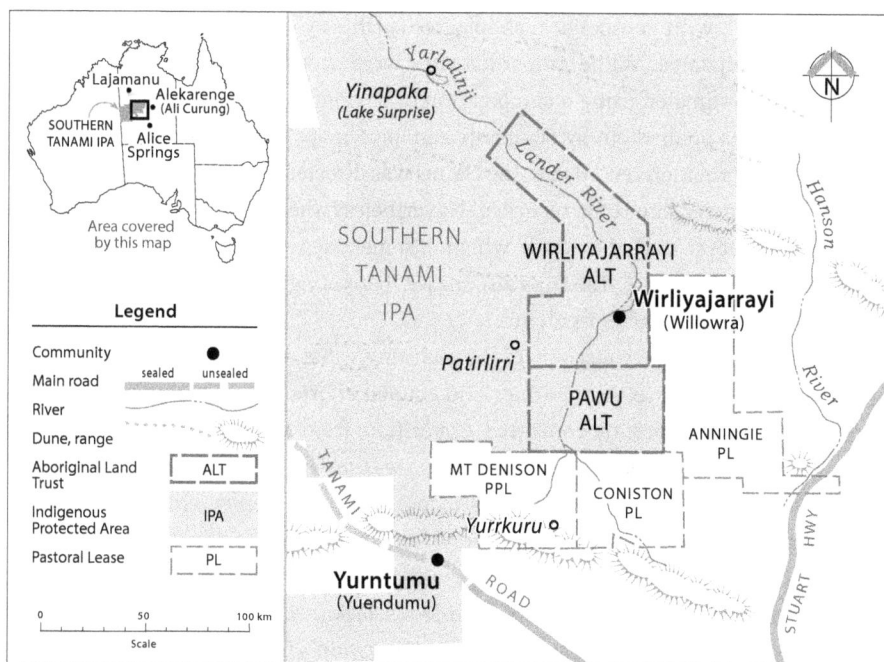

Figure 1. Map showing location of Wirliyajarrayi Aboriginal Land Trust (former Willowra PL), Pawu ALT (former Mount Barkly PL) and other key places mentioned in the text; shaded area is the portion of the Southern Tanami Indigenous Protected Area which encompasses the Lander River (map: Brenda Thornley)

successful and the majority of Lander Warlpiri land is now Aboriginal freehold, unlike the majority of adjoining Anmatyerr land, which is encompassed by non-Indigenous held pastoral leases (see Figure 1).[19]

Mapping country in land claims

In preparation of the above-mentioned land claims, the CLC employed anthropologists and linguists to research the claimants' system of land tenure. In the process they documented Dreaming tracks, sacred sites, and related ancestral stories, songs, and ceremonies. While constraints on time and resources limited the opportunities for country visits, the land claim maps provide the most extensive spatial record of sites in the Lander Warlpiri, Anmatyerr, and adjoining Kaytetye region that existed until recently. While the maps were impressive, a common refrain of elders at the time was that they didn't need "whitefella maps," because they held the knowledge in their heads (see also Peterson 2017; Sutton 2019).

Along with anthropological reports, maps showing place names associated with clan estates and Dreaming tracks became exhibits in claim hearings. Although professional and drawn to scale (Peterson 2017: 246), they lacked the topographic shading and colour of base

---

19 At the time of writing, a native title claim has been lodged under the *Native Title Act 1993* (Commonwealth) on Anningie station and in June 2018 a determination of Native Title was made for the Anmatyerr and Warlpiri custodians of Mount Denison PPL (perpetual pastoral lease).

maps now produced with geospatial technologies (such as GPS devices[20] and GIS software), which are readily updated. While numerous sites were accurately located, the positions of many others were estimated using a combination of techniques, including by taking compass bearings of locations pointed out by claimants and 'mud maps' drawn in the sand by Warlpiri men. Moreover, information recorded in the claims was directed to the legal process, which did not require every sacred site to be recorded. Nevertheless, the field trips provided important opportunities for people to visit country, which in some cases had not been revisited since the time of the Coniston Massacre. The trips also meant that younger people raised on settlements could experience their countries firsthand.

While researchers were conscious of the enduring value of the maps, little consideration was given to their future use. At the time, land council efforts were directed toward winning claimants' cases in the face of concerted opposition from various parties, including the Northern Territory Government. Looking back, it was an era of hope, when it was hard to imagine how the impacts of factors such as modernity, demography, changing government policies, and practices of dwelling on the land would affect people's lifeworlds. Moreover, the legal process involved in claiming land and granting property rights to Indigenous peoples is itself not without impacts (Povinelli 1993; Weiner & Glaskin 2007).[21]

Discussing the effects of the mapping and registration of Indigenous customary land in Australia and New Guinea, Weiner & Glaskin note that land claims are not just about securing land rights, but "also about creating a managerial and legal capacity for them through various processes of *incorporation*" [emphasis in original] (2007: 6). Commenting on the impacts of maps produced for Indigenous land claims in Belize and Nicaragua, Wainwright & Bryan observe that an effect of "the cartographic-legal strategy" was a "shift towards conceiving of rights to land in terms of *property*" [emphasis in original] (2009: 155).[22] Closer to home, Elias (2007) has explored the effects of gold mining on ways that Warlpiri people model relations to, and delimit, place in the Northern Tanami. He argues that the land rights and royalty regime has resulted in the reification of people's relationship to place, the objectification of place as space, and new forms of valuation. He notes, furthermore, that the influence of the latter is not insignificant: "It is at the centre of tensions and politicking between people to identify who is eligible to receive money from specific tracts of land, and the criteria upon which such eligibility is based, contested and upheld" (Elias 2007: 224).

The impetus for the Lander Warlpiri cultural mapping project

Over the past decade, many of the older generation who walked the land and gave evidence in land claims have passed away. Furthermore, while initiation, women's *yawulyu*, and other land-based ceremonies are still held, collective knowledge of large-scale ceremonies such as

20 Global Positioning System devices record points and routes to assist navigation.

21 The negative effects include issues arising from the fact that the burden of proof in claims is on Indigenous people with the "inevitable clash between indigenous and non-indigenous modes of proof" (Gray 2000: 1), and the non-recognition of claims by people who cannot satisfy the requirements of land rights acts.

22 On relationships between mapping, territorialisation, and/or property regimes, see Carter (1987), Nadasdy (2017) and Craib (2017).

Ngajakula and Jardiwanpa, has diminished. At the same time, younger people's lives have altered with their increasing entanglement with settler society and constraints imposed by the government income support system. The Lander Warlpiri region covers a vast semi-arid territory with limited road access. Most individuals cannot afford the properly equipped all-wheel drive vehicles required to access remote areas of country without risking lives. As few people have such suitable vehicles, knowledge of traditional country away from station tracks and roads has declined (Elias 2007; Peterson 2017).

Yet, while the nature of people's engagement with land has transformed, country remains central to their identity and spiritual wellbeing. While it is undoubtedly the case that land has acquired new forms of value as a result of compensatory payments from activities such as mining and leases, land is not regarded as a commodity. Nevertheless, as demonstrated by Elias (2007), the impact of the Australian territorial and property regime on Warlpiri is undeniable. To take an example from Willowra, prior to the commencement of the mapping project, Vaarzon-Morel overheard a young man refer to his father's country as "my station," as he demarcated clear boundaries in the sand. In doing so he conflated the anthropological term 'estate' with 'station' and attributed a non-permeable boundedness to the country that it does not possess for older generations.

During the same period, Willowra community underwent much conflict, some of which arose between families over payments made by the government for the compulsory tenure of land on which Willowra is located.[23] Elders attributed some of the problems to younger people's lack of knowledge about the complexity of people–land relations and conjoined responsibilities for country at a regional level. At the same time, a lack of knowledge of where one's group hands over responsibility of a Dreaming track to another meant that young people sometimes asserted rights beyond their traditional country. Younger people were also anxious about a decline in place-based knowledge with the passing of elders. While such concerns motivated the project, a related impetus was the desire to maintain "strong Yarlalinji Warlpiri" language. Although Yarlalinji or Lander Warlpiri is in the strongest position of the four main Warlpiri dialects[24] spoken today (O'Shannessy 2012), it is still vulnerable.[25] While lack of space prevents us elaborating here, place names, associated stories, and landscape terms index and contain important cultural information (Hercus & Simpson 2002; Burenhult & Levinson 2008).

The CLC was keen to support the project for two main reasons. Firstly the Lander region had not been subject to the same intensive mineral exploration and site survey activity as the northern Tanami, hence maps were not updated. Secondly Brian Connelly, former anthropology manager at the CLC, regarded the situated, bottom-up approach of the project

---

23 The leases were a condition for receiving basic infrastructure and services, a requirement of the 2007 Northern Territory National Emergency Response, which aimed to 'normalise' Aboriginal communities (Altman & Hinkson 2010).

24 The four main dialects are Southern (Ngaliya), Western Warlpiri (Warnayaka), Northern, and the eastern Lander River and Hansen River dialects (Laughren in preparation).

25 Willowra people's long-held resolve to maintain the vitality of Lander Warlpiri is demonstrated by their campaign to develop the bilingual education program at Willowra in 1976 (Vaarzon-Morel & Wafer 2017), their ongoing commitment to Warlpiri law and ritual, their funding of the Wirliyajarrayi (Willowra) Learning Centre (WLC), and now the cultural mapping program.

as a possible model for future mapping projects. Land councils throughout Australia struggle with issues concerning the dissemination of ethnographic material created during claim research. In addition to legal issues (see earlier), and amid large workloads involving traditional owner consultations, land agreements, and dispute mediation, most land councils do not have the funds or capacity to systematically undertake a meaningful repatriation process. In this instance the CLC was able to positively respond to the Willowra community's request for support, because – despite material disadvantage and competition for limited resources – the community allocated significant resources to the project. A related factor was the authors' long-term relationships with Willowra.

A vision takes shape

Although elders had long expressed concerns to Vaarzon-Morel about the lack of opportunities for younger people to learn about their countries in situ,[26] the project took shape in conversations with Teddy Long Jupurrula during research for a native title claim over Mount Denison PPL. At the time, Jupurrula and Kelly were discussing sites they had mapped on the PPL, when Jupurrula suggested creating a map of the entire Lander region, extending from Lake Surprise (Yinapaka) in the north to his country Yurrkuru, in the south, where the Coniston Massacre began.[27] Motioning to the end of the wide veranda of his house, he indicated the large scale and scope of the map. It would largely ignore boundaries imposed on the land such as pastoral leases and land trusts created through mechanisms of settler property regimes.

By chance, 'The Paruku Project' (Morton et al. 2013), a major exhibition showcasing scientific and Indigenous understandings of land around Lake Gregory, WA, had opened in Alice Springs. This gave Jupurrula an opportunity to tease out his vision with Kelly. Yet, as impressive as the exhibition was, there were few examples of what Jupurrula wanted. On the return trip to Willowra, while stopping at Ti Tree roadhouse on the Stuart Highway, Jupurrula sighted a mounted map depicting the highway snaking down Australia, dotted with names and images of towns and roadhouses. He indicated that he wanted something similar but larger, with the Lander River as the map's centrepiece. He also suggested graphic illustrations that depicted ancestral activity; for example, dust kicked into the air by ancestral Karnta Karnta 'Dancing Women' as they travelled through the region. Such a map would illuminate Warlpiri cosmography and the sensory experience of country conveyed through song, ceremony, and story. Unlike a sand map, Jupurrula wanted a 'modern' map to appeal to youth. While form was important, the underlying rationale was to use the map as a teaching tool: the telling of stories and reworking of cultural information by family groups while on their country was central to this process.

With the realisation that such a project would be a large financial and logistical undertaking, it was suggested that Vaarzon-Morel and Kelly apply to the Warlpiri Education Training Trust

---

26   For example, the late Maxie Jampijinpa would argue that elders should be supported to educate people about Jukurrpa. Elders also pondered why funds were directed to physical and not cultural infrastructure, that is, their intangible cultural heritage.

27   In 1928, Yurrkuru was on Coniston Station, but changes in PL boundaries mean that it is now encompassed by Mount Denison Station.

(WETT) for funding. In part, it was conceived as a community-building opportunity in the hope that it would empower people's sense of governance and help the process of repairing fractured social relations. Projects which had recognised the main families in Willowra, such as the painting of Jukurrpa panels in 2013 for the new Wirliyajarrayi (Willowra) Learning Centre (WLC), had demonstrated positive community impacts. While initially the project was funded for two weeks, it became apparent that a more substantial undertaking was needed. To this end, the authors successfully applied to WETT for larger grants. The Anthropology section at the CLC agreed to act as the project partner, and in principle support was provided by the WLC and South Tanami Indigenous Protected Area (STIPA).

Additional funding was provided by the Granites Mines Affected Areas Aboriginal Corporation (GMAAAC).[28] Funded and directed by Willowra community, the mapping project ran for 16 weeks from late 2014 to 2018.[29]

Methodology and the mapping process

In this section we describe the preparation of the physical map and sketch the mapping process and activities undertaken on the ground. We then provide a background to the legacy materials used in the project and present a case study to illustrate their incorporation.

Map preparation: the base, scale, orientation, and demarcation of Lander country

As Brotton (2012: 13) notes, all map making involves choices as to content that is included or excluded, the perspective, orientation, projection, and scale used, and how territories are demarcated. From the start, project participants agreed that the map should be large in scale and able to be laid on the ground and read like a sand map. This would facilitate group discussion about people's connections to places and each other and ensure that the map was collectively constructed. Furthermore, apart from the fact that internet connectivity is slow and unreliable at Willowra, no local person possessed computer-based geospatial mapping skills. Moreover, the use of such technology at this stage would have undermined elders' command of the mapping exercise. While people are open to learning digital mapping techniques, those techniques should complement Warlpiri geographic knowledge systems and "cartographic responses" (Palmer 2012). The digital imaging and mapping technology used on the ground was largely limited to cameras (including video and smartphones), printed satellite images, and GPS (handheld and mounted in cars).

---

28 Supported by the Community Development Program at the CLC, the GMAAAC committee constitutes an informal reference group who invite potential partners to submit community benefit project proposals. Funding is derived from compensation payments from mining in the western Tanami. The benefits of this approach for the community included the use of established CLC Community Development consultation processes, the involvement of community members in project design, and the responsiveness and accountability of project workers to the community.

29 WETT contributed $84,715 and GMAAAC a further $121,883. Funds covered fees for local participants in recognition that the project constitutes important 'work', as well as fees for consultants and costs incurred for vehicle maintenance, fuel, food, canvas painting, and recording equipment.

It was agreed to begin with a place names map, to be compiled during country visits and discussions at Willowra. Kim Mahood, who had worked on the Paruku project mentioned earlier, was employed to underpaint a large canvas on which she marked features in the Lander region. (The advantage of canvas was that it is durable, rollable, and easily moved.) Projecting a series of adjoining 1:250,000 topographic maps on a wall, she traced the course of the Lander River, from its rise in the south near Coniston to the flood-out in the north at Yinapaka (Lake Surprise). She drew visual landmarks such as mountains, sandhills, roads, station bores, and fencelines to help people calibrate distance and the relative positions of sites. Then, re-projecting the maps onto the canvas, she added names of well-known places for which we had geo-referenced data.

Encompassing the Lander River from north to south, the map extended east to neighbouring Kaytetye territory and west to the area where Lander Warlpiri territory merges with that of Warnayaka Warlpiri. There is in fact no hard and fast boundary demarcating Lander Warlpiri from other Warlpiri regions. According to Jupurrula, the map broadly covered the estates of Lander Warlpiri and Anmatyerr whose members traditionally intermarried, held ceremonies together and considered themselves "all one family." Just as the region cannot be precisely delineated, neither can individual estates within it. As anthropologists' reports for Warlpiri land claims observe, a clan's 'country' is comprised of the area surrounding clusters of named sites and Dreaming tracks with which patri-groups are affiliated (Peterson et al. 1978; Wafer & Wafer 1980).

Significantly, the orientation of the map along a north–south axis aligned with Lander Warlpiri geo-social groupings of estates. While not the case in every instance, the countries of several clan groups who belong to the patri-moiety containing the subsections Jungarrayi/ Nungarrayi–Japaljarri/Napaljarri[30] and Japanangka/Napanangka–Japangardi/Napangardi are located downstream surrounding the northern Lander. Several other countries belonging to clan groups associated with the opposite moiety, that is, Jangala/Nangala–Jampijinpa/ Nampijinpa and Jupurrula/Napurrula–Jakamarra/Nakamarra, are located upstream on the southern Lander River. Reflecting the spatial distribution of the two groupings, the following terms are used for the two moieties: *Ngurra Kurlarninyarra*, meaning 'camp across the north side' and *Ngurra Yatujumparra*, meaning 'camp across the south side' (Laughren 1982: 76). This arrangement has implications for ritual and social relations.

Mapping on the ground

This part involved visiting as many places as possible with *kirda* and *kurdungurlu* affiliated with the sites and surrounding country. Ownership of most Warlpiri estates and ritual property is passed down the generations through the male line, in what anthropologists variously refer to as patrilineal descent or patrifiliation (see Sutton 2003). Although women inherit their father's country, they do not pass on their same ownership rights to their children. Warlpiri refer to male and female 'owners' in the male line as *kirda*, whereas children of female members of the patriclan are called *kurdungurlu*. The latter act as ritual managers for their *kirda*. The relationship between *kirda* and *kurdungurlu* is complementary and reciprocal.

---

30   Men's subsection names begin with 'J', whereas women's start with 'N'.

Observing cultural protocol, estate groups did not map other people's countries. Nevertheless, the 'witnessing' of trips by non-estate members was critical, and the project facilitated various people participating as observers in order to learn about regional links. For the most part, we undertook day and overnight trips.[31] The number of sites visited varied each trip, depending on factors such as accessibility and time spent engaging with country, as people addressed ancestral spirits, cleaned soakages, fired country, sang, hunted, cooked, and performed other activities (see case study below). Many sites proved difficult to locate due to changes in vegetation and difficult terrain, resulting in flat tyres – sometimes seven or eight a day. Nevertheless, the process generated considerable enthusiasm, with young people becoming attuned to the spiritual landscape, reading the Dreaming topography with renewed vigour. This resulted in people locating soakages when hunting in private cars.

The on-ground mapping process blended scientific cartographic techniques with Warlpiri cartographic practices and navigation (see Nash 1998; Vaarzon-Morel 2016). For example, when explaining the location of a site, men sometimes drew a sand map. Employing cardinal points such as north and south to orient themselves (the absolute frame of reference), they indicated the position of sites in relation to one another. Depicting sacred sites and Dreaming paths as circles and lines respectively, these ground maps drew upon the iconographic system employed when painting designs on people's bodies, ritual objects, and acrylic paintings produced for the art market (Munn 1973; Sutton 1998a).

In keeping with Warlpiri methods of imparting cultural information, elders provided details of Dreaming places while in proximity to them. Observing age and gender restrictions, they pointed out topographic features such as rock formations, Dreaming trees, ridge lines, and creeks that revealed ancestral activity and paths of travel. Elders insisted that *kurdungurlu* accompany *kirda* on site visits and, as described below, on visiting a site, *kurdungurlu* would address ancestral spirits, announcing the identity of visitors and asserting their rights to be there.

While elders instructed younger people about the landscape, the anthropologists documented GPS locations, place names, mythology, the extent of sites, and the nature of people's affiliations to them. Elders, who had not visited some sites since their youth, benefitted from recourse to land claim maps. In addition, photographs and legacy recordings were employed to prompt people's memories of places, resulting in the recollection of stories, information, and ritual performances. Younger people videoed activities and recorded events on mobile phones, later sharing images with relatives, who circulated them on devices using applications such as Bluetooth. Back at the WLC, newly documented toponyms were marked in the correct locations on the canvas map, which was used to facilitate further discussions of people's relationships with places and Dreamings (see Figures 2 & 3). Data was entered in a spreadsheet and provided to the CLC geospatial unit to add to their database to produce revised maps.[32] Copies of photos and recordings were provided to participants on trips and uploaded to a designated

---

31   Not counting IPA trips (involving about 80 people), a total of 198 people participated in mapping trips. Of these approximately 25 per cent were 60 years plus, 40 per cent 30–50 years, and 35 per cent 16–30 years.

32   To give an idea of sites located on Mount Barkly and Willowra claim areas, 233 were recorded prior to the project, of which 49 were located. The project has since located 136 sites, of which 20 were not previously documented.

heritage computer at the WLC. Geo-referenced by place name and coordinates, the media is also stored at the CLC. On completion of the project, copies of material will be provided to the GMAAAC committee, who will discuss archival options for long-term preservation.

Figure 2. Cecilia Nampijinpa and Doris Napaljarri add place names to canvas map, Willowra Learning Centre (photo: Petronella Vaarzon-Morel)

Figure 3. Map talk at the Willowra Learning Centre. Elder Lucy Nampijinpa instructs Doreen Nakamarra and others (photo: Petronella Vaarzon-Morel)

Augmenting GMAAAC-funded mapping trips, we participated in two Warlpiri ranger and community country visits organised by the CLC Land Management section. In 2018, we camped for a week at Yinapaka, 80 kilometres to the north of Willowra. The area is part of an Indigenous Protected Area (IPA) in the Tanami region. Under the IPA plan of management, cultural values and practices are regarded as integral to natural resource management. Thus, while a key objective of expeditions was burning to regenerate country and promote biodiversity, the trips provided an opportunity for traditional owners to undertake cultural activities in their countries.

In addition to the ground-based burning of country, aerial burning was undertaken by helicopter in remote country and, when not required for burning, we employed the helicopter to locate sites. For example, on one occasion, navigating without a whitefella map, elder George Jungarrayi directed the pilot as we[33] followed the route taken by the ancestral *Mala* 'rufous hare-wallaby', hoping to locate *Mala* sites on the ground. Jungarrayi's method was first to orient himself to a known place, then taking cues from changes in topography and vegetation as we flew, he looked for distinguishing trees and features which 'marked' the places in question. In this way we located several sites. At night senior women led *yawulyu* singing sessions and instructed younger women about song items related to the identity and features of surrounding estates. The metaphorical nature of many songs means that information about places can remain opaque to those without firsthand knowledge of them. For example, *wurrpardi* 'spear bush' grows on the high sandhill which runs east–west for 13 kilometres on the northern side of Yinapaka. One song concerns an ancestral being who fashions ritual spears from *wurrpardi*. While straightening spears in the fire, the ancestor notices another being in sandhill country further to the east and calls out: "I'm Yinapaka, and I'm Warlpiri," to which the other ancestor replies, "I'm Ngunulurru and I'm Warlpiri." In this way they establish relations of similarity and difference. Song is an important mnemonic practice for Warlpiri, and such sessions stimulate multilayered understandings and poetic evocations of country.

As part of the project, one week was devoted to recording the Ngajakula songline. Ngajakula is owned by *kirda* belonging to the moiety associated with *Ngurra Kurlarninyarra* (see earlier) and is the reciprocal ceremony to Jardiwanpa, *kirda* for which belong to the opposite moiety. While it is beyond the scope of this chapter to elaborate, Ngajakula and Jardiwanpa songs encode cosmological details of places and link estate groups belonging to the same subsections. In so doing they invoke a level of social organisation beyond the local (Vaarzon-Morel in press). The intent of the Ngajakula session was to instruct young people about socio-spatial relations in the Lander region and relate places mentioned in songs to sites on the map.

Deeming the content of the songs and their performance too powerful to perform within the WLC, elders took the map to the ceremonial ground at Willowra, where they hung it from a Toyota correctly oriented (see Figure 4). Before instruction began, young men collected wood, constructed bough shades, and prepared the ceremonial ground, while elder George Jungarrayi carved clapping sticks. Teddy Jupurrula introduced the proceedings, explaining the purpose of the map. He spoke to the ethical imperative of understanding how far one's group takes a songline and not "jumping over" into other countries to claim royalties. He began:

---

33 Jungarrayi's daughters and Vaarzon-Morel.

I know a lot of young people and middle-aged people have still got to learn Law proper way. At royalty time people talk up but they don't know Jukurrpa from *warringiyi* (father's father). [Gesturing to the map.] You've got the proper story and Jukurrpa along these soakages and places. I bin thinking about this map a lot. I was the one behind the map. We've been working on this map with Napangardi (Vaarzon-Morel) and Jungarrayi (Kelly) a couple of years now. We've been putting all the waterholes and names.

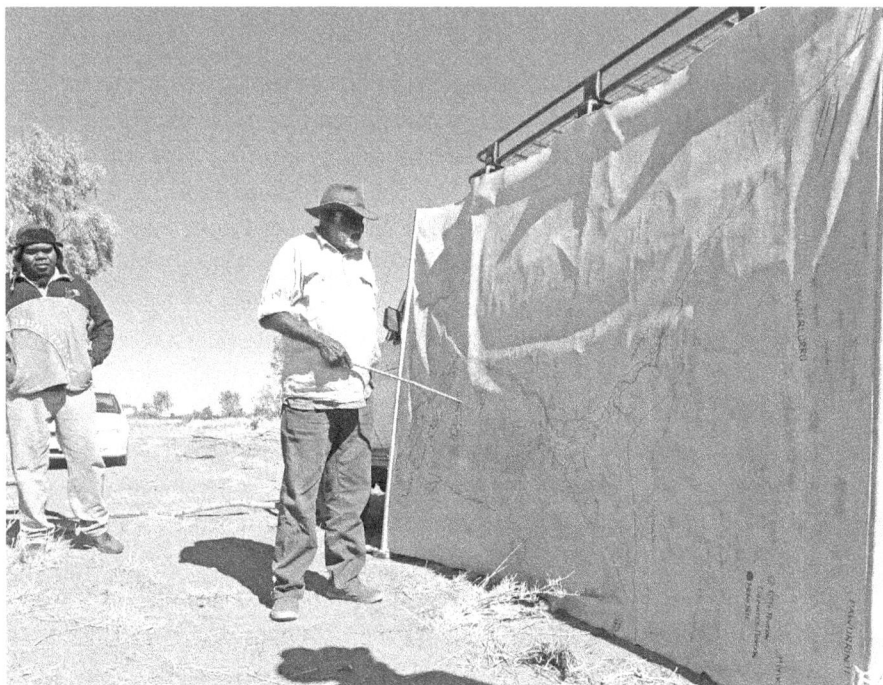

Figure 4. With the map correctly oriented on a north–south axis, Teddy Long Jupurrula instructs a group of men and women (out of sight, Dwayne Jupurrula on Teddy's left) about interrelationships between countries in the Lander River region (photo: Petronella Vaarzon-Morel)

After Jungarrayi traced the path of Ngajakula ancestors through the region, men sang the songline. In the event, over 60 song items were recorded on video. Subsequently, USBs with the recordings were provided to elders to share with family. Although a Ngajakula ceremony was filmed at Yuendumu in the 1970s (Sandall 1977), people wanted their songs documented in full as the songline may never be performed in its entirety again.

Use of archival materials

In this section we describe how Vaarzon-Morel's legacy collection of media relating to the Lander region is being incorporated in the mapping project. For background, Vaarzon-Morel has worked with Willowra community for over 40 years, firstly as a school teacher in 1976–1977, then conducting anthropological research for land claims, and housing, history, environmental, and social justice projects. Her collection, which documents Lander Warlpiri intangible cultural heritage, includes photographic images, audio and visual recordings of women's rituals, men's public ceremonies, and narratives, much of which was recorded during Vaarzon-Morel's PhD research in the 1980s. In the 1990s she collaborated on *Warlpiri women's voices*[34] with different generations of women, some of whom have sadly passed away. Their families still cherish the book, which describes events in the Lander region following colonisation.

Over the years Vaarzon-Morel had provided innumerable copies of photos and recordings to families at Willowra. However, the lack of suitable places to store material, combined with constant handling, heat and dust, and people's observance of protocols concerning the deceased (requiring them to destroy images or possessions of a person following his/her death), meant that material rarely survived long. Moreover, the equipment for playing old recordings was obsolete. Although the CLC had digitised some of Vaarzon-Morel's photos and placed them on their version of Keeping Culture KMS (keepingculture.com) for community access, no Aboriginal houses at Willowra currently have internet. While the internet became available for community use in 2013 when the WLC was established, low capacity makes it impractical to use Keeping Culture KMS and other cloud-based platforms for the sharing of digital cultural media.

In 2016, Vaarzon-Morel became Research Associate on an ARC Linkage grant[35] with partner organisations the CLC, the University of Sydney and the University of Melbourne. The aim of the project was to apply research on archiving and community access to find practical solutions to managing recorded cultural material of interest to the CLC and its constituents. This involved connecting collections to appropriate people and supporting CLC activities in land management and intergenerational knowledge transfer, and contributing to people's wellbeing. The linkage project enabled Vaarzon-Morel's Willowra collection to be digitised and reintegrated into the community, with instructions taken for long-term preservation and access.

After explaining what the linkage project was about, Vaarzon-Morel informed people about the content of the collection, from which they selected media that they wanted to listen to or view. On first encountering an item, an individual frequently chose not to share it. That access restrictions apply to secret-sacred, gendered materials also means that people need to view the contents of material before they can make informed decisions. In addition to the fact that "secrecy and economizing with knowledge is central to the relations between the generations" (Peterson 2017: 235), individuals do not want to violate protocols by revealing information to the wrong people. A fundamental principle of the system of protocols surrounding cultural property in Central Australia is that one should not speak for, and make decisions about, country, songs, ceremonies, or ritual objects for which one does not hold customary rights and responsibilities (Michaels 1986; Myers 1986; Sutton 2003). While the exercise of an individual's entitlement depends on seniority and context, a general rule is that cultural property should be managed by relevant *kirda* and *kurdungurlu*. As indicated by Napanangka, the latter should be close kin:

---

34 For a critique, see Grossman (2013).

35 LP140100806, 'Re-integrating Central Australian community cultural collections'.

> The people with the authority to make decisions [about archival material] are older and middle-aged persons. If people have passed away it should be their descendants, through mother and father, but with mother's side it should be close up, not distant people.[36]

While changing attitudes concerning the deceased means that families are now keen to have photos and recordings of deceased relatives, affective qualities of such media are apprehended differently, so that widows avoid material associated with deceased spouses or children. In keeping with customary mortuary practices, adult children manage photos and records of their parents. However, photos and recordings are not simply material objects, but are imbued with the persona of those who figure in them, and they can provoke deep emotions in viewers. For example, on first viewing footage from the 1970s of their relatives, senior women referred to them by their Dreaming names, in recognition of their ancestral status. They touched images with tenderness, weeping tears of joy and sorrow at reconnecting with 'dear ones'. In this manner they cleared the way to re-engage with the material much as they sweep places after an absence (see below), thereafter relating to them in quotidian ways. Listening to relatives discussing a Dreaming, Jeannie Nampijinpa remarked: "the old people are calling up we mob, and we still hold 'em [songs, stories, ceremonies]. This is good to have these stories and songs to teach young people." For her part, Vaarzon-Morel was relieved to know the media would be reused in ways long envisaged. The recordings awakened memories of good times, underscoring the women's enduring – if at times diffuse – involvement in each other's lives. While more can be said about the returns process, we make some general observations before addressing how material was put to work for the mapping project.

Where media featured groups of people performing public ceremonies, the return process was straightforward, involving Vaarzon-Morel consulting participants or, if deceased, close kin, as to what they wanted done. Invariably she was asked to copy material onto USBs and USB bracelets to distribute to nominated individuals for viewing on TVs, iPads, and PlayStations. Photos and recordings deemed suitable for wider community access were copied to computers housed at the WLC. Where media involved one or a few deceased persons, Vaarzon-Morel consulted their adult children (if not available, then other kin) about the material. After items were returned to individuals, other people quickly asked for copies, asserting their relatedness to people featured in them. Such demands of sociality can cut across other considerations. This was generally not a problem, as designated 'holders' of material became comfortable sharing with extended family. However, Vaarzon-Morel was sometimes instructed to withhold material from kin due to disputes.

The material brought back memories and provoked much discussion. People not yet born at the time of a recording were keen to learn more. While metadata was available for items, individuals frequently asked Vaarzon-Morel to sit with them while they listened to, or viewed, recordings and photos of relatives and country. This provided an opportunity to further annotate material. We also translated stories, songs and interviews, noting place names, Dreamings and other details relevant to the mapping project. During this process, individuals selected material to take with them when visiting their country.

---

36   That is, genealogically distant, e.g. MDDDD or S (man's daughter's daughter's daughter's daughter or son).

For example, a recording made in the late 1980s of a conversation between Vaarzon-Morel and the late Japangardi, senior *kirda* for Ngarnalkurru, contained important information about sites in his country. Listening to the recording, his daughter, Napanangka, was able to identify forgotten toponyms, thus enabling her to revive them. She discussed the places with her aging mother, Nampijinpa, who recalled their location, and when we visited them, remembered further details. Additionally, photos with descriptions of sites, some of which feature in *Warlpiri women's voices*, proved valuable to custodians. It also happened that while listening to old recordings, people identified unfamiliar language terms, which they followed up with elders. In this way, terms pertinent to earlier modes of relating to country were reintroduced to people's language repertoire.

The following provides a case study of a mapping trip. While incomplete and not addressing all the elements of the project, it nevertheless offers a view onto the multilayered process through which people are mobilising archival material to remake their sense of place. It shows how they reinscribe names, stories, and song in country, incorporating aspects of elders' knowledge into their own.

Case study: Visit to Patirlirri, 2018

Driving west from Willowra, we headed away from the Lander River toward the limestone country of Patirlirri. Patirlirri is the name for the assemblage of sacred places, Dreamings, and biophysical features that comprise the patrifilial country of the Kitson family, who we accompanied this day. While not the only trip to Patirlirri, it was the first on which elder George Jungarrayi had come to help locate elusive sites. Although Patirlirri is not his country, he knows it intimately, having visited the area on foot before settling at Willowra.

Jungarrayi holds primary responsibility for the countries Yinapaka and Ngunulurru which adjoin Patirlirri to the northeast. Linked by shared Dreaming tracks associated with the same subsections, these neighbouring countries are said to be in a 'company relationship'. *Kirda* for Patirlirri, Yinapaka, and Ngunulurru are associated with the Jungarrayi/Nungarrayi and Japaljarri/Napaljarri subsections, and *kurdungurlu* with Jupurrula/Napurrula and Jampijinpa/Nampijinpa subsections. That they share the same subsection affiliations means that the countries stand in an equivalent kinship relationship to each other.

As Jungarrayi is the senior surviving male of the related countries, *kirda* and *kurdungurlu* of Patirlirri deferred to his vast knowledge. On such trips there is a palpable sense of urgency to learn from elders. On their part, the elders demonstrate their deeply felt responsibility to uphold the law and sustain country by teaching younger generations. When not on their own country, and mindful of ancestral spirits, they are careful to deny their entitlement, exclaiming, as did Jungarrayi, "this is not my country, I'm just showing it, learning the younger ones."

During this trip we stopped at numerous places where Jungarrayi pointed out features and shared his knowledge of the cosmography. While younger people recorded events on cameras and phones, the anthropologists noted GPS positions, place names, features, stories, and details of people associated with places. Utilising Jungarrayi's sand maps and satellite photographs, we collectively checked newly recorded locations against those marked on land claim maps and calibrated likely positions of sites yet to be re-located (see Figure 5). Throughout, people learnt about country while sensorially immersed in it.

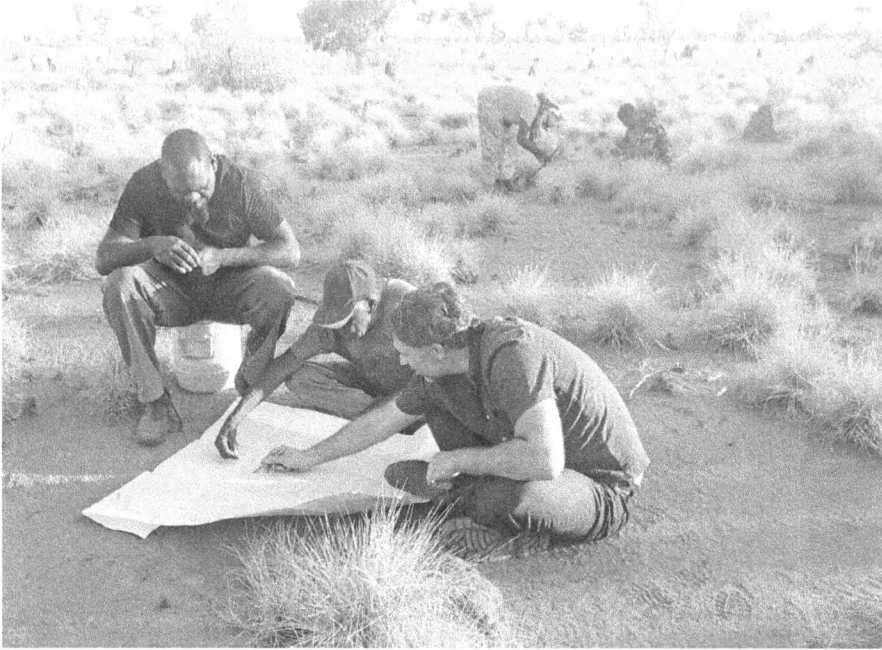

Figure 5. Dwayne Jupurrula, George Jungarrayi, and Luke Kelly discussing site locations (photo: Petronella Vaarzon-Morel)

On approaching sacred places, *kurdungurlu* would walk ahead, addressing ancestral spirits and identifying everyone present. They cleaned waterholes by digging out sand and burning surrounding grass. Such rituals are generally performed after considerable time has elapsed between visits. Places resonate with spirits and memories, and the death of a person connected to a site moves women to keen when first revisiting that place. Using eucalyptus branches, everyone would file past the site while sweeping the surrounds to erase traces of the deceased. Moving on, as we travelled from place to place, people collected bush medicine, hunted for food, fired undergrowth in order to regenerate the country, and otherwise engaged with the ancestral landscape.

On this occasion we travelled in two vehicles: men in one car and women in another. As we travelled through Patirlirri, Julie Napaljarri plugged a USB into the dashboard of the Toyota and played a recording of her late father, Jimmy Jungarrayi. It was one of the items digitised through the linkage grant that Napaljarri had suggested we take to remind us about places. It had been recorded 30 years earlier, when Jungarrayi had taken Vaarzon-Morel to Patirlirri to show her where he wanted to establish his outstation. Momentarily collapsing the passage of time that now separated them, Jungarrayi's voice could be heard teaching the young anthropologist about the country, calling out the names of places she now drove past with his daughters and grandchildren:

> Mijarrkunyangu—swamp, Nganawulpayi, Jamirdiwurduwurdu. We'll get along Rabbit Bore, going up Patirlirri area ... there's a bit of a creek starts in [the] spinifex – that's Ngatijirri Jukurrpa [Budgerigar Dreaming]. The little hill north, close to the road is Lirrapirtipirti, Ngatijirri starts there ...

Continuing his commentary, Jungarrayi described the paths taken by Dreaming beings as they deposited their spiritual essence and created the landscape through which we drove. He explained that the neighbouring countries Pawu and Yurrkuru stood in an in-law relationship to Patirlirri, meaning that they produce *kurdungurlu* or ritual managers for Patirlirri and vice versa. Through this emphasis, Jungarrayi stressed that the different countries in the Lander region were *jintangka* 'in one' and that "you can't cut 'em out," that is, treat them as unrelated. At the site Kulumalaji he recalled a ceremonial gathering during which young men played a game of *pulja*, in which players from opposing teams and generation moieties competed for possession of a hairstring football. As we approached Tipirnpa, Jungarrayi pointed out where his brother and three other relatives were shot by the whitefella Nugget Morton during the Coniston Massacre.

Continuing on, Napaljarri played another recording. This one featured her mother and sisters-in-law singing Ngatijirri *yawulyu* for Patirlirri country. They also sang related *yawulyu* for the neighbouring countries Yinapaka and Ngunulurru (*Wurrpardi* 'women's ritual spears', and *Jurlarda* 'bush honey' Dreamings respectively). Listening attentively, it was not long before the women broke into song, accompanying their now-deceased relatives, 'holding' the country, as we followed in their tracks. Sitting around the campfire that night, Dwayne Jupurrula, *kurdungurlu* for Patirlirri, recalled that earlier, when changing a tyre in the heat of the day, a cool breeze had struck his skin and he sensed the presence of *milarlpa*, spirits of the country. Napaljarri, his mother, reflected that they would have heard the voices of the Nungarrayis, her aunties, singing their country, and were looking after us.

Reflections

An advantage of working on the mapping and archival projects concurrently was seeing how intangible cultural heritage, such as place names, Dreaming tracks, stories, and songlines, can be rewoven in people's lives. What became clear is the multilayered, dynamic, and emergent nature of the process. By way of conclusion we briefly consider how archival returns may intersect with changing social formations and people's understandings of territoriality and landholding. Finally, we outline future directions for the project.

In the 1970s, people had little access to cars or telephonic communication, and memories of kin who lived far away could fade. Over time, those kin tended to become incorporated into the estate groups of people with whom they lived. In the past, being conceived and growing up in country could confer certain rights in places (Sutton 2003). However, now people who no longer live in their country can maintain contact with their families, and there is a shift toward a more codified landholding system. This is reflected in the following statement by Napanangka:

> We need family tree[s] because younger ones might lose that knowledge. We need to update them because it might have been made 10 years ago and we can add more people. We can put it in Willowra Learning Centre computer with the cultural mapping project. Some people have grown up in country and think it's theirs, but we take country through father and mother's father. (Pers. comm. to P Vaarzon-Morel, 2017)

Nevertheless, the need to engage with, and exercise responsibility for, country is regarded as important. And, against the background of the royalty regime, some people are concerned that people from the Warlpiri diaspora may use information gained from archives to "talk over" custodians living near, and caring for, country:

> you have to go and live in country and look and listen to the person talking and teaching you face-to-face. If they just listen to or read words and watch video, when royalty time comes the person who has been to country asks "have you been to that country?" … We have to look with our own eyes on country visits, in-person, listening to people telling a story and listening on country and to the country. (Napanangka, pers. comm. to P Vaarzon-Morel, 2017)

Another issue concerns variation in the weight assigned to heritage material according to factors such as a person's seniority, gender, and knowledge of country. For example, elders did not automatically accept as 'true' what someone said 30 years ago. They would listen to recordings to ascertain whether the person had the story 'straight'. At the other extreme, Vaarzon-Morel had requests from people who wanted photos of their father taken on land claim trips, because they said they were 'proof' that he spoke for country and had rights in it. In fact, he was there as a knowledgeable elder but did not claim the country as his own.

Yet, despite potential tensions and ambiguities surrounding heritage media, people recognise the need to preserve and archive cultural information for the future. In order to become better informed about possibilities, two Willowra women visited archives at PARADISEC[37] at the Sydney Conservatorium of Music and at AIATSIS in Canberra. Reflecting on PARADISEC, Napanangka stated:

> When I flew down here, I saw that the archive and digitisation process was real … we went to Lauren's computer … She clicked the NT and showed what you've [Vaarzon-Morel] been doing with my family and other people at Willowra when I was a little kid. She clicked Molly's recording – she was singing about *Mala Jukurrpa*. She showed us photos that you took of old people at *yawulyu* and ceremony, sharing and caring for each other, living a good life and being strong. We have only four Nampijinpas and two older Jupurrula left. It made us think how important it is that you did that work and that we have those old recordings. (Pers. comm. to P Vaarzon-Morel, 2017)

To date, the project has been intensive in terms of visiting places, recording, cataloguing, and returning information in the form of recordings to participants and reports to GMAAAC and the CLC. The next phase will focus on finalising the map to be hung in the WLC and developing Dreaming track and other maps that show connections between estate groups and countries.[38] It is planned to have the canvas map photographed by AIATSIS digitisation studio, enabling surrogates[39] to be made for display by the community (see Figure 6; Australian Broadcasting

37 The Pacific and Regional Archive for Digital Sources in Endangered Cultures. See www.paradisec.org.au.
38 For example, alliances between intermarrying countries and the Ngajakula songline.
39 Sponsorship is needed to fund reproduction of the map.

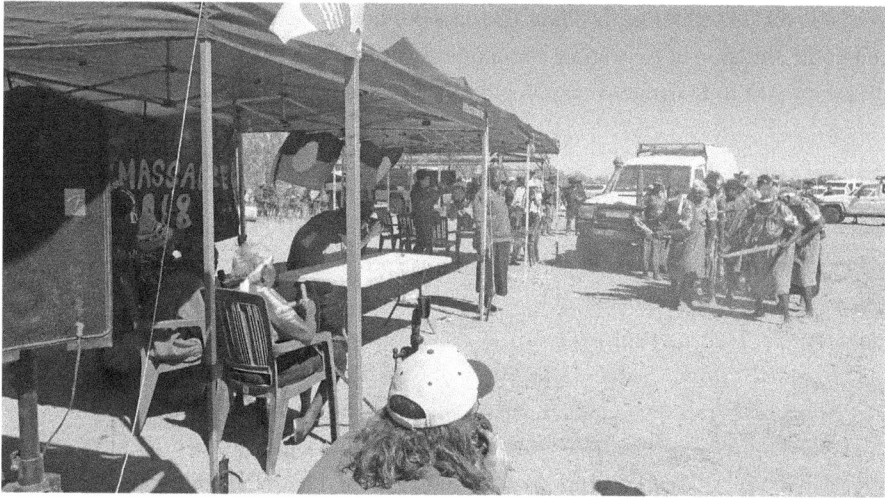

Figure 6. Warlpiri women performing *yawulyu* against the backdrop of the canvas map displayed at Yurrkuru during the 90th anniversary of the 1928 Coniston Massacre. The 2018 memorial event was held to commemorate the estimated 100 people killed during the massacre; the locations of killings are recorded on the map (photo: Petronella Vaarzon-Morel)

Corporation 2018). A high-megapixel shot will be archived at AIATSIS with access restrictions. As a way of disseminating information on country, the project will develop multiple booklets for estate groups based on John Bradley's (Bradley et al. 2010) atlas and the storied places model. It is also hoped to conduct mapping activities with the school. Additionally, four young adults are funded to receive training in digital mapping at the Indigenous Mapping Workshop 2019 to be held in Perth, WA. The long-term aim is to develop stand-alone computer maps that use the geographic coordinates recorded in the databases to attach cultural media to relevant place names, tracks, and songlines. The community has engaged linguist and anthropologist Jim Wafer to transcribe and translate Ngajakula songs with Willowra men as a step toward revitalising the material. Although there is no ongoing funding for the project after 2019, elders hope that we can find outside sponsorship for future activities, including a book and possible exhibition (see CLC 2018: 13).

Peterson (2017: 248) has questioned whether maps produced by anthropologists have a role to play in Warlpiri futures, observing that they "cannot substitute for 'traditional modes of cultural production'." We concur with this point but feel that cultural mapping projects such as the one we describe can play a significant role in place making and ongoing processes of "cultural production" (Ginsburg & Myers 2005). While the project may not resolve disputes over ownership of country, it can facilitate the renegotiation and sharing of knowledge.

Our chapter illustrates the importance of attending to the *process* of community mapping rather than simply focusing on cartography as an end in itself. In bridging different perspectival regimes and technologies, the mapping project is part of an ongoing process which involves the re-storying of places and refiguring of people's relations with each other and their environment. Cultural mapping complements, but cannot substitute for, other community-development activities. In recognising that a radical shift is needed in the way the government engages with the community, Teddy Long's vision for the Lander Warlpiri cultural mapping project calls for an "ethics of dwelling that is a politics of worldbuilding" (Zigon 2018: 150). Although the situation of Aboriginal communities varies,[40] we suggest that the project offers a positive approach to Indigenous mapping that may have wider applicability.

References

Australian Broadcasting Corporation. 2018. *Mapping the Coniston Massacre.* Podcast on
    Awaye! (https://www.abc.net.au/radionational/programs/awaye/2018-09-08/10209510)
    (Accessed on 8 September 2018.)
Altman, Jon C & Melinda Hinkson (eds.). 2010. *Culture crisis: Anthropology and politics in
    Aboriginal Australia.* Sydney: University of New South Wales Press.
Bradley, John, with Yanyuwa families. 2010. *Singing saltwater country: Journey to the
    songlines of Carpentaria.* Crows Nest, NSW: Allen and Unwin.
Brotton, Jerry. 2012. *A history of the world in twelve maps.* London: Penguin Books.
Burenhult, Niclas & Stephen C Levinson. 2008. Language and landscape: A cross-linguistic
    perspective. *Language Sciences* 30(2). 135–150.
Byrne, Denis. 2008. Counter-mapping: New South Wales & Southeast Asia. *Transforming
    Cultures eJournal* 3(1). 256–264.
Carter, Paul. 1987. *The road to Botany Bay: An essay in spatial history.* London, Boston:
    Faber and Faber.
Central Land Council. October 2018. Lander River map passes knowledge to children.
    Land Rights News Central Australia 8(3). 13. (http://www.territorystories.nt.gov.au/
    jspui/bitstream/10070/305766/1/CLC-Land-Rights-News-October-2018.pdf) (Accessed
    20 October 2019.)
Chambers, Kimberlee J, Jonathan Corbett, Peter C Keller & Colin JB Wood. 2004.
    Indigenous knowledge, mapping, and GIS: A diffusion of innovation perspective.
    Cartographica 59(3). 19–31.
Chapin, Mac, Zachary Lamb & Bill Threlkeld. 2005. Mapping indigenous lands. *Annual
    Review of Anthropology* 34. 619–638.
Craib, Raymond B. 2017. Cartography and decolonization. In James Akerman (ed.),
    Decolonizing the map: Cartography from colony to nation, 11–71. Chicago: University
    of Chicago Press. (https://www.academia.edu/34010438/CARTOGRAPHY_AND_
    DECOLONIZATION) (Accessed 19 October 2019.)
Dieckmann, Ute. 2018. *Cultural maps and hunter-gatherers' being in the world.* Panel 17,
    Twelfth International Conference on Hunting and Gathering Societies (CHAGS XII),
    School of Social Sciences, Universiti Sains Malaysia, Penang, 23 to 27 July 2018.
Elias, Derek. 2007. The measure of dreams. In James F Weiner & Katie Glaskin (eds.),
    *Customary land tenure & registration in Australia and Papua New Guinea:
    Anthropological perspectives* (Asia-Pacific Environment Monographs 3), 223–246.
    Canberra: ANU Press.

40   We note that other communities have expressed interest in undertaking similar mapping projects.

Ginsburg, Faye & Fred Myers. 2005. A history of Aboriginal futures. *Critique of Anthropology* 26(1). 27–45.

Gray, Peter RA. 2000. Do the walls have ears? Indigenous title and courts in Australia. *Australian Indigenous Law Reporter* 5(1). 1–17.

Grossman, Michele. 2013. *Entangled subjects: Indigenous/Australian cross-cultures of talk, text, and modernity* (Cross Cultures 158). Amsterdam: Rodopi.

Hercus, Luise & Jane Simpson. 2002. Indigenous place names: An introduction. In Luise Hercus, Flavia Hodges & Jane Simpson (eds.), *The land is a map: Placenames of Indigenous origin in Australia*, 1–23. Canberra: Pandanus Books in association with Pacific Linguistics.

Hirt, Irène. 2012. Mapping dreams/dreaming maps: Bridging indigenous and western geographical knowledge. *Cartographica* 47(2). 105–120. (ouverte.unige.ch/files/downloads/0/0/0/2/7/7/9/4/unige 27794 attachment01.pdf)

Ingold, Tim. 1996. Hunting and gathering as ways of perceiving the environment. In Roy Ellen & Katsuyoshi Fukai (eds.), *Redefining nature: Ecology, culture, and domestication*, 117–155. Oxford: Berg.

Koch, Grace. 2008. *The future of connection material held by Native Title Representative Bodies: Final report* (Native Title Research Report vol. 1). Canberra: Native Title Research Unit, AIATSIS.

Laughren, Mary. 1982. Warlpiri kinship structure. In Jeffrey Heath, Francesca Merlan & Alan Rumsey (eds.), *The languages of kinship in Aboriginal Australia* (Oceania Linguistic Monograph 24), 72–85. Sydney: University of Sydney.

Laughren, Mary (compiler). (in preparation). *Warlpiri–English encyclopaedic dictionary.* Draft ms. University of Queensland (electronic files accessed via Kirrkirr application).

Lempert, William. 2018. Generative hope in the postapocalyptic present. *Cultural Anthropology* 33(2). 202–212.

Louis, Renee Pualani, Jay T Johnson & Albertus Hadi Pramono. 2012. Introduction. *Indigenous cartographies and counter-mapping* 47(2). 77–79. (https://www.utpjournals.press/doi/abs/10.3138/carto.47.2.77)

Meggitt, MJ. 1972. Understanding Australian Aboriginal society: Kinship systems or cultural categories? In Priscilla Reining (ed.), *Kinship studies in the Morgan Centennial Year*, 64–87. Washington: The Anthropological Society of Washington.

Michaels, Eric. 1986. *The Aboriginal invention of television in Central Australia 1982–1986* (Institute Report Series). Canberra: Australian Institute of Aboriginal Studies.

Morgan, Rebecca & Helen Wilmot. 2010. Written proof: The appropriation of genealogical records in contemporary Arrernte society. *Land, Rights, Laws: Issues of Native Title* 4(5). (https://www.nintione.com.au/?p=3276)

Morton, Steve, Mandy Martin, Kim Mahood & John Carty. 2013. *Desert lake: Art, science and stories from Paruku.* Canberra: CSIRO Publishing.

Munn, Nancy. 1973. *Warlbiri iconography: Graphic representation and cultural symbolism in a Central Australian society.* Chicago: University of Chicago Press.

Munn, Nancy. 1996. Excluded spaces: The figure in the Australian Aboriginal landscape. *Critical Inquiry* 22(3). 446–465.

Myers, Fred. 1986. *Pintupi country, Pintupi self: Sentiment, place, and politics among Western Desert Aborigines.* Washington, DC: Smithsonian Institution Press.

Myers, Fred. 2000. Ways of placemaking. In Howard Morphy & Katherine Flynt (eds.), *Culture, landscape, and the environment,* 72–110. Oxford: Oxford University Press.

Myers, Fred. 2013. Emplacement and displacement: Perceiving the landscape through Aboriginal Australian acrylic painting. *Ethnos* 78(4). 435–463.

Nadasdy, Paul. 2017. Imposing territoriality: First Nation land claims and the transformation of human environment relations in the Yukon. In Stephen Bocking & Brad Martin (eds.), *Ice blink: Navigating northern environmental history,* 333–376. Calgary: University of Calgary Press.

Nash, David. 1998. Notes towards a draft ethnocartographic primer (for Central Australia). Unpublished manuscript. Canberra.

Nash, David. 2010. *An atlas of Indigenous country in central Australia?* Abstract. (http://www.anu.edu.au/linguistics/nash/abstracts/ICIPN2010-Nash-abstract.pdf) (Accessed 20 October 2019.)

Neale, Margo. 2017. The third archive and artist as archivist. In Darren Jorgensen & Ian McLean (eds.), *Indigenous archives: The making and unmaking of Aboriginal art,* 269–294. Perth: UWA Publishing.

Northern Territory v Griffiths et al. [2019] HCA 19. (Judgment of the High Court of Australia).

O'Shannessy, Carmel. 2012. *Report on children's Warlpiri in Willowra, NT.* University of Michigan. (https://www.youtube.com/watch?v=9RQi1xrg8lw) (Accessed 19 October 2019.)

Palmer, Mark. 2012. Indigenous cartographies and counter-mapping: Theorizing indigital geographic information networks. *Cartographica* 47(2). 80–91.

Peluso, Nancy. 1995. Whose woods are these? Counter-mapping forest territories in Kalimantan, Indonesia. *Antipode* 4. 383–406.

Peterson, Nicolas, Patrick McConvell, Stephen Wild & Rod Hagen. 1978. *A claim to areas of traditional land by the Warlpiri and Kartangarurru-Kurintji.* Alice Springs: Central Land Council.

Peterson, Nicolas. 2017. Is there a role for anthropology in cultural reproduction? Maps, mining, and the 'cultural future' in Central Australia. In Françoise Dussart & Sylvie Poirier (eds.), *Entangled territorialities: Negotiating Indigenous lands in Australia and Canada,* 235–252. Toronto: University of Toronto Press.

Povinelli, Elizabeth A. 1993. *Labor's lot: The power, history, and culture of Aboriginal action.* Chicago: University of Chicago Press.

Roth, Robin. 2009. The challenges of mapping complex indigenous spatiality: From abstract space to dwelling space. *Cultural Geographies* 16(2). 207–227.

Rumsey, Alan. 1993. Language and territoriality in Aboriginal Australia. In Michael Walsh & Colin Yallop (eds.), *Language and culture in Aboriginal Australia,* 191–206. Canberra: Aboriginal Studies Press.

Ryan, Simon. 1996. *The cartographic eye: How explorers saw Australia.* Cambridge: Cambridge University Press.

Sandall, R. 1977 [1967]. *A Walbiri fire ceremony, Ngatjakula* (motion picture). Canberra: Australian Institute of Aboriginal Studies.

Sletto, Bjørn Ingmunn. 2009. "We drew what we imagined": Participatory mapping, performance, and the arts of landscape making. *Current Anthropology* 50(4). 443–476.

Sutton, Peter. 1998a. Aboriginal maps and plans. In David Woodward & G Malcolm Lewis (eds.), *The history of cartography, vol. 2, book 3: Cartography in the traditional African, American, Arctic, Australian, and Pacific societies*, 387–416. Chicago: University of Chicago Press.

Sutton, Peter. 1998b. Icons of country: Topographic representations in classical Aboriginal traditions. In David Woodward & G Malcolm Lewis (eds.), *The history of cartography, vol. 2, book 3: Cartography in the traditional African, American, Arctic, Australian, and Pacific societies*, 353–386. Chicago: University of Chicago Press.

Sutton, Peter. 2003. *Native title in Australia: An ethnographic perspective.* Cambridge: Cambridge University Press.

Sutton, Peter. 2019. *The mapping of Aboriginal language countries.* (Paper presented in Session 7, Re-placing language and place, language keepers conference, National Library of Australia, 10 February 2019.) (https://youtu.be/-obX7huNnWk?t=2298) (Accessed 19 October 2019.)

Vaarzon-Morel, Petronella (ed. and compiler). 1995. *Warlpiri women's voices: Our lives our history.* Alice Springs: IAD Press.

Vaarzon-Morel, Petronella. 2016. Continuity and change in Warlpiri practices of marking the landscape. In William A Lovis & Robert Whallon (eds.), *Marking the land: Hunter-gatherer creation of meaning in their environment*, 201–230. New York & London: Routledge/Taylor and Francis.

Vaarzon-Morel, Petronella & Jim Wafer. 2017. 'Bilingual time at Willowra': The beginnings of a community-initiated program, 1976–1977. In Brian Clive Devlin, Samantha Disbray & Nancy Regine Friedman Devlin (eds.), *History of bilingual education in the Northern Territory: People, programs and policies*, 35–48. Singapore: Springer Publishing.

Vaarzon-Morel, Petronella. (in press). Sutton's model of underlying and proximate customary title and the Lander Warlpiri region. In Julie D Finlayson & Frances Morphy (eds.), *Ethnographer and contrarian: Biographical and anthropological essays in honour of Peter Sutton.* Adelaide: Wakefield Press.

Wafer, Jim & Petronella Wafer. 1980. *The Lander Warlpiri-Anmatjirra land claim to Willowra pastoral lease.* Alice Springs: Central Land Council.

Wafer, Jim & Petronella Wafer. 1983. *The Mount Barkly land claim.* Alice Springs: Central Land Council.

Wafer, Jim. 2017. Introduction: Everything got a song. In Jim Wafer & Myfany Turpin (eds.), *Recirculating songs: Revitalising the singing practices of Indigenous Australia*, 1–42. Hamilton: Hunter Press and Asia-Pacific Linguistics, ANU.

Wainwright, Joel & Joe Bryan. 2009. Cartography, territory, property: Postcolonial reflections on indigenous countermapping in Nicaragua and Belize. *Cultural Geographies* 16. 153–178.

Walsh, Fiona & Paul Mitchell (eds.). 2002. *Planning for Country: Cross-cultural approaches to decision-making on Aboriginal lands.* Alice Springs: Jukurrpa Books, IAD Press.

Weiner, James F & Katie Glaskin. 2007. Customary land tenure & registration in Australia and Papua New Guinea: Anthropological perspectives. In James F Weiner & Katie

Glaskin (eds.), *Customary land tenure & registration in Australia and Papua New Guinea: Anthropological perspectives* (Asia-Pacific Environment Monographs 3), 1–14. Canberra: ANU Press.

Wilkins, David P. 2002. The concept of place among the Arrernte. In Luise Hercus, Flavia Hodges & Jane Simpson (eds.), *The land is a map: Placenames of Indigenous origin in Australia,* 24–4. Canberra: Pandanus Books in association with Pacific Linguistics.

Zigon, Jarrett. 2018. *Disappointment: Toward a critical hermeneutics of worldbuilding.* New York: Fordham University Press.

Language Documentation & Conservation Special Publication No. 18
Archival returns: Central Australia and beyond
ed. by Linda Barwick, Jennifer Green & Petronella Vaarzon-Morel, pp. 139–151
http://nflrc.hawaii.edu/ldc/sp18
http://hdl.handle.net/10125/24881

7

(Re)turning research into pedagogical practice: A case study of translational language research in Warlpiri

Carmel O'Shannessy
Australian National University

Samantha Disbray
The University of Queensland

Barbara Martin
Yuendumu School

Gretel Macdonald
Yuendumu School

Abstract

Speech corpora created primarily for linguistic research are not often easily repurposed for practical use by the communities who participated in the research. This chapter describes a process whereby methods and materials collected for language documentation research have been returned to speakers in communities; this involves the implementation of professional development activities for Warlpiri educators in bilingual education programs. Documentation of children's speech took place in four Warlpiri communities in 2010. To make the research results available to educators in Warlpiri communities in an easily accessible way, the researcher produced short videos showing analyses of the children's speech. These online videos, along with audio recordings and written transcripts of the children's speech, were utilised by a team of linguists and educators at professional development workshops in the Northern Territory Department of Education. Educators actively worked with the materials, discussed issues relating to children's oral language development, and identified potential pedagogical practices. Through this process the materials were returned to the Warlpiri community and utilised in an active cycle of locally focused professional learning activities.

Keywords: Warlpiri, bilingual education, oral language, curriculum, children

Introduction[1]

Responsible linguistic research practice demands collaboration between communities and researchers (Czaykowska-Higgins 2009: 59; Dobrin & Schwarz 2016). Collaboration is manifested in a wide range of ways (Ahlers 2009; Benedicto et al. 2007), such as decision-making about research; training fieldworkers (Florey 2008); developing adult education programs (Little, Wysote, McClay & Coon 2015; Miyashita & Chatsis 2013); returning language documentation materials and the creation of community archives (Linn 2014); and the return of research findings in accessible forms for the creation of language resources. Documentation of children's language in endangered language contexts is important for understanding language maintenance and change, as the speech of children and young people is an indicator of ethnolinguistic vitality. Additionally, children may play a role in language innovation and shift, if change is occurring. However, the relationship between the data collected, research outputs, and ways to respond practically to community needs and wants might not be immediately clear.

This chapter describes a process whereby methods and materials from Warlpiri child language documentation research have been returned to speakers in communities and become the cornerstone of professional development activities for educators in bilingual education programs over several years. The education activities were enabled through a collaboration of Warlpiri and non-Warlpiri school-based educators and curriculum support staff.

The chapter sets out the context of the research, how research findings were communicated to community members through the creation of accessible audiovisual reports, and the collaborative process of repurposing the reports and transcripts of children's speech for professional learning cycles for Warlpiri educators, with a focus on the teaching and learning of oral language. The processes are more than a return of the materials. They involve interacting with the materials in cycles that enrich teachers' understandings of language structures, linguistic terminology, analysis of oral texts, identification of learning needs, and development of teaching activities. The teachers then moved beyond interacting with the materials provided, to creating their own recordings of children's speech and analysing those. In doing this, they transformed their teaching practices on their own terms. The repurposing of methods and materials was an innovative undertaking, drawing on specific speech corpora and collaborations of local educators, curriculum support staff, and researchers.

We begin by introducing the Warlpiri communities and their bilingual education programs, then detail the language data and its return in the form of audiovisual reports, audio recordings, and transcripts. We then explain the process of using these as a basis for a professional learning program, and the cycles of learning that have taken place over four years.

1   Our thanks to all Warlpiri educators, Warlpiri community members, and non-Warlpiri Northern Territory Department of Education staff who have collaborated in the professional learning project described in this chapter. Thanks also to the children, families, and Northern Territory Department of Education staff who were involved in the data collection that formed the basis for the professional learning project. Field research on the project was carried out as part of and within Ethical Research Approval by the Cooperative Research Centre for the project 'Cooperative Research Centre for Remote Economic Participation, Remote Education Systems, Warlpiri Triangle site' 2012–2016.

We conclude with a discussion of the ongoing and enduring research and practice relationship and collaboration that resulted, of the contribution such a collaboration can make to community and school-based language maintenance efforts, and the potential to use similar data in other language contexts.

Background to the Warlpiri communities and Warlpiri Bilingual Education Programs

Warlpiri–English bilingual programs operate in four remote Warlpiri communities in the Northern Territory (NT) (see Figure 1), forming the education- and language-related Warlpiri Triangle region. The populations of the four communities range from approximately 200–300 (Nyirrpi and Willowra) to 600–700 (Lajamanu and Yuendumu). The Warlpiri travel frequently between communities and are in constant communication with each other. Although Warlpiri is the main language spoken in the communities, they are multilingual environments. Other traditional Australian languages are spoken in the communities by relatives, friends, and visitors, and most people speak varieties of English. There is some evidence of English

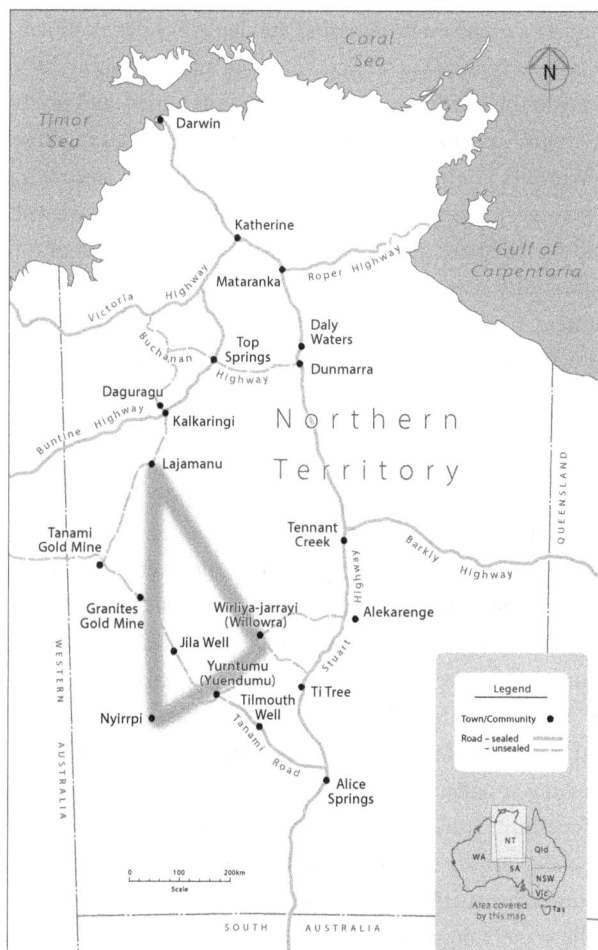

Figure 1. Map of Warlpiri Triangle region. Created by Brenda Thornley, 2019

influence on Warlpiri (Bavin & Shopen 1985; O'Shannessy 2012), and in Lajamanu community, young people speak a new mixed language, Light Warlpiri (O'Shannessy 2006, 2008, 2013, 2016), and also learn Warlpiri.

The Warlpiri schools' bilingual education programs are part of the Northern Territory Bilingual Education Program that began in the 1970s (Devlin, Disbray, & Friedman Devlin 2017), to enable Aboriginal children in remote communities to have "their primary education in Aboriginal languages" (Department of Education 1973: 1). The programs in the Warlpiri schools were among the first bilingual programs (Disbray 2014), with the program at Yuendumu beginning in 1975 (Ross & Baarda 2017). Community demand for bilingual education led to the development of programs at Willowra in 1976 (Vaarzon-Morel & Wafer 2017) and Lajamanu in 1981 (Nicholls 1998). The outstation schools established in the mid to late 1980s at Waylilinypa and Nyirrpi (later to become a community school) also ran Warlpiri programs. Since then, the political will to support the program has varied, but Warlpiri educators and community members have remained committed to teaching their language and culture in the schools, and the programs continue.

A challenge is that in the hustle and bustle of everyday planning and teaching in schools, Warlpiri educators are rarely able to take the time to develop their skills in the linguistic analysis of Warlpiri, or to set up the logistics involved in assessing oral language development. Most often, in contexts such as this one, the emphasis is on first language and English literacy, and mathematics. Development of oracy in the children's first language is assumed, and rarely evaluated carefully. Opportunities for the professional development of Warlpiri teachers are few, but some are provided by the annual Warlpiri Triangle and quarterly *Jinta-jarrimi* ('Becoming one') workshops. These workshops involve personnel from all the Warlpiri schools as well as community members, including elders. They are a key and enduring part of the program. At each workshop, educators and community members share the progress of their program, exchange teaching strategies and resources, plan together, and undertake professional learning. The current project, the development and delivery of professional learning on children's oral language development, took place in the context of these workshops.

Recording for research

The language documentation data used in the project was gathered by the first author, a researcher and former teacher-linguist at a Warlpiri school in one community, Lajamanu. She began documenting children's language in Lajamanu in 2002 (O'Shannessy 2005, 2008, 2013). Here, although a new variety of Warlpiri, Light Warlpiri, has evolved, the children still learn traditional Warlpiri. Having seen a dramatic change in children's language in one Warlpiri community, O'Shannessy was interested to know how Warlpiri children in the other communities were speaking. There are few cross-sectional studies of children's speech in Aboriginal communities, yet a snapshot of how children are speaking at one point in time can be a good reference for the community, especially teachers, and for future studies. A similar kind of project on a smaller scale had been undertaken earlier in the Warlpiri schools as part of the bilingual education program, and Warlpiri teachers had found it instructive to read through transcripts of children's stories and identify learning needs. The project described here built on the earlier method, in much greater detail and with more support for the teachers, several years later.

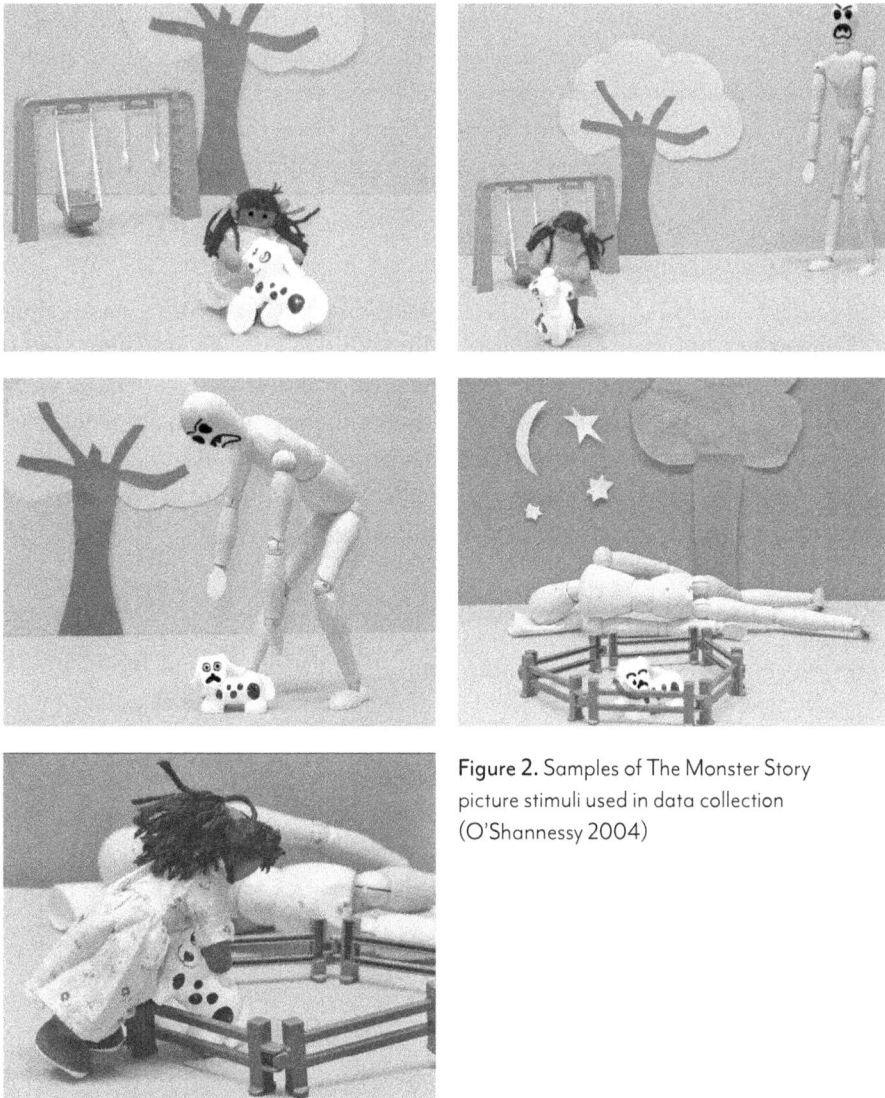

Figure 2. Samples of The Monster Story picture stimuli used in data collection (O'Shannessy 2004)

In 2010, 71 children aged 5–14 years, drawn from across the four Warlpiri communities, were recorded telling stories based on visual stimuli. Specifically, 15 children from Lajamanu, 14 from Willowra, 18 from Nyirrpi, and 24 from Yuendumu were recorded.

The aim was to enable a thorough picture of the children's language skills at that point in time. In the study, children and adults individually told a series of short narratives based on wordless picture books that had been created specifically for the documentation of morphosyntactic structures in varieties of Warlpiri (O'Shannessy 2004). In particular, the stories aimed to elicit overt subjects of transitive verbs during the telling of the stories, because one focus of the study was to understand how children made use of ergative case-marking (suffixes on overt subjects of transitive verbs) and word order in their speech. The question arose because of contact with English, which uses only word order to indicate grammatical relations, where Warlpiri uses ergative-absolutive case-marking. Recordings of spontaneous interactions would probably not have yielded enough tokens of overt transitive subjects, because cross-linguistically subjects of transitive clauses are more likely to occur as pronouns, or to be elided in null-subject languages, than to occur as lexical nouns and lexical noun phrases, i.e. lexical nouns with other features such as determiners or descriptive material (Du Bois 2003). In Warlpiri, transitive and intransitive subjects can be elided, so this method of creating contexts in which to produce them in a naturalistic manner was necessary, and proved to be effective.

The advantage of this method is that the speakers tell the stories freely in their own words, but opportunities to produce the target structures are optimised, and the structures of the stories can be compared across speakers, enabling a profile of speech across age groups in the communities. Since the pictures depict short narratives, many other structures and a variety of vocabulary are elicited at the same time. The children were recorded as they told the stories based on the picture books. The books have themes and settings familiar to the children, such as caring for sick people, going out hunting, and encounters with monsters. The illustrations are colourful and engaging, and children often told dramatic, rich, and exciting stories, using a range of expressive discourse features.

Returning the research findings

There were three stages in the return of the materials to the communities. First, at the time of data collection, each child's set of stories was copied to CD and the CDs distributed to the children to listen to at home (in more recent iterations of the method, the recordings are given to families on USB drives, as computers and other technology such as PlayStations and Xboxes have become more common than CD players). The families' responses to this were very positive, as it was a way of celebrating the children's speech. Schools are very focused on children's development of literacy, English, and mathematics in education, and on the quest for improvement of these skills. In this project, it was refreshing for the children, families, and educators to have their Warlpiri speaking skills celebrated.

The second stage was that several children's transcripts along with the picture stimuli were made into mini-movies (2–3 minutes long) and distributed to each school, and were viewed during the Warlpiri Triangle meetings in evening sharing sessions. At this point there was no structure to the viewing and the mini-movies were not presented in the main part of the meetings.

The third stage is the most important and is the focus of this chapter. In return for giving permission to the researcher to record children in school time, the Northern Territory Department of Education (NT DoE) asked for a report about the children's language. During the recording sessions, Warlpiri and non-Warlpiri teachers in each school expressed interest in the findings of the study. O'Shannessy opted to produce video reports instead of a traditional written report, because she wanted to express the findings in a way that made sense to, and was accessible to, educators in Warlpiri schools. It also meant that the reports were accessible to others in the NT Department of Education who do not have a background in linguistics. Few people would be likely to read a written report, but an accessible online resource might reach more people, and be more useful to those it reached. As the researcher had a strong existing relationship with the educators and solid experience with the school programs, she was able to contribute to, and work collaboratively with, the school and curriculum staff in their efforts to turn a resource developed from research into a practical school resource.

Each approximately 12-minute video includes a voice-over explaining grammatical patterns in Warlpiri, which are illustrated by examples from children's speech, using the children's anonymised voices. There are four videos in the same format, but each one has excerpts from the speech of children in one community, making it, to an extent, community-specific. The voice-over explains some features of Warlpiri structure, using both plain English and linguistic terminology, and gives examples from the children's speech, demonstrating the children's knowledge and use of these structures. Examples include complex Warlpiri verbs, grammatical structures of nouns and verbs, word order, and examples of code-switching and borrowing. This is illustrated in the following extract of the voice-over from a video report.

> One way that Warlpiri differs from English is in showing who is doing an action to someone or something else. In Warlpiri there's an ending on the word that shows who or what is doing an action, called the ergative ending. If someone says "*Karnta-wita-ngku ka mani maliki*" [extract of child's voice], we know that the woman did the action. In the children's Warlpiri, they do use the ergative ending most of the time. This is great, because it's an important Warlpiri element.

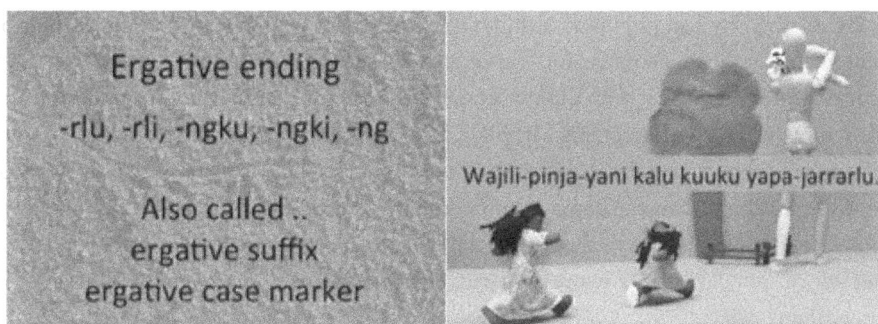

Figure 3. Two screenshots from Nyirrpi Children's Warlpiri Report 2012 (https://www.youtube.com/watch?v=FGYSCXmrpys)

The video reports were made available on YouTube, with the permission of the Warlpiri educators.[2]

Along with the videos, the audio recordings and transcripts of the stories were sent to each school and to the NT DoE curriculum support officer (the second author, then employed as regional linguist). She found that the videos were not widely viewed at that time but had the potential to be a useful resource.[3] For this to happen, it seemed that a context for really engaging

---

2   Nyirrpi Children's Warlpiri Report 2012 (https://www.youtube.com/watch?v=FGYSCXmrpys); Yuendumu Children's Warlpiri Report 2012 (https://www.youtube.com/watch?v=lh0dtH1Ugws); Willowra Children's Warlpiri Report 2102 (https://www.youtube.com/watch?v=9RQi1xrg8lw); Lajamanu Children's Warlpiri Report 2012 (https://www.youtube.com/watch?v=7nVry7Q_QG8).

3   By the time of writing, however, the videos have had between 300 and 1300 views.

with the reports had to be created. A proposal was made to the Warlpiri educators that the focus of the 2012 workshops might be oral language teaching and learning, incorporating the children's language video reports. The Warlpiri teachers and assistant teachers were keen to take this up. Between 2012 and 2016 educators took part in five professional learning cycles focused on oral language teaching and learning, and the video reports and transcripts provided the basis for these.

Turning research findings into professional learning opportunities for teachers

Five multi-day workshops with 18–30 school staff were facilitated by the second, third, and, later, the fourth author, all NT DoE personnel at the time. The curriculum officer communicated with the researcher, who regularly visits the communities and gave ongoing advice and support to curriculum and school staff. Workshop methods included cycles of watching the video reports, identifying key points, analysing transcripts, and planning learning activities for classes.

Each video covered the same grammatical structures, customised for each community, so the Warlpiri and non-Warlpiri educators were able to access the elements they needed most. For instance, Warlpiri educators already know Warlpiri, so the examples were meaningful to them. By relating English linguistic terminology to familiar language structures of their own first language, they had a context for learning the linguistic terms, e.g. verb, ergative, suffix. The non-Warlpiri educators, who did not know Warlpiri, were able to learn something about the structures of Warlpiri, explained in plain English, as well as the linguistic terminology. For instance, as shown above, the commentary in the video reports drew attention to endings on nouns in Warlpiri, their purposes, and the children's production of them. In the following example from a child's story, shown in the video report, there is the actor or ergative marker *-ngku*, an allative affix expressing movement towards something *-kurra,* plus a suffix meaning 'then' *-lku.*

Ngula	*kurdu-ngku*	drive-*manu*	*turaki*	*ngurra-kurra-lku.*
ANAPH	child-ERG	drive-CAUS	truck	home-ALL-then

'Then the child drove the truck home.'[4]

Learning the linguistic terms is important not only to provide a learning bridge between community members and the research, but also to enrich teachers' skills and knowledge. Both understanding and using linguistic terminology are crucial to a teacher's ability to make use of curriculum and assessment documents. Few professional learning opportunities address this. The Warlpiri child language videos provided information about children's language locally, as well as oral language development, language description, and teaching and monitoring more broadly.

---

4   Abbreviations: ALL 'allative'; ANAPH 'anaphoric'; CAUS 'causative'; ERG 'ergative'.

In the professional learning cycle, workshop participants identified what they found important from the reports. They noted, for instance, that children used a range of vocabulary, including different verb types, and that there was some English appearing in their verbs. The specific English words that appeared are actually widespread in adult colloquial speech, but seeing them in the video reports and transcripts brought them to the teachers' attention. After watching the reports, educators viewed a selection of the transcripts of children's speech from their respective communities. They were able to work on stories told by children in their own community, making the task more immediately relevant. They examined the transcripts and identified features that demonstrated the children's knowledge of Warlpiri and any learning needs that appeared. They identified features such as discourse markers and strategies, and pronunciation features found in colloquial speech styles. The amount of detail and speaker engagement in the children's stories varied, with some being rich in detail and excitement, and others less so.

These analysis sessions increased Indigenous and non-Indigenous teachers' linguistic knowledge and provided an intensive opportunity to better understand children's oral language development from a strengths-based perspective. Over the course of the workshops, the teachers' observations moved from noticing 'errors', or features that are more colloquial and not part of documented classic Warlpiri speech, to also noticing what the students did know. It is important to identify the students' language strengths, as well as needs, to evaluate their progress fairly and plan ways to build on the strengths. The video reports were developed to celebrate children's abilities, and so, in the workshops, it was easy to draw attention to what they revealed children can do, and do well. Workshop participants identified the 'best thing' about the workshops as "seeing that kids can speak strong Warlpiri" and "the videos [were] about children talking. It's good for kids to learn more Warlpiri and to share ideas and it's good to see work from kids" (Northern Territory Department of Education 2012: 59).

In a final step in the cycle, teachers mapped their observations about children's speech production to their teaching program, drawing on curriculum documents and establishing ways to teach and monitor oral language development.

The professional learning cycle became:

1. View video;
2. Identify key points and relevant linguistic terminology;
3. Analyse children's transcripts; and
4. Plan and implement teaching activities and monitoring methods.

The cycle was repeated in each workshop, tailored each time according to the feedback from educators on what would be helpful. Challenges were noted. In particular, the lack of follow-up or opportunity for Warlpiri educators to apply newly acquired knowledge back in schools was a barrier. To some extent, this was countered by the ongoing attention to oral language teaching and learning, which allowed teachers to refresh and take opportunities when they were available at their school.

Part of the professional learning cycle was to develop skills for critical listening. Repetition of the cycle allowed the teachers to develop these skills, as they revisited the texts and analysed them more deeply. Over time, more attention was paid to the kinds of language knowledge the students demonstrated, and the types of teaching and learning content that could follow. With this growing skill, the content was increasingly aligned to the relevant learning outcomes in the Northern Territory Curriculum Framework for Indigenous Languages and Cultures (NTCF ILC).[5]

The impacts of the professional learning cycles using the repurposed child language research data emerged incrementally but strongly. The third author and Warlpiri facilitator in the workshops explained that analysing the materials and transferring the analyses into practical teaching and learning strategies helped her to understand the children's oral language development better. Key components for her were the repetition of the cycle in consecutive workshops, and the analysis of children's transcripts. The professional learning cycles, learnings, and resultant planning were written up in the workshop reports, which are published as Northern Territory Department of Education documents (see, for example, Northern Territory Department of Education 2016; Northern Territory Department of Education 2017).

By the final cycle, the second author (Disbray) was no longer employed by the NT DoE, and was carrying out research. One of her research tasks was to reflect critically with O'Shannessy on the professional learning cycles to date, thus beginning a further research cycle. Disbray remained involved with the Warlpiri Triangle workshops, and Warlpiri educator Barbara Martin (third author) and newly arrived Yuendumu School linguist Gretel Macdonald (fourth author) collaborated to reflect on the professional learning to date, and to extend it. In this way, the research and practice interplay was enduring and ever emergent.

Under the stewardship of Martin and Macdonald, the final sessions focused on building familiarity with the characterisation of oral language structures and features in the NTCF ILC (Northern Territory Department of Education and Training 2002) in order to support assessment of, and reporting on, oral language. This aspect of the project provided a bridge between the child language research and the education infrastructure teachers and assistant teachers use. The sessions required familiarity with linguistic vocabulary and linguistic concepts, an awareness of which had been growing over prior sessions. In a sense, Warlpiri educators participating in the Warlpiri Triangle and *Jinta-jarrimi* 'Becoming one' workshops had been 'getting into the habit' of talking about oral language and were now in a position to apply this knowledge. They took a bottom-up approach, first analysing representative samples of student speech from different year levels and then drawing on teacher-as-native-speaker intuitions to identify whether this student was 'low', 'medium', or 'high' in their oral language proficiency. Finally they would make the connection between Warlpiri student speech samples and the language structures and features that characterised the relevant level for that year group in the NTCF ILC. In taking this approach, they showed their capacity to undertake the monitoring and assessment processes required by the NT DoE. This is important, as it positions Warlpiri language as a rigorously taught subject in the education system.

---

5   A revised Northern Territory Indigenous Languages and Cultures Curriculum is replacing the NTCF ILC. The revised curriculum has been drafted and was trialled in schools across the Northern Territory in 2018.

Conclusion

In this chapter we have described the process of repurposing a spoken corpus of child language data and a collaboration to make reporting back on research meaningful and useful to a community, well beyond the original research. We describe an enduring research and practice relationship, which sought out opportunities to share specific and relevant research knowledge with community members. This moved beyond observations about the language of individual children or children broadly in the community: with the involvement of education department staff, this collaboration sought to upskill educators, Warlpiri and non-Warlpiri, about Warlpiri child language development and metalanguage, and to apply this knowledge in the task of teaching and monitoring oral language as a core and valid learning area in school.

Warlpiri educators have expressed concern about potential language shift in their communities. In these contexts of language endangerment, professional learning which draws on accessible – e.g. multimodal, plain English, and locally relevant resources such as the videos – and clear processes is valuable because it can facilitate critical conversations at the community level about language shift. The video reports and the transcripts allowed educators to look closely at what individual children were actually saying, rather than relying on memory or intuition, and to celebrate their language skills. Ultimately, these types of resources have the potential to motivate action on language maintenance, based on observable evidence and skilled, careful reflection. These factors – an evidence base, increasing teacher expertise, and its application to a centralised curriculum – have in addition an important bearing on school-based language maintenance efforts. They give Warlpiri educators the tools to talk back to the system, strengthening their calls for greater support for Warlpiri teaching and learning. Thus, through this collaboration, Warlpiri educators and support staff increased their capacity to transform their teaching, as well as to advocate for pursuing Warlpiri teaching and learning on their own terms.

The approach taken in this collaboration, using child language recordings, can be used in other settings. In language revitalisation settings, for instance, such data could be similarly used to look at heritage language items or features children use in code-alternations, as a basis for planning teaching and learning. What is critical to success is the combined and varied skills of the team and the willingness to explore the potential of research data for community uses and to find ways to actualise this potential over time.

References

Ahlers, Jocelyn. 2009. The many meanings of collaboration: Fieldwork with the Elem Pomo. *Language & Communication* 29. 230–243.

Bavin, Edith & Tim Shopen. 1985. Warlpiri and English: Languages in contact. In Michael Clyne (ed.), *Australia, meeting place of languages*, vol. C-92, 81–94. Canberra: Pacific Linguistics.

Benedicto, Elena, Demetrio Antolín, Modesta Dolores, Cristina Feliciano, Gloria Fendly, Tomasa Gómez, Baudilio Miguel & Salomón Elizabeth. 2007. A model of participatory action research: The Mayangna linguists team of Nicaragua. In Maya Khemlani David, Nicholas Ostler & Caesar Dealwis (eds.), *Proceedings of FEL [Foundation for Endangered Languages] XI: Working together for endangered languages: Research challenges and social impacts*, 29–35. Bath: Foundation for Endangered Language.

Czaykowska-Higgins, Ewa. 2009. Research models, community engagement, and linguistic fieldwork: Reflections on working within Canadian Indigenous communities. *Language Documentation & Conservation* 3(1). 15–50. (http://hdl.handle.net/10125/4423)

Department of Education. 1973. *Progress report on the bilingual program in schools in the Northern Territory*. Darwin: Department of Education.

Devlin, Brian, Samantha Disbray & Nancy Friedman Devlin (eds.). 2017. *History of bilingual education in the Northern Territory: People, programs and policies*. Singapore: Springer Publishing.

Disbray, Samantha. 2014. Evaluating bilingual education in Warlpiri schools. In Rob Pensalfini, Myfany Turpin & D Guillemin (eds.), *Language description informed by theory*, 25–46. Amsterdam: John Benjamins.

Dobrin, Lise & Saul Schwarz. 2016. Collaboration or participant observation? Rethinking models of 'linguistic social work'. *Language Documentation & Conservation* 10. 253–277.

Du Bois, John. 2003. Argument structure: Grammar in use. In John W Du Bois, Lorraine E Kumpf & William J Ashby (eds.), *Preferred argument structure: Grammar as architecture for function*, 11–60. Amsterdam/New York: John Benjamins.

Florey, Margaret. 2008. Language activism and the 'new linguistics': Expanding opportunities for documenting endangered languages in Indonesia. In Peter K Austin (ed.), *Language Documentation and Description*, vol. 5, 120–135. London: EL Publishing.

Linn, Mary. 2014. Living archives: A community-based language archive model. In David Nathan & Peter K Austin (eds.), *Language Documentation and Description*, vol. 12, 53–67. London: EL Publishing.

Little, Carol-Rose, Travis Wysote, Elise McClay & Jessica Coon. 2015. Language research and revitalization through a community-university partnership: The Mi'gmaq research partnership. *Language Documentation & Conservation* 9. 292–306. (http://hdl.handle.net/10125/24644)

Miyashita, Mizuki & Annabelle Chatsis. 2013. Collaborative development of Blackfoot language courses. *Language Documentation & Conservation* 7. 302–330. (http://hdl.handle.net/10125/4597)

Nicholls, Christine. 1998. Serious business: Warlpiri aspirations, Indigenous land rights and the TESL curriculum. In Gary Partington (ed.), *Perspectives on Aboriginal and Torres Strait Islander education*, 294–308. South Melbourne, Victoria: Cengage.

Northern Territory Department of Education. 1990. *1990 Report from specialist staff in bilingual schools in the Northern Territory*. Darwin: Northern Territory Department of Education.

Northern Territory Department of Education. 2012. *Warlpiri Triangle report 2012* (Lajamanu School). Alice Springs: Northern Territory Government.

Northern Territory Department of Education and Training. 2002. *Northern Territory Curriculum Framework: Indigenous language and culture.* Darwin: Northern Territory Government.

O'Shannessy, Carmel. 2004. *The monster stories: A set of picture books to elicit overt transitive subjects in oral texts* (Unpublished series). Nijmegen, The Netherlands: Max Planck Institute for Psycholinguistics.

O'Shannessy, Carmel. 2005. Light Warlpiri: A new language. *Australian Journal of Linguistics* 25(1). 31–57.

O'Shannessy, Carmel. 2006. *Language contact and children's bilingual acquisition: Learning a mixed language and Warlpiri in northern Australia.* Sydney: University of Sydney. (PhD Thesis.)

O'Shannessy, Carmel. 2008. Children's production of their heritage language and a new mixed language. In Jane Simpson & Gillian Wigglesworth (eds.), *Children's language and multilingualism*, 261–282. London: Continuum.

O'Shannessy, Carmel. 2012. The role of code-switched input to children in the origin of a new mixed language. *Linguistics* 50(2). 305–340.

O'Shannessy, Carmel. 2013. What younger speakers have to teach us: A case study of Light Warlpiri speakers. (Paper presented at the 3rd International Conference on Language Documentation and Conservation [ICLDC], Hawaii.)

O'Shannessy, Carmel. 2016. Distributions of case allomorphy by multilingual children speaking Warlpiri and Light Warlpiri. *Linguistic Variation* 16(1). 68–102.

Ross, Tess & Wendy Baarda. 2017. Starting out at Yuendumu School – Teaching in our own language. In Brian Devlin, Samantha Disbray & Nancy Friedman Devlin (eds.), *History of bilingual education in the Northern Territory: People, programs and policies*, 247–257. Singapore: Springer Publishing.

Vaarzon-Morel, Petronella & Jim Wafer. 2017. 'Bilingual time' at Willowra: The beginnings of a community-initiated program, 1976–1977. In Brian Devlin, Samantha Disbray & Nancy Friedman Devlin (eds.), *History of bilingual education in the Northern Territory: People, programs and policies*, 35–48. Singapore: Springer Publishing.

8

Language Documentation & Conservation Special Publication No. 18
Archival returns: Central Australia and beyond
ed. by Linda Barwick, Jennifer Green & Petronella Vaarzon-Morel, pp. 153–172
http://nflrc.hawaii.edu/ldc/sp18
http://hdl.handle.net/10125/24882

"The songline is alive in Mukurtu": Return, reuse, and respect

Kimberly Christen
Washington State University

Abstract

This chapter examines the return, reuse, and repositioning of archival materials within Indigenous communities and specifically within the Warumungu Aboriginal community in Central Australia. Over the last 20 years there has been an uptake in collecting institutions and scholars returning cultural, linguistic, and historical material to Indigenous communities in digital formats. These practices of digital return have been spurred by decolonisation and reconciliation movements globally, and at the same time catalysed by new technologies that allow for surrogates to be returned and concurrently reinvented, reused, and reimagined in community, kin-based, and place-based social and cultural networks. Examining the creation, use, and ongoing development of Mukurtu CMS, this article focuses on the implications for digital return as a type of repatriation that promotes decolonising strategies and reparative frameworks for engagement.

Keywords: digital return, archival studies, repatriation, digital archives, Warumungu

Opening[1]

In May of 2017 I sat with several Warumungu and Warlmanpa women in the Cultural Resource Room at the Nyinkka Nyunyu Art and Culture Centre in Tennant Creek, Northern Territory (NT), Australia, listening over and over again to Milwayi and Mungamunga songs recorded by researchers over several decades. The women were from several family groups in the Barkly region, related through these songlines. The connections were known intimately by the women, and their responsibility for the songs, the country, the language, and their ancestors wove through those connections (Barwick et al. 2013: 198–203). After the deaths of several senior women and knowledge-holders for these songlines in 2011, this group of women embarked on a process to both repatriate recordings and associated materials related to the songlines and record new versions of the songs, body decorations, and dances that make up the bundle of knowledge surrounding the songlines. After the bulk of the material had been repatriated from scholars and archives, and the recordings the women had made with a professional filmmaker were completed, the focus turned to providing appropriate access to the digital corpus – now and in the future.

We were accessing and listening to the songs that day through the most recent version of the Mukurtu Wumpurrarni-kari Archive, a community resource and digital access platform that had been in use since 2007. Up to this point, however, the majority of the community material uploaded and circulating using Mukurtu had been photographs. Indeed, the catalyst for the platform's creation had been the repatriation of hundreds of photos from the Aboriginal Inland Mission (AIM). The reason for our meeting and listening session that May afternoon in 2017 was to begin a more in-depth conversation about the potential of using the newly updated Mukurtu CMS platform to provide access to the songs as well as the videos, photos, and documents that made up the newly repatriated and assembled collection. The women had had many discussions over the previous years of work to define the protocols for access and use through a more static hard drive, but the potential for more interactive usage and modes of sharing through Mukurtu prompted another set of discussions (K Webeck, pers. comm., 2017).

---

1   This article was written as part of my collaboration with the Warumungu community, who are the traditional
    owners, caretakers, and stewards for the country in and around the present-day town of Tennant Creek,
    in the Northern Territory of Australia. I pay my respects to Warumungu people past, present, and future
    and acknowledge their ongoing connections to and relationships with their country, kin, and ancestors
    and the continuing knowledge they hold for their country. I want to thank E Nelson Nappanangka, K Fitz
    Nappanangka, E Graham Nakkamarra, D Dawson Nangali, TR Nappanangka, Dianne Stokes Nampin,
    LG Namikili, Rose Graham Namikili, Patricia Frank Narrurlu, Ruby Frank Narrurlu, Michael Jones Jampin,
    and Jimmy Frank Juppurula for their time, patience, and willingness to share. Any omissions or mistakes are
    mine. Kim Webeck and Samantha Disbray have been fantastic collaborators, interlocutors, and dinner mates
    in and around Tennant Creek and I appreciate their willingness to work together on our many overlapping
    projects. My graduate assistant, Jesslyn Starnes, produced the references and formatted the article and
    so much more; her labour was central to this piece seeing the light of day. The ongoing development and
    support for Mukurtu CMS is provided by an amazing team of dedicated developers at the Center for Digital
    Scholarship and Curation led by Alex Merrill, Steve Taylor, and Michael Wynne. Finally I owe a debt of
    gratitude to my colleague and friend, Dr Jane Anderson, whose intellectual rigour, compassion, and depth of
    knowledge about how to enact acknowledgement is something I strive for daily.

Table 1: Brief timeline of Mukurtu's development and distribution

Release type	Year	Distribution	Core features/updates
Mukurtu alpha – MySQL server and PHP scripting	2007	Warumungu	Local protocol-based access; community commentary
Mukurtu beta – LAMP stack Linux Centos 5.4, Apache 2, MySQL and PHP	2009	3 Plateau tribes (USA)	Expanded metadata + Dublin core; audio/video comments
Mukurtu .5 Drupal 7.08	2011	6 Plateau tribes (USA)	Community records; expanded admin roles
Mukurtu 1.0 Drupal 7.22	2012	Australia, New Zealand, USA	Integrated sharing/ cultural protocols w/user roles; additional media; multipage documents
Mukurtu CMS 1.5 Drupal 7.24	2013	Australia, New Zealand, USA, Canada, Thailand 100+	External hosting options; Mukurtu mobile app; document viewer
Mukurtu CMS 2.0 Drupal 7.3	2015	Global 300+	Round-trip sync; TK Label customisation; SCALD media integration
Mukurtu CMS 2.1 Drupal 7.6	2018	Global 800+	Nested collections; dictionary; customisable front page

The discussions then centred on how access, use, reuse, and transmission might operate through the Mukurtu platform as one point of return. Initiated in 2005 from a community-driven conversation around the circulation of and access to Warumungu community-specific material previously held in national archives, libraries, and museums (Christen 2007, 2011, 2012), Mukurtu has grown into a free and open-source content management system and community digital access platform used by Indigenous communities around the world.

The impetus for Mukurtu's transformation from a one-off, locally hosted community platform in Tennant Creek to a flexible and customisable software package was the similar concerns that Indigenous communities worldwide have expressed regarding community-based protocols for the circulation, access, and use of cultural materials, traditional knowledge, and language.[2] It was fitting then that we were at Nyinkka Nyunyu having these conversations about digital return and access. As we listened to the songs, watched videos, and viewed archival photos, the conversations turned to the circulation of the songs – through these women as stewards, caretakers, and knowledge-holders, and in many formats. So, when one Mungamunga track ended and Dianne Stokes Nampin spontaneously announced that

---

2   This table provides a brief history of Mukurtu's development and its shift to a technical platform base through Drupal and a browser-based model for access. Mukurtu's code is open source and freely available on GitHub. From 2011 onwards, the Mukurtu team delivered workshops in Indigenous communities in the United States, New Zealand, Canada, Thailand, Mexico, and Central America.

"the songline is alive in Mukurtu," I was struck by her positioning of the Mungamunga songs within a larger set of circulation routes that include physical and digital spaces, recorded and live performances, tracks over the land, and tracks playing from the MP3s.

I use this quote to frame this chapter in order to foreground the dynamic, coexisting spaces, histories, and networks in which archival returns take place, move, and are negotiated. Nampin wasn't suggesting some type of anthropomorphism, nor am I. Her spontaneous assertion that the "songline is alive in Mukurtu" was at once a recognition of the primacy of orality, listening, and group circulation, and at the same time a nod to the multiplicity of networks through which knowledge can travel, change, be extended, and grow. Her statement also frames the capacities of Mukurtu CMS as a platform designed to facilitate both the return of and access to cultural heritage materials in culturally responsible ways. That is, the primary role of Mukurtu is to function as part of a network of already existing cultural exchange that includes humans, non-human ancestors, geographical places, analogue systems, and digital technologies and platforms. In this article, I examine a series of archival returns within the Warumungu community that spurred the development of Mukurtu CMS and subsequently were catalysts for the production of cultural materials, expanded collections, and extended relationships. By exploring the specific engagements and the networks created through these digital returns, I situate digital return, reuse, and repatriation as modes of decolonising practice, aligning it more generally with global debates and discussions about repatriation, sovereignty, and decolonising movements with, in, and through potentially reparative archival returns.

Return

This section returns to the beginnings of Mukurtu in order to trace the history of its development both locally and within larger conversations and concerns about archival practices, scholarly research priorities, and social and cultural policies related to Indigenous collections, repatriation, and traditional knowledge. I started working with and collaborating on recording and documentation projects with Warumungu women in 1995 as a graduate student. A senior group of women including K Fitz Nappanangka, E Nelson Nappanangka, D Dawson Nangali, E Graham Nakkamarra, and D Stokes Nampin invited me to record songs and stories about their homelands and traditions with the express intent of passing these recordings on to their children and grandchildren. They specifically asked me to record audio and video of places they were raised, stories of their ancestors, songs about their countries, and the many languages they spoke. Between 1995 and 2005, I worked steadily with this group of women and their extended kin to record oral histories, songs, dances, and stories that were significant to them (Christen 2009). As we did so, we also made trips both to the women's country – specific tracks and sites in and around Tennant Creek – and to national and regional archives, libraries, and museums to complement the women's stories.

Recording at the locations of ancestors and kin was never in doubt. The interest in connecting archival collections to these places emerged as a small group of women and I set out to retrace a specific ancestral track that connected three waterholes they traversed when young. As we were doing so, two of the women recalled similar trips in the early 1970s as part of the Warumungu land claim effort (Christen 2009). I contacted the Central Land Council office in Tennant Creek and located a set of the full land claims transcripts at the Tennant Creek library. Sifting through thousands of pages of testimony, I found the passages the women recalled and together we were able to use these to help us further connect physical tracks. As we traced the tracks of their non-human ancestors over the landscape, we also traced the tracks of their kin in the pages of the land claims case – connecting the two and positioning the archival documents within the present as both evidence and knowledge.

During this time Warumungu traditional owners were planning the design of the Nyinkka Nyunyu Art and Culture Centre in town – built on the ancestral Dreaming track of the Nyinkka (spiky tailed goanna). As part of the planning phase, community members made several trips to museums, archives, and libraries throughout Australia to view materials taken from Warumungu country, with the goal of repatriating some of these physical materials for the community. Once the centre opened in 2002, the work to bring cultural materials home continued. In 2004, I accompanied a group of Warumungu men and women to the National Archives in Darwin to locate materials. After an emotional few days in the archives, we left with a stack of photocopied documents that would be housed at Nyinkka Nyunyu and the promise of digital photos that would be returned via a hard drive. On the drive back to Tennant Creek, Trisha Frank Narrurlu suggested we stop at the house of former missionaries Richard and Sue Davies. Many of the community members present remembered them fondly from their time in Tennant Creek in the late 1970s and early 1980s. It turned out that Mr Davies was in possession of the entire collection of the Tennant Creek photos from the AIM from the 1930s to the 1980s and he had been slowly digitising them. In boxes and now on his computer's hard drive was a partial 50-year community history that Warumungu community members had yet to see. Trisha told him about Nyinkka Nyunyu and the plans for a community cultural resource room located within the centre to house Warumungu archival materials and provide a space for community members to engage with and reuse the materials in various contexts (Christen 2007). Mr Davies was eager to provide us with the digital files. With some trepidation, I loaded some 700 digitised images on to my laptop and we took them back to Tennant Creek.

I spent the following weeks in Tennant Creek with community members, family by family, clicking through the photos on my laptop reviewing the images and sorting them into folders by family. In the community cultural resource room at Nyinkka Nyunyu, Michael Jones Jampin – one of the cultural managers and a senior knowledge-holder in the community – had already defined access protocols for the physical archival materials returned. On the metal file cabinet in the resource room Jampin affixed a sign reading: "Restricted men only: Permission applies (contact Mr Jones)." As I sat with Jampin, he made it clear that these newly returned photos needed to be managed within the existing social and cultural protocols the community already had for viewing and circulating cultural materials. These protocols are based on a number of factors, with family and country being among the most important. The application of the protocols is, in practice, dynamic and depends on specific contexts. When we discussed the digital materials that had been returned by the missionaries and now school teachers as well, Jampin and Trisha confirmed they wanted this same notion of permissions and community access applied to these newly returned digital materials. She reviewed and explored other software options, but none met the criteria for the fine-grained access levels that were needed. With a view to creating a local community digital access point, we therefore set out to create a platform that would allow for digitally returned materials to be accessed, viewed, managed, and circulated within the community following their own clearly articulated set of community protocols and kin-based knowledge system.

Over the next two years we worked together – myself, designers, software engineers, workers at Nyinkka Nyunyu, and Warumungu community members – to design, test, and implement the Mukurtu Wumpurrarni-kari Archive to meet the specific cultural needs and social values of the community, modelling the architecture itself on the dynamic information and knowledge transmissions already in place.[3] Jampin gave the name Mukurtu, which means dilly bag in Warumungu, to the platform we were creating. We had seen a dilly bag at the South Australian Museum on one of our trips to view Warumungu belongings in the museum. Some of the younger Warumungu community members in their 20s and 30s had not heard the word, nor seen one before. Jampin explained to us that in the "old days" elders kept sacred items in the dilly bag. Novices had to approach the elders who had the obligation and social responsibility to "open up" the items – to share the knowledge that went with them. He said, "See in them old days, it was hard law, you couldn't look." But, Jampin also reminded us that elders had to "open them up" under the proper conditions – through respectful and "right-way" relationships (M Jampin Jones, pers. comm. to K Christen, 2004). It is through ongoing dialogues and interactions between kin that knowledge transfer and generation take place. The dilly bag – *mukurtu* – embodies these dynamic relations and one of its primary roles is prompting, strengthening, and maintaining relationships of respect within the community and between generations. Those relationships can also be strained and tested in the face of emergent social systems and political structures.

Jampin choose Mukurtu as the name for the platform we imagined because it denotes a set of relationships, obligations, and ongoing intergenerational knowledge sharing based on systems and networks of reciprocity and respect recognised by community members. The dilly bag, he translated further, is a "safe keeping place" – not only physically secure, but a safe space for "holding up" relationships and knowledge. We needed a system that could uphold and embody (not replicate) the same types of social relations and cultural protocols. The technology was not a replacement for kin and territorial relations. But it was the networks of kin, country, and ancestors that animated the design and development process. Over two years I flew back and forth with versions of the platform, testing the features with people and managing expectations – what the system could and could not do. In 2007, we launched the Mukurtu Wumpurrarni-kari Archive at Nyinkka Nyunyu. Within the Mukurtu platform, community members defined viewing and access of country, family, and kin, based on their own cultural and social protocols, and using a detailed user-profile system. At the time, the community designated eight protocols for access, and all content had to be tagged with at least one family and one country. Unlike most content management platforms of the time, we had designed Mukurtu to foreground social relationships – not items, collections, or records.[4]

---

3   For other such work, see Verran & Christie (2007), Becvar & Srinivasan (2009), Gardiner et al. (2011), Geismar
    & Mohns (2011), Hennessy et al. (2012), Bohaker et al. (2015), and Powell (2016).

4   On the limits of standard content management systems and the systems of cataloguing, classification, and
    metadata they rely on to encompass Indigenous knowledge and exchange systems, see: Toner (2003), Hunter
    (2005), Salmond (2012), Rowley (2013), Littletree & Metoyer (2015), O'Neal (2015), and Ghaddar (2016).

At the same time as we were building the Mukurtu platform, Trisha and Jampin, as the cultural managers at Nyinkka Nyunyu, were engaged in a series of digital return and repatriation projects. Trisha had created a detailed list of school teachers, missionaries, academics, lawyers, and others who had worked in Tennant Creek and she was relentlessly following every lead to have their materials digitally returned to Nyinkka Nyunyu. The filing cabinets in the resource room grew, with CDs and the iMacs expanded with digital files, all sorted by family. As mentioned above, the structure outlined for the Mukurtu Wumpurrarni-kari Archive was designed with family and country as the primary modes for defining access: thus any material uploaded was required to have a family and country protocol, with subsequent protocols such as elders, male, or female only added as needed. The protocols, importantly, could be mixed and matched to provide very granular levels of access, say for women from one kin group, all of whom had obligations to a certain country. I trained the staff in the then labour-intensive process of uploading – our maximum at that time was set at 50 images – and the inputting of metadata fields was all one by one. Although this would change radically in future iterations, we learnt through that process that literacy and cultural values around the significance of metadata guided the process more than did the technical infrastructure. People were simply less interested in defining file types than in naming family members.

Reuse

In the first few days, weeks, and months after the AIM photo collection was returned to the Warumungu community, there was a flurry of activity. The excitement was palpable. This was coupled with a sense of Warumungu pride and purpose that accompanied the opening and programming at Nyinkka Nyunyu Art and Culture Centre. Community members working there set in motion a series of projects, ventures, and collaborations that were all grounded in the vision of Nyinkka Nyunyu as a hub for Warumungu people – and a larger Barkly region Aboriginal community – to narrate, reframe, create, and share their stories, histories, knowledge, art, and culture. It was during this time that the senior women with whom I had been collaborating expanded the notion of the book they originally envisioned. They wanted to use the photos and videos taken during our excursions, the archival materials repatriated from the National Archives in Darwin and the South Australian Museum, and the photos from the Davies as well as one of the school teachers, Peter Brand, to create a community DVD and book, *Anyinginyi manuku apparr: Stories from our country.*

It was two of the most senior women, K Fitz Nappanangka and E Nelson Nappanangka, who drove the production of the DVD as a necessary part of the "paper stories" we had already been writing and collecting. Diane Stokes Nampin framed some of their intentions for both the initial recording and the viewing later this way:

> Well, a lot of children, a lot of children who see us sitting in front of old ladies, want to do painting on us, we get strong, the kids really want to join in and take part in dancing and take part in painting. So, kids feel happy 'cause they want to learn, for when they see their mother or their auntie or their grandmother in the front there they want to get up and dance. So, they want to dance so they feel happy and we feel happy that they going to

learn. We want them to get up and do something, we don't say no to them, we want them to learn, we want them to come in there and sit down and do the paintings on their chests. (D Stokes Nampin, pers. comm. to K Christen, 2003)

These sessions (which I attended) moved between instruction, to teasing and scolding for missteps, to larger conversations about 'holding' and upholding the knowledge of country and ancestors embedded within the songs, body designs, and dances. We completed the DVD in 2004, and multiple copies circulated between the women for years (Christen 2005). I uploaded this corpus of videos and audio we created together along with the digital copies of archival materials we amassed during our work together into the Mukurtu Wumpurrarni-kari Archive in 2007 for access by the women. Instead of only the edited clips on the DVD, we uploaded the complete video and audio files into Mukurtu to provide access to the women and girls. This, in turn, spurred the women to direct Nyinkka Nyunyu cultural resource staff, led by Trisha Frank Narrurlu and Rose Graham Namikili, to seek more materials specific to women, especially Mungamunga. Watching and listening to these recordings created an interest among the women to record more – especially family histories. Rose was also using the growing content uploaded to Mukurtu to produce booklets for the new Wumpurrarni Tours offered through Nyinkka Nyunyu. Rose took tourists to Kunjarra – a site just outside of town – and took them on bush tours and told them about the Mungamunga women and the importance of the site to Warumungu people.

Through these multiple returns, cultural materials were repurposed, reused, and reimagined as vehicles for community empowerment, re-narrating misunderstood events, and reconnecting family histories.[5] I was able to go with Rose on a few tours in 2007 and 2009 and record her as she narrated the history of Kunjarra. In May 2017, I sat with Rose at the Training Centre in town (she no longer worked at Nyinkka Nyunyu), and we watched videos of her mother, and my mentor, E Nakkamarra Graham. I wasn't sure at first if she would want to watch the videos, since her mother had passed away in 2014 and protocols over viewing are more and more dependent on individual preference. She was not only interested in watching, she also sat with me for hours as we translated one of her mother's videos from Warumungu into English. In the video Nakkamarra discussed the "old ways" women from all over the region came together to sing and dance:

Old people coming from everywhere to dance, we show them that this *yawulyu* is our own. We only dance one time to share with others and after people scatter going back to their country, from camp to camp. They take that *yawulyu* to another country to show them. (E Nakkamarra Graham, pers. comm. to K Christen, 2007)

We watched the full video several times, along with others from earlier trips out bush. On one of the videos we watched a trip to a nearby soakage where both E Graham Nakkamarra and D Dawson Nangali described the movements of their kin and wove in stories of ancestral tracks and the movements of settlers in the area. We laughed too at the children on the video as they darted in and out of the frame variously listening and telling their own stories. Rose

5   See Barwick et al. (2013) for more on reuse within Central Australian communities.

commented, "See, that was good, taking them kids out to that place, they're happy I reckon." The intention of that elder group of women was not only for instruction – passing on their knowledge – it was also to stimulate new knowledge, connections, and relations to country and kin. This use of the technology was decidedly purposeful.[6] This particular group of women knew that part (not all) of their legacy would be mediated through new forms of capture, return, and circulation. It was their kin who were now watching, listening, and reusing these materials to reach outward, within and between their community, families, and different publics.

Access and circulation

By 2015, Mukurtu CMS was at a 2.0 release with much more functionality than previous iterations – particularly around displaying content, adding traditional knowledge, and linking content across the platform (Christen et al. 2017). While people were familiar with, and comfortable, accessing the content on Mukurtu through the Nyinkka Nyunyu staff, there had not been much content added to the site in the previous few years. While Nyinkka Nyunyu was going through its own set of financial and organisational challenges and changes, fewer staff meant that the archive was a lower priority and that original excitement was absent. During this time, Nyinkka Nyunyu also expanded its focus to the larger Barkly region. Extended relations across the region have always been evident and acknowledged by community members through their own family and social networks, as well as through the structures of ceremonial systems. During meetings at Nyinkka Nyunyu in 2015–2016, we discussed the varied stakeholders, and the types of contributions to the content and knowledge in the Mukurtu site up to that point. As we looked over the photos and documents in the current Mukurtu site, Jampin explained:

> See, this is for all Wumpurrarni people, some of the photos we have we don't know the
> people 'cause they weren't from here. We have photos from the Barkly region here, we
> have some photos here of old Alyawarr people, you got Warlpiri, we got those Warlmanpa
> lot too, their stuff is here. (M Jampin Jones, pers. comm. to K Christen, 2016)

Because the scope had expanded over the last 10 years, with digital collections being returned from researchers, national, and regional archives, and school teachers, Jampin suggested a new name for the Mukurtu site: *Wurrppujinta Anyul Mappu – a gathering place*. With the updated name, we also took the opportunity to rethink the categories, the structure of the site, and how – once it went online – people could access the site from their homes, on their phones, or at other organisations in addition to Nyinkka Nyunyu. When Nyinkka Nyunyu temporarily closed for renovations in 2017–2018, the need for more access points became even more relevant. And successive layoffs of staff in the preceding years had slowed the addition of content to the site, highlighting the need for more trained staff across a range of organisations.

---

6   For specific discussions of Indigenous communities' use of technology within and beyond return projects
    see Cha chom se nup et al. (2013), Hollinger et al. (2013), Hennessy et al. (2012), Lempert (2018), Nakata et al.
    (2014), and Solomon & Thorpe (2012).

We'd been having discussions around making Mukurtu accessible online for years. In 2006–2007 when we were in active development of the original platform, the idea of having content accessible via the internet was impractical. In the ensuing decade, the digital infrastructure, including broadband access, in Tennant Creek – and the Northern Territory more broadly – changed alongside the rapid uptake of mobile devices by Aboriginal people. In fact, where once I was continually asked for prints of photos, and then CDs, now it is a "stick" – a USB or flash drive. While it is still the case that personal computers are rare in Aboriginal homes in Tennant Creek, gaming devices such as the Xbox and mobile phones are prevalent. People are adept at using Bluetooth-enabled devices to share, copy, and circulate digital files, including photos and audio and video files.

Reflecting the expanded purview of the new Wurrppujinta site, we were able to use the updated architecture of Mukurtu CMS to emphasise the types of contributors and returned collections in a way that we were not able to do in previous iterations of the software. Since the new site was to be online, there was a conscious decision to delineate the types of public materials on the site. The main page now highlights the contributions to the site that Aboriginal organisations, researchers, and others have made. So, for example, within the 'Aboriginal Organisations' track, there are currently three organisations in town that are contributing content. Similarly, researchers who may have collections deposited in national archives can also upload copies to Wurrppujinta to allow for easier community access. The original family materials that formed the core of the content over the last decade remain viewable only by family members and those protocols are defined and updated by them. During 2018–2019, I returned to Tennant Creek and walked through the new functionality with various stakeholders and traditional owners. Some were eager to use the platform, while others preferred to watch. The continued lack of training opportunities to upload materials – as opposed to accessing them – remains a challenge.

At the same time as we were updating the Wurrppujinta site, linguists Samantha Disbray and Jane Simpson, who had both worked in the community for decades, started work with community members "to repatriate and repurpose a collection of Warumungu language audio materials" that had been digitised from the Prith Chakravarti collection at the Australian Institute of Aboriginal and Torres Strait Islander Studies (AIATSIS) (S Disbray, pers. comm. to K Christen, 2018). In fact, Samantha and I coordinated several of our field trips and worked simultaneously with community members. As I was showing people videos and we were looking at old photographs on Wurrppujinta, Samantha was playing the Chakravarti recordings and soliciting transcriptions of the materials. The Chakravarti recordings include "language materials, such as wordlists, sentence elicitation and explanation, along with oral history, personal narratives, descriptions of cultural practice, country, flora and fauna, and an extensive range of dreamtime stories" (S Disbray, pers. comm. to K Christen, 2018). The tapes had been largely inaccessible to the community and so their digital repatriation was welcome, for both linguistic content as well as the knowledge they held about people, places, and kin.

The audio repatriation project will ultimately produce several aural and visual products. In December 2018, I was able to meet with several Warumungu artists at Barkly Arts who have now created new paintings depicting their renditions of several of the stories recounted on the recordings. Samantha was eager to allow more people to hear the recordings and so after securing family permissions to play some of the recordings for others, in 2017 she worked with several community members to produce a SoundCloud playlist of the recordings and set up a listening station at the Desert Harmony festival – a set of public events in and around town. We also uploaded a few of the recordings to the Wurrppujinta site to allow those I was working with to listen to them directly. Once the project is completed and the protocols are defined by those families, the recordings will be available through the Wurrppujinta site – with the option to 'save to USB' as part of the functionality. Community members, once logged in to the site, will also be able to access copies on their own devices. It has become fairly routine in the last five years for people to use mobile phones to store (temporarily) and access media of all types.

Protocols and process

The update to the Wurrppujinta site overlapped with discussions about access, use, and reproduction of the repatriated Mungamunga and Milwayi collections with which I opened this chapter. While there had been discussions about accessing songs and other ceremonial material using the Mukurtu Wumpurrarni-kari Archive since its inception in 2007, the platform had in practice been used almost exclusively for photos and documents, the bulk of which were under family-based protocols. That is, the majority of the materials were primarily accessed through family protocols, whereas the songs and other ceremonial material would require a more granular set of protocols for access and sharing based on territorial knowledge and ritual status. From a software structure perspective, not only was this possible, it was exactly what the platform was designed to do and many communities in North America using Mukurtu CMS had done just that.

The process for implementing cultural protocols within Mukurtu CMS requires discussions and decisions about social relations and circulation expectations prior to upload. Because all materials uploaded are required to have a cultural protocol (regardless of the type – that is, even if it were 'public') decisions about what cultural protocols to add must be determined in advance of ingestion of content to any site. Amelia Wilson, the director of the Huna Heritage Foundation in Alaska, discussed how they are implementing Mukurtu CMS to provide responsible access to their archival materials:

> In Tlingit culture songs have protocols for sharing. And so, much like copyrights, I can't sing a song from another clan without having permission. I belong to the Chookaneidí, the Bear Clan. But say we have something from another clan, the Kaagwaantaan, the Wolf Clan, in our archives, and I approach the clan leaders and they say, "We would like the site to house our songs and our stories, but we don't want other people, or other clans even, to be able to access those." So, the protocols that are available on Mukurtu, then, makes that possible. We can make sure that the right clans and clan members have access. (Wilson et al. 2017)

What Wilson points to is the underlying structure of Mukurtu that has been built to facilitate diverse sets of access, circulation, and exchange models and systems grounded in Indigenous relationality. Similarly, Jason Wesaw, the archivist for the Pokagon Band of Potawatomi, worked with members of his community to define not only the ways materials should circulate, but also how they imagined Mukurtu building from and working within their own social, moral, and linguistic system. They thus named their Mukurtu site Wiwkwébthëgen and sought to define their goals from this established set of values. Jason explains:

> So, Wiwkwébthëgen, in our language is just basically talking about a bundle. All of our tribal communities, in one way or another, use bundles. So, bundles are physical things where a man might keep their pipe, [a] woman might keep a water bundle, a young girl that is transitioning into womanhood might have a certain kind of bundle that helps her in that time of life. So, it's a physical thing, but it's also like a spiritual, emotional, knowledge-based thing. So that's what the Wiwkwébthëgen Mukurtu site is, because we are trying to connect all of these dots in the minds of our community, and how you can use technology to help push that knowledge forward. We want to be able to use the history, the photographs and the objects as a way to help people understand that story of how our people lost our land and how [we] lost our federal recognition and the way that we used our culture to regain that. Because the culture is a huge aspect of our sovereign status as a nation and how we have to hold on to it if we are going to keep that status. (Wilson et al. 2017)

For the Pokagon, Mukurtu is a part of a social and cultural system of tribal values. It is one tool to express sovereignty and tribal status by retelling a story of loss and at the same time narrating a history of survival – linguistic, cultural, and political.

In Tennant Creek, the repatriated Mungamunga and Milwayi materials – which included content from researchers (including myself) deposited in the original Mukurtu Wumpurrarni-kari Archive – prompted a set of discussions by women and men about the potential to use the new Wurrppujinta site for storing, accessing, and circulating ceremonial materials, which up to that point had not occurred.[7] While most of these discussions in previous years had centred on community control and family decisions, this newly repatriated content led to conversations that ranged from contemplating unique shared sets of passwords, to restricting copying and downloading of some materials while allowing for in-person viewing at the centre, and to the need for shared sets of understandings about how access is defined between the performance and the digital recordings. As community members grappled with these questions, both in our in-person meetings and between themselves, we created several different versions of access and use scenarios within the Wurrppujinta site to provide viewable examples of the scenarios through which the materials could be accessed. The biggest sticking point was around the ability to download materials. Everyone wanted to be able to download content for which they

---

7   It should be noted that Mukurtu CMS is an access platform and as such is one part of any necessary digital ecosystem in which preservation and access are two necessary and separate processes. The Mukurtu support site has documentation suggesting that access files should be created from originals or high-quality master files for ingestion and uploading into Mukurtu CMS. Through the Mukurtu CMS web interface, access to and use, annotation, and curation of content is possible. The preservation of original or master files (TIFFs, WAV files and the like) is either handled by another institution, the original source (as is the case for much of the repatriated material), or through tiered systems built for the hosting institution.

were stewards to their own devices. They also wanted to protect very sensitive materials from being downloaded. However, within one instance of Mukurtu there is no means to disable functionality for some but not all content. That is, protocols to define access cannot manage whether download is an option for some but not all materials. If the download function is enabled, it would apply to all materials across that instance of Mukurtu, and could not be selectively applied to any songline material within it. Therefore, either they could not upload the most sensitive material, or they had to disable download for all materials. No one was happy with the choices.

In December 2018, after the initial conversations and successive meetings with the women in 2017, we added a test track within the Wurrppujinta site for *Winkarra* 'Dreaming' materials to demonstrate how access and use could work through Wurrppujinta. Over a week, Kim Webeck, from the Central Land Council, and I held demo and listening sessions with men and women both in separate and mixed groups, walking them through the site to show how materials could be accessed using collections and sub-collections and protocols throughout. Webeck had worked with the women on the Mungamunga and Milwayi repatriation project and had been part of discussions about how, or whether, to use Mukurtu to provide access to the materials. Several senior men were keen to discuss the possibility of having men's songs within Wurrppujinta. At one meeting, Michael Jampin Jones noted that Mukurtu could be used now so that younger generations could listen with elders to songs on their phones. Another Warumungu senior man wanted to embark on a similar repatriation and recording project as the women had, and as we showed him the Wurrppujinta site, he noted the possibilities for continued access in town, and also worried about having the materials on the same platform as the women's materials.

Hopi scholar Trevor Reed notes that replaying archival songs within Indigenous contexts, especially those of songs still in use, can perform "a kind of meaningful connecting that acquire[s] affective power through the revoicing of the past into the present" (2018: 5) – wherever that present moment takes place. When negotiating digital return, concern around access unfolds in many ways. In her work in Western Australia, ethnomusicologist Sally Treloyn suggests that in the Australian case, "it is important to note that songs and repertories traditionally fall in and out of usage" (Treloyn & Emberly 2013: 165). That is, individual songs and song repertories don't necessarily die, although of course they can. But what is "of more concern is a decrease in opportunities for elder and younger generations to share knowledge about songs and the information attached to them" (Treloyn & Emberly 2013: 165). Indeed, the conversations with Warumungu women that I participated in centred more on how to provide a space for intergenerational sharing and learning within the context of a life that is mostly based in town. That is, they were worried that "young girls" wouldn't have the time or space to listen and learn. Ethnomusicologist Linda Barwick documented these concerns in 2010 in a series of interviews specifically directed at understanding the sustainability of women's *yawulyu* (country-based ceremonies) – of which Mungamunga songs are one. In Tennant Creek, Barwick worked with the same women who were part of the Mukurtu projects. She found that the senior women expressed "anxiety about the extent to which the younger generations would be able to uphold the traditional performance practice" (Barwick et al. 2013: 201). Some of their anxiety came from how to facilitate both the showing and sharing of the materials in spaces that would allow younger generations to get over some of their fear of not knowing, or not being able to perform properly (Barwick et al. 2013; Christen 2006). One aspect of having the materials digitised and accessible within Mukurtu was to ensure not only that cultural protocols could be applied, but also that this specific group of women could access and view the recordings in their own spaces, on their own time, and share them as needed – through mobile phones, on USB drives, or on other networked devices.

As I was leaving Tennant Creek in December of 2018, I got an urgent text message from Trisha. She wanted to know if there were any photos of "that old woman" within Wurrppujinta or on any of my hard drives. Her follow-up text provided more clues and I was able to piece together that she was seeking photos of a senior woman who had just passed away that week. I did a quick search and found several photos within the Wurrppujinta site and I also opened up several of the remaining files we had been organising and cleaning up for upload and found several more. I loaded them onto a flash drive and met Trisha at Nyinkka Nyunyu for one last look through the site. We did indeed find more photos by searching some alternative names she suggested. I recalled discussing this practice a few years earlier with TR Nappanangka, who was working at Nyinkka Nyunyu in the community resource room. She said that one of the most popular uses of the Mukurtu Wumpurrarni-kari Archive at the time was families looking for images of deceased relatives. She said that funerals almost always prompted a search through the archive for photos to use on the handouts at the service. Similarly, as I was showing a group of related Warumungu women photos of their families in the Wurrppujinta site in order to add in family names, stories, and any other information, a black and white photo from the "mission days" came up and one woman whispered the name of her deceased brother. I hadn't heard her, and I did not know he had passed away, so I asked her to repeat what she said so I could add it to the metadata correctly. More whispers ensued and I began to understand why. Then Trisha said loudly, "Sing out, you gotta say that name for the archive, it will be here in 50 years, you won't." I was somewhat taken aback by Trisha's insistence, but at the same time I understood her point. Who would be there to pass on that old man's name for future generations? The women spoke to each other and after some more hushed conversation they spelled out his name for me, letter by letter, as I typed it into the name field and clicked save.

Repatriation

Although Mukurtu CMS was primarily envisioned as an access platform, what it has become is a platform for access, return, reuse, and repatriation. That is, while the return of digital materials from archives and other collecting institutions is a primary reason that Indigenous communities use Mukurtu CMS, return is imagined as a whole set of practices that include future access, use, and circulation. Getting archival materials back from collecting institutions is not limited to an ingestion model where content and metadata are understood as a complete, or even trustworthy, source of knowledge. In fact, distrust in these materials is part of the reason for wanting their return (Koch 2018; McKemmish et al. 2011). Archival returns are motivated by histories of surveillance, dispossession, violence, and documentation (O'Neal

2015; Sanborn 2009; Thorpe 2014), and that scaffolding thus needs to be replaced before return can rightly move to reparative repatriation work.

Part of the return process that Mukurtu can facilitate is a repositioning and reframing of materials, through expanded and enriched metadata, customisable categories and vocabularies, and a focus on Indigenous knowledge through fields that are not wholly reliant on text, but can include video and audio as metadata. We have developed import and export functions that provide avenues for return based on Indigenous systems of circulation. Notable among these are a suite of tools known as 'round-trip' that allow both content and metadata to be imported and exported using a CSV spreadsheet that comes prepackaged in the software. As a part of round-trip, the selective sync option allows Mukurtu CMS users to define which metadata fields they want to share with institutions. A feedback loop is thus created whereby communities can receive content and metadata, enhance the institution's metadata, and return it – or parts of it – to the institution to update their records.[8] For example, it could be that Warumungu women add annotations to some of the songlines for their own knowledge sharing. They may also add map markers and names of singers for specific caretakers, and in the traditional knowledge metadata field they might add an audio file of discussions between senior women about the Dreaming track. If they want to share the content (the songs) as well as any of the metadata they have added, they can choose which metadata fields within the Mukurtu export spread-sheet to share, and only the fields they choose and the information they permit to be shared will be exported. The effect is reparative in that the knowledge, values, social systems, and protocols of the communities drive the display, circulation, and access, thus undoing the emphasis on archival or scholarly notions of value and valuable data, metadata, content, and information.

Within this framework of digital return, digital repatriation thus explicitly acknowledges histories of dispossession and disruption as a fundamental part of the return practice. That is, digital repatriation is one mode of return that overtly acknowledges histories of taking along with the harm done to individuals and communities. In her work returning cultural materials including films, photos, and documents to Native communities in the United States at the National Museum of the American Indian, Grande Rhone scholar-archivist Jennifer O'Neal remarked that:

> Thus, the physical and the digital form must work together and complement one another to achieve the major goals of the diverse needs of each tribal community that seeks for the preservation and reinvigoration of traditional knowledge for future generations. (2013: 180)

In these cases, the harm – and violence – is reflected in the categories, metadata, and clas-sifications that define the collections and must be undone, recreated, and directed through Indigenous systems and protocols. Digital repatriation as a restorative process must therefore include: recognition and documentation of harm; collective solutions towards remaking and undoing settler colonial structures of classification and categorisation; pathways for Indigenous metadata to expand, replace, or update records; options for updating or replacing copyright or other intellectual property rights that function to dislodge Indigenous stewardship; and a

---

8   Linda Barwick (2004: 260) notes the need for this type of distribution model and decentralised system as new digital platforms and archives are created.

commitment to developing ongoing relationships of stewardship. Digital repatriation includes practices framed by purposeful acts of restitution and repair that include multiple types of exchange and are dependent on creating new types of relationships. Ts'msyen scholar Robin Gray argues that, "The politics of Indigenous repatriation – whether it involves human remains, objects, or songs – requires that it be restorative so that the source community can find a sense of resolution from historical injustices" (2018: 1). What that resolution may look like from community to community – and within communities – varies and can only be shaped through long-term engagement (Treloyn & Emberly 2013; Campbell 2014; Gray 2018; Reed 2018). And indeed, resolution may only be partial: returning, as a single act, is not digital repatriation. Instead, digital repatriation takes on local meaning according to different histories and needs, and the types of materials being returned and restored. As Hopi scholar Trevor Reed argues:

> Repatriation need not be only a mode of remedying misappropriation of culturally affiliated properties, but may be a way of enabling voices of the past to become present again within Indigenous communities. (2018: 21)

Reed's work leading the Hopi Music Repatriation Project highlights the flexibility and possibilities associated with sonic repatriation when positioned alongside the challenges posed by western legal systems through which Indigenous archival music collections remain owned and governed. Reed argues against defining repatriation as "property transactions between two sovereigns" (2018: 2); instead he suggests an inscription of sonic/musical repatriation processes through Indigenous networks that do not replicate notions of ownership, authority, or authorship derived from western systems and legal frameworks.

In the last 10 years since we created Mukurtu CMS, issues of digital return and repatriation have been even more closely aligned with specific goals of effecting the decolonisation of museums, archives, and libraries as part of the explicit expressions of Indigenous sovereignty and self-determination movements globally. Decolonisation movements are not new, nor are critiques of collecting institutions as colonial storehouses. However, the specific focus on reparative return in these calls for decolonisation is more expressly manifested in global networks, and is tied to legacies of territorial dispossession. It is linked to the current resistance to sustained disenfranchisement and continued expressions of rights to, and stewardship over, lands, resources, cultural materials, traditional knowledge, and languages (Christen & Anderson 2019).

Respect

It was just a year after Nyinkka Nyunyu officially opened in 2003 that Michael Jampin Jones and I walked through the exhibit space with my then one-year-old son toddling in front of us. We talked about our families and caught up on events in town, and then we discussed the permanent Punttu exhibit that Jampin and other Warumungu community members had created. *Punttu* is routinely translated as 'skin' in English and it is part of the larger kinship system signifying the subsection within the moiety system of which all Warumungu people are a part. Non-Warumungu people who have long-term relationships with the community are often given a skin as well. I still remember the bumpy Toyota ride off the side of the Barkly

Highway when E Graham Nakkamarra gave me my skin: Namikili. The Punttu exhibit is a series of self portraits, each depicting one of the 16 skins. As we talked, Jampin's commentary moved between the relationships people have with one another, to those they have with ancestors and country. He talked about his stockman days and about the close connections he still had to places throughout the region. As we walked past the land claims display, he paused. "See," he took in all of the centre and the landscape outside with one swipe of his arms, "respect is the ground we walk on."

The decolonisation of museums and archives – in their physical and digital forms – begins with a recognition of the harm and hurt caused not just by removal, but by ongoing erasure through systems of cataloging, categorisation, curation, and circulation. Maori scholar Moana Jackson argues that "museums are dangerous places because they control the storytelling" (Jackson, cited in Cairns 2018). The danger that Jackson names is the power of naming, in itself, to reroute local understandings, places, and people, through many subtle or explicit acts. Museums are not the only dangerous places in this sense. When practices of return are grounded in Indigenous sovereignty and self-determination, they demand a recognition of territorial rights, autonomous political structures, ongoing systems of governance, and communal forms of stewardship over cultural resources and knowledge. Decolonising strategies must move from recognition toward repair – from acknowledgements to action. These moves can be a part of return practices where Indigenous knowledge and naming systems and structures are foregrounded within curatorial conventions to refocus on Indigenous understandings rather than perpetuate fictions of erasure and invisibility. Warumungu women continue their discussions of how best to access, use, circulate, and exchange their repatriated materials, well after the return of the digital files. This is another reminder that digital return, in whatever form, is always part of larger systems of accountability, attribution, and acknowledgement grounded in place, in ancestral relations, and through kinship networks that span generations and continue to be animated in the present by multiple types of relations.

As an access platform, Mukurtu CMS extends and overlaps with existing, embodied kinship networks and territorial relations. Mukurtu is a tool, one part of a number of cultural toolboxes that can be used to meet some of the needs and desires of community members as they envision and enact returns and futures. Like mobile phone applications for learning language, or GIS maps on tablets that are used to document ancestral tracks, digital access platforms and other newer technologies are part of a continuum of technology that works with, alongside, in relation to, and as a part of conscious Indigenous future-making (Ginsburg 2018; Lempert 2018). The multiple futures imagined by Indigenous communities and their collaborators are constrained by political, economic, and social structures enacted by nation-states and filtered through violent histories. Within this landscape, an 'ethics of possibility' opens up different types of mediated futures (Ginsburg 2018: 225). It is sometimes easy to fall back on the old versus the new, or narratives of tradition versus modernity, especially when it comes to technology. I was reminded again of how this false binary has endured, when, in December 2018, I sat discussing the Wurrppujinta site with Jimmy Frank Juppurula, a Warumungu man and cultural manager at Nyinkka Nyunyu in Tennant Creek. We had been working all week together. As the days unfolded, more and more community members interacted with Mukurtu and discussed what they wanted to do with it. As we listened, what we heard was that the possibilities for what Mukurtu could become, and enable to happen, were not limited by any one overriding sense of tradition or technology. As we wrapped up our talk that evening, Jimmy said to me, "People always talk about bringing the new to the old, but I think we have to bring the old to the new." And it struck me that this was exactly what digital repatriation as a decolonising strategy could be, at its best – a way to dislodge both technological determinism and technological utopianism. A way to insist on seeing a cultural continuum. It could be a way of intentionally entangling the old and the new, of making technology traditionally modern.

References

Barwick, Linda. 2004. Turning it all upside down … imagining a distributed digital audiovisual archive. *Literary and Linguistic Computing* 19(3). 253–263.

Barwick, Linda, Mary Laughren & Myfany Turpin. 2013. Sustaining women's *yawulyu/awelye*: Some practitioners' and learners' perspectives. *Musicology Australia* 35(2). 191–220.

Becvar, Katherine & Ramesh Srinivasan. 2009. Indigenous knowledge and culturally responsive methods in information research. *The Library* 79(4). 421–441.

Bohaker, Heidi, Alan Ojiig Corbiere & Ruth Phillips. 2015. Wampum unites us: Digital access, interdisciplinarity, and indigenous knowledge – situating the GRASAC knowledge sharing database. In Raymond A Silverman (ed.), *Museum as process: Translating local and global knowledge*, 44–66. New York: Routledge.

Cairns, Puawai. 2018. *"Museums are dangerous places" – challenging history* (blog post). Museum of New Zealand Te Papa Tongarewa. (https://blog.tepapa.govt.nz/2018/10/19/museums-are-dangerous-places-challenging-history/) (Accessed 10 January 2019.)

Campbell, Genevieve. 2014. Song as artefact: The reclaiming of song recordings empowering Indigenous stakeholders – and the recordings themselves. In Amanda Harris (ed.), *Circulating cultures: Exchanges of Australian Indigenous music, dance and media*, 101–128. Canberra: Australian National University Press.

Cha chom se nup (Earl J Smith), Heekus (Victoria C Wells) & Peter Brand. 2013. A partnership between Ehattesaht Chinehkint, First Peoples' Culture Council, and First Peoples' Culture Council's FirstVoice™ Team to build a digital bridge between the past and future of the Ehattesaht Chinehkint language and culture. *Museum Anthropology Review* 7(1–2). 185–200.

Christen, Kimberly. 2005. Gone digital: Aboriginal remix and the cultural commons. *International Journal of Cultural Property* 12. 315–345.

Christen, Kimberly. 2006. Tracking properness: Repackaging culture in a remote Australian town. *Cultural Anthropology* 21(3). 416–446.

Christen, Kimberly. 2007. Following the Nyinkka: Relations of respect and obligations to act in the collaborative work of Aboriginal culture centers. *Museum Anthropology* 30(2). 101–124.

Christen, Kimberly. 2009. *Aboriginal business: Alliances in a remote Australian town.* Canberra: Aboriginal Studies Press.

Christen, Kimberly. 2011. Opening archives: Respectful repatriation. *American Archivist* 74. 185–210.

Christen, Kimberly. 2012. Does information really want to be free? Indigenous knowledge systems and the question of openness. *International Journal of Communication* 6. 2870–2893.

Christen, Kimberly, Alex Merrill & Michael Wynne. 2017. A community of relations: Mukurtu hubs and spokes. *D-Lib Magazine* 23(5–6).

Christen, Kimberly & Jane Anderson. 2019. Towards slow archives. In JJ Ghaddar & Michelle Caswell (eds.), *Archival Science special issue: Towards a decolonial archival praxis* 19(2). 87–116.

Gardiner, Gabrielle, Jemima McDonald, Alex Byrne & Kirsten Thorpe. 2011. Respect, trust and engagement: Creating an Australian Indigenous data archive. *Collection Building* 30(4). 148–152.

Geismar, Haidy & William Mohns. 2011. Social relationships and digital relationships: Rethinking the database at the Vanuatu Cultural Centre. *Journal of the Royal Anthropological Institute* 17(s1). S133–S155.

Ghaddar, JJ. 2016. The spectre in the archive: Truth, reconciliation, and Indigenous archival memory. *Archivaria* 82. 3–26.

Ginsburg, Faye. 2018. The road forward. *Cultural Anthropology* 33(2). 224–232.

Gray, Robin RR. 2018. Repatriation and decolonization: Thoughts on ownership, access, and control. 2018. In Frank Gunderson, Robert C Lancefield & Bret Woods (eds.), *The Oxford handbook on musical repatriation*, 1–16. Oxford Handbooks Online. (http://www.oxfordhandbooks.com/view/10.1093/oxfordhb/9780190659806.001.0001/oxfordhb-9780190659806-e-39) (Accessed 1 January 2019.)

Hennessy, Kate, Ryan Wallace, Nicholas Jakobsen & Charles Arnold. 2012. Virtual repatriation and the application programming interface: From the Smithsonian Institution's MacFarlane Collection to Inuvialuit living history. In Nancy Proctor & Rich Cherry (eds.), *Museums and the web 2012*. San Diego: Archives and Museum Informatics.

Hollinger, R Eric, Edwell John Jr, Harold Jacobs, Lora Moran-Collins, Carolyn Thome, Jonathan Zastrow, Adam Metallo, Günter Waibel, & Vince Rossi. 2013. Tlingit-Smithsonian collaborations with 3D digitization of cultural objects. *Museum Anthropology Review* 7(1–2). 201–253.

Hunter, Jane. 2005. The role of information technologies in Indigenous knowledge management. *Australian Academic & Research Libraries* 36(2). 109–124.

Koch, Grace. 2018. "We want our voices back": Ethical dilemmas in the repatriation of recordings. In Frank Gunderson, Robert C Lancefield & Bret Woods (eds.), *The Oxford handbook of musical repatriation*, 1–16. Oxford Handbooks Online. (http://www.oxfordhandbooks.com/view/10.1093/oxfordhb/9780190659806.001.0001/oxfordhb-9780190659806) (Accessed 1 January 2019.)

Lempert, William. 2018. Indigenous media futures: An introduction. *Cultural Anthropology* 33(2). 173–179.

Littletree, Sandra & Cheryl A Metoyer. 2015. Knowledge organisation from an Indigenous perspective: The Mashantucket Pequot thesaurus of American Indian terminology project. *Cataloging and Classification Quarterly* 53(5–6). 640–657.

McKemmish, Sue, Shannon Faulkhead & Lynette Russell. 2011. Distrust in the archives: Reconciling records. *Archival Science* 11. 211–239.

Mukurtu CMS. 2019. (https://mukurtu.org/) (Accessed 18 January 2018.)

Nakata, Martin, Duane Hamacher, John Warren, Alex Byrne, Maurice Pagnucco, Ross Harley, Srikumar Venugopal, Kirsten Thorpe, Richard Neville & Reuben Bolt. 2014. Using modern technologies to capture and share Indigenous astronomical knowledge. *Australian Academic & Research Libraries* 45(2). 101–110.

O'Neal, Jennifer R. 2013. Going home: The digital return of films at the National Museum of the American Indian. *Museum Anthropology Review* 7(1–2). 166–184.

O'Neal, Jennifer R. 2015. The right to know: Decolonizing Native American archives. *Journal of Western Archives* 6(1). 1–17.

Powell, Timothy. 2016. Digital knowledge sharing: Forging partnerships between scholars, archives, and Indigenous communities. *Museum Anthropology Review* 10(2). 66–90.

Rowley, Susan. 2013. The reciprocal research network: The development process. *Museum Anthropology Review* 7(1–2). 22–43.

Reed, Trevor. 2018. Reclaiming ownership of the Indigenous voice: The Hopi Music Repatriation Project. In Frank Gunderson, Robert C Lancefield & Bret Woods (eds.), *The Oxford handbook of musical repatriation*, 1–30. Oxford Handbooks Online. (http://www.oxfordhandbooks.com/view/10.1093/oxfordhb/9780190659806.001.0001/oxfordhb-9780190659806-e-35) (Accessed 1 January 2019.)

Salmond, Amiria. 2012. Digital subjects, cultural objects: Special issue introduction. *Journal of Material Culture* 17(3). 211–228.

Sanborn, Andrea. 2009. The reunification of the Kwakwaka'wakw mask with its cultural soul. *Museum International* 61(1–2). 81–86.

Solomon, Maui & Susan Thorpe. 2012. Taonga Moriori: Recording and revival. *Journal of Material Culture* 17(3). 245–263.

Thorpe, Kirsten. 2014. Indigenous records: Connecting, critiquing, and diversifying collections. *Archives and Manuscripts* 42(2). 211–214.

Toner, Peter. 2003. History, memory, and music: The repatriation of digital audio to Yolngu communities, or, memory as metadata. In Linda Barwick, Allan Marett, Jane Simpson & Amanda Harris (eds.), *Researchers, communities, institutions, sound recordings*. Sydney: University of Sydney. (http://hdl.handle.net/2123/1518)

Treloyn, Sally & Andrea Emberly. 2013. Sustaining traditions: Ethnomusicological collections, access and sustainability in Australia. *Musicology Australia* 35(2). 159–177.

Verran, Helen & Michael Christie. 2007. Using/designing digital technologies of representation in Aboriginal Australian knowledge practices. *Human Technology: Interdisciplinary Journal on Humans in ICT Environments* 3(2). 214–227.

Wilson, Amelia, Jason Wesaw & Ashley Sexton. 2017. Introduction to Mukurtu Content Management System (CMS): Providing digital access to cultural collections. (Panel discussion, International Conference of Indigenous Archives, Libraries, and Museums, Santa Ana Pueblo, New Mexico, 10 October 2017.)

Language Documentation & Conservation Special Publication No. 18
Archival returns: Central Australia and beyond
ed. by Linda Barwick, Jennifer Green & Petronella Vaarzon-Morel, pp. 173–191
http://nflrc.hawaii.edu/ldc/sp18
http://hdl.handle.net/10125/24883

9

"For the children ...": Aboriginal Australia, cultural access, and archival obligation

Brenda L Croft
Australian National University

Sandy Toussaint
The University of Western Australia

Felicity Meakins
The University of Queensland

Patrick McConvell
Australian National University

Abstract

For whom are archival documents created and conserved? Who is obliged to care for them and provide access to their content, and for how long? The state, libraries, museums and galleries, researchers, interlocutors, genealogists, family heritage organisations? Or does material collected long ago and then archived belong personally, socially, emotionally, culturally, and intellectually to the people from whom the original material was collected and, eventually, to their descendants? In a colonised nation, additional ethical and epistemological questions arise: Are archives protected and accessed for the colonised or the colonisers, or both? How are differences regarding archival creation, protection, and access distinguished, and in whose interest? Is it for future generations? What happens when archives are accessed and read by family members and/or researchers, and what happens when they are not? A focus on two interrelated stories – firstly an experiential account narrated by Brenda L Croft about constructive archival management and access, and secondly a contrasting example relating how the Berndt Field Note Archive continues to be restricted from entitled claimants – facilitates a return to three interrelated questions: for whom are archives created and conserved, who is obliged to care for, and authorise access to, them, and to whom do they belong?

Keywords: cultural ethics, Australian museums, Gurindji, Indigenous autoethnography, provenance

Introduction[1]

> It's an important thing for us, to see the things in the [Berndt] museum in WA. We want to know or we want to see ... things we haven't seen for a long time.
>
> (Gus George, video interview, Karungkarni Art and Culture Aboriginal Corporation, Kalkaringi, March 2016)

Archives matter – most of us know that – but the question of to whom they most matter interweaves the discussion that follows by contextualising and identifying distinctive and overlapping voices. Drawing attention to the personal, cultural, political, and ethical issues that evolve when the matters of archival ownership and access arise, we interpolate the impact on personal experience and dignity by recounting Brenda L Croft's story when she undertook an archival search and gaining access became a reality. Croft's story emerged within, and can be distinguished from, a contrasting example where the opposite occurred and archival access was denied. We conclude by showing, through these examples, why certain archives were not created with inbuilt obligations to future generations, and outline how an opportunity was lost when a significant change could have resulted in a productive outcome for all. Considered, too, is how and why archival access denial has resulted in both insult and obstruction, most especially for subsequent generations of Australian First Nations families, such as Gurindji families of Northern Australia. Presented also are thoughts for future generations of Indigenous and non-Indigenous families and researchers whose intentions for their own research are likely to matter far more to the people with whom they worked, rather than to themselves. Brenda L Croft's opening story, relating the profound immediacy of successfully searching for family through the archives, draws readers into the deep archival well that is explored.

Drawing from an archival well, and (re)finding loved ones

Brenda L Croft

For as long as I can remember, I have always been drawn to the archives, initially those closest to home, the personal archives of my family, and in more recent decades, those in, and of, the 'public' domain – designated official documents and material.

---

1   At the heart of this chapter are those to whom content most matters. Thank you in particular to Gurindji Elders who respectfully endeavoured to gain access to the Berndt Field Note Archive and to organise a visit to the Berndt Museum in 2016. Particular thanks to Gus George, Violet Wadrill Nanaku, and Ronnie Wavehill Wirrpnga, and to Penny Smith at the Karungkarni Art and Culture Aboriginal Corporation in Kalkaringi, Northern Territory. We are grateful to Erika Charola for transcription and James Marshall for film documentation. Sincere thanks also to Ali Abdullah-Highfold, Shane Agius, and Lea Gardam at the South Australian Museum for all their assistance. We have also benefited from independent legal advice, and wish to thank the *Language Documentation & Conservation* editorial team, and two reviewers, for their thoughtful and constructive feedback on our original chapter.

Both types, private and public, house profound histories – filed away in folders and boxes containing letters, notebooks, microfiche, photographs, negatives, transparencies, audio tapes, film, miscellaneous documents, and ephemera, all dependent on the knowledge holders sharing their recollections, providing the methods and means with which to decode their contents.

My mother, Dorothy, inspired the archivist in me, organising regular family slide nights, adding captions to books, papers, photographs, and slides, filing away letters, cards, and notices that held resonance for her, which she felt would hold significance for someone in our family down the track.

She was also determined to create a personal archive for my father, Joe, whose past seemed a blank beyond a certain point in his early childhood. A member of the Stolen Generations, he professed not to remember anything before the age of seven years.

This included any memory of his mother, Bessie, from whom he had been removed at the age of five in 1931, where they were interred at Kahlin Compound in Darwin. He was sent south to government-run children's homes in the Katherine and Central Australian regions, before being sent to boarding school in Queensland in 1940.

It was there that my father assumed Bessie had died, when correspondence she sent to him during his time at All Souls Anglican School in Charters Towers, central Queensland (1940–1943), c/- Native Patrol Officer, Bill Harney Senior, ceased during World War II. Harney had kept an eye on my father, not only in his role as a native patrol officer but also because of his own connections with Charters Towers, having been born there in 1895.

How was my father to know that following the Japanese bombing of Darwin in 1942, all women and children had been evacuated to southern states? How could he not assume his mother was dead?

The birth of an(other) archive

Sandy Toussaint

It was also in the 1940s Northern Territory that newly trained anthropologists Catherine and Ronald Berndt visited the Gurindji, a language group associated with Croft's father's family and community, at Jinparrak, or Wave Hill Station. At that time, specifically 1944, and with seemingly good intentions on all sides, Gurindji women, men, and children acknowledged the young married couple on their traditional lands and welcomed them into their homes and lives. Conversations began, and interviews and ethnographic descriptions were recorded in notebooks. Richly woven dilly bags became the property of the Berndts, a point we develop further below. With Catherine and Ronald as interlocutors, language learning apparently commenced. It is likely that they required assistance with translations. During a two-month research time frame, cultural and linguistic material was collected, becoming information that years later informed reports and a book about the poor conditions Gurindji pastoral workers were living in, a matter that became publicly known and nationally recognised through the Equal Wages Pastoral Award in the late 1960s (Berndt & Berndt 1987). The recognition of traditional land ownership in 1976 through the *Aboriginal Land Rights (Northern Territory) Act 1976* was also a factor that drove efforts to obtain improved living conditions and rights in land for Aboriginal families, including for the Gurindji.

Gurindji men and women (and associated Malngin, Mudburra, Bilinarra, Ngarinyman, Warlpiri, and others) continued to struggle for improved working conditions and the return of their traditional lands. But the cultural and linguistic artefacts and material information recorded by Catherine and Ronald at Wave Hill, as well as at other parts of the Northern Territory (especially Yirrkala in northeast Arnhem Land and Birrindudu on the border of Western Australia and the Northern Territory),[2] remained in their notebooks to be later stored at the University of Western Australia's Berndt Museum of Anthropology. The notebooks eventually became known as the Berndt Field Note Archive.

Ronald Berndt passed away in 1990. Catherine Berndt died four years later. A 30-year embargo, commencing from the point of Catherine's death in May 1994, was placed on the release of their fieldnotes, meaning that none of the cultural information they had collected would be available to the families with whom they had worked until 2024. In the case of Gurindji families, this meant that the cultural information imparted to the Berndts in 1944 would not be available in response to access requests from their descendants for at least 80 years (Toussaint 2017).

Other Indigenous families have also been disaffected by the embargo but are increasingly making their concerns publicly felt. Smith, Jackson, Gray & Copley (2018), for instance, write about the embargo's impact on the Ngadjuri group of South Australia. Also in 2018, the Federal Court of Australia in the matter of *Mumbin v Northern Territory of Australia*, Griffiths J issued orders to the University of Western Australia (UWA) to provide non-party discovery documents in the Berndt Museum Collection relevant to the Katherine (Jawoyn/Dagoman) Native Title claims (FCA 2018).

The Berndt Field Note Archive was not only restricted from Gurindji and other Indigenous groups; it was also restricted from non-Aboriginal scholars working on behalf of Aboriginal people to undertake research for native title claims, such as the Kalkaringi Claim, begun in 2000 by the Central Land Council for the township where many Gurindji live. Language documentation and analysis, oral history studies, material culture research, and family inquiries indicate further reasons for which access to archival material is sought. In such a restrictive process, the Berndt Field Notes were effectively 'owned' by the Berndt Museum and decidedly kept from the descendants of the 1944 families: clearly the Berndts and later museum management did not feel obliged to make available fieldnote content to the families of the people from whom the original information had been collected.

Returning, in uneven parallel, to a more collaborative and productive, albeit emotionally anguished, archival encounter, we continue with Croft's telling story.

---

2   A quantity of brown paper drawings was also collected by the Berndts at Birrindudu, a small community
     that remains a pastoral station on the northern border of Western Australia and the Northern Territory.
     While collected in 1944 and/or possibly early 1945, the collection of Birrindudu artworks was not formally
     accessioned into the Berndt Museum's Collection until 2012 (Toussaint 2015a).

No words necessary

Croft continues …

In an audio interview from the National Library of Australia archives that historian Peter Read conducted with my father in 1989 as research for his biography on renowned Eastern Arrernte/Kalkadoon activist Charles Perkins, my father described himself as an orphan, an assumption he had made following the cessation of letters from his mother in 1942.

He had continued thinking he had no family until he married my mother in 1962. Following their marriage in Sydney they moved to Perth, remaining there until 1968, when my parents made the decision to return to the eastern states.

In order to apply for employment my father needed a birth certificate, which he did not have, so he wrote to Harry Giese, Director of Social Welfare, Welfare Branch, NT Administration. Giese's response included news that his mother was alive. Taken aback by this revelation, my father resumed contact through letters, although he was not reunited with my grandmother until May 1974.

My family travelled to Darwin to be with her when it was clear that she was terminally ill. Prior to this, on 13 February of that year, my father wrote to Giese seeking his assistance to bring my grandmother to Brisbane Hospital for treatment, which was close to where we lived just over the border in NSW.

It is with thanks to a colleague, Luke Scholes, that this information became known to me. Luke came across my father's correspondence in February 2015 while conducting research in Harry Giese's files in the National Archives of Australia NT Archives Centre (NAA NTAC) in Milner, Darwin.

When Luke sent digital copies of my father's letter to me via email I immediately recognised the typewriter font. My mother had typed the letter on her Facit typewriter, which was then signed by my father in his beautiful Copperplate script. There is something visceral, almost physical, in the recognition of the mark making of loved ones no longer here.

Viewing the letter felt like being sucked down a time tunnel, transported to the moment when the paper was in the typewriter, the keys clacking under my mother's swift fingers, as my father dictated his concerned words. Recognition of the font also brought the memory of learning to type on that machine in our kitchen in Canberra four decades ago.

Giese's reply on 1 March 1974 states that he does not think that my grandmother will agree to leave her home at Retta Dixon to go into hospital. This was the impetus for my parents selling their newsagency in order to fund our trip to Darwin two months later.

This recollection brings to mind another memory, that of me sitting in the viewing room at the NAA NTAC at Milner on 5–6 November 2014. I am the lone occupant and the document I am reading is the Timber Creek Police Book NTRS 2771/P1, Police Book (PB) 256, 1926–1928.

The book is so fragile that the brittle pages partially disintegrate in my hands as I turn them, no matter how careful I am. Am I the first person to open this book of matter-of-fact horrors in nearly 90 years? Turning to pages 35–36, I read:

Yearly report on Aboriginals, 1st July 1927: ... The following half-castes were sent to Darwin Half-Caste Home ...,[3] Joe (Quadroon), & his half-caste mother named Bessie ... Report by JK Hemmings.

The black Indian ink script of the policeman in charge at Timber Creek on 1 July 1927 is the inverse reflection of my father's signature at the end of his poignant request to Giese nearly 46 years later. Echoes rebound down the four decades hence, growing fainter with each reverberation.

This is the earliest record I have found of my father and grandmother. The breath leaves my body, like a sucker-punch to the stomach. I stand up and start pacing. I've rung someone, I can't recall who, but I'm talking gibberish. I don't realise that tears are streaming down my face, but the staff do, having been watching me through the glass walls of the room.

One staff member enters quietly, walks to where I am again sitting reading the page over and over, places a box of tissues beside me with unspoken compassion, then silently leaves the room, no words necessary.

The museum, the university, and the Gurindji request

My name's Ronnie Wavehill Jangala, I'm full Gurindji ... we want to look at that – what's it, paper, in the book ... if they've got it from Aboriginal people in the early days ... I was only a little boy at the time ... I saw those two *kartiya* [a reference to non-Aboriginal people, such as Ronald and Catherine Berndt] ... they took them, talking man-to-man ... sometimes it's secret ... if they've got it in a book, let somebody read it to me, some of it's for men's business, secret – women can't hear it, kids can't hear that information, you know ... sometimes it's alright [open], sometimes it's ceremony way ... if somebody gets that book, and reads it to me, read it, sometimes it's alright, sometimes I'll say, "No, don't share it out, it's secret business," when it's in a book, it's like that, that's all I can say ...[4]

(Ronnie Wavehill Wirrpnga, video interview, Karungkarni Art and Culture Aboriginal Corporation, Kalkaringi, March 2016).

Toussaint continues ...

The discipline of anthropology began at UWA in the mid-1950s, whereas the Anthropology Research Museum, later known as the Berndt Museum of Anthropology, was established

---

3   Name redacted at the request of the Northern Territory Police, Fire and Emergency Services, 8 May 2017.
4   Transcription by Erika Charola, 20 May 2016.

20 years later in 1976.[5] The Berndt Field Note Archive is stored at the museum and its governance comes within the purview of the museum director or associate director. Records show that the Berndt Museum, and the later RM and CH Berndt Research Foundation established as part of the Berndt Bequest to the university, have received a number of formal and informal access requests to review the Berndt Field Note Archive. These have mostly come from Indigenous groups and associated researchers. Requests have increased since the implementation of the federal government's *Native Title Act 1993*, in response to the High Court's momentous 1992 *Mabo* decision that rejected the fiction of *terra nullius*, and acknowledged Indigenous customary law in lands and waters.[6] On all but one occasion a request to access the fieldnotes was denied by both the Berndt Museum and the University of Western Australia's legal office, citing will conditions: it was argued that the fieldnotes were not to be released until 30 years after Catherine Berndt's death.[7] It remains unclear why Catherine and Ronald embargoed their fieldnotes for three decades, to begin after Catherine's death.[8] But it does not seem to have been for the benefit of the descendants of the Indigenous women, men, and children who so generously provided them with substantial cultural information and other materials when they visited their homes at Jinparrak in 1944.[9]

In 2016 the Gurindji[10] decided to formally approach the Berndt Museum and the Berndt Foundation to gain access to the Berndt Field Note Archive and to the information contained in the fieldnotes it held, which had been collected from their forebears eight decades earlier.[11] Lodged carefully and respectfully, their request did not ask for repatriation, but for viewing

5   In a report titled 'Berndt Museum and the American Museum of Natural History in New York' to UWA's deputy vice-chancellor and director of Development and Alumni, Toussaint (2015b) advised that the Berndts sold 130 artefacts they had collected in the 1940s–1950s. The artefacts were sold for the equivalent of A$7000 in an arrangement made between the AMNH and UWA with the aim of assisting the establishment of anthropology at UWA. Toussaint, alarmed by documentation about the 1957–1958 sale, visited the AMNH in 2015 and later advised relevant organisations about the find. It was unclear whether any of the artefacts were from Wave Hill. This matter, like the embargo, remains unresolved.

6   AIATSIS has a wealth of information about the High Court's 1992 *Mabo* decision and the *Native Title Act 1993*. (https://aiatsis.gov.au/explore/articles/mabo-case.)

7   On one occasion only was a request acquiesced and this was due solely to a 1998 Federal Court Order in the South Australian Hindmarsh Island Bridge Case listed as *Kartinyeri v Commonwealth*. A highly supervised visit was arranged for an anthropologist to view and interpret relevant fieldnotes at the Berndt Museum, without adverse outcomes for any party.

8   Certain progress has been made with regard to policies and legislation relating to repatriation, but with the focus consistently placed on the return of human remains and sacred objects. (http://www.collectionslaw. com.au/1repatriation.)

9   See, for instance, Toussaint (2017, 2018) and Tonkinson (2007) for further discussion of Catherine and Ronald's life and research.

10 The renowned 'From Little Things, Big Things Grow' by Kev Carmody and Paul Kelly eloquently renders the Gurindji struggle. The first lands to be symbolically and actually returned to the Gurindji are also iconically connected to senior Traditional Owner Vincent Lingiari and the 1972–1975 Labor prime minister, Gough Whitlam.

11 The Berndt Museum and Berndt Foundation were both approached because of Brenda L Croft's successful application for a scholarship to the foundation, which listed research related to the museum as one of its aims.

and recording access only. It was accompanied by a compelling audiovisual film with senior Gurindji Traditional Owners explaining their profound concerns for their need to obtain access, combined with a support letter from the Karungkarni Art and Culture Aboriginal Corporation (2016), and another from the co-trustee of the Catherine Berndt Estate, Sandy Toussaint.[12]

The access request was initiated through artist, curator, and practice-led researcher Brenda L Croft, who had been competitively selected from a range of applicants for a research grant from the university's Berndt Research Foundation (funds for which were provided in Catherine Berndt's will and bequest to assist anthropological, archaeological, and linguistic research in Aboriginal Australia). Curiously, the Berndt Foundation Committee, while supporting Croft's application for an $8000 research grant to undertake research toward a doctorate and an accompanying exhibition, did not support her or any combined Gurindji requests for access to the 1944 fieldnotes. Only one foundation committee member cogently advocated for Gurindji access.[13]

Further, a long-planned and agreed visit that Croft organised as part of her Berndt Postgraduate Award to view objects and material in the collection with Gurindji community members in 2016 was cancelled at short notice. The reason given, that proposed museum renovations would prevent access, was not followed with any suggested alternative date. Croft indicated that she considered her originally approved award aims were being deliberately eroded, which also affected the award outcomes.

The relationship between Croft, on behalf of the Gurindji community and the Karungkarni Art Centre, and the Berndt Museum initially began in 2015, at which point it had been both positive and encouraging. Close liaison around Croft's intended aims and outcomes, and the museum's realisation that the collection also held a series of crayon drawings, along with a number of vibrant dilly bags the Berndts collected so long ago at Wave Hill, was both exciting and revelatory. There was a great deal of communication back and forth via email between the Berndt Museum, Croft, Meakins, and McConvell, the latter providing much needed background. Digitised copies of the drawings were sent from the museum and McConvell showed them to, and discussed them with, senior men in the Jinparrak Community during preparations for the planned 50th anniversary commemoration of the 1960s Gurindji Walk-Off from Wave Hill Station. The invaluable information McConvell collated was then provided back to the Berndt Museum. McConvell also collated who could access which drawings according to the cultural information provided. Here was a clear example of two-way collaborative access that was

---

12 In 1993, Catherine Berndt, and Catherine's physician brother, asked Toussaint to become an estate trustee. Following Catherine's death in 1994, her brother asked Toussaint to become co-trustee (personal correspondence, Sandy Toussaint, CH Berndt Estate File). John Stanton, director of the Berndt Museum for 30 years, was co-trustee and the Berndt's literary executor.

13 In a 2016 letter to Sandy Toussaint, who supported Gurindji access and managed the Berndt Museum between October 2013 and December 2015, UWA's deputy vice-chancellor advised her that "UWA's decision is based on the intent expressed within Paragraph 6.1(a) of the Will of Catherine Berndt to impose a 30-year embargo on access to the field notes. That will be lifted in 2024. From the perspective of understanding and interpreting the Will, there is no ambiguity to that embargo. I understand that this view is in fact shared by your Co-Trustee in the estate, Dr John Stanton" (Reference F82517). Some opine that Stanton was a 'protégé' of the Berndts (see Smith et al 2018). There is no evidence to support this claim.

of prospective mutual benefit to both parties. Despite the potential embedded in a possible collaboration, it became obvious in 2016 that circumstances had changed, and museum access was denied to Croft and a planned Gurindji Elders visit thwarted. The silence from the Berndt Foundation was deafening; museum emails to Croft and others caused confusion and were unnecessarily bruising.

The denial of access to all Gurindji material held in the collection – not just the 1940s fieldnotes – short term or long term, impacted everyone involved, but to Croft, in particular, it felt like a resounding slap in the face: communication completely shut down. Surely the community's written and audiovisual requests, with accompanying support material, to access deeply significant cultural knowledge in the archived fieldnotes could be addressed with positive and mutually beneficial outcomes?

It is possible that the Berndts were cautious about revealing their fieldnotes in case this generated criticism from other anthropologists and/or Indigenous groups, perhaps because of the contested role some anthropologists played in the 20th century. But 30 years? While it is known that certain archives need to be restricted because of gender and ritual sensitivities, most museum and gallery staff in the 21st century follow clear guidelines to protect restricted, gender-specific material. Interestingly, these rely heavily on significant Indigenous traditional protocols; this highlights how the Berndt Museum has lost an additional opportunity to involve senior Gurindji women and men and their associate researchers in the language and culture of a decision-making process relating to the Field Note Archive.

Archival and museum access denied to Gurindji

Linguist Felicity Meakins, who was working with the Gurindji community alongside linguist and anthropologist Patrick McConvell at the time of the request, has a long history of interaction with local families. They further help to contextualise and explain the difficult consequences of denied access, not only to the archived fieldnotes, but also to the material items Catherine and Ronald collected that the Berndt Museum retains, and the effect on the local community and broader, interrelated research interests.

Felicity Meakins and Patrick McConvell

Although our attempts to access the Berndt Archive are turned down, we nonetheless rely on earlier communications from the museum that there were 21 crayon drawings and four dilly bags created by Gurindji people in the collection.[14] As visual objects, they have some potential for the *Still in my mind: Gurindji experience, location and visuality* exhibition Brenda L Croft is curating. We also see this as another opportunity to develop a collaborative process with the Berndt Museum with a view to repatriate and enrich the Berndt collection. We envisage researchers who have the trust of relevant Indigenous communities acting as points of mediation between the museum and these communities. Due to the short length of time that Ronald and Catherine spent in so many and varied locations, we believe it is reasonable to assume that there is still a lot of work to be done to both uncover and understand the 1940s

---

14   See also Toussaint (2016), who discusses inquiries relating to, and display of, the dilly bags.

collected objects and documented knowledge. The process we outline aims to resuscitate the Berndt collection in a culturally appropriate manner.

We receive what little metadata is available from the museum for the crayon drawings. The digitised images of the drawings that staff had previously sent include a few pencil annotations only, but these assist in clarifying the content and function of the drawings. It is not known whether the annotations are made by Catherine or Ronald. The arrival of the scans immediately engenders unease with Patrick McConvell as they include stick figures of spirit beings drawn by senior men. It is unclear how 'open' these drawings really are, despite the fact that they are apparently listed as 'open', or non-restricted, in the Berndt Museum's database. We consider whether it is likely that some of the crayon drawings depict acts of sorcery designed to cause harm through the very process of drawing them. There are examples of sorcery drawings in the rocky gorges close to Daguragu, where the Gurindji workers and their families had settled after they'd walked off Wave Hill Station. It becomes increasingly evident that access to the fieldnotes would give us a better sense of how to proceed with any possible knowledge repatriation, in addition to whether the drawings could be appropriately included as display objects in the *Still in my mind: Gurindji experience, location and visuality* exhibition.

Although the dilly bags are unlikely to belong to the realm of the secret and sacred, they are equally perplexing. The bags are made from modern fibres and dyes, and weaving is also not a practice among the Gurindji or their close neighbours. How did Gurindji women on Wave Hill Station come to be making string bags? The bags clearly have a story to tell, but it is likely to be one of broader regional connections between Aboriginal groups or perhaps some rapport between *kartiya* (non-Aboriginal) and *ngumpin* (Aboriginal) station women. While the dilly bags present somewhat of a mystery, the crayon drawings become a site of contestation.

Gurindji trust of outside researchers and museum staff becomes paramount in the discussion process. It is decided that Patrick McConvell, as a man with a longstanding connection to Gurindji people, is the best placed person to mediate between the archive and the community, to better understand the provenance and purpose of the crayon drawings. McConvell has also had prior experience with the problem of access to the Berndt fieldnotes when working with the Gurindji and others at Daguragu and Kalkaringi for the Central Land Council.[15]

We time the trip to coincide with the long-planned 50th anniversary celebration of the Wave Hill Walk-Off, the landmark event of 1966 that, as noted above, strongly aided the delivery of the equal wages to the pastoral industry and resulted in the establishment of the *Aboriginal Land Rights (Northern Territory) Act 1976*.

Patrick works with two senior men, Ronnie Wavehill and Robbie Peter. The fragility of knowledge is palpable. The age of this small group, all senior custodians of knowledge in their respective societies, adds an urgency to the task. We are reminded that knowledge is only as strong as the bodies that carry it. They gather around the drawings, trying to understand the minds of the men from 1944. Many other Gurindji men might have been able

---

15   McConvell notes that while he and the Gurindji community were denied access to any fieldnotes when working on the claim through the CLC, then museum director John Stanton suggested that he could have access to drawings the Berndts collected at Wave Hill. An arrangement was made to meet at Kalkaringi in the Northern Territory, but the meeting did not eventuate and McConvell heard nothing further from the museum.

to provide significantly more information, since they were adults at the time Ronald and Catherine undertook fieldwork. But they have since passed away. Ronnie Wavehill is one of the oldest culturally knowledgeable men, but he was born in 1936, so he was only eight at the time Catherine and Ronald undertook fieldwork. Robbie is also a knowledgeable Elder, but considerably younger than Ronnie. How much longer will Gurindji Elders and senior academics with connections to the community be able to make sense of the esoteric figures in the drawings, let alone the wealth of knowledge held in the fieldnotes? We report this information back to the Berndt Museum and Foundation in our application for access, and in the audiovisual film we send.

Four of the images are clearly identified by Ronnie and Robbie as depictions of men's secret ceremonies and sacred objects. The remaining 17 images are deemed to be unrestricted and can be shown to the general public. A number of these are included in the *Still in my mind: Gurindji experience, location and visuality* exhibition. The provenance of the dilly bags is belatedly identified by Gurindji artists Ena Oscar and Kathy Wardill at the exhibition's opening at UNSW Galleries in Sydney in May 2017. They remember Elsie Jalyawuk Nangala used to make them with a manager's wife on neighbouring Vestey station of Limbunya.

The information about the crayon drawings and dilly bags is written up and sent to the Berndt Museum. Notwithstanding seeming opposition to fieldnote access and its painful implications, we are confident that with regard to the crayon drawings, we have successfully trialled a collaborative model of repatriation and enrichment. But we receive word later that year that the 30-year fieldnotes embargo will definitely hold until 2024, and that no access to the rest of the collection will be granted to Gurindji people and their research associates.

What of the effect of the passing of time on the cultural value of the collection, of the knowledge and information recorded by Ronald and Catherine Berndt that dates back to 1944? Their visit was brief, but some important publications resulted from it, such as the co-authored *End of an era* (1987), and *Women's changing ceremonies in Northern Australia* (1950) by Catherine Berndt, drawn from her Master of Arts thesis on women's secret love songs, which unfortunately put these songs into the public domain (as was not uncommon practice at the time). It is likely that these publications contain only a fraction of the knowledge senior Gurindji men and women gave to the Berndts, and no doubt only the portion that the Berndts, as young, inexperienced anthropologists at the time, could make sense of when they visited Wave Hill Station. In 2024, when the embargo is lifted, Ronnie Wavehill will be 88 years old. Senior ceremony woman Topsy Dodd will be 90. The ongoing tragedy is that neither is likely to be alive by then. If they are, and live long enough to see the embargo lifted, it may not be possible for them to fully recall and recount their cultural expertise with younger generations and researchers to elucidate meaning from the fieldnotes. A more probable scenario is that younger generations will be wary of the fieldnote and crayon drawing contents, particularly the extent to which the knowledge should be publicly available. A further outcome is that a permanent embargo will be placed on the fieldnotes, but this time it will be Gurindji-imposed.

When archival access evolves into another sort of grief

Croft continues ...

My anticipation was embodied as I wrote to the Archives Section at the South Australian Museum (SAM) on 28 May 2014, requesting copies of the images of my grandmother. I had already been liaising with SAM's Archives Section in relation to Norman B Tindale's Aboriginal Languages map, when I came across the reference to Bessie.

Finally, I'd be able to see an image of her when she was a young woman, before her face was distorted by illness, to see if my father resembled her, if I looked like her. I submitted the required indemnity form outlining my relationship.

Two days later Ali Abdullah-Highfold, Family and Community History consultant, rang to advise me that the images were part of medical records. In my excitement to see images of Bessie, I didn't really take his warning on board.

When the digital images arrived via email I opened them and was taken aback to see a partial photograph of my grandmother's face from the bridge of her nose down to her neck, with her eyes out of frame (Figure 1). The second image was of my grandmother's misshapen, 'boomerang' legs, and that was when the truth hit home.

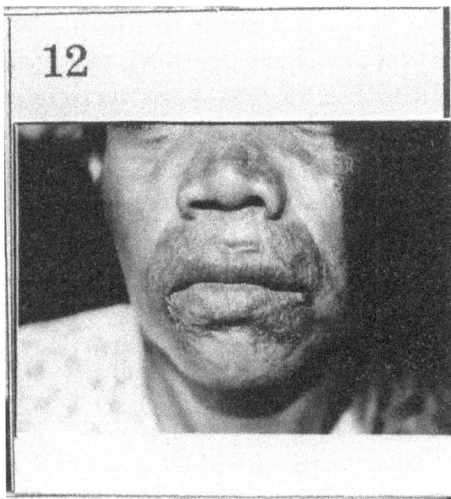

Figure 1. Cecil J Hackett, Proof number 11–12 Annotated 'Bessie Croft Chinese/native'. H/C. AA122/15/1/5/12, Hackett Collection, South Australian Museum Archives

She was the medical research subject of the photographer and doctoral researcher CJ Hackett (1905–1995). Subjected to abject debasement, dehumanised, stripped of dignity, savaged by and through the lens. My eyes burned with anger, my heart ached for her, for me not being able to see her face in full. My hope had been to see my father and myself reflected in her face, but that was denied me.

The image of her truncated face was etched into my mind. I was torn between fury with Hackett and bittersweet appreciation that he had bothered to note her name, the date, and the place where the photograph was taken – Kahlin Compound, 17 May 1934 – and most intriguingly, her racial classification – half-caste/Chinese. The latter ethnicity was news to me, and either my grandmother provided this information to Hackett, or he surmised it from her mixed-race appearance.

Following this experiential encounter, arrangements were made to visit and view the SAM archives in early September 2014 with Felicity Meakins, following a field research trip we had undertaken to Wave Hill. Felicity was viewing material in the archives as part of her research for *Yijarni: True stories from Gurindji Country*, to which I was contributing photographs.

As I viewed Hackett's fieldnotes and proof sheets relating to the images of my grandmother, I was struck by how less confrontational they appeared 'in the flesh'. Proof sheet strips of 35 mm glued into a small exercise book did not have the overwhelming impact of a high-resolution scan of my grandmother's sectioned face appearing full screen on my laptop.

I was also able to read Hackett's hand-typed publication, 'Another letter or a trip across Australia, 15 March to 6 September 1934, vol. 1 & 2' (Cambridge, 1936), which read like a Boys' Own Adventure journal of his travels through Central and Northern Australia, conducting medical research in Aboriginal communities, and in one disturbing instance, recording his gleeful grave-robbing of a recently deceased woman's skeleton afflicted with 'boomerang legs', both via text and photography.

In comparison, Hackett's thesis 'Boomerang legs and yaws in Australian Aborigines with a description of bone lesions resulting from yaws', which was submitted to the University of Adelaide in July 1935, was bloodless – ironical given its subject matter. A year later it was published as *Boomerang leg and yaws in Australian Aborigines* (Royal Society of Tropical Medicine and Hygiene, 1936).

I managed to secure copies of the latter two publications, but not copies of 'Another letter ...', nor, frustratingly, locate the negatives of his proof sheets in the South Australian Museum archives. Whether they were with the original deposit could not be ascertained.

Hackett's degradation of my grandmother impelled the creation of a major artwork, *shut/mouth/scream* (2016b) (Figure 2), as a visual call and response to his disturbing image. I had a similar image taken of myself, using wet plate collodion processing onto tin, then scanned the image and overlaid both images with text.

My reworked image of my grandmother referenced Hackett's notes – his racialised description of my grandmother and the date he took the photograph at Kahlin Compound; my image included my birthdate – exactly three decades after Hackett's – my silent, visual howl, echoing over eight decades, giving my grandmother a voice, where she had so long been denied the chance to speak, my gift to her.

The relationship developed with the South Australian Museum since first accessing Hackett's material has proved extremely positive for both of us. My work *shut/mouth/scream* has been included in the exhibitions *Defying Empire: 3rd National Indigenous Art Triennial*, at the National Gallery of Australia, touring nationally, and my practice-led doctoral research exhibition *Still in my mind: Gurindji experience, location and visuality*, also touring nationally. My reworked image of my grandmother has also been reproduced on the cover of *Visualising human rights* (2018).[16]

---

16 https://uwap.uwa.edu.au/products/visualising-human-rights; see also Lydon (2018).

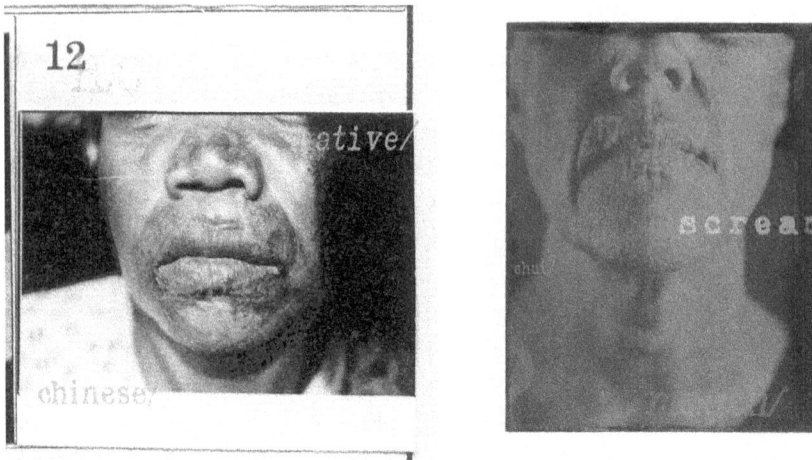

Figure 2. Brenda L Croft, *shut/mouth/scream* (2016b)

The Adelaide venue for *Still in my mind: Gurindji experience, location and visuality* will be the South Australian Museum in October 2019 as part of the city-wide First Nations visual arts and cultural festival Tarnanthi. A public panel is being proposed, with the focus on the importance of First Nations individuals and communities being able to access First Nations material held in public archives.

Other Gurindji material held in the South Australian Museum archives included data cards and photographs collected at Inverway Station by Norman B Tindale in 1954 (see Figure 3), a decade after the Berndts visited Wave Hill Station. Some of the data cards were reproduced in the *Still in my mind: Gurindji experience, location and visuality* exhibition and *Mayarni-kari Yurrk: More stories from Gurindji Country*, and copies of the material have been repatriated to Karungkarni Art and Culture Aboriginal Corporation.

Figure 3. Joseph B Birdsell, AA346/4/22/1. 'Inverway Station data card. Image R1317 Old Limbunya, Jack Pingkiyarri Jurlama, 1954. R1317'. Board for Anthropological Research Collection, South Australian Museum Archives

It was stated at the outset that the Berndt Museum, along with the Lawrence Wilson Art Gallery, is part of the University of Western Australia's Cultural Precinct. I had hoped that either or both institutions may have been possible venues for the Western Australian component of the *Still in my mind: Gurindji experience, location and visuality* touring exhibition. Initial inquiries received positive interest. At the same time that access to Gurindji 1940s fieldnotes was denied, and arrangements to visit the Berndt Museum were rescinded in 2016, so too interest in hosting the collaborative Gurindji exhibition lapsed.

The welcome and productive relationship that developed with the South Australian Museum, when compared to the shutdown of the relationship with the Berndt Museum, provides a stark contrasting example of how it is possible to generate a profoundly consequential two-way cultural exchange that creates something bigger together, as opposed to separately.

But we are not alone in our desire and despair about accessing First Nations' cultural assets held in the Berndt Museum archives. As referred to above in the article by Smith et al. (2018) titled 'Who owns a family's story? Why it's time to lift the Berndt fieldnotes embargo',[17] a mirror to my community's struggle appeared. Clearly outlined is the anger and sense of injustice experienced, in particular, by Ngadjuri Elder and Adjunct Associate in Archaeology at Flinders University Vincent Copley.

For Copley, the denial of access to fieldnotes of his grandfather's cultural knowledge that Ronald Berndt collected between 1939 and 1944, just before Ronald and Catherine Berndt undertook field research at Wave Hill, was highly distressing. Eighty-one-year-old Uncle Vince had been a friend of my late father, Joe, and his intense frustration and personal pain at being denied access to knowledge that is his birthright was unmistakable.

I was compelled to contact him, and during our telephone call we shared our exasperation at what seems a bloody-minded 21st century rendition of paternalism and control. For Uncle Vince – as with Gurindji Elder Ronnie Wavehill – six years felt like an eternity.

By the time the Berndt-imposed embargo is lifted – 2024 – it is unlikely that many, if any, of our Senior Custodians, who possess the required depth and breadth of classical Gurindji knowledge with which to decipher what is held in the Berndt archive from information collected 80 years ago, will still be here.

By that time what is held in the archives will be truly dead. It is too much to bear, it is much too late.

"For the children ..."

It's important for this country [that] we teach our children culture. That's why we want the important [information], for the children. We have to teach them, culture, law, everything.

(Violet Wadrill Nanaku, video interview, Karungkarni Art and Culture Aboriginal Corporation, Kalkaringi, March 2016)

---

17 Smith et al. (2018) (https://theconversation.com/friday-essay-who-owns-a-familys-story-why-its-time-to-lift-the-berndt-field-notes-embargo-94652)

Official archives, like academic institutions, vary in form, management and purpose. Archival collections in all their guises can also be places of contradiction for Indigenous Australians: women and men often feel desperate about what can seem foreboding metaphorical and literal doors, seeking knowledge and illumination of individual and collective histories, especially about family, and, where accessed, find the results tangible, precious, revealing. Those doors can sometimes seem impenetrable, however, or only open to a select few who have access to the language of the academy.

With regard to how the Gurindji request for access to the Berndt Field Note Archive and the Berndt Collection was ultimately handled, no consideration was given to the problems associated with a legal document found wanting several decades after it had been so poorly designed, and due consideration was not given to the Australian Indigenous groups most affected by its inequity. The high-level value of adding much-needed provenance was also sorely under-estimated, perhaps indicating a museum preference for the management of objects and collections.[18]

As we have described and analysed, generations of Indigenous women and men are still often personally, culturally, historically, and ethically excluded. Eager for discovery, seeking information about families, communities, language, and culture, Indigenous people search for what might be uncovered, while also being wary because that which might be revealed may lead to more pain and heartache for selves, families, and communities.

The Federal Court of Australia's orders to the University of Western Australia and the Berndt Museum in *Mumbin v Northern Territory of Australia* (2018 FCA 1646) referred to above add further depth and breadth to the myriad difficulties and implications of the Berndt embargo for Indigenous groups and associated researchers. The denial of archival access through instruments such as the embargo not only diverts access to the deep cultural heritage, knowledge, history, and expertise of First Nations groups, it also casts aside issues of collaboration and knowledge-strengthening, as so many senior people pass away each year. The high rates of Indigenous morbidity and mortality impact the Gurindji people as they do so many others. Opportunities to engender positive ways of enabling and facilitating access, developing relationships, reviving the original archives, and investing communities with power and pride are missed on so many critical, ethical, and subsequently important levels, despite the significance of the High Court of Australia's 1992 *Mabo* decision.

Via the interpolation of several interrelated stories, we have articulated through the unresolved Gurindji request and others in relation to the Berndt Museum that this archive was not created for the children of those from whom the material was originally collected. Ronald and Catherine Berndt, museum staff, and the university apparently felt little obligation to investigate fully, or find a legal, ethical, and culturally responsible means to advocate for, Gurindji requests for access. The Berndt Foundation Committee was also found wanting. The outcome has been a continuing grief through struggle, alongside resilience and greater confidence in Gurindji decision-making in the future, a confidence likely to inspire and hopefully empower other groups and researchers.

18   Toussaint (2017) also makes plain that universities in the future must consider whether they should accept collections tied to such unfair conditions, such as with the 30-year embargo accepted by UWA.

We have also shown that when family access to archives does occur, and archival and museum management is both positive and productive to applicants whose requests are underpinned by due cause, that it can and often does result in a generation of meaningful memories and connections, alongside the potential value of collaboration and expansion of the provenance of archival and other materials. While these experiences sometimes generate another layer of reflection and grief, they eventually find their way back to the loved ones of the persons to whom the intellectual and cultural copyright rightfully belongs. But these qualities are distant, suspended in light of dated and inequitable thinking and practice when an embargo such as that upheld by the Berndt Museum is reinforced in the face of a counter qualitative and rigorous argument about the value of provenance-adding, intertwined with attention to cultural ethics and human rights recognition in an increasingly enlightened nation.

For Croft, as family and community member, as well as scholar, artist, and applicant, the whole experience of receiving such varied archival access generated ongoing sorrow, grief, anger, frustration, illumination, and occasional joy. Both the struggle and the outcome also impacted upon Croft's practice-led collaborative doctoral research and exhibition project. For Toussaint the specificity of the Berndt embargo resulted in an increasing disquiet, one shared by many of her peers, at a circumstance that put the profession before the Gurindji people's substantive case for access. The process determined through the Berndt Museum, the Berndt Foundation, and by Toussaint's co-trustee, and the university's strategies that so discourteously and, on this occasion, so dismissively, discarded the request, also furthered her existing resolve to repatriate her own fieldwork materials, with Traditional Owner access and guidance. For Meakins and McConvell there was profound disappointment at the way in which the Berndt Museum and Foundation undermined the possibility of working collaboratively with Gurindji and associated researchers to add cultural and linguistic depth to the Wave Hill materials held in the museum collection. McConvell also tells how it was not the first time that he and the people among whom he conducted linguistic and cultural research had been denied access to the Berndt Museum.

The archives and access matter has become yet another chapter for Gurindji men, women, and children, including, and most especially, in the scenario we have described for Croft and her family. The experience adds to an already memorable, patient, and resilient Gurindji history. The words of Ronnie Wavehill best sum up a situation where so many people have been waiting for far too long ...

> We don't want to wait for too long. Some people [like] me are not too good now. We don't want to keep it for another couple of years more ... whatever information is in that book ... we don't want to wait, too long, couple of years, six years, ten years ... I don't think we'll live that bloody long, that many years ... not too good now ... that's all I can say.

(Ronnie Wavehill Wirrpnga, video interview, Kalkaringi, March 2016)

References

Berndt, CH. 1950. *Women's changing ceremonies.* Paris: L'Homme.

Berndt, RM & CH. 1987. *End of an era: Aboriginal labour in the Northern Territory.* Canberra: Australian Institute of Aboriginal Studies.

Charola, Erica & Felicity Meakins (eds.). 2016a. *Yijarni: True stories from Gurindji Country.* Canberra: Aboriginal Studies Press.

Charola, Erica & Felicity Meakins (eds.). 2016b. *Mayarni-kari Yurrk: More stories from Gurindji Country.* Batchelor, NT: Batchelor Press.

Croft, Brenda. 2016a. Retrac(k)ing country and (s)kin: Walking the Wave Hill Walk Off Track (and other sites of cultural contestation). *Westerly* 61(1). 76–82.

Croft, Brenda. 2016b. *shut/mouth/scream,* artwork featured in *subalter/N/ative dreams,* Sydney: Stills Gallery, 2016; *Still in my mind: Gurindji experience, locality and visuality,* Sydney: UNSW Galleries, Brisbane: UQ Art Museum, 2017 (touring nationally through to 2021); *Defying Empire: 3rd National Indigenous Art Triennial.* Canberra: National Gallery of Australia, 2017. *shut/mouth/scream* also featured on the cover of Jane Lydon (ed.). 2018. *Visualising human rights.* Nedlands: UWA Publishing.

Croft, Brenda. 2017. *Still in my mind: Gurindji experience, locality and visuality.* (Exhibition catalogue.) University of New South Wales Art and Design and the Karungkarni Art Centre: Sydney and Kalkaringi, Northern Territory.

Federal Court of Australia. 2018. Griffiths, J in the matter of *Mumbin v Northern Territory of Australia.* (http://www.judgments.fedcourt.gov.au/judgments/Judgments/fca/single2018/2018fca1646) (Accessed 19 October 2019.)

Hackett, Cecil J. 1934. Another letter or a trip across Australia, 15 March to 6 September, vol. 1 & 2. Cambridge. (Hand-typed copy held in South Australian Museum Archives.)

Hackett, Cecil, J. 1936. *Boomerang leg and yaws in Australian Aborigines.* Adelaide: Royal Society of Tropical Medicine and Hygiene.

Karungkarni Art Centre. 2016. Audiovisual recording to the Berndt Museum's Associate Director and the Berndt Foundation Committee when seeking access to the Berndt Field Note Archive. Jinparrak, NT.

Lydon, Jane (ed.). 2018. *Visualising human rights.* Nedlands: UWA Publishing.

Smith, Claire, Gary Jackson, Geoffrey Gray & Vincent Copley. 2018. Who owns a family's story? Why it's time to lift the Berndt field notes embargo. *The Conversation,* September. (https://theconversation.com/friday-essay-who-owns-a-familys-story-why-its-time-to-lift-the-berndt-field-notes-embargo-94652) (Accessed 5 October 2018.)

Tonkinson, Robert. 2007. Ronald Murray Berndt (1916–1990). *Australian dictionary of biography.* (http://adb.anu.edu.au/biography/berndt-ronald-murray-12202) (Accessed 19 October 2019.)

Toussaint, Sandy. 2015a. Berndt Museum Report. Unpublished report to UWA's cultural precinct director and deputy vice-chancellor (Community Engagement). UWA, September.

Toussaint, Sandy. 2015b. Berndt Museum and the American Museum of Natural History, New York. Unpublished report to UWA's deputy vice-chancellor and director of UWA Development and Alumni/ Berndt Museum. UWA, November.

Toussaint, Sandy. 2016. A mix of emotion. *Westerly* 61(1). 73–75.

Toussaint, Sandy. 2017. A letter to Catherine Berndt: Cultural politics and the preciousness of time. *Griffith Review*. (https://griffithreview.com/multimedia/a-letter-to-catherine-berndt/) (Accessed 19 October 2019.)

Toussaint, Sandy. 2018. Catherine Helen Berndt (1918–1994). *Australian dictionary of biography*. (https://www.google.com/search?client=safari&rls=en&q=catherine+helen+berndt,+national+australian+biography&ie=UTF-8&oe=UTF) (Accessed 19 October 2019.)

Language Documentation & Conservation Special Publication No. 18
Archival returns: Central Australia and beyond
ed. by Linda Barwick, Jennifer Green & Petronella Vaarzon-Morel, pp. 193–216
http://nflrc.hawaii.edu/ldc/sp18
http://hdl.handle.net/10125/24884

10

Working at the interface: The Daly Languages Project

Rachel Nordlinger
The University of Melbourne, ARC Centre of Excellence for the Dynamics of Language

Ian Green
The University of Adelaide

Peter Hurst
The University of Melbourne, ARC Centre of Excellence for the Dynamics of Language

Abstract

In this paper we present the Daly Languages Project (www.dalylanguages.org), funded by the ARC Centre of Excellence for the Dynamics of Language, and in collaboration with the Pacific and Regional Archive for Digital Sources in Endangered Cultures (PARADISEC), which has developed website landing pages for all of the languages of the Daly region of northern Australia. These landing pages provide a useful and usable interface by which a range of users can access primary recordings, fieldnotes, and other resources about the Daly languages; they are powered by a relational database which allows for easy updating, ensuring consistency across the website and allowing for an immediate response to community requests. Moreover, since the website is built with a commitment to open source, it is available for other researchers to adapt to their own projects and language groups. In this paper we discuss the goals and outcomes of the project, the design and functionality of the website landing pages, and advise readers on how they can access and adapt the open-source framework for their own purposes.

Keywords: Daly languages, language repatriation, landing pages, website, heritage recordings

Introduction[1]

The development of sustainable, accessible corpora of small languages has been an increasing focus of language documentation in recent years (see Henke & Berez-Kroeker 2016 for a summary of developments). Central to this has been the discussion of best practice in making good language records, and in archiving them appropriately to ensure their longevity and availability for future generations (e.g. Johnson 2004; Thieberger & Berez 2012). One important goal of such archives is to provide access to these language records, most importantly, for language communities and their descendants, and for other researchers. However, the ways in which such accessibility is best achieved are not yet well understood and have only recently become a focus of language documentation research (see, for example, Holton 2014).

In this paper we present the Daly Languages Project (www.dalylanguages.org), funded by the ARC Centre of Excellence for the Dynamics of Language, and in collaboration with the Pacific and Regional Archive for Digital Sources in Endangered Cultures (PARADISEC [www.paradisec.org.au]; see also Thieberger 2014; Thieberger, Barwick & Harris 2015), which has developed website landing pages for all of the languages of the Daly region of northern Australia. These landing pages provide a clear and easy-to-use interface for the extensive corpora of Ian Green, including recordings, fieldnotes, and manuscripts of 11 languages across the region, most of which are no longer spoken fluently. The websites are powered by a relational database which allows for easy updating, ensuring consistency across the website and allowing for an immediate response to community requests about the information contained on the various pages.

We believe the Daly Languages Project provides a useful interface model for other researchers, showing how corpora can be packaged and presented in a way that is usable and accessible for both community members and other researchers. In this paper we discuss the goals and outcomes of the project, the design and functionality of the website landing pages, and advise readers on how they can access and adapt the open-source framework for their own purposes.

Daly Languages

For this project, we use the term 'Daly Languages' to cover a group of 22 language varieties of the Daly region of the Northern Territory of Australia, southwest of Darwin. These languages (excluding Murrinhpatha) were first discussed as a group and proposed as a single language family in Tryon's (1974) volume, which provides brief sketches of each language and, for many, still represents the key published resource on the language. However, Tryon's evidence

1   We would like to thank Nick Reid, Stefan Schnell, and Nick Thieberger for useful discussion of the issues involved in designing and building the Daly Languages website, and lots of invaluable advice. We also thank Brighde Collins, Chris Venning, Kate Charlwood, and Geneva Goldenberg for research assistance support in digitising materials and entering content into the database, and audiences of the Australian Linguistics Society 2016 conference and corpus workshops run by the ARC Centre of Excellence for the Dynamics of Language, as well as two anonymous reviewers for useful feedback and suggestions. We are grateful to PARADISEC for support in digitising and archiving the Daly language materials, and the ARC Centre of Excellence for the Dynamics of Language (Project ID: CE140100041) for funding the project and the 2016 repatriation trip.

for considering these languages to be a single family appears to be largely typological (Tryon 1974: 304) and subsequent work, most notably by Ian Green (e.g. 2003) and Mark Harvey (e.g. 2003a; 2003b), has revised this picture. The current understanding of the relationships between the languages of the Daly region (see Nordlinger 2017) is that the 22 language varieties can be grouped into 10 different languages belonging to five language families. It is not clear whether there are any superordinate relationships among these five families, apart from proto-Australian, and indeed Evans (2003) suggests that (some of) these Daly families may be early offshoots of the proto language itself. Harvey (2003a) suggests a possible remote connection between the Eastern Daly group and the Gunwinyguan languages of Arnhem Land to the east, but this has yet to be definitively established.

The languages of the Daly region (except perhaps for Murrinhpatha) are greatly under-represented in the Australianist literature, and, beyond a brief chapter in Tryon (1974), many have had only limited description. One of the goals of the Daly Languages Project is to collect all available materials on these languages and make them accessible wherever possible to help redress this dearth of available resources. Nordlinger (2017) provides references to all available linguistic materials on the Daly languages, many of which are also available on the Daly Languages website that is the focus of this paper. Unfortunately, Murrinhpatha is now the only language of the region that is still being acquired by children: it is still being used by around 2500 people for daily communication in the community of Wadeye (Port Keats) and is acquired by all Wadeye children as their first language. All other languages of the region are highly endangered; many have only a handful of elderly speakers left and some (for example, Marramaninjsji, Yunggurr) have no fluent speakers left at all.

Ian Green's materials

During the period of 1980 through to 1996, the second author worked in the Daly region and amassed over 157 hours of recordings from 11 of the Daly languages. These recordings were accompanied by 23 books of handwritten fieldnotes and transcriptions. Many of the people Green worked with and recorded were among the last fluent speakers of their languages – languages now no longer spoken regularly in their communities – and all have long since passed away. Apart from Marrithiyel, which was the focus of Green's PhD thesis (Green 1989), most of these languages have been the subject of very little description, and available materials on the languages range from limited to non-existent. It was therefore very difficult for community members to access any information about their heritage languages, making Green's corpus a precious resource for communities. At the inception of the Daly Languages Project, the large majority of these materials were in analogue form, unarchived and unpublished, although well-maintained and safely stored in Green's home office. The original Green corpus is made up of the recordings and resources listed below.

Recordings

There is a total of 157 hours of recordings for 11 languages, as listed below. All recordings have now been digitised and most are available on open access in PARADISEC (http://www.paradisec.org.au).

- Marrithiyel, 32 hours, including texts and elicitation (grammatical, phonological, lexical)
- Marri Tjevin, 6 hours, grammatical elicitation
- Magati Ke, 3 hours, grammatical elicitation
- Marri Ngarr, 36 hours, elicitation (grammatical, phonological, lexical)
- Marramaninjsji, 6 hours, elicitation (grammatical, phonological, lexical), some texts
- Batjamalh, 2 hours, elicitation
- Merranunggu, 10 hours, including texts and elicitation (grammatical, phonological, lexical)
- Menthe, 7 hours, elicitation
- Emmi, 2 hours, elicitation
- MalakMalak, 36 hours, elicitation (grammatical, phonological, lexical)
- Matngele, 17 hours, elicitation (grammatical, phonological, lexical)

Fieldnotes, transcriptions, and analyses

Accompanying these recordings are 23 books of handwritten fieldnotes, transcriptions, and grammatical analyses. Each book has been scanned and added to the PARADISEC archive as an individual item. Where these notebooks contain transcriptions of field recordings, these pages have additionally been added to the same item as the recording in PARADISEC, so that the recording and the associated pages of the field notebook can be accessed together. Unpublished manuscripts laying out linguistic analyses, wordlists, and historical analyses have also been scanned or uploaded as required and are archived in PARADISEC.

Goals of the Daly Languages Project

The overall goals of the Daly Languages Project are (i) to protect the Daly language resources and ensure their longevity through digitisation and archiving in PARADISEC and (ii) to ensure their accessibility to community members and other researchers by providing a simple and functional online interface to these archived resources. More specifically, we wanted a digital portal that would be clear and simple for all users, both academic and non-academic; that would provide the content relevant to different user groups, including community users and researchers; and that would be easy to maintain and update without requiring the assistance of a programmer, so that we would minimise the risk of it becoming a graveyard website over time. A further goal was to provide a site where all the available information about each language could be brought together in one place – recordings, fieldnotes, published sources, language learning materials, cultural information, photos, and more. So, while the initial impetus was to protect and make accessible Ian Green's corpus, we have expanded the scope of the project to include any available materials on the Daly languages (subject to accessibility and copyright). Currently this amounts to another 60 resources, but we will continue to add more as they become available. Finally, in order to ensure maximal accessibility, it was important that the portal have functionality across multiple digital platforms (computer, mobile phone, tablet) and also in offline mode,[2] given that most community members live in remote locations where internet connections are not reliable or readily available.

A second aspect of the project was to repatriate Green's recordings to the families and communities of the people that he worked with in the 1980s and 1990s and, in doing so, to inform the communities of the digital portal where they could access materials about their languages, discuss access conditions and permissions, and get input on the functionality of the portal and suggestions for improvement.

We developed the Daly Languages website (http://www.dalylanguages.org/) to achieve these goals. It consists of landing pages for all of the languages of the Daly region of Australia and links to digitised copies of Green's recordings, his fieldnotes, dictionary materials, unpublished manuscripts containing grammatical description and linguistic analyses of most of the languages, as well as historical reconstructions. Our purpose in this paper is to discuss the design and functionality of this website and the associated database in case it may be of use for other researchers to adapt for other language areas. Firstly we discuss the design of the website landing pages, and then the administration of the website and its construction. In addition, Green and Nordlinger undertook a repatriation trip through the Daly region in July 2016. This trip and its outcomes are discussed in the final section.

The Daly Languages website

The primary functionality of the Daly Languages website (Figure 1) is to provide information about each of the languages of the Daly region, links to their primary and secondary resources (recordings, fieldnotes, etc), and a unified means of navigating the website as a whole. In this section we describe both the functionality and content of our website, including website navigation and the language pages.

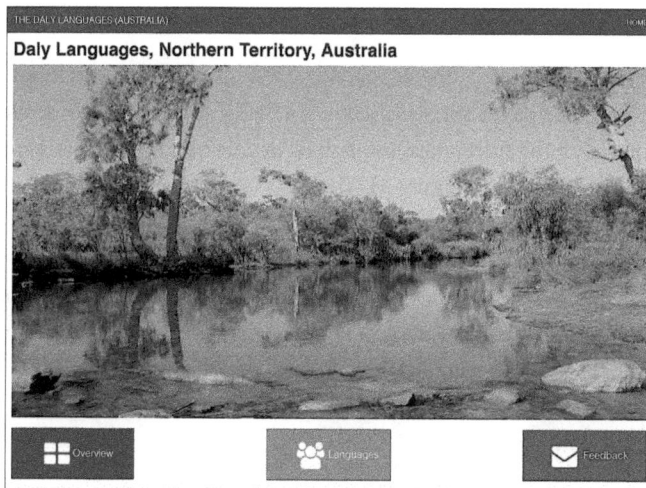

Figure 1. Home page of www.dalylanguages.org

---

2   We have not yet created a fully functional offline mode for the website, apart from the fact that all the resources are downloadable, but hope to develop this in the future.

Website navigation

Navigation toolbar

Every page on our website has the same navigation mechanism. This is a toolbar located at the top of each web page. The consistency of this navigation toolbar across all pages is intended to simplify engagement with the website and make it easier for the user to navigate around it.

Figure 2. The navigation toolbar as it appears on a desktop

This toolbar allows a user to access all areas of the public website. Note that the presentation of the toolbar (but not its functionality) changes depending on the device used to access the website. When viewed on a smaller device, the navigation toolbar is reconfigured to that shown in Figure 3:

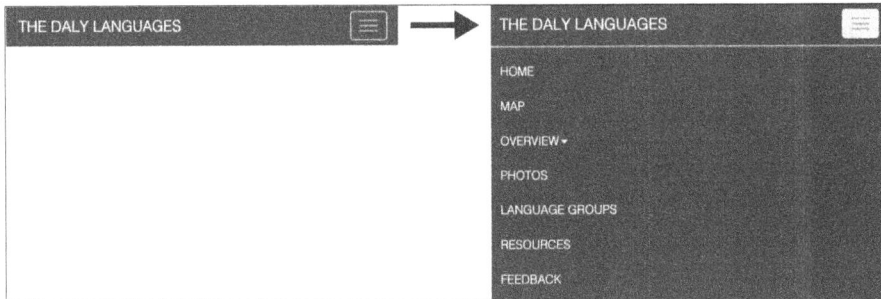

Figure 3. The navigation toolbar as it appears on a mobile phone

Map

The typical means by which language pages are accessed is via the language map. This map is reached either from the 'Map' tab in the navigation toolbar, or by clicking on the 'Languages' button on the entry page of the website (see Figure 1). The map is a customised Google map that displays each language and its general location.

A nice feature is that this map is dynamically resized depending upon which device a visitor uses to access the website. For smaller devices, the map of Australia is moved above the main map to give the user more screen space to access the region containing the language names, as shown in Figure 5.

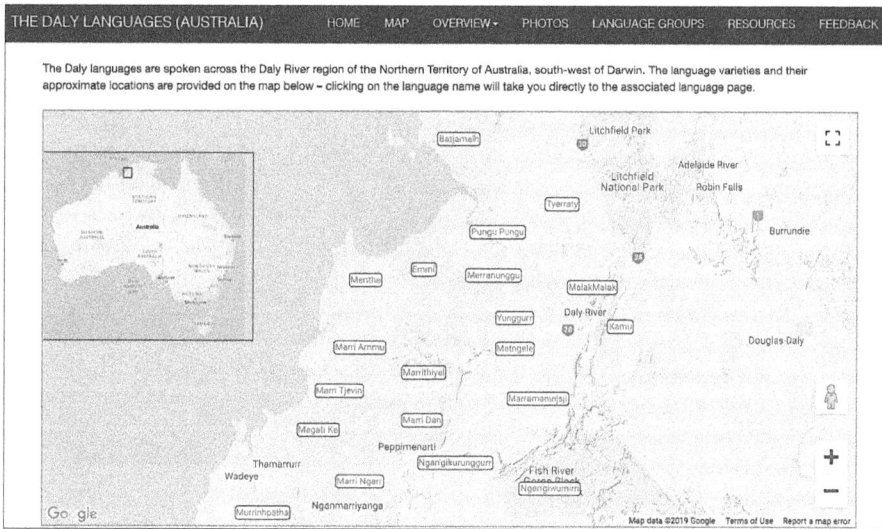

Figure 4. The language map: the language names are active links and direct the visitor to the relevant language page (see Figure 6)

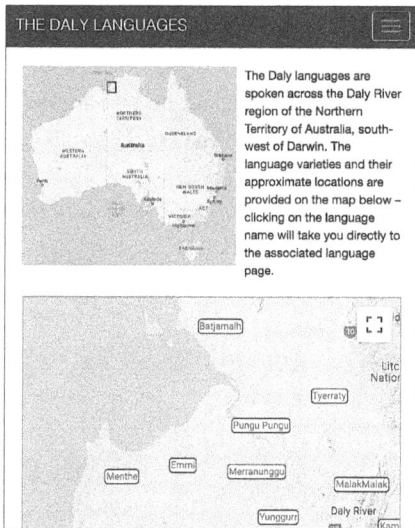

Figure 5. The resized map on a mobile phone

Language pages

The language pages contain most of the website's content. For each language we provide basic information about its relationships with other languages, alternative names and spellings, information about the language's location and speakers, and pictures of country and people, where possible. The layout of each language page is consistent, to ensure ease of navigation: the basic layout is shown in Figure 6. Below we discuss the various features in more detail.

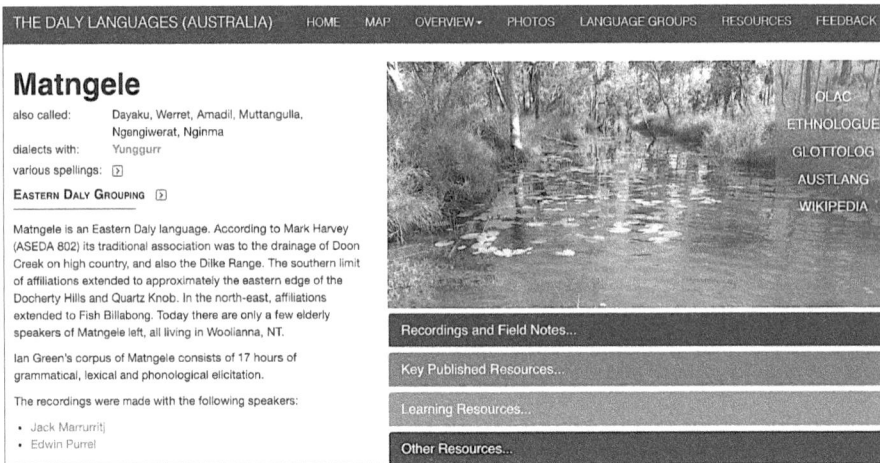

Figure 6. The Matngele language page

Although the layout of the language pages appears clean, it hides a deceptively large amount of information. This is by design, as many of the language details will not be relevant to most users – as such they don't appear unless clicked, reducing visual clutter. This allows us to focus on the most important information for most users – namely the name of the language, what material is available and who is recorded.

Figure 6 is the view a visitor would see when accessing the language page from a desktop. For smaller devices, the information is moved to be more suitable to the vertical scrolling they utilise, as shown in Figure 7.

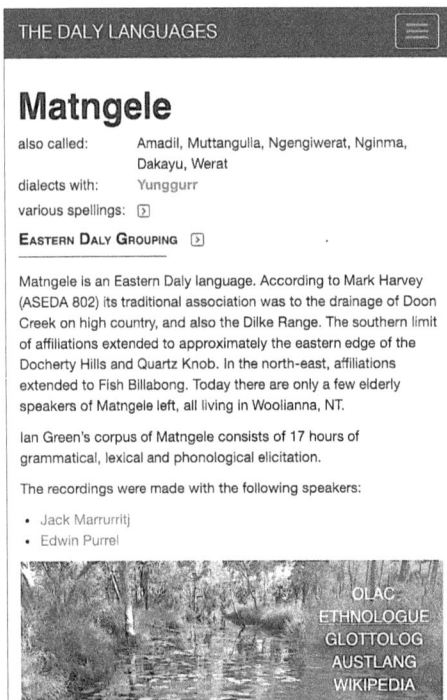

Figure 7. Matngele language page on a mobile phone

Speaker information

Through our community consultations on the repatriation trip it was clear that many users are particularly interested in accessing recordings by speaker, rather than by language. In other words, they may be interested in finding all of the recordings involving a particular family member, rather than all of the recordings in a particular language. Thus, every language page lists the speakers that feature in the available recordings of that language. If a speaker's name is clicked, the visitor is directed to that speaker's web page, which includes links to their audio recordings, any other resources they worked on, and a list of other community members with whom they were also recorded, as shown in Figure 8.

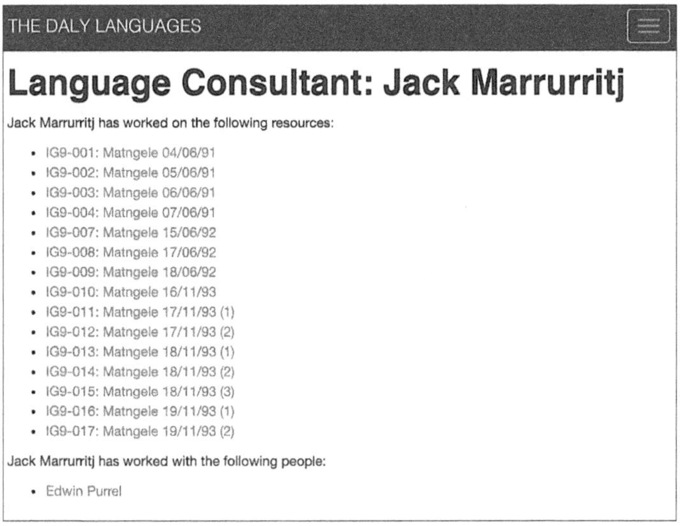

Figure 8. Example language consultant page

Alternative names and various spellings

Many Australian languages are known by different names with various spellings. This causes difficulties in web searches, since available resources for a language may not be identified if the user searched with an alternative name or spelling. We therefore attempted to include all alternative names and spellings that we were aware of for each language variety so that the information in the website is more likely to be found on web searches.

This naming information is split into two groups, *alternative names* and *various spellings*. The 'alternative names' section is used to display alternative language names that bear no similarity to the name we have taken as standard. Some of these alternative names are ones that have contemporary currency in the Daly region – for example, *Matngele* is also known as *Dakayu* or *Werat* – and others are alternative names from the historical literature. These alternative names are always visible as we can't assume that a visitor to the website will know a language by the name we use.

The 'various spellings' link lists all the known spellings of the language names. By default this information is hidden from a visitor as it is not usually needed. Should a visitor want to view this information, they must expand the associated list by clicking the 'various spellings' link:

---

various spellings: ☑

    Madngala, Madngela, Madngele, Madngella, Matngala, Matngela, Matngelli,
    Muttangella, Weret, Werat

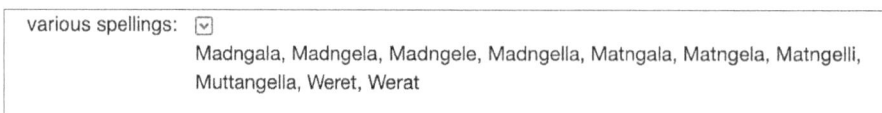

Figure 9. An expanded list containing the different spellings for Matngele

Recording these various spellings and grouping them together allows search engines to associate these different spellings with the language web page. For example, a Google search on 'Madngela language' returns as a search result a link to the Matngele language page shown in Figure 6 above, despite the fact that Madngela spelling is not used as the standard spelling for the language name on that page. This functionality is important as it greatly increases the chances of someone discovering the website and its resources, even if they search on an alternative language name or spelling.

Dialectal information

Language varieties that are considered (by linguists) to be in a dialectal relationship with each other are linked in the 'dialects with' section. No one of these language varieties is given a privileged status in this respect – they are treated identically, with each being listed as a dialect with the other – which is important so that the website provides a neutral perspective equally acceptable to all heritage communities. For example, on the Matngele page, Matngele is listed as being a dialect with Yunggurr, and on the Yunggurr page Yunggurr is listed as being a dialect with Matngele.

Language group information

Our current understanding of the diachronic relationships between the various Daly language varieties is reflected in the 'Group' name on the language page, which can be expanded to show the details of the relevant group. This information is also accessible via the 'Language Groups' tab in the navigation bar at the top of the page.

WESTERN DALY GROUPING ☑

Western Daly

Marramaninjsji	Merranunggu	Marri Ngarr	Marri Dan
	Emmi	Magati Ke	Marrithiyel
	Menthe		Marri Tjevin
			Marri Ammu

Figure 10. Language group information

Each language is associated with one of five language groups, based on our current understanding of how these languages are related to each other (Nordlinger 2017). As further historical comparative work is undertaken, this information may be revised. Distinct but related languages are listed horizontally (for example, Marramaninjsji, Merranunggu, Marri Ngarr above). Each vertical stack of language varieties represents those that we consider to be related as dialects (for example, Marri Ngarr and Magati Ke), although it is important to remember that this is a linguistic classification rather than a community-oriented one. Each language name is an active link, and so the user can easily move between the pages of related languages as they wish.

Information links

Overlaying the photo of country, we have five hyperlinks which link to major online sites which provide additional information and material about the languages: OLAC, Ethnologue, Glottolog, Austlang, and Wikipedia. Should one of these resources have no information about a particular language, the corresponding hyperlink does not appear.

Resource links

We have categorised the resources associated with a language into four groups:

- Recordings and fieldnotes
- Key published resources
- Learning resources
- Other resources

These titles are fairly self-explanatory, but these categories were created to best suit the different users of the website. Community members are generally more interested in hearing recordings and accessing learning resources (such as posters, learner's guides, storybooks). Academics and other researchers may additionally want to access key published resources which reference the language.

An important aspect of the project design is that all primary resources are appropriately archived, and that nothing is stored only on the website. To ensure this, we link directly from the website to the archived item wherever possible. Thus, the items under the 'Recordings and Field Notes' button link directly to the associated items in PARADISEC (see Figure 11). The disadvantage of this is that it requires new users to undertake a two-step process to access the recordings: they must first sign up (or sign in) to a PARADISEC account before they can access the Daly language recordings, and this can make the access more complex for users unfamiliar with the PARADISEC interface. However, it has the advantage of ensuring that the recordings have a level of protection from spurious use that they wouldn't have if they were immediately accessible by an internet search.

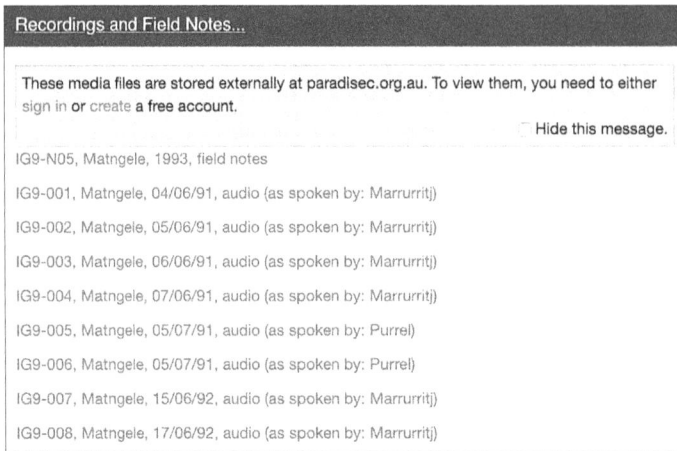

Figure 11. Snapshot of Matngele recordings and fieldnotes

The 'Key published resources' includes 5–6 published linguistic resources for each language. We have not attempted to include every single publication here, but simply to identify the key published resources, and to make them available online wherever possible. For some languages, there are very few published resources, and so the information provided varies significantly for each language.

The full set of resources listed on the whole Daly Languages website can be accessed via the Resources tab in the navigation bar at the top of each page – along with the type of resource (pdf, recording, etc) and the language(s) to which it relates. Where the resource is an audio file, we also note the language consultant. This means that the recordings can be found by community members using a search engine. For example, when searching for Worumbu, a speaker of Marri Tjevin, the search results include links to every audio recording featuring Worumbu on our Daly Language website (although the user still needs a PARADISEC account before being able to access them, as discussed above). This functionality is very appealing to non-linguist users who may not know to search particular language archives (such as PARADISEC or AUSTLANG, for example) for resources, but might just use a general search engine such as Google. Thus, this significantly increases the visibility and accessibility of these Daly language materials for community stakeholders.

Website administration

The website was designed from the outset to be easy to administer and update so that it could be maintained easily without requiring programming or specialised web design skills. In the next section we discuss the design of the website and the nature of the relational database that drives it. In this section we briefly describe the administration side of the website.

The administration side of the website allows content to be added, edited, and deleted. The two main administration pages control information regarding languages and resources. The administration pages are only available to users who have a username and password to access this part of the website. We decided not to implement individual username/passwords, instead using the functionality offered by web hosts to create password protected folders on a website.[3] This simplified the design of the website, and still offers a practical and straightforward means to control access to the administration pages of the website.

On logging into the administration web pages, the user sees the following menu:

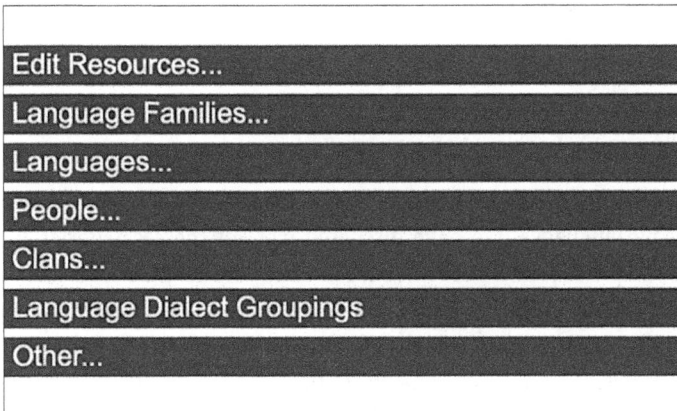

Edit Resources...
Language Families...
Languages...
People...
Clans...
Language Dialect Groupings
Other...

Figure 12. The administration control panel

Each of these links has the same functionality, allowing the administrator to add, edit, or delete information. For example, clicking on the 'Languages...' tab reveals:

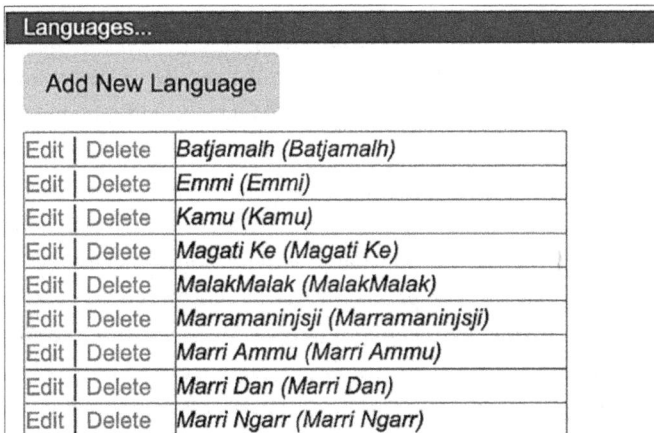

Languages...

Add New Language

Edit	Delete	Batjamalh (Batjamalh)
Edit	Delete	Emmi (Emmi)
Edit	Delete	Kamu (Kamu)
Edit	Delete	Magati Ke (Magati Ke)
Edit	Delete	MalakMalak (MalakMalak)
Edit	Delete	Marramaninjsji (Marramaninjsji)
Edit	Delete	Marri Ammu (Marri Ammu)
Edit	Delete	Marri Dan (Marri Dan)
Edit	Delete	Marri Ngarr (Marri Ngarr)

Figure 13. Administration of languages

Languages

Each language area in the database contains the following information:

- Linguistic name (the most commonly used name for the language)
- Traditional name (if different to linguistic name)
- Language family

---

3   For a typical example of how this is accomplished see https://www.a2hosting.com/kb/cpanel/cpanel-security-features/password-protect-directories.

- URLs to information in OLAC, Ethnologue, Glottolog, Austlang, Wikipedia
- Alternative language names
- Alternative spellings
- Related dialects
- Photo of country URL and caption
- Public notes
- Private notes
- Geographical location (the latitude and longitude for where the language is spoken, for positioning on the map)

Administrators may enter this information if adding a new language to the website or edit the information for existing languages. We have discussed most of these categories in the section above. The public and private notes are textboxes in which the administrator can write whatever relevant material they require. The public notes appear on the web page associated with the language and can be marked up in HTML. The general information about Matngele visible in Figures 6 and 7 above, for example, comes from the public notes. The private notes never appear on the public website and may be used by administrators to record workflow notes or other housekeeping information that may be useful. The geographical location is used to locate the language on the map page.

Resources

We have developed a relatively extensive web page for managing resources, since this is the major purpose of the website. Beyond basic attributes such as the resource's creation date, citation, and URL, we also categorise resources by type (fieldnotes, recordings, published works, and other) and how they relate to the different languages. A resource can relate to various languages in many different ways. For example, an article could be a key published resource for one or two languages, containing transcripts etc, whereas it might only tangentially mention another language (in which case it would appear in the 'other resources' section for the web page for that language). The resource page allows an administrator to specify how a resource relates to a language (Figure 14, left), and also to give a more specific citation for that language as well (such as a specific chapter). As the documentation of a resource can take some time, we have included an option which allows the administrator to create a resource in the database, but not to include its information in the public website. This feature is useful when waiting on a copyright holder's permission to use a resource online.

The creator (author, etc) and language consultants are associated with the resource, drawing upon a list of people's names. This ensures that all references to people are consistent in spelling (Figure 14, right).

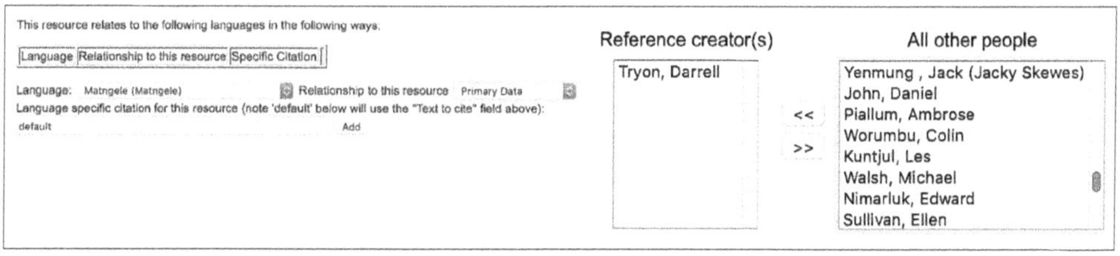

Figure 14. Interface for associating a language (left) and a creator (right) with a resource

Construction of the website and relational database

Although people commonly consider a website's usefulness in terms of the content it contains, the design and construction of a website contribute significantly to its utility. A well-designed website will help users locate the content they want, when they want to find it. Furthermore, over the longer term, the utility of a website comes not just from the information it contains, but from the fact that this information is updated regularly so as to be current. In constructing the Daly Languages website, we had four major design goals, namely that the website be: maintainable, extendable, optimised for the user, and reusable.

Maintainability

For a website to be useful to a community it needs to be maintained. Users of websites typically consider maintenance to be principally concerned with the addition of new content – however, the maintenance of websites revolves around both content and infrastructure.

Maintaining website content

Beyond the addition of new material, content also needs to be updated and occasionally deleted. For static websites, it is the updating and/or deletion of material that is particularly time consuming, especially on larger websites. Consider what happens if a resource (say a book) is deleted from a static website. This requires that the book be removed not only from the list of resources, but also from every language page that may reference that book. Likewise, changing the spelling of an author's name (or even one of the languages) requires every reference to that name in the website to be updated. In reality, in a large static website, mistakes are made and slowly accrue – authors' names may have different spellings on different pages, or a web page may reference a resource that has been deleted. These types of errors are not harmless, as searches on the data contained within the website may return inaccurate information.

Database-driven websites offer a solution to this problem at the cost of more initial programming in the creation of the website where administration web pages are built to allow the website to be easily updated. Thus, we decided to create a relational database to store our content, and a specialised content management system to drive our website that would allow administrators to easily add and delete information and to maintain consistency across the various pages. The basic workflow is shown in Figure 15.

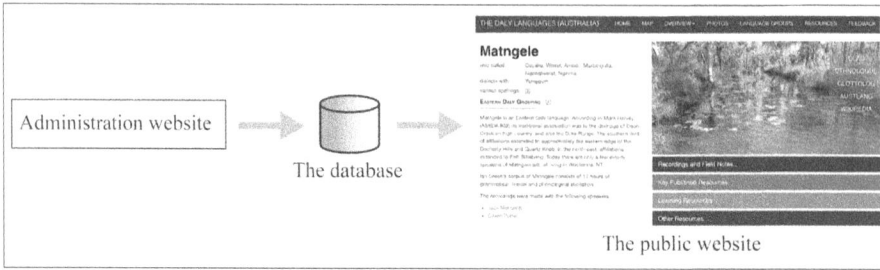

Figure 15. Overview of website and workflow

For example, as part of the administration web pages, an administrator can view all the languages entered into the database, and choose whether to add a new language, edit one, or delete one, as we saw above. If choosing to add a new language, they see a new web page, allowing them to add the information regarding the new language:

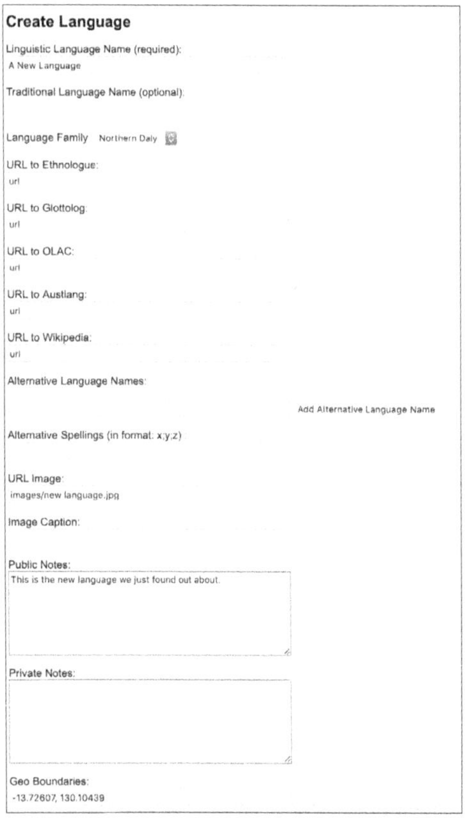

Figure 16. Adding a new language to the database

Once this information has been added, the new language is immediately added to the map and a new language page is created, as shown in Figures 17 and 18. Note that the new language page even includes a new family tree for the Northern Daly family (since we selected this as the Language Family when we entered information about the new language in Figure 16).

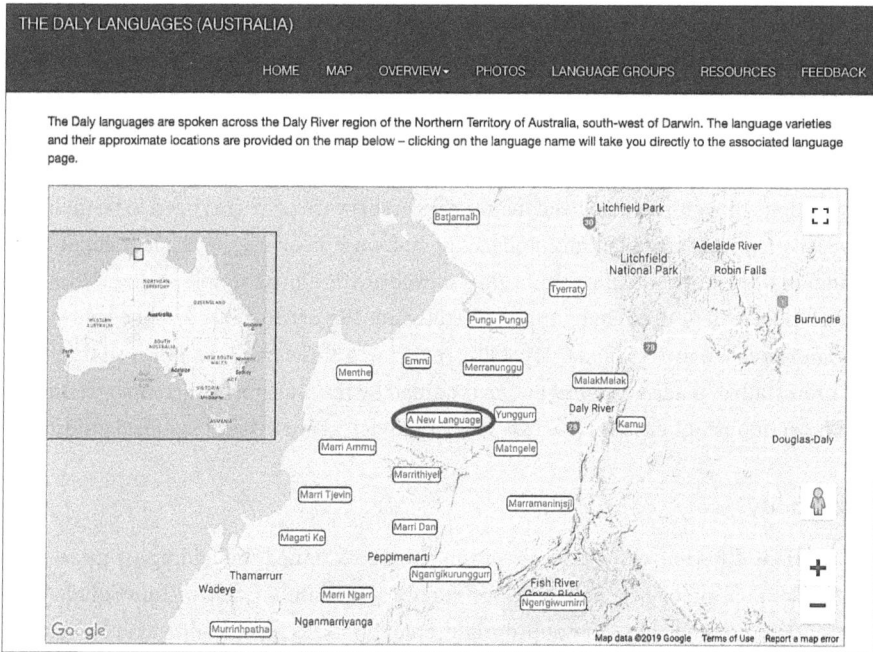

Figure 17. Map with new language added

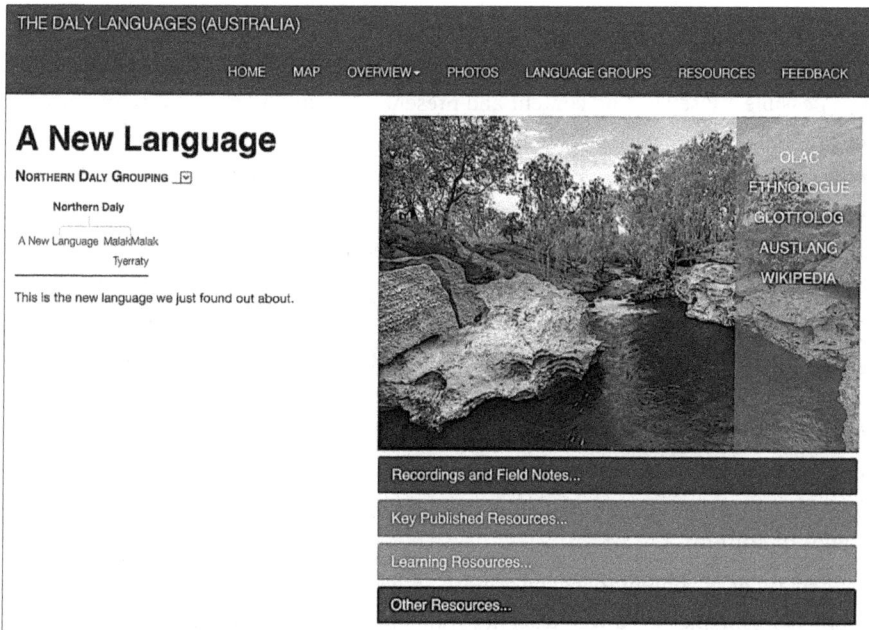

Figure 18. New language page generated

Additional information about the language and the resources can then be added by the administrator as required, via the administrative tools discussed in the section on website administration above.

Maintaining website infrastructure

The foundations of websites also need maintenance: software packages need to be updated and have security updates installed and underlying software needs to be made compatible with new standards. The key to making this aspect of website design as simple as possible is to build a website upon widely used and supported software. We discuss this further below, but the core technologies we use (PHP and MySQL) are de facto standards – so much so that they are usually preinstalled, made available, and maintained by the website host company. This means that the most important updates (such as security updates) are usually installed automatically.

Extendability

There are three different ways that a website can be extended, by adding (i) more content, (ii) new functionality, or (iii) new types of content. The administrative functionality of our website allows anyone with the appropriate credentials to easily add, modify, and delete content, as described and demonstrated in the discussions above.

New functionality

We have designed the website with the view to making it extensible. This is accomplished, as much as possible, by separating content and presentation, and by not duplicating functionality. For example, the key way visitors to the website navigate to the different languages is by using the map. However, a future web-designer might prefer to have the languages also listed in the navigation toolbar. Although the toolbar functionality appears on every web page, it is actually only created once in a file called 'publicheader.php'. Consequently, any new functionality added to this file is automatically included over the entire website. Note, too, in this particular instance no new data is needed to create the functionality as the list of languages is already stored within the database. The creation of new functionality requires a programmer with some basic web skills in PHP, MySQL, and Javascript. However, advanced skills in these languages are not required and it is generally not difficult to find someone with enough knowledge to add this type of functionality.

New types of content

Adding new types of content to a database-driven website would be the most complex type of extension. For example, say a web-designer wants to add information about the communities that speak these languages. This requires three additions to the website:

- An extension to the database that stores information about the communities and links them to the language(s) they speak.
- An extension to the administration web pages allowing an administrator to add, edit, and delete information about the communities.
- An extension to the public web pages to display the community information.

The creation of this type of functionality would require a programmer. However, their job is simplified by the availability of a database schema (a formal description of the database and how the information is linked together) and existing administration pages that could be used as a basis for new functionality (see http://dalylanguages.org/feedback.php for details).

Optimising user experience

A primary goal of website design is that visitors to a website should be able to find the information they want easily, regardless of which browser and which device they use to access it. For example, whether a visitor uses Safari, Chrome, Firefox on a desktop, tablet, or mobile, the website needs to display information clearly on their device. We accomplish this by using Bootstrap – an open-source framework that helps web page designers create pages that automatically reposition content so that it appears appropriately on different devices. Another important aspect of the users' experience with the website is that they should only be presented with information that is relevant to them. Rather than displaying all the possible information at once, we show only the most crucial or interesting information. For example, the languages pages display a photo of country, some basic information about the language, and who we have recorded speaking it. Should visitors want to view additional information (such as other resources, alternative spellings, language groupings, etc), they click a link to do so. This link does not redirect the visitor elsewhere, rather it is used to reveal (or hide) the additional information on the existing page. For example, language groupings are mainly of interest to linguistic researchers and so this information is initially hidden. However, if clicked, this information is revealed:

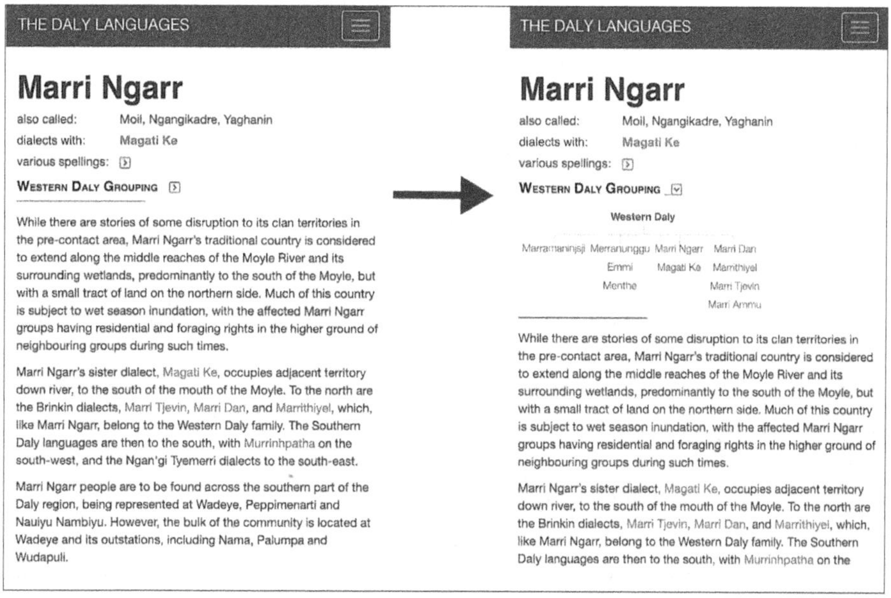

Figure 19. Expansion of language grouping information

Reusability

As noted above, the primary functionality of our website is to associate different languages to their relevant resources and provide a means of easily navigating amongst them. This means that potentially anyone with similar needs could make use of our code. This is possible because one of the design principles we followed was, as much as possible, separating content and presentation so that information about content (such as a language-specific information) and resources are stored in the database whereas how that information is presented is specified separately. Consequently, if someone wanted to create a similar landing page website for any other language group, they could do so with only minor modifications to our code. Such reuse would require a person with basic programming skills and take a day or two to have up and running.

Technologies used

As mentioned above, our database and website are constructed with open-source software. Open-source software is licensed in such a way that anyone may use it, and anyone may also *alter* it. Although there was no need for us to alter the software we used, the ability for others to do so is important. This is because widely used open-source projects (such as we used) have a large community of developers working on the software, creating updates where deficiencies have been identified and adding new features from time to time. Ultimately this means the foundations of our project are maintained by a community of altruistically minded developers. Most of the widely used open-source software for the web is supported by website hosts – including the automatic installation of security updates etc. This further simplifies the ongoing maintenance of the project.

As indicated, we made use of the following open-source software:

- MySQL – the database software
- PHP – a scripting language that allows web pages to access and modify data in a database and present it in a web page
- jQuery
- Bootstrap.

jQuery and Bootstrap are programming languages which run inside the browser. jQuery is a specially written programming language that is designed to work on many different browsers (such as Chrome, Firefox, Safari, etc), as well as older versions of these same browsers. Bootstrap (which itself is built on jQuery) is a software framework that allows web pages to dynamically resize themselves depending upon what device they are being viewed on. This means that a page will appear one way when viewed on a desktop, another on a tablet and yet another when viewed on a mobile, as we have demonstrated for our website in various places above. Utilisation of such sector-standard, open-source, regularly updated software, with an operational capacity that well exceeds the projected size of the site database, makes for page load speeds that easily meet industry benchmarks.

Readers interested in using our framework for their own projects can find all the relevant information about licensing, source files and contacts at http://dalylanguages.org/feedback.php.

Repatriation and community consultation

While it is important to archive primary data to ensure its longevity and future accessibility, of equal importance is how we ensure that target communities are aware of the archived material and its ability to be accessed. In recent years the field of documentary linguistics has moved towards participatory models for linguistic archiving which "break traditional boundaries between depositors, users, and archivists to expand the audiences and uses for archives while involving speaker communities directly in language documentation and archival processes" (Henke & Berez-Kroeker 2016: 428; see also Holton 2014 and many other papers in Nathan & Austin 2014). A key objective in the Daly Languages Project is the repatriation of language recordings back to community, so that people have ownership of their language and their family's recordings, and so that these can be used in community-based language maintenance and revitalisation efforts. We also wanted to consult with these communities about the website and the accessibility of materials to ensure that our design was maximally usable. In July 2016, Ian Green and Rachel Nordlinger (accompanied also by fellow Daly linguist Nick Reid) travelled through the Daly region of the Northern Territory, visiting communities and returning language recordings. On this trip, we distributed to family members and community organisations more than 40 USBs containing language recordings Green made in the 1980s and 1990s. The USBs were also printed with the Daly Languages website address. A story about the trip was published by Melbourne University's *Pursuit* magazine (https://pursuit.unimelb.edu.au/articles/preserving-precious-indigenous-languages), and photos are available on the Daly Languages website under the Photos tab.

Figure 20. Project USB worn by a family member (photo: Rachel Nordlinger)

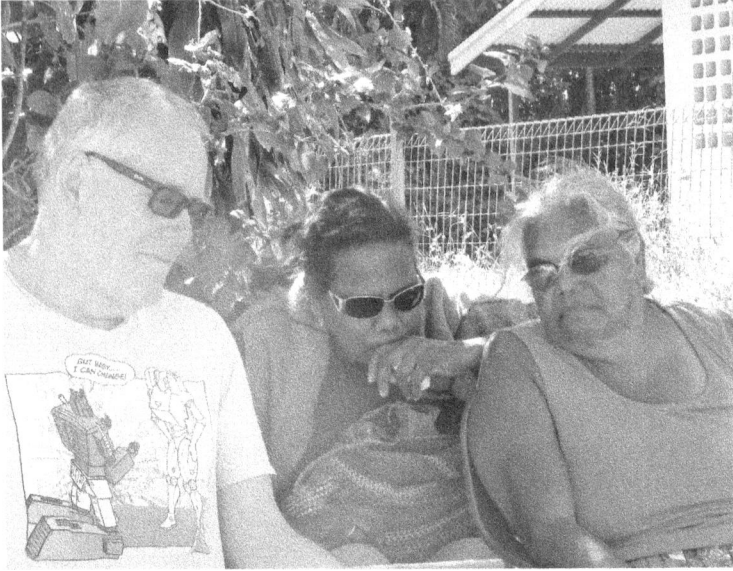

Figure 21. Ian Green listens to Marrithiyel recordings with members of Bill Parry's family (photo: Rachel Nordlinger)

A secondary purpose of the trip was to discuss the Daly Languages website with community stakeholders; confirm permissions and access conditions for the recordings to be archived in PARADISEC; and seek stakeholder input on the design and functionality of the website. This ended up being much more difficult to do than we initially anticipated, given the limited access to computers and internet in many of the remote communities we visited, although those who were able to access the website were generally very positive and found it generally easy to navigate. A number of the website features discussed above arose through this consultation process, since community members were primarily interested in hearing recordings of their own family members, seeing photos of country and people, and, given that these languages are no longer spoken, accessing learning materials that might help them relearn some of their heritage language. In order to respond to these user needs, we added language consultant names associated with each relevant resource to our database, so that users could search for a family member's name to find all associated resources, as discussed above. We also categorised our resource lists and included a 'Learning resources' category for each language, so that learners could more easily identify the relevant materials for their needs from among the list of resources for each language. The fact that the website was easily navigable on mobile phones was crucial to many of these community stakeholders since access to computers is so limited in remote communities.

We also discussed access conditions for the recordings archived in PARADISEC with family members. All families, apart from one, were happy with recordings being on open access in PARADISEC to ensure that the recordings would be accessible to their descendants into the future. One family wanted open access for family members only, a condition that is very difficult for us to implement long term since we can't know who the family members will be in the future. We are still in discussions with this family to negotiate a practical arrangement that they will be comfortable with, so for the time being these recordings are not accessible from the Daly Languages website.

On the other hand, community response to the repatriation of recordings was emotional and overwhelming, reinforcing the importance of researchers ensuring they return recordings to the communities they work with. In general, people were quite overcome to hear the recordings of their past family members; to hear languages that they had often not heard since childhood; and to obtain their own copies on the USBs. They were also astounded and appreciative of our efforts to find them in what were often very remote locations and return the recordings in person. For those of us engaged in language documentation, archiving our recordings is now an important step in our workflow. However, we cannot simply assume that our responsibility to return the recordings to the communities we work with ends there. Community stakeholders are often not aware of linguistic archives and how to access them, and they may not even be aware of the possibility that there are recordings of their languages available online. We therefore need to build repatriation trips into our language documentation workflow as well, if we are to complete our responsibility as researchers to the communities who share their languages and cultures with us.

Conclusion

The Daly Languages Project aims to provide a useful and usable interface by which a range of users can access primary recordings, fieldnotes, and other resources about the Daly languages of the Northern Territory. Moreover, since the website is built with a commitment to open source, it is available for other researchers to adapt to their own projects and language groups. We have attempted to create a resource that will be longlasting and adaptive to the needs of different user groups (community members, language learners, researchers), although we are of course limited by the fact that we can't know what the demands for such resources will be in the future. The database-driven website provides a user-friendly interface to archival records and is easy to maintain and update in response to community requests. Details more likely to be of interest only to other researchers (such as language family relationships, typological features of the languages, academic linguistic resources) are included in clearly separate parts of the website so that each group of users can easily access exactly the information they are after without having to search through other information of less relevance. Combined with the repatriation trip to return heritage recordings to language communities throughout the Daly region, we believe the Daly Languages website provides a useful model for the mediation of archival language materials (Holton 2014) so that they may be readily accessible and usable by speaker communities as well as by other researchers.

References

Evans, Nicholas. 2003. Comparative non-Pama-Nyungan and Australian historical linguistics. In Nicholas Evans (ed.), *The Non-Pama-Nyungan languages of Northern Australia*, 3–25. Canberra: Pacific Linguistics.

Green, Ian. 1989. Marrithiyel: A language of the Daly River region of Australia's Northern Territory. Canberra: Australian National University. (PhD dissertation.)

Green, Ian. 2003. The genetic status of Murrinh-patha. In Nicholas Evans (ed.), *The Non-Pama-Nyungan languages of Northern Australia*, 125–158. Canberra: Pacific Linguistics.

Harvey, Mark. 2003a. The evolution of verb systems in the Eastern Daly language family. In Nicholas Evans (ed.), *The Non-Pama-Nyungan languages of Northern Australia*, 159–184. Canberra: Pacific Linguistics.

Harvey, Mark. 2003b. The evolution of object enclitic paradigms in the Eastern Daly language family. In Nicholas Evans (ed.), *The Non-Pama-Nyungan languages of Northern Australia*, 185–201. Canberra: Pacific Linguistics.

Henke, Ryan & Andrea L Berez-Kroeker. 2016. A brief history of archiving in language documentation, with an annotated bibliography. *Language Documentation & Conservation* 10. 411–457.

Holton, Gary. 2014. Mediating language documentation. In David Nathan & Peter Austin (eds.), *Language documentation and description, vol. 12: Special issue on language documentation and archiving*, 37–52. London: SOAS.

Johnson, Heidi. 2004. Language documentation and archiving, or how to build a better corpus. In Peter Austin (ed.), *Language documentation and description, vol. 2*, 140–153. London: SOAS.

Nathan, David & Peter Austin (eds.). 2014. *Language documentation and description, vol. 12: Special issue on language documentation and archiving*. London: SOAS.

Nordlinger, Rachel. 2017. The languages of the Daly River region (Northern Australia). In Michael Fortescue, Marianne Mithun & Nicholas Evans (eds.), *The Oxford handbook of polysynthesis*, 782–807. Oxford: Oxford University Press.

Thieberger, Nicholas & Andrea L Berez. 2012. Linguistic data management. In Nicholas Thieberger (ed.), *The Oxford handbook of linguistic fieldwork*, 90–118. Oxford: Oxford University Press.

Thieberger, Nick. 2014. PARADISEC, building methods for preserving ethnographic fieldwork recordings and providing long term access. *Australian Sound Recording Association Journal* 39. 45–53.

Thieberger, Nick, Amanda Harris & Linda Barwick. 2015. PARADISEC: Its history and future. In Amanda Harris, Nick Thieberger & Linda Barwick (eds.), *Research, records and responsibility: Ten years of PARADISEC*, 1–16. Sydney: Sydney University Press. (http://purl.library.usyd.edu.au/sup/9781743324431)

Tryon, Darrell T. 1974. *Daly family languages, Australia*. Canberra: Pacific Linguistics.

Language Documentation & Conservation Special Publication No. 18
Archival returns: Central Australia and beyond
ed. by Linda Barwick, Jennifer Green & Petronella Vaarzon-Morel, pp. 217–238
http://nflrc.hawaii.edu/ldc/sp18
http://hdl.handle.net/10125/24885

11

"We never had any photos of my family": Archival return, film, and a personal history

Fred Myers
New York University

Lisa Stefanoff
University of New South Wales

Abstract

The film *Remembering Yayayi* emerged from a project to return raw 16mm film footage shot in 1974 at the early Pintupi outstation of Yayayi, near Papunya, by filmmaker Ian Dunlop, with Fred Myers as translator and consultant. Two subsequent remote Pintupi communities, Kintore and Kiwirrkura, were involved in the footage's return. The material had not been available for research (or other) purposes until 2005, when VHS copies were made from the workprint deposited in the National Archives of Australia. In 2006, Myers and Stefanoff took this rare historical visual material in Pintupi language to Kintore and Kiwirrkura, showing it to individuals and family groups and holding community screenings. Responses were overwhelmingly positive. The tapes quickly became regular entertainment for patients undergoing lengthy renal dialysis sessions and Myers received multiple requests for copies. Over several years, one of Myers' long-term Pintupi friends, Marlene Spencer Nampitjinpa, came to provide a moving personal commentary on the footage, enabling a feature documentary to be produced from it. This chapter draws on a conversation between Stefanoff and Myers to reflect on how the repatriation project became a catalyst for memory and produced new Pintupi community historical knowledge, particularly about outstation life, early efforts at developing local forms of self-determination and the transformation of lives and wellbeing over a 40-year period.

Keywords: Pintupi, memory, archive, repatriation, film

A prologue in two voices[1]

Fred Myers:

Archival returns have many forms and functions. They can be highly personal, interpersonal, collaborative or contested, and the materials can be various. The project we discuss in the interview below relates to the return, in 2006, of film footage that was shot by internationally renowned Australian filmmaker Ian Dunlop in 1974 at the remote Northern Territory Government–supported Yayayi outstation. The footage was returned to Pintupi communities whose members had been the subjects of the filming, but who had never seen it. This footage was very meaningful to me, as I had been living at Yayayi, undertaking my doctoral fieldwork, when it was shot. Forty-three years later, in 2017, Lisa and I recorded a conversation exploring how and why repatriating this material had led to the production of the documentary film *Remembering Yayayi* that I co-produced in 2014, and the value of this film as a Pintupi perspective on Pintupi history.

Remembering Yayayi was one product of an Australian Research Council (ARC) Linkage grant 'Pintupi dialogues: reconstructing memories of art, land and community through the visual record'. Initially, it was called 'the Yayayi Footage Project', and became known officially as 'Pintupi Dialogues' in grant-writing. The ARC grant and a separate AIATSIS (Australian Institute of Aboriginal and Torres Strait Islander Studies) grant funded my collaboration with the mainly Pintupi Aboriginal–owned artists company, Papunya Tula Artists Ltd, Peter Thorley of the National Museum of Australia, and Nicolas Peterson and Philippa Deveson of the Australian National University (ANU). Our collective undertaking aimed to use film and photographic records "to animate historical consciousness" by using visual records to reflect with members of the remote Western Desert Pintupi communities of Walungurru (Kintore) in the Northern Territory and Kiwirrkura in Western Australia on a pivotal period in the history of the Pintupi people with whom I began research in 1973. The ARC grant extended from 2010 to 2013, but the project began much earlier. It involved not only returning to my earliest ethnographic work in Pintupi communities (see Myers 1986), but also looking further into the historical context of the policy of self-determination in Australia as it was elaborated in the early 1970s. There were further historical significances to the return of the visual materials: in 1964, a decade before he shot the Yayayi footage, Ian Dunlop, accompanying then patrol officer Jeremy Long, had photographed Pintupi people as being among the last Aboriginal people still living a nomadic life in Australia's Western Desert. And, at the other end, while working on the return of this archival material, I became engaged in consulting on another project of archival significance, on the Museum and Art Gallery of the Northern Territory (MAGNT) collection of early Papunya paintings and the restrictions of what can be shown (Myers 2017a).

---

1   We acknowledge the support of the Pintupi communities of Walungurru (Kintore) and Kiwirrkura in this project, as well as Papunya Tula Artists, the National Museum of Australia, and the Australian National University. Thanks to Ian Dunlop, Pip Deveson, Peter Thorley, and Nic Peterson for their many contributions, and to Howard Morphy, especially for housing this project at the ANU and helping with legal support. Grant support is acknowledged elsewhere, where appropriate.

Lisa Stefanoff:

Fred co-supervised my graduate studies at New York University (NYU) in the late 1990s and then also my PhD fieldwork in Central Australia at CAAMA (Central Australian Aboriginal Media Association, 2002–2006). In 2000, we sat down together in the NYU Program in Culture and Media's then-new digital editing suite with some of Fred's 1970s fieldwork photographs and some High-8 video footage taken at the landmark Asia Society exhibition of Aboriginal art in New York.[2] The footage showed Papunya-based artists Michael Nelson Jagamara and Billy Stockman Tjapaltjarri creating, consecrating and performing *yinma* 'ceremony' around a beautiful ground painting constructed on site using sand mixed with red cement, brought in from Long Island. This was combined with footage Fred shot that same year with painters at Yuendumu, Kintore and Kiwirrkura to show how Aboriginal life and culture had made its way to New York.

Together, we edited a little film called *From the Dreaming* (or *Tjukurrtjanu* in Pintupi), with the subtitle 'Aboriginal art comes to New York', meant to highlight 'culture-making' (Myers 1991, 1994) and draw attention to the movement of culture through what Myers was analysing as different "regimes of value" (Myers 2001). The Asia Society material captured the artists' improvisational energy in a new and unconventional ceremonial environment and also provided a small window onto some of the transactional social exchange between them and a host of non-Aboriginal people and circumstances. Our small early editing experiment included a clip of Michael and Billy explaining to the female anchor of the US PBS *MacNeill/Lehrer* NewsHour TV program that they were sharing *tjukurrpa* through the exhibition, and that all of the work in the exhibition was *tjukurrtjanu*.

In a sense, the film *Remembering Yayayi* should be understood as one outcome of another, further experiment in returning to archival material – a series of research activities to construct history, and more fully to document participants' storied recollections of lively lived memories. This project aimed to generate historicising reflections through a cultural-history-making practice of repeated looking at, listening to, and talking about footage of past times and places.

I was thrilled when Fred invited me to help him and Ian Dunlop take some of Ian's never-seen 1970s footage to show people in Kintore and Kiwirrkura in 2006. I was just finishing my fieldwork at CAAMA and was attuned to the value of desert audiovisual archives as precious community history and cultural property. Sadly, Ian wasn't able to make the repatriation journey due to an accident that made lengthy car travel difficult. He missed the direct experience of hearing Marlene Nampitjinpa Spencer and her family exploding with joy upon seeing some of Ian's old footage on the small laptop the team had set up on the dining table in the Finke River Mission house, where we had been given lodging in Kintore. Likewise, indelibly burnt into my memory was the sense of the whole Kiwirrkura community and all its dogs coming together in their freezing cold hall to watch the footage projected as large as we could make it, two nights in a row. The kids' exuberant shadow play across scenes full of their elders and ancestors seemed a vital and possessive claim (see Figure 1). The footage clearly mattered, in ways that were yet to be revealed.

---

2   This exhibition was *Dreamings: The art of Aboriginal Australia.*

Figure 1. Kids engaging with projection of archival footage, Kiwirrkura community hall, 2006 (photo: Lisa Stefanoff)

Fast-forward a decade, to 2017. *Remembering Yayayi* was completed and had received a great reception in New York, and the wonderful *Tjuŋuṇutja* exhibition on which Fred had been a consultant was about to open in Darwin (where I was living and he was visiting). We sat down on 30 June and recorded about an hour of conversation about the making and impacts of the film. The text presented here is an edited version of that recording.[3]

Conversation

I started by asking Fred to explain the origins of the project.

Fred: I'll explain what the footage was, first. I was a PhD student from 1973 to 1975, in Yayayi, one of the first small breakaway outstation communities in Central Australia. The community had moved away from Papunya under the framework of the new federal policy of Aboriginal self-determination. After I had been there almost a year, Ian Dunlop – who was already known to me as a very distinguished filmmaker who had made a wonderful award-winning film called *Desert People* [1967] about Western Desert people – came to Yayayi with the idea of perhaps making a film with people he had met 10 years before, when he was doing research for that film. Many people at Yayayi were among those whom he'd first seen coming in from the bush. He wanted to follow up what had happened. When I say "coming from the bush," they were people who had been living a traditional hunting and gathering life, who were

---

3   Original audio interview is available at https://rememberingyayayi.com/remembering-yayayi-the-project-of-archival-return-fred-myers-interview-with-lisa-stefanoff/

coming to live in the government settlement of Papunya. So, Ian came out there, I agreed to help him in some way, and then he came back in June that year [1974]. He shot maybe 12–13 hours of colour 16mm sync-sound footage with the idea that he would make a film, but he couldn't really figure out what the film would be. It didn't turn out that what people were doing was something that he had hoped to see – the situation [at Yayayi] was a little rougher and more complicated. He couldn't figure out what the narrative would be. I went to Sydney with two Pintupi men, friends of mine, and we translated all 12 hours of the footage, and that was it.[4] We never made a film.

I stayed friendly with Ian for a long time. We used to talk about that material. I always wanted to see it again. I wanted to take it back to the community, but it was too expensive to take it, and it only existed as a workprint, which wasn't easy to screen. Then, in the early 2000s, after Ian had retired and given his material to the National Archives [of Australia], they transferred it to video and then eventually to a digitised [format]. He called me and told me. I got access to the material [through him], and he and I decided that we would love to take it out and show it to the community because it was now more portable and possible to show. So, we arranged this trip; it was all set up. It wasn't that easy, but it was set up. You, Lisa, and Basil, your then-fiancé, were going to be our helpers in driving out there [from Alice Springs].

Ian broke his hip and he couldn't go. We went out anyway. We took the digitised material to Kintore and Kiwirrkura. We screened it on two nights at Kiwirrkura. People were incredibly responsive. They loved it. They were very excited. They wanted to keep it. We left copies with Sister Annie [Dixon] at the clinic. By the time we got back to Alice Springs, we were getting messages about how people were responding to it. At that point I thought I really needed to do something more with that material.

I went back out to Kintore the following year,[5] and started to make some plans. We got money, first from the National Museum of Australia [NMA], to re-digitise the original footage. We got [other] grants. The idea was to take the film footage back. I was really interested in people's memories of that time, because in Australia by 2007 the period of self-determination and the policies of Aboriginal self-determination had come under really severe criticism by conservatives and others as a failure. I felt, in reading this material, that people had not actually been there, they didn't understand what it was like, how much it [self-determination] meant to people.[6]

Yayayi – the community where I had lived – was the first of the communities to be created under that policy. I thought if we could develop that film [material] and people's response to it [i.e. the documentation project, not the 'film' we ended up making] and their understandings of self-determination and their lives at the time, that would be some kind of

---

4   The two Pintupi men were Freddy West Tjakamarra and George Yapa Yapa Tjangala.

5   For the opening of a new art studio in that community, for Papunya Tula Artists, the artists company that began the acrylic painting movement (see Myers 2002).

6   This period and the Pintupi case are discussed in Myers (2016). The article and book (Peterson & Myers 2016) were part of the results of a Pilot and Linkage grant from Australia Research Council (2010–2013), and an earlier research grant from the Australian Institute of Aboriginal and Torres Strait Islander Studies (2009), both entitled 'Pintupi Dialogues'.

a documentation of what it really was, as opposed to the ideological positions.[7] That was the political and anthropological take. But secondly I also had really strong memories of that time, and my friendships with people there and the sociality, the nature of everyday life, which I never felt I could capture in print. I always wanted a film [a documentation] that allowed you to listen to people talking. I loved the elegant ways in which people spoke Pintupi, the way they interacted with each other and I thought, "Wow, in this film you could see it." That would be something that really squared the circle for me about my experience and my sense of life in an Indigenous community. Those were the goals, but it was a lot harder to carry it out. Also, I should say that we didn't set out to make 'a film'. We set out to produce historical documentation of people's understandings and attitudes of the time and what their responses were. They were people who, for the most part, did not have visual records of their own lives and their past, so this was also an attempt to see what a visual archive could mean for a community that hadn't had the experience of that. It was a kind of exploration of memory and what memory could mean and what it meant to people there, so it was a kind of open-ended project to go back out there. Thus, the title of our chapter, from the words of our main narrator, Marlene Spencer Nampitjinpa: "We never had any photos of my family, there, at Yayayi."

Although Ian was unable to travel, he was very interested and supportive of this venture. His former brilliant editor and research assistant, Pip Deveson, who was based at the ANU, became my film partner in this. We also collaborated with Peter Thorley, a curator of the National Museum of Australia whom I had first known when he was a teacher-linguist at Kintore in 1988. Peter was also, therefore, able to mediate this work and material to the Australian archival and museum world. The final part of this plan was to work with the National Museum: I hoped it could offer a means through which the Pintupi archive and materials would have a permanent location that people could continue to access. These are remote communities and they have limited resources, so even if I were to give them [Pintupi communities] the material, they would have no place to store it. The museum seemed to be a proper storage place with responsibilities to the community where this material could be lodged when we were done.[8]

Lisa: This project of repatriation generated a new film based on the old material. Let's talk about how that unfolded.

Fred: The 'film' was an issue for us – whether we would actually make a 'film' – because the project was really envisioned as returning the raw footage and documenting people's understandings of it as history. When we did return it, people watched it [from] beginning to end, saw pictures of themselves. As part of the documentation project, we worked with four different [Pintupi] consultants initially,[9] to comment on the film and to re-translate parts and to talk about what they saw [see Figure 2]. As a result of that, we arrived at several themes that

---

7   A significant example of the criticism of the self-determination policies and outstations was Hughes (2007), but see Altman (2012), one of the strongest defenders of remote communities.

8   In fact, we did give communities copies of the footage more than once, as well as digitised collections of my own photographs taken over the years.

9   The consultants were Bobby West Tjupurrula, Jimmy Brown Tjampitjinpa, Irene Nangala and Monica Robinson Nangala.

Figure 2. Irene Nangala, Monica Robinson Nangala, with Ian Dunlop and wife Rosemary, Pip Deveson, Peter Thorley, and Fred Myers consulting on the archival project in Canberra, 2010 (photo: Fred Myers)

all consultants independently saw in the material.[10] But we couldn't figure out, really, if there was a way to link things together in a shorter version that might be easier to have available for people, and to circulate more broadly in the world, if that were possible.

On our first trip, in 2006,[11] on our way back from Kiwirrkura, we stopped at Kintore and I bumped into a woman who had been in the film, who was a very good friend of mine, Marlene Spencer Nampitjinpa. She wanted to know if we had any pictures. I said, "Well, I have this film footage, but I'll show it to you in the house." She brought all her relatives over, all these young kids and her husband and other people. We sat down with the laptop and watched it [see Figure 3]. It was just extraordinary to watch how people were energised by looking at it and seeing who people were. Marlene saw herself as a young girl, and she explained to the younger kids who the people in the film were and their relationship to them. Then I thought, "Wow, she is just an amazing presence."

Lisa: You had the foresight to quickly set up a small video camera on a tripod behind that viewing. People can actually see those precious moments in the new film, which is quite extraordinary.

Fred: Yes, it was. It was very poor quality. You need to have more than one person if you're really going to be engaged in a project like this. And you were knocked out with a migraine that day!

10 There were four themes articulated: (1) the significance of relatives, (2) the health of the people, (3) the strong leadership indicated by meetings in the community where the elders "spoke strong" and "looked after" people, and (4) sharing or exchange.

11 This is the trip Lisa shared. It was a personal journey on my part, not supported by research grants but nonetheless passed through NYU Human Subjects research ethics review.

Figure 3. Marlene Spencer Nampitjinpa and family watching archival footage in Kintore, 2006 (photo: Fred Myers)

Fred: So, we had this new footage. But Marlene is very busy and we never could find a time in the first three years of the project to talk to her. I always wanted to interview her more formally and to talk to her about it, because I was always very drawn to her as a person and to her family.

Towards the end of the project, Pip and I flew up to Alice Springs. We knew where Marlene was staying there. She had come to work with the renal dialysis project and she was in town for a board meeting.[12] So, we met in a hotel room and we videotaped a conversation with her, with the material, in one day. All in one day. We set up the camera, she looked at the camera, and we said, "Just start telling us who you are." She looked at the camera, and she said [in English], "My name is Marlene Nampitjinpa, and I was born in the bush." I just felt the hairs on the back of my neck tingle. We had just started this conversation and I felt that her memories and her explanation to me and Pip, as her interlocutors for this moment, was a thread to tie the film together. The other people we had videotaped and interviewed were informative and very interesting, but they didn't have the same screen presence. Marlene has real presence. She is used to talking to people. Even when she was a young woman and she was still breastfeeding a child, she was a person who was mediating for her community. Pip and I then realised that we had a film, and that Marlene's subjectivity, her memories, her way of talking about what she saw, drew people into a Pintupi presence, and what it meant to people who were of that community and that time. Many things in the old footage perhaps

---

12   The 'Purple House' Western Desert Dialysis Project, or *Nganampa Walytja Palyantjaku Tjutaku*, 'to keep our relatives healthy' in Pintupi-Luritja, that was first developed through the initiative of the Pintupi communities at Walungurru and Kiwirrkura, and Papunya Tula Artists in 2000.

look to outsiders as signs of an impoverished community, and people living on the edge of a modern world, but you don't feel that from Marlene. You feel her family, you feel her presence. In the footage, you hear people joking and teasing each other. They are aware of the camera. Marlene's pleasure in the presence of her past and present relatives in these scenes is palpable.

Lisa: You also recorded interviews with other people, about what they could see in the old footage.

Fred: They were all taped with the idea that if it worked out, the 'interview' might be employed in 'the [new] film'. We had four other Pintupi consultants, and we also interviewed all of the non-Indigenous people who had been present in the community and were in the film, to have their memories.[13] These recordings were often very interesting, but they became something that was more important as research documentation. Really, the film is 'remembering Yayayi'. It is Marlene's memories. Other people's memories are very interesting and they're now in the archival record, but they seemed much less important than the local point of view.

Lisa: How did you and Marlene communicate throughout the research and production process? What did it mean for the project that you each held memories of the same past places, times and people, connected through shared language?

Fred: I had several conversations with Marlene, beginning with showing her and her family some of the raw footage in 2006. Then, at the opening of the new art studio in Kintore in 2007, and the celebration of the 30th anniversary of the founding of Walungurru [2011], we watched the footage together again. Since it has been some years since I spoke Pintupi regularly, Marlene and I speak in Pintupi-Luritja and English, as we needed clarifications. Recording with her in Alice Springs in 2013 for the film, she and I spoke in Pintupi-Luritja mostly and she moved back and forth between English and Pintupi to include Pip in the conversation, often repeating in English what she said to me in Pintupi.

A good deal of the conversation that I had with Marlene during the filming was built around our shared memories and histories of people and events. I cannot separate the results from our shared experiences, stand outside of our mutual knowledge. The recording is undoubtedly mutually produced. Her explanations and discussions usually assume I know who the people are and what the events might be, as when she discusses the meeting about alcohol use when the Yayayi leaders go to Papunya. You can see her nodding and looking for my acknowledgment at various times in the film. Pip was watching me and Marlene to decide when fragments were completed or we were moving on to a new topic. One of Marlene's gifts is her ability to recognise what her listeners may not share as background, not always a common quality. Marlene was pretty good at making sure Pip was following, quite amazing, really. In fact, her on-the-spot translations for Pip are very important for the film, since the most likely audience might be non-Pintupi speakers.

---

13   These included Jeffery Stead (then the community advisor), Ken and Leslie Hansen (linguists from Summer Institute of Linguistics and long-time residents), Terry Parry (Yayayi schoolteacher), Dick Kimber (local historian and once-manager of Papunya Tula Artists), Peter Fannin (manager of Papunya Tula Artists in 1974), and Ian Dunlop himself.

I think I mention in the film that when we returned a year after the initial screening of raw footage, I learnt that the copies of the footage were being watched continuously by patients having renal dialysis at Kintore, as part of the then-new program of remote dialysis. The nurses recognised me from the footage, and told me how much the Pintupi patients enjoyed watching their relatives and hearing their language. The language spoken by most of the people in the film is actually an older variant of Pintupi, spoken by that senior generation. Many of the younger people now do not speak in what some have called 'classic Pintupi', which involved more bound morphemes (as with pronouns) as well as a vocabulary and avoidance registers.

When I have spent time with Pintupi friends away from Central Australia, they prefer to watch the film and the film footage over almost anything else, slipping into the familiarity of their relatives and the language. Making something with the old film [footage] was exciting for the possibility of showing how people had actually interacted, told stories, narrated things. It was really important, perhaps the most important value of the film. It had an effect on the final edit; for example, I wanted to keep as much as possible of the meeting in which the Yayayi Community Council were speaking, in order to show how people showed 'respect' in speech, the diplomacy of daily life.

Lisa: One of the things that Melinda Hinkson [2016] explores in her substantial review of the film in the *Australian Journal of Anthropology* is the shifting temporality of the story. You've made a film of memory, of Marlene Spencer's memories specifically. Significantly, the archival film material has evoked and provoked the memories the film collects. You also appear in that old footage as a young fieldworker. Yayayi was your first desert home, it was the place that made you an anthropologist. What was it like looking back and seeing yourself in the midst of that time gone?

Fred: Well, I think that an anthropologist seeing himself in the field is not so enjoyable. I'm very aware of all of my discomforts and anxieties that are maybe not so visible in the film. I'm smoking like a chimney in the film because there are many things happening that I follow imperfectly and I get very fatigued. But also, I wanted to have something to share with people; cigarettes were something [to share]. I can see myself in the film avoiding being drawn into intercultural relations about money and resources and trying to work out my situation. In making the film [in 1974], I always said to Ian, "My first relationships are with the people here. I know you after I know them and my obligation is to them. I'm never going to do anything for you that isn't really suited to them." I tried to maintain that in all my fieldwork there.

I see myself taking notes at various times and wandering around. There is one scene of me that we included in the film for reasons that have to do with the significance of some of the activity at Yayayi. Yayayi was one of the communities that was involved in Papunya Tula Artists, the beginning of the acrylic painting movement which became very significant in Australia. There's a scene in which Ian filmed me very soon after he got there, documenting a painting. It was one of the things I did at Yayayi. Papunya Tula is an Aboriginal-owned co-operative [company]. The manager, Peter Fannin, couldn't keep up with the documentation of the paintings, and so I was providing that information for their records. There is a scene, a kind of classic anthropological scene, of me with my notebook and a painting, and the painter John Tjakamarra [Wingantjirrinya]. I'm collecting the work's ancestral story, the Dreaming story, *tjukurrpa*, and Tjakamarra's sitting there. Of course, as in most Aboriginal settings, he's not alone. There are other Aboriginal men sitting there too. Tjakamarra was noteworthy for his lack of communication and was very, very soft-spoken. Another man who was a very close friend of mine was kind of interpolating for us there. Other people were offering their views about what the story is about, because they are related to that country. So, I think you kind of wonder there [about the story]. I remember very distinctly that event. I was listening to all of them, trying to figure out different people's views and writing on the side, I was really trying to figure out whose version of the story was most appropriate for this case. It's all being channelled into my notebook of the moment. That painting was purchased by the art co-operative [company], and with my documentation sent out, annotated in that way, as part of its provenance and its significance.

When we had an exhibition of early Papunya paintings in New York in 2009,[14] we included footage from our project of me taking that documentation down and my notebook as a way of trying to show something about the ways in which Indigenous art makes its way into the world. So in the film you can see that. Even though it's a very remote community and they are very 'traditional' – among the last people to be living a hunting and gathering life shortly before this time – agents of the Australian government and various institutions are part of their world: the art advisor, the people from the Aboriginal Art Board, who had given a grant to help support this enterprise, come out there and they interact with them. It was very important for us to be able to show – and that footage is very powerful – something about the way in which a contemporary life was lived in a remote community at that time.

Lisa: We see you as a quiet presence in the film. You're listening. You've written about listening and also the imperative to help people, which was a local structure of meaning around your presence there. Could you say something now, reflecting on that time, and through your career, on the role and the aesthetics – the ethics – of listening as fieldwork practice? It's very evident in how we see you in that film.

Fred: I had a wonderful teacher [Jane Goodale] when I prepared to do fieldwork, who emphasised very much the need to listen to people and to try to understand them. It's not an easy thing to learn. When I got to Central Australia and got to that community, I was so appreciative of their acceptance of me that modesty and humility seemed appropriate at every level. But also, I learnt very early on that only some people really have the right to speak about a variety of things, and that I should probably not be voicing my opinions too much about things that Aboriginal people should speak for. This is also the period of early self-determination. The very few times when I did try to tell them what I thought was going on – because I thought I knew what was going on with the government and other things – they would just basically say, "You just don't understand," and I realised that there wasn't anything to be gained. So, I spoke to people a lot. I learnt the language, I hung out with people. The circumstances that were filmed [in 1974] were events in which I was peripheral, or I had a particular role. It doesn't represent my everyday life of sitting down and talking with people about what

---

14 The exhibition, 'Icons of the Desert: Early Aboriginal Paintings from Papunya', had an excellent catalogue of the same name. See Benjamin (2009).

we were doing and what was going on, but I did learn that I needed to listen, and it was hard for me. I did learn Pintupi, informally, pretty well, but it was always a challenge to be sure I was following things. Fundamentally, I think, as an anthropologist you are there to learn and to listen, but it was doubly so for [working with] Aboriginal people. Especially at that time, because it was very common for people to assume they knew better than them [i.e. Yarnangu, 'Aboriginal people'] about everything, and that people would constantly speak *for* them. On the occasions when I might have mis-stepped on that, I was reminded by people that I was a 'whitefella', and that these things were *their* business. Often, they would ask me what I thought. It didn't mean that they accepted my views when they did, but they were very open. I realised that there were people there who had authority; there were people there who should be speaking. I also saw how they responded to people who talked *over* them. You can see in the film, people's body posture when other people are not giving them the opportunity to speak. It's one of the great things I learnt from them, really: how to be a respectful person. In Pintupi, there is a substantial discourse, a set of understandings, about what a respectful person is. The word in Pintupi is *kunta*. It can mean 'shame' but it also means 'respectful', and people who speak out of place or inappropriately are said to be 'lacking shame', or that they should be 'embarrassed'. That made a lot of sense to me as I learnt it, and it's something very valuable. So, to some extent my practice, if you want to call it that, was really learning to be Pintupi. The proudest moment I ever had there, and it happened sometimes, was people would say, "This is Tjapanangka" – that was my subsection, my kinship classification – "He's different. He listens. He shares. He's from Yayayi." That is really a part of my identity. I worked with Pintupi people in many other places later, but that early time – I lived there for two years – is really, in a way, who I am for them, and in a way who I am for myself in that situation.

Lisa: That aesthetic, that ethic of respectful listening, carries over into the film *Remembering Yayayi*, in that we have, as you've been describing, Marlene Spencer Nampitjinpa as the narrator. The film uses quite a tight close-up on her face throughout. It pulls out a bit at the end, and we see her more in conversation with you. The film steadily draws the viewer into a very intimate listening relationship. This is partly assisted by her visual presence in that close-up, but we can't help but have absolute attention to her voice and to her narrative. It builds to a point towards the end of the film where Marlene becomes quite emotional about the changes she's seen in the course of her life, the loss of people who are close to her, and it's very, very moving [see Figure 4]. The film has played to audiences in Australia, in the United States – in New York at the Margaret Mead Film and Video Festival, in Paris and in some other places. Can you say a little bit about how that evocation, that drawing-in-to-listen, has worked in other places?

Fred: Well, there are two different experiences. There's the experience when Marlene has been present at a screening, which was extraordinary because she talks to the image and to what she sees in the film, just as she does in the film itself. When the film is played, she's engaging with it as a present context. That allowed people [viewers] to trust their own responses to her and to the humour in the film. I think when people see films about other people, other cultures, they don't necessarily know how to respond. We try to give them cues. It takes longer in the film, but when she was there, present at the screening, that was great.

Figure 4. Marlene remembering, close-up (still image from *Remembering Yayayi*)

The film progresses from a lot of humorous things, and then towards the end of the interview with Marlene, she starts to reflect more about her time there at Yayayi and the people that she sees in the footage[15] and she says, "I remember ..." She starts talking about the fact that people died. She remembers one person, and she says, "He's gone," and then you can see her emotion is building up. I intervened at this moment in our filming. It had actually been provoked by my asking her – I wanted to get her to go back to Yayayi and the closure of Yayayi – so I asked her. Usually you don't ask people about the deaths of their close family members, but I wanted to get her to think about this. I said, "Your father died at Yayayi, right?" and then she just sort of steps back for a moment, and I thought, "Oh, that wasn't so good." She starts to think about the deaths, and then I said, "But you know, those people, they lived a good, long life," because the people she mentions actually didn't die young. Many people are dying young now, with a huge epidemic of kidney failure and obesity and so on, but in the film, everybody's really healthy. She's remembering the loss of them, and I said – to try to make her feel better – "But those old people, they lived a good, long life." It just had no effect on her, she just rolled right past that. I felt it was a kind of tin-eared response from me, and it's embarrassing, actually, to see it in the film, but it is real, and then she continues. At the end of the film, she's really taking up a position that I recognise as a very Pintupi location of 'grief' [*yalurrpa*], and she starts rubbing her eyes with her sleeve. When people are grieving, this is exactly what they do. Pip looked over at me and signalled, "Should I turn it off? Should I leave it on?" But Ian [Dunlop] always said this one thing, "Don't turn the camera off." So, we kept the camera on, and Marlene continues to talk. Then, she pulls herself up, and she says [in English], "That really touched me, this video. I know [knew] all the men, all the women, and people, when I was a young girl in Yayayi." We were nearly crying ourselves, at that point. But that's the moment that I had always hoped for in this. That there would be some kind of connection [with the old footage]. There's something about the moment of my being in front

---

15 Indeed, she remarks that she can see them in the footage as if they are still alive, a presencing that clearly affects her.

of the camera with her. I do share her feelings. Not to the same extent, but those were people who really made my life what it is. So, to the extent that that happened and is there, I felt we had accomplished something that I wanted viewers to have, and some engagement with an Aboriginal world through them. She [Marlene] has the great capacity to provide it to us.

Lisa: It's a beautifully edited film, and of course it builds to that emotional climax at the end. Pip Deveson, as you've mentioned, is a brilliant and very experienced editor. How much input did you or did Marlene have into the editing of the film and the shape it takes?

Fred: The film is structured fundamentally around the themes I mentioned before that had been set up by the four other consultants. These are themes that Marlene hit as if she were hitting her mark in some kind of performance. The others all responded in very similar ways. So, we knew that we had something that resonated with the community of Pintupi viewers. One of the disappointments is that none of the Pintupi people we talked to had any interest in being involved in the editing. They really saw that as our business and that they would see it afterwards. So, Pip edited it, sending it back and forth to me, and I fine-tuned the translations throughout. Then, when Marlene was in Canberra on other business, Pip was able to show her the rough cut. She loved it and then we did take it out and show it to people.

My friend Bobby West, who had been the chairperson of Kiwirrkura – he was my oldest friend from the beginning of my time at Yayayi – was another advisor on this. We had him look at all of the film, and 'okay [approve] it', or not. We had a few concerns that he had raised, that we adjusted in the film: a few things that he thought Marlene had said that might be confusing to people. In terms of the editing, we did not have the kind of dialogical editing[16] that we might have hoped for.

I think it's an interesting issue that people in that community don't have that much experience with [audio]visual material. The truth of the matter is, I believe they would always prefer to see the raw footage where nobody is edited out, even if they're in the corner of the image. The film is, in that way, a kind of a compromise between the necessities of its circulation and the uses of its circulation, in a shorter form. But also, as the film project evolved and because of Marlene's identification with the dialysis project that's helping so many people in Central Australia, the original response of the people who saw the film was "How healthy we were then!"[17] They're living in the midst of an epidemic now.

At the time of the original filming, they were all thin; they were healthy. They looked good; they were lively. Because of Marlene's presence and also because two of the other consultants were also heavily involved with the dialysis project, I felt that I didn't want to just make a film that was an ethnographic film, something that was simply for an [outside] audience. I thought, "That's not enough." But I also felt that they [the community] already have the footage itself; maybe they don't need any more. Papunya Tula Artists, which is involved in this [film footage] project, also has helped develop the project of remote dialysis, so I thought that given the communities' response to the film and what it means, that this film

16 I drew this concept from my friend and former colleague Steve Feld (1987).

17 The film became more and more devoted to this project through its reception by Pintupi as a sign of their prior health.

Figure 5. Panel at a public screening of *Remembering Yayayi* at the National Museum of Australia, with Peter Thorley, Sarah Brown (Purple House), Ian Dunlop, Pip Deveson, Monica Robinson Nangala, Marlene Spencer Nampitjinpa, and Fred Myers, 2015 (photo: Fred Myers)

could have two uses, really. One, in publicising in some way what self-determination really meant to people then (and now). That question is up there in the footage. It's not there as my opinion, but present in all of its complexity, its presence in events. And two, the health issue. When we screened the film at the National Museum of Australia, the people from the Purple House came [see Figure 5]. It was a venue in which donors could be sought out to support the dialysis project. Marlene and another one of our consultants, a middle-aged woman [Monica Robinson Nangala], came to talk about the importance of this and the health crisis. The Purple House will also screen it later in Alice Springs.[18]

I felt that this is a project that has some value for the community. When I wrote my book, the first book,[19] I felt it had some value in the context of land rights, but nobody working with Aboriginal people since the 1970s as an anthropologist can feel that making simply an academic project out of the work is enough. It's not always possible for us to do more, but Aboriginal people do expect that you're not just there to get information from them: that if you're there and taken in as a member of the community, as someone 'from Yayayi', for example, you have obligations towards them, to help them and to do things. What form that can take is always a question and not always obvious, but I have felt, through my whole academic career, an obligation, something that I can never repay them, for the many things that they have given to me. I think many people working with Aboriginal people feel this incredible debt for being included so much in people's lives. That debt is not just a kind of abstraction. With this film, I wanted it to do something for them. One thing it can do is to mobilise people around the issues of health. Another would be that the National Museum of Australia now holds their cultural property, so it won't be lost. That was important to me.

Lisa: Cultural property, another big topic that threads itself through this work and through a lot of your thinking over the last couple of decades. Some of the [audiovisual] material in this

---

18   The film screened in Alice Springs on 4 and 5 July 2017 as part of local NAIDOC week celebrations.

19   See Myers (1986).

Figure 6. Ian Dunlop and Fred Myers discussing Marlene's presence in the archival footage, Canberra (still image from *Remembering Yayayi*)

film we wouldn't be able to share as an audio clip in a podcast. Some of it might be easier to share. Can you say something about the early footage and the cultural properties in it? And what you had to do to make this film, because it's actually a feat in the management of very complex relations around cultural property in film.

Fred: When we started the project, we went through two sets of university Human Subjects Research ethics approvals. Internal review boards, agreements about what rights people would have in the material, what ethical obligations we had, and so on. The original footage, we understood, Ian Dunlop had shot for Film Australia, which eventually has become Screen Australia, a government organisation, but he continued to have rights to his own projects. That's how we understood it. The National Archive was very happy for us to use the material as a research tool, so that's what we were doing. We weren't planning to make a film.

When we decided to make a film, we edited it [the original footage] and we did all of this work. We had all the agreements. Papunya Tula Artists, the Aboriginal communities Kintore and Kiwirrkura were all involved, they were very happy with all this. Very late in the process, Ian Dunlop and Pip Deveson went to the National Film and Sound Archives [NFSA] – the agency that controls the copyright of the footage and manages its usages – with the proposal to make a film to be added to Ian's other film work, that would be free for them [NFSA] and that could be included [with Ian's corpus of other work]. They said, "You don't have the right to make the film." Ian was completely taken aback, because his understanding was that it was his material [and therefore he held authorial rights] even though it was lodged in the archive. That commenced quite a long process in which we had to negotiate with them.

Part of my current research interest, of course, is the issue of rights in cultural materials, and what had happened in Australia. Archival material like that was actually being freely shared with people who had permissions of the communities. That is, the National Archives recognised that communities had rights to their material, and if you had permission from them you could use it. But now, because the Australian Federal Government had removed most of the funding from the archives, the NFSA had to make money from their collections. We would call that a return to neo-liberalism, in which institutions had to earn their keep. They were obliged to charge us money, and it was quite a lot per second, commercial rates. They said, "Well, we'll allow you to do it at academic rates," which is still very costly.

Initially Ian was quite upset because [as already indicated] he believed that he had authorial rights, as he was the creator of the film material, which in most copyright circumstances would give him control over it, even if he shared it [the film and the rights in it] with the community. But now, the government had a claim to it. So, we had some money in the grant, and we paid for the right to screen it in festivals. However, the film is marred, in some sense, by the necessity of including a stamp on it that says 'Property of National Film and Sound Archives', on all of the archival footage. It's not terrible, but it does hinder its visual ability. Eventually, Ian rediscovered the Memorandum of Understanding that he had with Film Australia when he retired, which made it pretty clear, I thought, that he had rights to the material to use in his own projects, and he was a co-producer of this project. In the end, we needed a lawyer. The Australian National University legal team wrote to the National Film and Sound Archives about the rights. So, you have two government bodies basically hashing it out about the rights to this. Actually, ideally and theoretically, it belongs to the Pintupi communities themselves, and to Ian as a creator. In the end, the significance of the creator's copyright privileges was allowed to stand. With the community's agreement and the agreement of Ian, we were allowed to go forward without having to pay these horrendous fees. It's quite an interesting story about the bureaucratisation of these protocols for establishing who has ownership rights in cultural material.[20]

Lisa: One of the ideas that you've developed over at least the last 25 years of your work is what you call 'culture-making' (Myers 1994) for desert people, and also as an idea that's helpful in anthropological theorising. You've also emphasised the value of thinking about anthropology as a social practice that is, at times, itself involved in, or enabling of, culture-making. You've gone so far in a paper in 2006 (Myers & Ginsburg 2006) to say that there are emancipatory potentials in culture-making for people. Does this film fit into that trajectory of Pintupi culture-making as you've understood it? And if it does, in what ways might we think about it as emancipatory?

Fred: I drew on this concept as I was struggling also with issues of 'Primitivism', which are always used to judge Aboriginal people's work [art, performance] as whether it's 'traditional' or whether it's 'contaminated' [see Myers 1991, 2006]. I think the emancipatory part is that it allows people to understand others as reaching towards you, as offering you a way into their worlds, to the extent that they are willing to do so. It allows them to *make* their cultural understandings through time. Because of the technology of the film, I think the question you asked about the editing is really to the point. It is not as much a product of their [consultants']

---

20   See Myers (2017b).

activity as I would have hoped. That is to say, if we had had more time, if I could live in Kintore for six months – which I can't because of family circumstances – it might have been more played out through time, where they could have had more input. Input, as deep consultation, takes a long time for Aboriginal people. You can't do it in two weeks. The process of consultation is longer. We did have an extended time. I think many scholars and activists have concluded that the idea of 'collaboration' is not simple. I have come to prefer 'accountability'. Anyway, [this project] is collaborative in many respects, but collaboration is limited by people's skills, and an understanding of a medium. The medium of film is something that most of the people in the two communities don't have sufficient experience of to make judgments of the kind that they might make. Perhaps if you showed it and you could reshow it and play it back and cut it and so on. There is some of that: the Pintupi communities had been watching the film for several years, so we did have the advantage of their understandings of the material, but our ability to train people to participate and to collaborate in the ways that we would have hoped, and the limitations of our own resources and our own family situations, made that, I think, less than it might have been. I don't want to say it was a perfect project. It is a project. I would have liked nothing more than to spend more time out there and let it play out in that way, which is what I did in my two years of fieldwork and later long periods. [But] people's lives become more complicated. Some of the constraints are the realities of our lives. It is a big issue in anthropology – no matter who you are at a point in your life.

I have 40 years of history. It's right now 44 years almost to the day [19 July 1973] when I went to Yayayi for the first time, and I can remember it as if it were yesterday. Bobby West was my first friend. I met him on the first day I was there [in Yayayi]. Now, he's coming to open up this exhibition [*Tjunguṇutja* – 'From Having Come Together']²¹ that's about to happen here in Darwin. I think that history and time has earned me some trust from people, and also some knowledge of the signs of people's hesitations. I am always worried about pushing into things that I should not be. That's why that moment of asking Marlene about her father rings to me as a bit insensitive, although I actually was meaning to provoke her to reflect. And I do know that, despite the fact that there is a well-known taboo on the names of the dead, that taboo is often suspended for the practicalities of the moment and among people who know each other very well, with some indication that you respect their relationship to it. From that point of view, I think maybe if there's an emancipatory potential in this film, it is [to give a value in the present] to the sweep of anthropology which was engaged with questions of land rights and the documentation of a way of life that will never [again] be what it was. And that our friendships can be helpful.

Lisa: I think that's a really great place to end this discussion. Thanks Fred, it's been a pleasure listening.

---

21   We are referring here to the opening of the exhibition at the Museum and Art Gallery of the Northern Territory (MAGNT), 1 July 2017, in Darwin. *Tjunguṇutja* was a retrospective of the collection of early Papunya Tula paintings held by MAGNT, curated by Luke Scholes (curator of Aboriginal Art, MAGNT) in collaboration with five senior artists of Papunya Tula Artists – Bobby West Tjupurrula, Michael Nelson Jagamara, Long Jack Phillipus Tjakamarra, Sid Anderson, and Joseph Jurrah Tjapaltjarri.

Conclusion

This discussion has two key frames of reference in the contemporary field of visual anthropology and it is through these that we figured the movement of our discussion when we caught up to record an interview/conversation in Darwin in 2017.

Firstly we are attuned to (and bothered by) the glorified banality of the term 'collaboration'. As a gloss for 'working together' it can too easily elide entangled histories of engagement and shifting distributions of power and agency. It oversimplifies the real conditions of possibility and multiple practices involved in co-creative projects (Haviland 2017), and it risks sidestepping a serious working through of complex participatory identities.[22] A banal conception of collaboration threatens to become, in many invocations, little more than another box to tick in the policing of imagined boundaries. The second frame, discussed more explicitly here, is that of the 'memory'-making capacity and tendency of archival 'returns' in the present lives of people whose generational successions have been threatened or disrupted dramatically within living memory. As Indigenous filmmakers like Rachel Perkins and Frances Peters-Little emphasised in telling the stories of the political struggles of an earlier generation, the Pintupi consultants want this film to illustrate or illuminate Indigenous strength, commitment and cultural practices, which they see as having guided their history from the settlement at Papunya back to their own country.

These two frames are linked. Archival 'return' – as a collaborative practice involving multiple 'stakeholders' working together on both sides of the equation – begins and ends with respecting the community protocols for designing, planning and carrying out the work of retrieval, consultation, sharing, receiving back and caretaking. Simultaneous with this social-ethical imperative, the cultural/material ends of repatriation cannot be predicted because enacting the primary respect for cultural privacy, authority, safety and aspiration is performative across multiple locations and times, via a variety of people and rule-bound processes. The case of the Dunlop footage is iconic in this respect: the relational negotiations around 'return' proved to be as fraught at the highest levels of our national cultural institutions as they are at the local levels of desert communities around the question of who can and will speak about the past and its value in the present, and to whom and to what ends. The exercise of taking, or shaping, power at any one point only opens up the necessity of renegotiating at another point.[23]

Anxieties surrounding the circulation and control of archival images are by no means solely the emotive terrain of people who might re-meet their ancestors and past family on screen. Archives can themselves be active agents in the displacement, projection and amplification of this anxiety, converting culturally significant recorded 'national' history into a price-per-second value. The *Remembering Yayayi* project reminds us that if, as Marilyn Strathern (1999) pointed out many years ago, property – and therefore culture as property – is

---

22 See *Apmere Angkentye-kenhe: Language as a music playing us* (Sometimes 2018), a recent innovative arts practice-led Aboriginal language-based research project in Mparntwe (Alice Springs) that thoughtfully enacted this kind of working through. Also, the report '*Ngapartji Ngapartji* – the consequences of kindness' (Palmer 2010), on the Big hART project of the same name.

23 We thank Steve Feld for helping to formulate this insight.

foundational to sociality and relationality, we should attend closely to its movement, its play of meanings and uses. The social life of cultural property (Appadurai 1986) mitigates against the reduction of co-creative relationships to the cold interface of a business contract, no matter how legally binding the latter may be. Shared pleasures in the recognition of historically emerging connections can be intense, and happily so. They spring up irrepressibly and unpredictably. They foreground and spill beyond the transactional discipline of 'partnerships' and 'collaboration'. Most importantly, they do a lot to ensure the survival of the deal, to keep the spirit of a project going. Such shared pleasures inspire inventiveness in the management of memory-based co-creative projects, eliciting a strong sense of purpose when red tape feels all too constricting and constraining.

Individuals experience social memory as a shared place of relatedness. Archival 'returns' have powerful intergenerationally affective dimensions. As the social life of the *Remembering Yayayi* project has shown, archival 'returns' that involve creative collaboration also inherently carry the potential to galvanise new relationships within and beyond communities. In Central Australia at the present moment these kinds of projects have a particular potency as people whose childhoods were in part shaped by the dramatic social transitions and cultural transformations of the 1970s move into roles as elders within their communities.

A range of what we might term 'memory machines' – processes, practices and productions that gather, curate and remake memory stories in visual and other media – are key here. They are mimetic in the sense that they create likenesses of what was. They are revelatory, remaking the past from the perspective of a precarious present, and casting it into an uncertain future. They suggest in equal measure personal nostalgia, community and research salvage, and enduring historical values.

As with the landmark MAGNT exhibition and accompanying film of the earliest Papunya paintings, '*Tjunguṉutja* – from having come together' (Scholes 2017), and similar retrospectives, films such as *Remembering Yayayi* provoke pleasure, sorrow and pride. It was no coincidence that we recorded the interview for this chapter at the time of the opening of this remarkable revelatory and revisionist Western Desert art show. Out of footage at risk of fading into obscurity, Marlene and the project's other key Pintupi consultants, together with Fred, Pip, Ian, Peter and others, made new memory narratives for desert people and for all who have been involved in their histories up close or at a distance. As they themselves grow older, what becomes of these memories in the imaginations of near and far away audiences remains to be seen.

References

Altman, Jon. 2012. People on country as alternate development. In Jon Altman & Sean Kerins (eds.), *People on country: Vital landscapes, Indigenous futures*, 1–25. Sydney: Federation Press.

Appadurai, Arjun. 1986. Introduction: Commodities and the politics of value. In Arjun Appadurai (ed.), *The social life of things*, 3–63. Cambridge: Cambridge University Press.

Benjamin, Roger (ed.). 2009. *Icons of the desert: Early Aboriginal paintings from Papunya*. Ithaca, NY: Cornell University Press.

Feld, Steven. 1987. Dialogic editing: Interpreting how Kaluli read *Sound and Sentiment*. *Cultural Anthropology* 2. 190–210.

Ginsburg, Faye & Fred Myers. 2006. A history of Indigenous futures: Accounting for Indigenous art and media. *Aboriginal History* 30. 95–110.

Haviland, Maya. 2017. *Side by side? Community art and the challenge of co-creativity*. New York: Routledge.

Hinkson, Melinda. 2016. 'That photo in my heart': *Remembering Yayayi* and self-determination. *TAJA* 20. 386–397.

Hughes, Helen. 2007. *Lands of shame: Aboriginal and Torres Strait Islander 'homelands' in transition*. Sydney: Centre for Independent Studies.

Myers, Fred. 1986. *Pintupi country, Pintupi self: Sentiment, place, and politics among Western Desert Aborigines*. Washington, DC: Smithsonian Institution Press.

Myers, Fred. 1991. Representing culture: The production of discourse(s) for Aboriginal acrylic paintings. *Cultural Anthropology* 6(1). 26–62.

Myers, Fred. 1994. Culture-making: Performing Aboriginality in the Asia Society Gallery. *American Ethnologist* 21(4). 679–699.

Myers, Fred. 2001. Introduction: The empire of things. In Fred Myers (ed.), *The empire of things: Regimes of value and material culture*, 3–64. Santa Fe: SAR Press.

Myers, Fred. 2006. 'Primitivism,' anthropology and the category of 'primitive art'. In Chris Tilley, Webb Keane, Susanne Kuechler, Michael Rowlands & Patricia Spyer (eds.), *Handbook of material culture*, 267–284. New York: Sage Press.

Myers, Fred. 2016. History, memory and the politics of self-determination at an early outstation. In Nicolas Peterson & Fred Myers (eds.), *Experiments in self-determination: Histories of the outstation movement in Australia*, 81–103. Canberra: ANU Press.

Myers, Fred. 2017a. Exhibiting culture at the boundary: The fetish of early Papunya boards. In Luke Scholes (ed.), *Tjunguṉutja: From having come together*, 196–210. Darwin: Museum and Art Gallery of the Northern Territory.

Myers, Fred. 2017b. Whose story is it? Complexities and complicities of using archival footage. In Jane Anderson & Haidy Geismar (eds.), *Routledge companion to cultural property*, 168–193. New York and Oxford: Routledge Press.

Palmer, Dave. 2010. *Ngapartji Ngapartji – the consequences of kindness*. Melbourne: Big hART / Perth: Murdoch University. (https://www.bighart.org/wp-content/uploads/2017/03/BIghART_Evaluation_ConsequencesofKindness.pdf) (Accessed 12 April 2019.)

Peterson, Nicolas & Fred Myers (eds.). (2016). *Experiments in self-determination: Histories of the outstation movement in Australia* (Monographs in Anthropology). Canberra: ANU Press.

Scholes, Luke (ed.). 2017. *Tjunguṉutja: From having come together*. Darwin: Museum and Art Gallery of the Northern Territory.

Sometimes, Beth. 2018. *Apmere Angkentye-kenhe: Language as a music playing us*. Melbourne: University of Melbourne. (MA Research thesis.) (https://minerva-access.unimelb.edu.au/handle/11343/213464) (Accessed 12 April 2019.)

Strathern, Marilyn. 1999. *Property, substance, and effect: Anthropological essays on persons and things*. London: Athlone Press.

Films

Deveson, Pip, Ian Dunlop & Fred Myers (directors). 2014. *Remembering Yayayi*. Documentary Educational Resources.

Dunlop, Ian (director). 1967. *Desert people*. Film Australia.

Language Documentation & Conservation Special Publication No. 18
Archival returns: Central Australia and beyond
ed. by Linda Barwick, Jennifer Green & Petronella Vaarzon-Morel, pp. 239–262
http://nflrc.hawaii.edu/ldc/sp18
http://hdl.handle.net/10125/24886

12

Return of a travelling song: *Wanji-wanji* in the Pintupi region of Central Australia

Myfany Turpin
Sydney Conservatorium of Music, The University of Sydney

Abstract

This chapter discusses responses to the return of legacy recordings of Pintupi singing made in 1976 and the collection of further metadata about the song *Wanji-wanji* featured on the recordings. *Wanji-wanji* was once a popular entertainment song that was performed across the western half of Australia, as can be seen by the many recordings of it held in archives. Custodianship of the song is unknown; the earliest reference to its performance dates back to the 1850s, where it is described as a 'travelling dance' (Bates 1913–1914) and so in terms of copyright its status may be comparable to 'public domain', i.e. outside of copyright. Responses to hearing the recording were emotional. Those who knew the song recalled the place and time in which they had heard it long ago. There was great interest in how widely it was known though little interest in the meanings of the lyrics. On the whole, responses to access and proposed uses of the recordings, as well as the future possible uses of the song, reflected its public domain status. Nevertheless, the confidence in people's responses varied depending on whether the individual knew the song, had experience in using archival recordings, and whether they perceived community interest and support for classical Aboriginal singing practices.

Keywords: Aboriginal song, Indigenous ceremony, Pintupi, entertainment songs, Australian Aboriginal ceremony

Introduction[1]

In 2017, I set out for Pintupi country to consult with people about audio recordings of a ceremonial song that could be described as a 'travelling corroboree' (Hercus 1980: 17). The ceremony was labelled *Wanji-wanji* and the recording had been made in 1976 at the now abandoned outstation of Kungkayurnti, 'Browns Bore', some 80 kilometres southwest of the community of Papunya in Central Australia. The five singers on the recordings were Pintupi men and women, now all deceased. Four were well-known artists who sang together on one recording: Mick Namarari Tjapaltjarri, Wintjiya Napaltjarri, Tjunkaya Napaltjarri, and Muwitja Napaltjarri. The other, who sang solo, was the renowned Nosepeg Tjungkarta Tjupurrula OBE, who entranced a series of filmmakers, politicians, and academics with his wit, knowledge, and charisma.[2] The two recordings, totalling 1 hour and 20 minutes of singing *Wanji-wanji*, were high quality and well documented and had been archived in public institutions. They had been made by musicologist Richard Moyle, who had spent a total of 12 months at Kungkayurnti documenting Pintupi musical life in the mid 1970s (Moyle 1979).

The songs were of the *turlku* ceremonial genre,[3] a Pintupi and Kukatja word meaning 'social corroboree' (Hansen & Hansen 1974: 200) or what Moyle (1979: 19) describes as "an informal song ... with occasional dancing" whose principal function is entertainment, and which has no associated sacred objects. In the neighbouring language Kukatja, in whose lands R Moyle recorded a further version of the song in 1982, the entertainment genre was called *tjulpurrpa* (Moyle 1997: 90), a term Hansen & Hansen (1974: 230) define as "a ceremony open to women and children." Moyle compares *tjulpurrpa* with "the 'corroborees' seen or heard in camps by scores of early visitors to central Australia. Now largely forgotten through non-performance, the names and a few songs alone are remembered" (1997: 90). The word 'corroboree', originally from the Darug language of Sydney, was well-established in English by the time

1   I wish to acknowledge the Indigenous consultants who contributed their views and knowledge in the interviews. In particular, Aileen Napurrula, Barbara Napangarti, Brenda Napaltjarri, Bundy Rowe, Charlie Tjapangarti, Clara Rowe, Elizabeth Marks Nakamarra, George Tjungurrayi, Irene Napangarti, Janelle Larry, Jeannie Pegg Nakamarra, Joe Young, Josephine Brown, Josephine Napurrula, Linda Anderson Nakamarra, Michael Nelson, Monica Robinson, Nanyuma Napangarti, Napurla Scobie, Nguya Napaltjarri, Noya Napaltjarri, Pamela Tolson, Patrick Oolodoodi†, George Lee, Mitjili Napurrurla, Eunice Napanangka Jack, Anmanari Napanangka, Alice Nampijinpa, Simon Dixon, Richard Pegg, Robert Nanala Tjapaltjarri, Rubilee Napurrula, Tatuli Napurrula, and Xavier Tjapanangka. I thank Peter Bartlett, Cindy Gibson, Lyle Gibson, Robin Granites, Jess Bartlett, Marlene Spencer Nampitjin, Richard Moyle, Fred Myers, Marina Strocchi, Luis Miguel Rojas Berscia, and the Purple House, who assisted in the logistics, translation, and consultation for this research. I thank Ben Deacon, Robert Nugent, and Felicity Meakins, who assisted with recording the interviews. I also thank Jason Gibson and two anonymous reviews for their insightful comments and suggestions. Funding for this research was provided by an Australian Research Council Future Fellowship (FT140100783) and Linkage Project grant in partnership with the Central Land Council (LP140100806). Ethical clearance for both projects was obtained from the University of Sydney (2015/081, 2015/544) and permits to enter Aboriginal Land from the Central Land Council (51332, 41434, 30791).

2   Nosepeg features in numerous movies, three biographical films and countless published writings. Nosepeg and Mick are discussed by Khan (2016).

3   The spelling of Pintupi/Kukatja words, including skin names, follows that in Valiquette (1993); for people who identify as Warlpiri I have followed standard Warlpiri spellings.

Howitt (1887: 327) used it to refer to Aboriginal song, the accompanying dances and the social gathering in which they are performed. Elkin (1970: 249) describes this genre as "secular or 'everyday' camp music." Most Indigenous groups across Australia have an equivalent term for this genre (e.g. Elkin 1970: 249; Treloyn et al. 2016: 96).[4] In Aboriginal English the term 'corroboree' or sometimes 'playabout' (Egan 1997: 100) is used for this genre in contrast to 'ceremony' or 'business', which refers to the more serious land-based performance genres.

My interest in the *Wanji-wanji* recordings stemmed from working on a project with linguist Felicity Meakins and Karungkarni Art Centre (Turpin & Meakins 2019) to document the traditional entertainment songs the Gurindji people of the Victoria River District (NT) perform. According to the Gurindji singers, some of their entertainment songs had come to them via Balgo, including one called *Laka*. Balgo had once been a hub of ceremonial exchange, and anthropologists Ronald and Catherine Berndt (1988: 383) described how ceremonies came from "all directions: the Canning Stock Route to the west, the east Kimberleys to the north." Richard Moyle had documented Aboriginal songs at Balgo in the 1980s, and *Laka* was indeed the name of a "largely forgotten song" (1997: 43, 90).[5] Moyle recorded Kukatja/Pintupi man Donkeyman Lee Tjupurrula singing and talking about *Laka* for 13 minutes. '*Wanji-wanji*' is one word that appears in a verse of *Laka*, as sung by the Gurindji. Moyle's extensive set of recordings includes two long performances of a song Nosepeg refers to as *Wanji-wanji* (1979: 19). With my interest piqued, I wrote to Richard Moyle requesting permission to hear both the Kungkayurnti and Balgo recordings performed some 580 kilometres and eight years apart (see Figure 1).[6]

My analysis of these three performances finds, based on the fact that they contain many of the same verses, that *Laka* and *Wanji-wanji* are alternative names for the same song. A summary of this analysis is presented in the next section.

---

4   Equivalent terms in neighbouring languages are *purlapa* in Warlpiri, *inma* in Pitjantjatjara, *wajarra* in Gurindji, and *junba* in Jaru and other languages across a vast area of northwestern Australia (Treloyn 2003: 209; Turpin & Meakins 2019). In Pintupi the word *turlku* is also used to refer to 'song' in a general sense, such as when the genre is unknown or unspecified (Valiquette 1993: 297).

5   Two other songs we recorded at Kalkaringi, *Tjuntara* and *Kamul*, were also recorded by Richard Moyle at Balgo, suggesting widespread ritual exchange between these regions (Turpin & Meakins 2019).

6   Both Richard Moyle's monographs contain a vast number of song texts; but these are only a fraction of the songs he recorded. Many, such as *Laka/Wanji-wanji*, did not make it into the published volumes, which focus on more well-known songs.

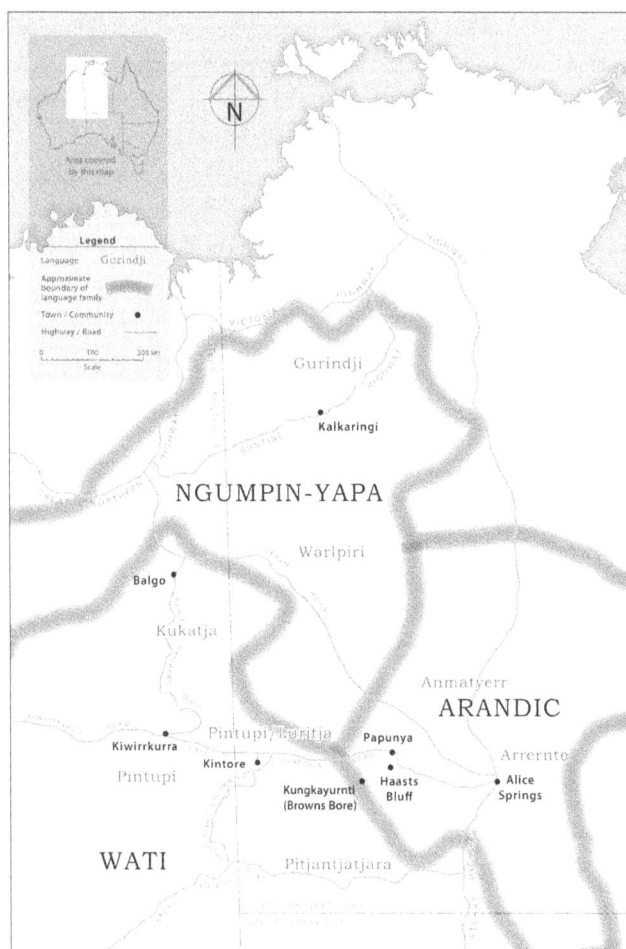

Figure 1. Map showing the communities where the three recordings of *Wanji-wanji/Laka* were made: Balgo, Kungkayurnti, and Kalkaringi

A comparison of the three recordings of the song

In this article I use the word 'song' to refer to the same entity that some musicologists call a 'song set' or 'repertory' (e.g. O'Keeffe et al. 2018: 141), which some ethnographers call a 'ceremony'. I use the word 'verse' for the contrastive units that make up a song and I use 'song item' to refer to the multiple tokens of each verse, a structural feature ubiquitous in Central Australian Aboriginal song.[7]

Although called by two different names, *Laka* and *Wanji-wanji* (henceforth 'the song') have many of the same verses. By 'the same' I am referring to the fact that the rhythmic-texts of the verses are indistinguishable, although their melodies may differ. This is based on my linguistic and musical analysis of the verses, but it is also supported by comments from Aboriginal singers who upon listening to these state that they are 'the same' and make comments such as "We sing it this way, but they sing it that way."[8] The remarkable stability

---

7   A song item is the smallest unit of singing and usually last 30–60 seconds.

8   On one occasion this was even accompanied by different patterns of higher and lower hand gestures, reminiscent of the way hand gestures are sometimes used to accompany a musical pitch system such as solfege.

of the rhythmic-texts is characteristic of other Aboriginal songs, including songs that are not understood by the people who sing them (Berndt & Berndt 1988: 384; Dixon 2011: 55; Roth 1897: 168; Turpin & Meakins 2019: 19, 166).

On the Kungkayurnti recordings there are 25 unique verses of the song, 13 of which also recur in the Balgo and Gurindji recordings of the song. This is shown on the top row of Table 1. On the much shorter Balgo recording, there are seven verses of the song, five of which are also on the Kungkayurnti and Gurindji recordings. On the Gurindji recordings, there are 15 verses of the song, 12 of which are also on the Balgo and Kungkayurnti recordings.

Table 1. A comparison of *Wanji-wanji/Laka* song recorded at three different places

Recording	Date	No. of verses	No. of verses common to the other two recordings
Kungkayurnti *Wanji-wanji*[9]	1975	25	13
Balgo *Laka*[10]	1981	7	5
Gurindji *Laka* (Turpin & Meakins)[11]	2015 & 2016	15	12

Table 2 shows the number of verses that are common to each of these three performances. The total number of verses in each performance is bolded along the diagonal (25, 7 and 15); and matching two performances along the X and Y axis gives the number of verses common to these two performances. For example, the Gurindji and Balgo performances have four verses in common.

Table 2. Number of verses in common across the three different recordings

3 performances	Kungkayurnti	Balgo	Gurindji
Kungkayurnti	**25**	5	12
Balgo	5	**7**	4
Gurindji	12	4	**15**

Ten verses of this same song can be heard on five other archival recordings made across Western Australia and South Australia by four linguists.[12] When we include these recordings in the comparison, we find even more verses common to other performances: a total of 19 of the 25 verses on the Kungkayurnti recordings can be heard on other recordings and six of the seven verses on the Balgo recordings can be heard on other recordings.

---

9   AIATSIS archive tapes Moyle_R03_Aus 80, 81, and 76.

10   AIATSIS archive tapes Moyle_R23_Aus 659/2.

11   Deposited at AIATSIS but yet to be accessioned.

12   The five recordings are held at AIATSIS. They are from Marble Bar, WA (Klokeid_T01-000669 [1967]), Roebourne, WA (OGrady_G02-000799 [1954/1955]), Norseman, WA (Von-Brandenstein_C04-002159A [1970]), Port Augusta, SA (Hercus_L03-001003B [1967]), and Maree, SA (Hercus_L27-004315A [1973]). The 'elsewhere' also includes a recording made with Pitjantjatjara speaker Nellie Patterson in 2017 that yielded an unelicited singing of one of the verses sung at Kalkaringi (Verse 29).

Table 3. Number of verses on the Kungkayurnti and Balgo recordings common to all other recordings

No. of verses/ Performance	Total	Occurring in other performances
Kungkayurnti	25	19
Balgo	7	6

The Kungkayurnti and Kalkaringi performances of the song contain by far the most verses and have the longest duration out of all the corpus of recordings located to date.[13] Across all the recordings of the song, there are a total of 33 different verses. These verses are listed in column 2 of Table 4 (Verse id.), each identified with a unique numeric id between 22 and 54.[14] Twenty-one of these verses occur on more than one recording. These are the verses in the shaded rows of Table 4. Put another way, 64 per cent of the verses across these recordings are the same, while 36 per cent of verses are unique to only one recording. This suggests that *Laka* and *Wanji-wanji* are alternative names for the one song.

Table 4. The distribution of the 32 verses of *Wanji-wanji/Laka* across the three recordings and five from elsewhere ('other'); 21 verses are sung on more than one recording (shaded)

Recording	Verse id.	Number of verses
Kungkayurnti (K)	41, 42, 43, 49, 51, 52	12 verses on only one recording
Gurindji (G)	36, 37, 39	
Balgo (B)	23	
Other	53, 54	
K & G	26, 27, 38, 30, 31, 32, 33, 35	21 verses on recordings from more than one location/time
K, G & B	24, 25, 28, 34	
K & B	47	
K & other	40, 44, 45, 46, 48, 50	
G & other	29	
B & other	22	

The verses on the recordings are not performed in the same order, which is not uncommon for genres of Aboriginal song. Having discovered that the Pintupi and the Gurindji, some 800 kilometres away, sing the same song, the next question was what sort of song this is. Thus,

---

13   The past manager at Pitjantjatjara Yankunytjatjara Media organisation (then called Ernabella Video and Television), Neil Turner, recalls playing a recording of this song at Ernabella "which caused great excitement in 1986" (email communication, June 2018). This recording has recently come to light. It has only two verses, both of which occur on the Pintupi recordings.

14   The numbering commences at 22 because my numbering system for verses is based on sequential ordering of verses in a single performance, which in this case was the Gurindji performance. This performance began with a different song before *Laka*, and thus the first *Laka* verse was 22. As can be imagined, a comparison of the same verse across multiple songs and performances requires a stable unique id. The numbering given here is an abbreviated form of my longer verse id system, which indicates the genre, song set, and unique verse.

my intention was to see whether contemporary Pintupi could shed light on the origins and nature of this travelling song, as well as provide contemporary views on access and publication.

Travelling songs

The term 'travelling corroboree' was first used by Roth in 1897 to refer to the '*Molonga* corroboree' from Queensland (Roth 1897; Elkin 1970: 260), which had been passed on over huge distances, and was sometimes known by a different name, such as *Tjitjingalla* in Arrernte territory, as noted by Gillen in 1898 (Mulvaney et al. 2001: 432).[15] Even before this, Howitt (1887: 329) described how some Aboriginal songs were "carried from tribe to tribe" and that the distance of one such song was "about five hundred miles in a direct line, but it by no means gives the length of the course followed by the song in its travels."

Various ethnographers have used the term 'travelling' plus either 'corroboree', 'ceremony', 'song', 'ritual', or 'business' to refer to Aboriginal traditions that have circulated well beyond their place of origin (e.g. McCarthy 1939). Elkin (1970: 260) observes that in addition to the traditional trade of ceremonies, since the time of colonisation ceremonies have also spread as people sought employment on cattle stations or townships and as they moved onto Aboriginal settlements far from their own tribal country.

Many German ethnographers who were interested in cultural diffusion referred to such ceremonies as 'Wanderkulte', wandering cults or mobile rituals (see Kolig 2017; Widlok 1992). Petri (2014 [1952]: 161) refers to such songs as being "carried from tribe to tribe until finally the precise meaning of the words and the original source of the songs fall into oblivion." Widlok (1992: 116), discussing three such ceremonies, argues that these are not limited to particular named genres (e.g. *turlku, yawulyu* in Pintupi), but are rather any "part of a traditional local repertoire (secret-sacred rituals or more profane poetry) [that has] become a mobile ritual" (see also Elkin 1970: 259–261). If we assume that any genre of ceremony can travel, we can understand how ceremonies might easily be recontextualised across time and place, as musicologist Wild (1987: 109) observes.

Wanji-wanji

The name *Wanji-wanji* was first used by ethnographer Daisy Bates, who witnessed what she called a 'travelling show' or 'travel dance' at Eucla on the south coast of Australia (Bates 1913–1914). Like the *Molonga*, this was known by different names in the regions through which it travelled. Bates believed it was the same song as what was called *Wanna Wa* in the southwest of Western Australia (WA).

The extent of the *Molonga*'s travels has been widely documented (Beckett & Hercus 2009: 11; Gibson 2017: 149; Hercus 1980; Kimber 1990; Mulvaney 1976; Skinner 2017: 340); however, this has not been the case for the *Wanji-wanji*. Unlike the *Molonga*, there were no known audio recordings of *Wanji-wanji*, and so comparisons of it until now have been based solely on Bates'

---

15 It was subsequently recorded on wax cylinder in 1901 at the Stevenson Creek in South Australia and a film of the associated dance was made in Alice Springs soon after. The unpublished notes and recordings of the *Tjitjingalla* ceremony recorded by Baldwin Spencer and Frank Gillen are discussed by Gibson (2015).

notes and anecdotal evidence. The archaeologist and museum anthropologist Fred McCarthy proposed a route for both travelling songs in a 1939 article based on Bates' work, and personal communication with Elkin, who had "heard of it" in the Musgrave Ranges, northwest of South Australia (McCarthy 1939: 86). German ethnographer Helmut Petri, drawing on Bates' work (2014 [1952]: 164), referred to it as 'secret ceremonial'; however, this is not attested elsewhere and appears to be based on a misreading of Bates, as her description of it involves men and women. Later, Petri (2018 [1967]) refers to the 'Wandji-kurang-gara' ceremony which he documented, yet a comparison of this with *Laka/Wanji-wanji* shows a completely different set of verses.

In 1975, Richard Moyle was the first researcher to record a performance of *Wanji-wanji* and document it as such. Previous recordings of some verses existed, though these were either hidden among linguistic recordings, documented as 'a corroboree song', or, in the case of Hercus, who was aware of the *Wanji-wanji* ceremony, recorded as individual's rememberings of it, rather than a full performance. Moyle noted that Daisy Bates had also heard a song of this name at Eucla, WA in 1913; nevertheless, he concluded that the Pintupi *Wanji-wanji* was not the same song that Bates had witnessed, based on the different meanings and social context that Bates attributes to it (Moyle 1979: 19).

Moyle did not publish any analysis of his *Wanji-wanji* or *Laka* recordings. My analysis of these, and a comparison with Daisy Bates' fieldnotes, reveals that the 'opening' verse of *Wanji-wanji* (Bates 1938: 126) is identical to a verse performed by the Gurindji and the Pintupi (Verse 33). Further examination of her written notes reveals an additional 11 verses that resemble verses performed by the Pintupi: Verses 23, 24, 25, 29 and 37 (Bates 35-20T), Verses 22 and 47 (Bates 35-20T), Verse 50 (Bates 35-23T), Verse 40 (Bates 35-24T), Verse 30 (Bates 35-25T) and Verse 31 (Bates 35-27T), as well as two verses on other recordings: Verses 54 (Bates 35-18T) and 53 (Bates 35-20T).

While we know nothing about the music to which the verses sung at Eucla in 1913 were set, Bates' transcription of the verses show *Laka* and *Wanji-wanji* are the same song (i.e. they have many of the same verses). This raises a number of questions. Where did the *Wanji-wanji* come from? Why did it travel? How did it travel over such a large distance? Was this a common thing? Do songs still travel today? Could some verses have come from different locations, and have been added on or forgotten over the course of time? Do people today still perform the song? Are people aware of the large geographic extent over which it was known? And more specific to the Pintupi, do they know of the existence of these recordings, and others made by Richard Moyle? Scant attention has been paid to this song in the literature; and the whole notion of what are essentially Aboriginal 'folk songs' (songs that are so old and have travelled so widely that their origins are unknown) has not been addressed. It was with these questions in mind that I engaged in community meetings to seek contemporary understandings of the song, and contemporary views on access and use of the recordings, consulting with both descendants of the singers and contemporary Pintupi ceremonial leaders.

These recordings are somewhat unusual in Indigenous Australia in that they contain creative work – considered also intangible cultural property – whose custodianship (composer and/or owner) is unknown, yet the identity of the performers is known. Bates' reference to the song dates its performance back to 1850 and, additionally, no person, clan, or language group claims ownership of the song that I am aware of. If we consider such material in terms of Australian copyright law, such songs are 'traditional' or what is also referred to as 'public domain', which means that the musical works and lyrics are out of copyright. In contrast, for most other Indigenous songs that have been recorded, custodianship can be identified through family lineage to either the original composer or to some other political unit, such as the clan, Dreaming line, or language group (e.g. Barwick & Turpin 2016; Gallagher et al. 2014; Gibson 2018; O'Keeffe et al. 2018: 141; Strehlow 1955). Furthermore, if all the descendants of the group pass away, custodianship can also be handed on to a neighbouring group or related unit. The trading and sharing of songs throughout Indigenous Australia has long been documented in the ethnographic literature (Howitt 1887; McCarthy 1939; Elkin 1970).

The song is also traditional in the sense of it being an Indigenous musical genre rather than an imported genre, in contrast with, for example, classical or popular music genres. Traditional music is characteristically music and dance whose origins are many generations in the past, and that is passed on "mostly unchanged between generations of informal players, usually without notation, and played mostly by ear."[16]

This article considers contemporary Pintupi people's responses to these recordings of this relatively little-documented genre, and the process by which further information about the songs and the singers was obtained. Across Australia the repatriation of song recordings to their communities of origin has been a common research practice for musicologists (Brown 2014; Brown et al. 2017; Treloyn et al. 2016; Turpin 2005; R Moyle, pers. comm., 2018). It is also of ethical concern that 'cultural stakeholders' have knowledge of and access to the results of past and present research, as Treloyn et al. (2016) point out. The outline of this chapter is as follows. In the next section I describe the methods used for seeking people's views on access, usage and further information about the recordings; then I analyse the main responses to hearing the recordings and summarise the sorts of memories and knowledge people have of the songs and the significance of these. Finally I summarise cultural stakeholders' views on access to and usage of the recordings.

Methodology

After obtaining copies of the recordings, I transcribed the verses and compared them with recordings of the same song from elsewhere, as summarised in the Introduction. I also worked with a team of people to translate the speech on the recordings.[17] Preliminary research on who to consult began by talking with people who had worked in Pintupi communities and with Pintupi people in Alice Springs.[18] After assembling a list of the descendants of the singers and cultural leaders, I then set out to undertake the consultations in partnership with a field

---

16 http://www.traditionalmusic.org/traditionalmusicdefinition.shtml (Accessed 18 March 2019.)

17 Peter Bartlett, Robin Granites Japanangka, Lyle Gibson Tjakamarra, Nancy Gil, and Cindy Lee Gibson translated the speech on the 1981 recording.

18 The abovementioned people plus Marina Strocchi, Fred Myers, Ken Hansen, Jeff Hulcombe, Sarah Brown, Sally Hodson, Jill Hodson, and Boyd Wright.

recording assistant and in most cases also an interpreter.[19] In Alice Springs these were done at the 'Purple House' (an accommodation centre for Pintupi people on dialysis),[20] outside the Dialysis Unit and at Papunya Tula, while in the communities these were done at the art centre, on people's verandas, or in a quiet location outside of the communities. Information about people's whereabouts and additional people to consult was continually updated throughout this process.

My primary questions were about access, usage and sharing information about the song. In consultation with community members I put forward a number of uses, including my own request for radio broadcast of excerpts and the release of the recordings as an album. I asked people if they wanted access to the recordings and, if so, whether there were any restrictions on who could access them, and if they wanted copies kept at the Central Land Council based in Alice Springs (the CLC is the primary representation body for Aboriginal issues relating to land in the region) – in particular, in the CLC's digital cultural media database, which can be accessed online and/or in a local institution.[21] In addition, I wanted to create new recordings with people who knew about the songs or the singers to get a better understanding of the nature of the songs and the lives of the people who sang them.

My approach was to inform people about the recordings and explain that I was seeking further information about them. Some people wanted to hear the song before agreeing to be part of the interviews. For older people it was usually enough for me to casually sing one of the lines of the main verse and they would immediately recognise it, while for others I played part of the recording on a speaker and we would then schedule an interview for later in the day or the following day. The interviews involved between one and eight people in a public place outdoors listening to the recordings in two different ways. One was with headphones, so the songs could be heard properly (there were often noise distractions in the external environment), and so that people's responses could be heard clearly (Figure 2). The second way was with speakers, which had the benefit of more than one person listening simultaneously (Figure 3). Sometimes other people would come by to listen briefly (see Figure 4).

All but two interviews were recorded. Depending on the person's interest, one or more verses would be played; rarely were all 24 verses played. In all, 30 people were consulted, predominantly descendants of the singers, but also elders who knew the songs, as well as local interpreters.

---

19 Recording assistants were Robert Nugent, Ben Deacon, Felicity Meakins, and Shanay Hubmann and interpreters were Jessie Bartlett, Cindy Gibson, Marlene Spencer Nampitjinpa, Irene Roberts, and Robert Tjapaltjarri.

20 The Purple House is described as a "home away from home for patients forced to relocate from remote communities for dialysis treatment." (https://www.purplehouse.org.au/alice-springs) (Last accessed 9 November 2018.)

21 https://clc.keepingculture.com/welcome (Accessed 18 March 2019.)

Figure 2. M Nelson, with headphones on, listening to the *Wanji-wanji* recordings at Papunya, May 2018 (photo: Robert Nugent)

Figure 3. Listening to the *Wanji-wanji* recordings on speaker at Kintore, July 2017. B Napaltjarri, R Napurrula, N Napaltjarri, J Napurrula, M Turpin, T Napurrula, and J Young (photo: Ben Deacon)

Figure 4. Listening to the *Wanji-wanji* recordings at Kiwirrkurra, July 2017. Nangala, C Tjapangarti, J Larry, P Oolodoodi†, and M Turpin (unknown man standing and boy sitting stopped to listen briefly) (photo: Ben Deacon)

Responses to hearing the recordings

Emotional responses

On hearing the recording, people were immediately transported back to a time and place of their childhood. This was a bittersweet feeling, as the song was associated with joyful social occasions yet it evoked nostalgia for the song and for the people who once sang it. Clearly the song had not been heard or performed for many years. Those who knew the song recalled the accompanying dances and specific performances they witnessed. Michael Nelson, born c. 1945–1949, recounts:[22]

> I used to see my mother at Haasts Bluff, even at Yuendumu. They used to dance like that – ah really good! ... Some visitors [would be] sitting around and they [others] used to run around and woman used to sing – oh really good! I remember, you know, because I was a little boy ... But we still love that big corroboree ... [They had a] head thing you know ... and puttem red, white, black. Oh gees! But nothing's happening now, all gone. Nothing, no corroboree now, only ceremony, that's all.[23] [02:45–05:28, 20180522]

People of Michael's age provided eyewitness accounts of a full *Wanji-wanji* performance – a show with costumes and dances put on because of a visiting group. The song was vaguely familiar to a few younger people, who recalled older relatives singing it in a more casual environment. Such people lamented the loss not so much of this song in particular, but the loss of such singing in everyday life. That is, while traditional Aboriginal singing is still heard in the local land-based ceremonies, entertainment songs are now rare, possibly because they have been replaced with western genres of song. Linda Anderson Nakamarra, born in 1962, paints the following picture of her childhood while listening to the recording of her father singing:

> We used to wake up every morning when they sang. Like food would be cooking and we would listen to old people singing as we waited for whatever was cooking. Just like nowadays we wake up to radio being played in the morning, well we used to listen to them singing. Beautiful singing from elders, you know. Nice, soft, it's like going on a journey ... I used to love going to corroboree night. Old women used to call out, "Hey children, it's corroboree time" and I used to be the first one sitting, cause I really liked the singing ... Women are missing out on that and it's really, you know, sad when that is not happening anymore. Because our children missed out a lot on that and their children are going to miss out on that unless it is introduced back. [07:50–12:00, 20180523]

Bittersweet feelings from listening to the recordings were not only stirred by thinking about a bygone era, but for some they were stirred by thinking about relatives that were sorely missed.

---

22   The quotes are presented here with minor grammatical alterations to assist understanding. This involves modification to ensure agreement of person, number and tense, as well as deleting repetition. Ellipses are reserved for substantial content that is not included in order to keep to the point.

23   Here the word 'ceremony' refers to land-based or sacred ceremonies and is being contrasted with 'corroboree', presumably referring to shared entertainment ceremonies.

For Nakamarra, hearing her 'two grandmothers' (her father's mother and father's mother's sister) brought to mind fond memories of growing up at Kungkayurnti, yet also sadness as she missed them.

> *Kunya* ['poor things'], my two grandmothers singing! [0:51] ... They told me to sing that song: "When you grow up, when you get old, you sing this song." But, all my [only(?)] memories now. It was a good time at Kungkayurnti with my grandmothers, singing, telling stories ... Sometimes I don't like to hear them, sometimes I get worried about them. I cry, because I've heard their voices. [18:38–21:30, 20181522]

One Pintupi interpreter highlighted how important it was to be 'on country' when listening to a recording of an ancestor; that is, to be on the homelands of the person whose voice is being heard. This was not because nearby places were being referred to on the recording; on the contrary, the spoken explanations of the seven verses were general and did not refer to specific locations. Some of the explanations included things such as travelling up sandhills, dancing with two hairstrings and two emus looking back.

> It's good you put that song on of Tjapangarti. Tjapanangka, his son is listening on his own countryside, where his father walked around singing that song. If you had met Tjapanangka anywhere else, that would be out of place. Right here, look. This is right. Old man sings and you look around, how he went through, walking up everywhere. [16:40–17:20, 20180520a-1, personal names have been replaced with skin names]

This resonates with comments from Indigenous people further west on the need to bring archived song recordings "back to Country" (Treloyn et al. 2016: 97).

Antiquity of the song

An overwhelming response from those who knew it was that it was an 'old' song. Tjungurrayi, born c. 1935–1943, exclaimed after hearing the first verse "That long, long time [ago]! All passed away now" (20160716), further explaining that this was in the times before there were houses and when people were naked; when his grandfather was alive (21:35—22:05, 20170703-1).

Michael Nelson described the time he saw it as "early days, Native Affairs days," which suggests some time prior to 1968.[24] On the 1981 Balgo recording, the speaker says that he heard the songs when he was a young boy, which dates the performance to some time between 1920 and 1935. In the interviews, the many unsolicited comments on the antiquity of the song contrast sharply with people's comments on other types of songs, such as the women's land-based songs (*yawulyu*) and songs associated with initiation. Rarely do people comment on the age of such songs;[25] instead people comment on the places, custodianship and meanings

---

24   Between 1968 and 1972 the Native Affairs Branch (established 1939) became the Department of Aboriginal Affairs.

25   Some singers have commented on the age of specific verses of a *yawulyu* song, but not on the age of the song as a whole.

associated with such a song. How then should one interpret comments on the antiquity of *Wanji-wanji*?

While it may be that *Wanji-wanji* is older than other songs, there are two other possible interpretations. It seems likely that land-based songs have continued to be performed, albeit less frequently and in some cases with less detail, whereas *Wanji-wanji* must have ceased being performed at some early date, as it is largely unknown to people born after 1945.[26] Thus comments on its old age may refer not to the time of its creation, but to when it had its heyday. A further aspect to this is that land-based songs are perceived to have always existed, although particular verses are sometimes regarded as new (see, for example Turpin & Ross 2013: 3; Turpin 2005: 69). In contrast, *Wanji-wanji* is described as having been brought in by people from elsewhere, like a traded item (Elkin 1970: 260; Mulvaney 1976). The lack of specific knowledge of the song's origin is presumably because it came in to being so long ago and because it travelled far from its specific place of origin.

Memories of the song

Social context in which it was performed

All accounts of *Wanji-wanji* concur in its public status;[27] however, for certain verses women and children were not permitted to see the associated action and so women would lower their heads and close their eyes, and children would dive under a blanket (e.g. Verse 32).[28] This was also required when male dancers adorned in ceremonial attire took their place 'on stage'. Their approach could not be viewed but once in position the audience were then instructed to open their eyes, creating an effect similar to that of raising the stage curtain. Hansen and Hansen (1974: 230) similarly describe the *tjulpurrpa* ceremonial genre as one where women can be present "but are covered with blankets, for certain performances." The detailed descriptions by Bates of the *Wanji-wanji* she witnessed at Eucla in 1913 have similar 'restricted' verses.

The Pintupi people interviewed commented on the public nature of the song. Tjakamarra, who recalled being in his mother's lap and watching men and women dance, associated it with when there were visitors:

> You know some visitors, might be from Willowra and some people from west, you know. From Balgo, somewhere around that area. I used to see them. Really good dance they had ... Oh just a big corroboree dance, you know, to make them happy, instead of going out somewhere like that. Better off just having a big *Wanji-wanji* ... They used to dance together, people used to just come in from another place, from north. [5:40–12:30]

---

26 This date no doubt varies from place to place, as its last performance date would have varied. Indeed at Kalkaringi people performed it in 2015.

27 All contemporary accounts and all but one historical account observe it was performed by men and women. The only exception is Petri (2014 [1952]: 164), who describes it as "secret ceremonial ... analogous to the Djanba dances of the northwest"; however, there is no evidence that Petri observed this ceremony himself.

28 Similar visual restrictions for particular verses were also observed for another travelling ceremony that entered the Pintupi region from the west, *Tjulurru*, which was performed at Kintore in the 1970s (Jeff Hulcombe, pers. comm., November 2018).

This is also suggested in the words of the speaker on the 1981 Balgo recording where Donkeyman describes it as a song that "we would take out everywhere."[29]

Origins of Wanji-wanji

While *Wanji-wanji* is known as a song that was brought from elsewhere, when asked how such songs come into being, people reflected in general about how *turlku* songs are created by the spirits of deceased people and are often discovered by traditional healers,[30] who get them in a dream. Such songs are often associated with a specific person, time and place. No one interviewed, however, had any knowledge about which specific people or places were associated with the original 'dreamers' of *Wanji-wanji*.

It is uncertain where *Wanji-wanji* originally came from. Bates (1938: 125) states it had come from the north of Eucla, "along the Fortescue, Gascoyne, Ashburton and Murchison rivers, east of the goldfield," yet no place of origin is convincingly suggested. In addition to the Pintupi recordings discussed here, there are archival recordings of the song from Port Augusta and Wilcannia in the southeast, Roebourne and Marble Bar in the west and Norseman and Eucla in the southwest,[31] distances that span over 1000 kilometres.[32] Today the song is also remembered by people from the Kimberley (Nyikina, Karajarri, Walmajarri, Nyangumarda language groups), the Pilbara (Nyiyaparli, Kariyarra, Nyamal, Warnman, Manyjilyjarra), and Central Australia (Pitjantjatjara, Yankunytjatjara, Ngaatjatjarra, Warlpiri, Arrernte, and Anmatyerr).[33]

When tracing the origins of a song it is important to trace the verses themselves rather than simply the name of the song. Names vary from region to region and a single name may refer to different ceremonies in different regions. As noted previously, *Laka* is the name used by Gurindji, as well as people from the Pilbara and desert regions, yet *Laka* is also the name of a mortuary ceremony performed by older Mardu (Tonkinson 2008: 38), and there is another ceremony called *Laka* on Mornington Island (Nancarrow & Cleary 2017); the verses of these songs are not the same though. Conversely, the travelling song discussed here is called by different names in different regions. It is called *Kulkalanya* by Pitjantjatjara people, *Wanajarra* by Nyangumarda and *Wanji-wanji* in Port Augusta and Alice Springs. In addition, *Wanna Wa* is said to be its name among the Noongar living in the southern regions of Western Australia (Bates 1938: 125).

In 1960 and 1963 Petri documented a ceremony called 'Wandji-kurang-kara' with the Nyangumarda people in the southern Kimberley. Although Petri equates it with Bates'

---

29   Translated from the Pintupi.

30   In some other parts of Australia this genre is similarly regarded as having been created by the spirits of deceased family members (Treloyn et al. 2016: 97).

31   The Norseman recording and another almost identical recording, both recorded by von Brandenstein, have been analysed by Bracknell (2015), who first drew a connection between these and the songs witnessed by Bates at Eucla and the Pintupi recordings by Moyle (1979).

32   Most of these are short recordings of a single verse or handful of verses amid longer recordings of spoken language or other songs. Only the Pintupi and Gurindji recordings consist solely of a long performance of *Wanji-wanji*.

33   Based on my own fieldwork in these regions in 2017 and 2018 and Nick Thieberger's in 2017.

Wanji-wanji (2018 [1967]: 32–33), there are no similarities between any of the 19 texts written out by Petri (2018 [1967]) and those by Bates (1913–1914).[34] As mentioned, Nyangumarda refer to the travelling song as *Wanajarra* and there is no secret aspect to it in this region, as evidenced by the Nyangumarda women on the 1954–1955 archival recordings and my own fieldwork in this region. It is quite likely that the ceremony documented by Petri in the 1960s and that discussed here are two different ceremonies.

In terms of its musical form, *Wanji-wanji* is clearly Central Australian in style (Ellis 1985). In terms of its linguistic form, many of its verses appear to be in a language of the Western Desert or higher-level Wati linguistic subgroup (see Figure 1), which includes some 15 named varieties. Identifying any single variety within that group is difficult for three main reasons. First, songs are frequently in a language other than that associated with their place of origin. Second, words that are identifiable tend to be common to multiple language varieties (e.g. *pu-* 'hit', *-rna* '1sg are very widespread). Third, vowels are modified in song, and thus contrasts that occur in spoken varieties can become non-contrastive when sung (e.g. 'hill' is *purli* and *pirli* in different varieties yet both vowels are realised as [i] when sung). It is also possible that verses may differ in their language and place of origin. Some verses may be local 'add-ons' to the song; for example, one verse is only heard on the recording from Roebourne while another verse is only sung by the Gurindji.

What is known is the direction from which the song came to the Pintupi. Nosepeg at Kungkayurnti, directly west of Alice Springs, said that the song was a *"Turlku* from Alice Springs. Down south, bin come up, this one bin come up, *Wanji-wanji,* go that way, Petermann Range" (Aus 076 6:37).[35] The archival recordings from South Australia also suggest that it went north. The late Tjungurrayi recalled it was performed at places southwest of Kiwirrkurra, including near Tjirrkarli and spread northeast (presumably along the Canning Stock Route) to Nganju, west of Jupiter Well, and Nyinmi, east of Jupiter Well. He recalls Manyjilytjarra, Ngaanyatjarra and Ngaatjatjarra groups singing the song. He also recalled the names of 12 people who used to sing these songs who left the Gibson Desert, some going south, others going north, east and west.[36] From this evidence it seems likely that the songs originated somewhere in the Wati region and spread out in all directions, one of which involved a route south, then east, and then north in to Central Australia. This is compatible with Daisy Bates' fieldnotes, which are cited in McCarthy (1939: 85). McCarthy hypothesises a route that shows the song originating in the Kimberleys and doing a singular journey south, then east through Eucla to Port Augusta, then northwards into the Centre (1938: 84); however, it seems more likely that the song originated in the Pilbara or desert region of Western Australia and radiated out, taking multiple routes rather than a singular route.

---

34 The recordings made by Petri are restricted, and thus I have not heard them.

35 The Peterman Ranges is some 250 kilometres southwest of Kungkayurnti and located in Pitjantjatjara country (Monaghan 2003: 86).

36 These were Kurinying Tjakamarra, Pikirri Tjakamarra, Kurdirr Tjakamarra (married to Wintjiya Napaltjarri, who sings these songs on R Moyle's 1976 recordings Aus 080 and 081), Mulyarta Tjapangarti, Pungkurra Tjapangardi, Kiilpa Tjapangarti, Kunturru Tjapangarti, Yawulyurru Tjapangarti and his wives, Wamiya Nampitjin, Nginana Nampitjin, and Pampartu Nampitjin (MT fieldnotes 20170704).

Like others, the Pintupi people consulted in 2017 and 2018 were surprised at how widely known the song was. At Kiwirrkurra, Tjapaltjarri, who had some familiarity with the song, gave the following explanation as to how the song might have come to be so widely known.

> We might be all different clans and we've got our own boundaries, but we got the one song. We all come in at a certain time of the year for this singalong and go back home then ... Kukatja, Luritja, Pintupi, Mardu ... It says here [referring to the words of the Kukatja/Pintupi man on the 1981 recording] about two emu men meeting and moving with their arms, when emus had their arms first. When they use their arms, that's how this song is nationwide in Australia here. [35:30–38:00]

The interviews did not reveal any known custodianship of the song, either an individual, clan, or language group – no doubt the basis for the public status of the song.

Meanings of the song

Few people commented on the meanings of the song. Only one archival recording includes any interpretations of the verses and song – the recording from Balgo. These meanings were not known to the Pintupi with whom I consulted, nor did they provide any alternate meanings. The Balgo recording is of Kukatja/Pintupi man Donkeyman Lee Tjupurrula (born 1925) singing and talking about seven verses of the song.[37] Yet even with discussion, the meaning of the verse is cryptic. As an example, the first 38 seconds of the recording, consisting of speech, singing of one verse and speech that leads into the second verse, is shown below.[38]

00:09	*Ngula nanta yunganyini, nganayi, Laka, lirrpirrparlangku-junngu, kurlu?*
	Wait, shall I tell you about the story of what's it, Laka?
	(RM: *Yuwayi*)
00:17	*Yananyirna Ngarirli-kutu.*
	I'll go towards Ngarirli (could be a place or Dreaming)
00:20	(sings the following verse, identified by the author elsewhere as m-laka28)

Tjarrarna-ngkurra jarrali yananya x 2
Ngarirli-ngarirli jarrali yananya x 2
(repeats)
(Possible gloss:)

Tjarra-rna-ngkurra	*tjarra-li*	*yana-nya* /	*Ngarirli-ngarirli*	*tjarra-li*	*yana-nya*
two-1SG-REFL	two-1DU.S	go-PTT	place_name-RED	two-1DU	go-PTT[39]
'We two take ourselves off	/		We two go (to) 'Ngarirli'		

00:39	*Pakalaya ngaalji tarraparing*
	Then they go up like this to avoid something
00:41	(sings the verse identified as m-laka22)

---

37   It is possible that this speaker is instead Wimintji Tjapangarti (born 1915).

38   Translation by Lyle Gibson Tjakamarra, Robin Granites Japanangka, and Peter Bartlett.

39   Linguistic glosses of the putative Western Desert song text are as follows: 1SG 'first person singular'; REFL 'reflexive'; 1DU.S '1 inclusive dual subject'; PTT 'presentational tense'; RED 'reduplication'.

Here, the listener may be left wondering who the referents of the 'we two' are, where the place Ngarirli is, and why they are going there. The non-specific nature of the text, its first person reference and its simple imagery are typical of Aboriginal song. Later in the recording Donkeyman explains another verse as being about "two emu men/leaders who walk away and look back over their shoulder."

No one in the interviews claimed to know what the song or even particular verses were about; one man who knew the song even said he had never considered the meaning of the song before. However, some people volunteered particular words in the verses, generally common words for which they provided English equivalents. For example, while listening to the main verse Michael Nelson volunteered the following:

(listening to verse m-laka 33)

Warriwarnkanya, Warriwarnkanya Kapanala wanji-wanji wanpanarra

Oh good song that one, very good. 'Warri' mean cold. Wind blowing.

(listening to verse m-laka 23)

Jiwirdila jimarnta x 2

Kurakura jimarnta x 2

Western people. '*Jiwirdi*' mean some little wood that gets burnt, for fire, after when
they have that big corroboree and they dance around. That's what my mother told me.
[19:00–21:00]

Other people suggested words and their meanings, following prompts by me made by picking out a string of word-like syllables from the song text and asking if it had any meaning. For example, a number of people volunteered independently words such as *puyu* 'smoke', *purli* 'hill', *tali* 'sandhill' and *jilka* 'prickle', as well as the verbs *yani* 'go' and *nyina* 'sit', which are all words from Western Desert languages.

Tjungurrayi was unusual in that he interpreted the words in songs, such as *purli* 'hill' and *tali* 'sandhill', as if they referred to specific places. It is not clear whether he meant these as original meanings, or whether he was deriving meanings relevant to the context in which he had heard the songs or how they had been explained to him. Part of the skill in interpreting Aboriginal songs is being able to draw out contextually relevant meanings, in the same way that preaching can be about bringing contemporary relevance to parts of the bible.

Given its well-travelled history, a lack of meaning is not surprising, as Berndt & Berndt point out in relation to such songs at Balgo:

As one woman at Balgo pointed out, when pressed for specific interpretation of every word
in a series to clarify inconsistencies in translation, "We don't see the people who started
these songs, we can't ask them: we get them from others in between, and they are the ones
who tell us." The nearer the place of origin, the greater the likelihood of finding someone
who knows the language in which they are composed; but some songs travel well beyond
the reach of such intermediaries, and attempts at word-for-word translation may be no
more than guesses. (Berndt & Berndt 1988: 384–385)

Views on access and usage

Most of the people consulted wanted to have the recordings included in the Central Land Council's collection, especially younger people who had worked with local media organisations or had used the Pitjantjatjara digital database Aṟa Irititja.[40] In terms of local access in communities, people struggled to identify a place where a copy of the recordings could be left. Presumably this was because people could not identify a building in the community that was available for public use and that had the facilities (e.g. computer, headphones) and personnel that could assist with access or could be approached for this.[41] This was important as not everyone has access to a device that could 'play' a USB, or the know-how to use one. Furthermore, a USB would not last forever. Indeed, at one community I was approached by someone who no longer had the USB that I had given them five weeks previously. In Alice Springs, staff at the Purple House were keen to have a copy so that they could provide these to their clients should they get the request.

Everyone was happy for the archival recordings to be included in the radio broadcast and many were happy to have their own responses included on the broadcast. Most people liked the idea of publishing the recordings as an album and a number of younger people wanted to work on such a production. Only one person hesitated at this idea because of concerns that other people might learn and sing the songs. It was possible that she was uncertain how the past practice of trading and sharing ceremonies of this type might play out today.

Nearly everyone consulted requested a copy of the recordings on USB, which was provided. A number of people at Kintore said that they wanted personal copies, as they hoped to learn the songs so that they could perform them (and suggested I could then come back to record them).

Conclusion

The confidence with which people responded to my enquiries about the songs varied significantly according to whether they sang along with the recording (and often independently of it) or whether they only listened. 'Listeners' were more hesitant to comment on access and usage, perhaps uncertain or unconvinced that the song had moved beyond local circulation. Without having personal historical experience, and being unfamiliar with the song texts, it would be unlikely they could deduce on the spot that the many recordings of the songs were indeed the same song. In contrast, 'singers' would exclaim emotively, revealing their astonishment at hearing recordings of the song from well beyond Pintupi country, such as from Kalkaringi and Port Augusta. Many commented on how good the song was, as if the extent of its travels were evidence of this.

Since discovering the Kungkayurnti, Balgo and five further recordings in the archives from other places in Western Australia, Northern Territory and South Australia as discussed

---

40 In contrast, recent fieldwork at Haasts Bluff showed that some Pintupi people there did not want these recordings to be available through the Central Land Council.

41 One possible local access place might have been PAW Media and Communications (Pintubi Anmatjere Warlpiri Media and Communications, Yuendumu); however, this was not suggested.

above, I have also undertaken fieldwork that revealed the song to be known among older generations throughout Central Australia, the Pilbara, and the Kimberley. It is not known how many other recordings of the song may exist hidden in the archives, as the recordings I found were not located by searching the archives by the various names of the song. Rather, they were located by methodically listening to open access recordings that included singing from regions where I suspected the song would have been known. Without the ability to search on verse texts and song titles (notwithstanding songs often having multiple names), as well as being unable to access many restricted collections that may include materials with a range of different statuses, discovering recordings of a specific song is a difficult task.

A number of Aboriginal people I consulted requested assistance in finding out if recordings of other songs they had in mind might similarly exist. In my experience of working on songs in Central Australia over the past 20 years, it is not uncommon for Aboriginal people to listen to archival recordings to help recall a forgotten verse, gain certainty over a song text and clarify the structure of particular verses. Archival recordings play a role similar to that of song books and lyrics websites (such as https://genius.com/ and https://www.azlyrics.com/). In this sense they are valuable tools for learning, as a number of researchers have noted (e.g. Hercus & Koch 2017; O'Keeffe et al. 2018; Treloyn & Morumburri Dowding 2017).

In the Kimberley there is a revival of a travelling song known as *Tjulurru*, a ceremony that was traded over large distances (Glowczewski 1983, 2014; Kolig 1989: 85; Poirier 2014; Widlok 1992). *Tjulurru* was sung in Broome at the 2018 Native Title conference (without dancing) and prior to that was performed at the Kimberley Aboriginal Law and Culture Centre (KALACC) festival in 2017.[42] Many years had passed since it was last performed in this region. KALACC and a number of other Aboriginal organisations have been instrumental in achieving this revival. In Central Australia it is uncertain whether any organisations could assist in such a revival. Certainly the availability of recordings of the song would be crucial for this task, as there are now few people in the communities who know these verses well enough to sing them 'right through'. Yet even then the task of revitalisation is possibly much harder than it appears, as the verses are not in everyday speech and it is unclear who would drive and support the revival of what Tjapaltjarri refers to as 'national wide song'. The song does not reflect land-based identity at a local level and so there may be fewer reasons to revive it, yet in contexts where there are no known land-based songs that can be publicly performed (the politics of performing these are sometimes difficult), *Wanji-wanji* might be attractive for revival, just as *Tjulurru* has been in the Kimberley. Whether the *Wanji-wanji* is similarly revived remains to be seen.

References

Barwick, Linda & Myfany Turpin. 2016. Central Australian women's traditional songs: Keeping *yawulyu/awelye* strong. In Huib Schippers & Catherine Grant (eds.), *Sustainable futures for music cultures: An ecological perspective*, 111–145. New York: Oxford University Press.

---

42 https://ictv.com.au/video/item/5373 (Accessed 18 March 2019.)

Bates, Daisy. 1913–1914. Series 2.6. Songs and dances of the last Wanji-wanji – Eucla (3 p., 5 p.), transcribed by Jane Walkley. Daisy Bates Papers MSS 572.994 B32t Series 2: 'Native Testaments of old natives'. Adelaide: University of Adelaide.

Bates, Daisy. 1938. *The passing of the Aborigines*. London: John Murray.

Beckett, Jeremy & Luise Hercus. 2009. *The two rainbow serpents travelling:* Mura *track narratives from the 'Corner Country'* (Aboriginal History Monograph 18). Canberra: ANU E-Press.

Berndt, Ronald & Catherine Berndt. 1988. *The world of the first Australians*. 5th edn. Canberra: Aboriginal Studies Press.

Bracknell, Clint. 2015. *Naatj Waalanginy* (What singing?): Noongar song from the south-west of Western Australia. Crawley, WA: University of Western Australia. (Unpublished PhD thesis.)

Brown, Reuben. 2014. The role of songs in connecting the living and the dead: A funeral ceremony for Nakodjok in Western Arnhem Land. In Amanda Harris (ed.), *Circulating cultures: Exchanges of Australian Indigenous music, dance and media*, 169–201. Canberra: ANU Press.

Brown, Reuben, David Manmurulu, Jenny Manmurulu, Isabel O'Keeffe & Ruth Singer. 2017. Maintaining song traditions and languages together at Warruwi (western Arnhem Land). In Jim Wafer & Myfany Turpin (eds.), *Recirculating songs: Revitalising the singing practices of Indigenous Australia*, 257–274. Canberra: Pacific Linguistics.

Dixon, RMW. 2011. *The languages of Australia*. New York: Cambridge University Press.

Egan, Ted. 1997. *Sitdown up north*. Marrickville, NSW: Kerr Publishing.

Elkin, AP. 1970 [1938]. *The Australian Aborigines: How to understand them*. 3rd edn. Sydney: Angus & Robertson.

Elkin, AP. 1994. *Aboriginal men of high degree*. 2nd edn. Rochester, Vermont: Inner Traditions.

Ellis, Catherine. 1985. *Aboriginal music: Education for living. Cross-cultural experiences from South Australia*. St Lucia: University of Queensland Press.

Gallagher, Coral, P Brown, Georgia Curran & Barbara Martin. 2014. *Jardiwanpa yawulyu: Warlpiri women's songs from Yuendumu* (including CD). Batchelor, NT: Batchelor Press.

Gibson, Jason. 2015. Central Australian songs: A history and reinterpretation of their distribution through the earliest recordings. *Oceania* 85(2). 165–182. (DOI:10.1002/ocea.5084)

Gibson, Jason. 2017. *Urrempel men. A collaborative interrogation of T. G. H. Strehlow's collection*. Clayton, Victoria: Monash Indigenous Centre, Monash University. (Unpublished PhD thesis.)

Gibson, Jason. 2018. Ethnographic sound collections and Australian Aboriginal heritage: Kaytetye song traditions remembered. *International Journal of Heritage Studies* 25(6). 537–552. (https://doi.org/10.1080/13527258.2018.1518255)

Glowczewski, Barbara. 1983. Manifestations symboliques d'une transition économique: Le Juluru, culte intertribal du cargo (Australie Occidentale et Centrale) [Symbolic manifestations of economic transition: The Juluru intertribal cargo cult (Western and Central Australia)]. *L'Homme* 23(2). 7–35.

Glowczewski, Barbara. 2014. From academic heritage to Aboriginal priorities: Anthropological responsibilities. In *Australian Aboriginal anthropology today: Critical perspectives from Europe*. Musée du quai Branly Jacques Chirac. https://journals.openedition.org/actesbranly/526 (Accessed 20 October 2019.)

Hansen, Kenneth & Lesley Hansen (compilers). 1974. *Pintupi Dictionary*. SIL International. (https://www.sil.org/resources/archives/3495) (Last accessed November 2018.)

Hercus, Luise. 1980. 'How we danced the Mudlungga': Memories of 1901 and 1902. *Aboriginal History* 4. 5–32.

Hercus, Luise & Grace Koch. 2017. Lone singers: The others have all gone. In Jim Wafer & Myfany Turpin (eds.), *Recirculating songs: Revitalising the singing practices of Indigenous Australia*, 102–118. Canberra: Pacific Linguistics.

Howitt, AW. 1887. Notes on songs and songmakers of some Australian tribes. *Journal of the Anthropological Institute of Great Britain and Ireland* 16. 327–335.

Khan, Kate. 2016. Looking back: The story of a collection. The Papunya permanent collection of early Western Desert paintings at the Australian Museum. *Technical Reports of the Australian Museum, Online* 25. 1–95. (ISSN 1835–4211.) (https://australianmuseum.net.au/uploads/journals/35041/1647_complete.pdf) (Accessed 20 October 2019.)

Kimber, Richard. 1990. Mulunga old Mulunga: 'Good corroboree,' they reckon. In Peter Austin, RMW Dixon, Tom Dutton & Isobel White (eds.), *Language and history: Essays in honour of Luise A. Hercus* (Pacific Linguistics Series C), 175–191. Canberra: Research School of Pacific Studies, Australian National University.

Kolig, Erich. 1989. *Dreamtime politics: Religion, world view, and utopian thought in Australian Aboriginal society*. Berlin: Dietrich Reimer Verlag.

Kolig, Erich. 2017. Doing research in the Kimberley and carrying ideological baggage: A personal journey. In Nicolas Peterson & Anna Kenny (eds.), *German ethnography in Australia*, 383–412. Canberra: ANU e-press.

McCarthy, Fred. 1939. 'Trade' in Aboriginal Australia, and 'trade' relationships with Torres Strait, New Guinea and Malaya (continued). *Oceania* 9(4). 405–438; *Oceania* 10(1). 80–104.

Monaghan, Paul. 2003. Laying down the country: Norman B. Tindale and the linguistic construction of the North-West of South Australia. Adelaide: School of European Studies and General Linguistics, University of Adelaide. (Unpublished PhD thesis.)

Mulvaney, DJ. 1976. 'The chain of connection': The material evidence. In Nicolas Peterson (ed.), *Tribes and boundaries in Australia*, 72–94. Canberra: AIAS.

Mulvaney, John, Howard Morphy & Alison Petch. 2001. *My dear Spencer: The letters of F. J. Gillen to Baldwin Spencer*. Melbourne: Hyland House.

Moyle, Richard. 1979. *Songs of the Pintupi: Musical life in a central Australian society*. AIAS Press: Canberra.

Moyle, Richard. 1997. *Balgo: The musical life of a desert community*. Nedlands, WA: Callaway International Resource Centre for Music Education.

Nancarrow, Cassy & Peter Cleary. 2017. Finding laka for burdal: Song revitalisation at Mornington Island over the past 40 years. In Jim Wafer & Myfany Turpin (eds.),

Recirculating songs: Revitalising the singing practices of Indigenous Australia, 245–256. Canberra: Pacific Linguistics.

O'Keeffe, Isabel, Linda Barwick, Carolyn Coleman, David Manmurulu, Jenny Manmurulu, Janet Mardbinda, Paul Naragoidj & Ruth Singer. 2018. Multiple uses for old and new recordings: Perspectives from the multilingual community of Warruwi. *FEL XXI Alcanena 2017: Communities in Control*, 140–147. Hungerford, UK: Foundation for Endangered Languages.

Petri, Helmut. 2014. *The Australian medicine man* (translated by I Campbell). Perth: Hesperian Press. [Translation of Petri, Helmut. 1952. Der Australische Medizinmann. *Annali Lateranensi* (16), 159–317.]

Petri, Helmut. 2018. *Wandji-kurang-gara*: A mythical complex of traditions from the Western Desert of Australia (translated by C Romuss). [Unpublished translation of Petri, Helmut. 1967. *Wandji-kurang-gara ein mythischer Traditionskomplex aus der Westlichen Wüste Australiens. Baessler-Archiv* (15). 1–54.]

Poirier, Sylvie. 2014. Places, performative kinship and networking in the Western Desert: A contemporary perspective. In *Australian Aboriginal anthropology today: Critical perspectives from Europe*. Musée du quai Branly Jacques Chirac. (http://actesbranly.revues.org/530) (Accessed 20 October 2019.)

Roth, Walter Edmond. 1897. *Ethnological studies among the north-west-central Queensland Aborigines*. Brisbane: Edmund Gregory, Government Printer.

Skinner, Graeme. 2017. Recovering musical data from colonial era transcriptions of Indigenous songs: Some practical considerations. In Jim Wafer & Myfany Turpin (eds.), *Recirculating songs: Revitalising the singing practices of Indigenous Australia*, 336–360. Canberra: Pacific Linguistics.

Strehlow, TGH. 1955. Australian Aboriginal songs. *Journal of the International Folk Music Council* 7. 37–40.

Tonkinson, Myrna. 2008. Solidarity in shared loss: Death-related observances among the Martu of the Western Desert. In Katie Glaskin, Myrna Tonkinson, Yasmine Musharbash & Victoria Burbank (eds.), *Mortality, mourning and mortuary practices in Indigenous Australia*, 37–53. Farnham, England; Burlington, VT: Ashgate.

Treloyn, Sally. 2003. Scotty Martin's Jadmi Junba: A song series from the Kimberley region of northwest Australia. *Oceania* 73. 208–220.

Treloyn, Sally & Andrew Morumburri Dowding. 2017. Thabi returns: The use of digital resources to recirculate and revitalise Thabi songs in the west Pilbara. In Jim Wafer & Myfany Turpin (eds.), *Recirculating songs: Revitalising the singing practices of Indigenous Australia,* 56–67. Canberra: Pacific Linguistics.

Treloyn, Sally, Matthew D Martin & Rona G Charles. 2016. Cultural precedents for the repatriation of legacy song records to communities of origin. *Australian Aboriginal Studies* 2. 94–103.

Turpin, Myfany. 2005. *Form and meaning of Akwelye: A Kaytetye women's song series from Central Australia*. Sydney: University of Sydney. (PhD thesis.)

Turpin, Myfany & Felicity Meakins. 2019. Songs from the stations. Wajarra as sung by
    Ronnie Wavehill Wirrpnga, Topsy Dodd Ngarnjal and Dandy Danbayarri at Kalkaringi.
    Sydney: Sydney University Press.
Turpin, Myfany & Alison Nangala Ross. 2013. *Antarrengeny Awely. Alyawarr women's
    traditional songs of Antarrengeny country.* Batchelor, NT: Batchelor Press.
Valiquette, Hilaire (ed.). 1993. *A basic Kukatja to English dictionary.* Balgo, WA: Luurnpa
    Catholic School.
Widlok, Thomas. 1992. Practice, politics and ideology of the 'travelling business' in
    Aboriginal religion. *Oceania* 63. 114–136.
Wild, Stephen. 1987. Recreating the Jukurrpa: Adaptation and innovation of songs and
    ceremonies in Warlpiri society. In Margaret Clunies Ross, Tamsin Donaldson & Stephen
    Wild (eds.), *Songs of Aboriginal Australia* (Oceania Monograph 32), 97–120. Sydney:
    University of Sydney.

Language Documentation & Conservation Special Publication No. 18
Archival returns: Central Australia and beyond
ed. by Linda Barwick, Jennifer Green & Petronella Vaarzon-Morel, pp. 263–284
http://nflrc.hawaii.edu/ldc/sp18
http://hdl.handle.net/10125/24887

13

Never giving up: Negotiating, culture-making, and the infinity of the archive

Sabra Thorner
Mount Holyoke College

Linda Rive
Ara Irititja Aboriginal Corporation

John Dallwitz
Ara Irititja Aboriginal Corporation

Janet Inyika
Ngaanyatjarra Pitjantjatjara Yankunytjatjara Women's Council

Abstract

Archival returns are a significant issue of concern for Indigenous peoples in many settler-colonial contexts. This chapter focuses on one example from Central Australia, Ara Irititja, to reflect on how an archive might simultaneously preserve 'culture' and also reflect, accommodate, and inspire cultural change. We feature the words of an Aṇangu 'senior law woman', Janet Inyika (affectionately known as Mrs Never-Give-Up), and our co-authorship is consistent with this community archive's commitment to co-production, yet also extends Inyika's social justice work into the future. Together, we argue that a collaborative, intercultural approach to archiving, in conjunction with the affordances of digital media, facilitate negotiations that are culturally appropriate, and not threatening. Ara Irititja is inspiring the production of a new genre of archival metadata: advance directives on what to do with representations of a person upon his/her death. These words are urging a shift in protocols for the correct treatment of photographs, asserting new domains of individual authority, and establishing the archive as the proper medium through which these should occur. The archive is also a site through which culture-making is never complete, always ongoing – indeed, infinite.

Keywords: Central Australian Indigenous people, digital media, intercultural productions, access protocols, archives

Reimagining archives, extending returns[1]

Ara Irititja is an archive built to manage photographic and other media collections in Ngaanyatjarra, Pitjantjatjara, and Yankunytjatjara (NPY) speaking communities in Central Australia. The archive originated in the early 1990s as an extension of land rights activism in the region in the 1970s–1980s: elders were becoming increasingly aware of the existence of photographs, taken by missionaries, teachers, visiting doctors and nurses, and others, and then taken away to be stored elsewhere. Two men, Peter Nyaningu and Colin Tjapiya, enlisted the help of an anthropologist (Ushma Scales), an archivist (John Dallwitz), and information technology (IT) professionals (Martin Hughes and, later, Douglas Mann) to seek their return. These efforts were grounded in growing political activism across Australia to reinstate Indigenous peoples' control over their own lives and representations.

Photographs, in the context of Ara Irititja and its origins, are objectifications of Anangu knowledge, culture, relationships, custodianship of and responsibility for land, community, and personhood.[2] Indeed, they are things with a unique status. In this chapter, we suggest that negotiations over their 'return', including keeping them 'open' to or 'closed' from viewing, preserving analogue originals, and circulating digital replicas, are ongoing and offer a particularly rich view into contemporary culture-making (Myers 1994).

Photographs are both iconic and indexical, re-presenting a moment in time and also, always, standing in for multiple (hi)stories. Photographs have a long history in Australia. Photographic technologies arrived on the continent in the 1840s: the oldest extant photograph of Aboriginal people is from 1847; and images have been used both in colonial discourses to represent Indigenous people as 'others' and taken up to recontextualise and redress those histories (Edwards 2001; Lydon 2005; Pinney & Peterson 2003).[3] Once they enter the digital archive, photographs – unlike their analogue form – are also infinitely replicable without any loss of quality or fidelity to an original.

For a group of people who sought the return of photographs as a reclamation of control over their own lives, infinite replicability poses a great challenge: who is in control on the ground? How is control negotiated and renegotiated over time? What does control look and/or feel like? Who has responsibility for what? Ara Irititja is a digital archive, a term that stands for both an infrastructure developed and maintained to facilitate this control, and a mechanism for the preservation of its contents for an imagined perpetuity into an indefinite future. Via Ara

1 As co-authors, we have given much thought to how best to acknowledge our respective contributions to this piece. Sabra Thorner has taken the lead on the academic argument. Linda Rive has worked with Anangu since 1980, has done extensive oral history and translation work for Ara Irititja, and has generously translated, clarified, and/or contextualised uses of the Pitjantjatjara language throughout this chapter. John Dallwitz, the manager of Ara Irititja from the beginning, is deeply committed to the power of culturally responsive archival practice. Janet Inyika – 'Mrs Never-Give-Up' – is quoted at length below, and we recognise her words, in pursuit of social change, as shared authorship. We – Sabra, Linda, and John – write in honour of Janet, and in so doing seek to follow her urging to keep her work alive beyond her lifetime.

2 Anangu is the Pitjantjatjara term for 'person' or 'people'.

3 There were earlier representations – watercolour paintings, engravings, and drawings from the late 18th century (see Smith 1988: 133–158; Donaldson & Donaldson 1985). These are important precursors in establishing visual media as significant in producing knowledge about Australian Indigenous peoples.

Irititja, photographs have become a significant medium of Aṉangu cultural reproduction, including both the reinforcement of traditional norms and their continuous reinvention.

From its earliest days, Aṟa Irititja has been both an archive in the conventional sense – an apparatus storing knowledge – and a reflexive attempt to expand this orthodox institution from one of state control and surveillance via the preservation and retrieval of texts (Stoler 2009) into a permeable place and a dynamic process where knowledge could be produced, activated, and transmitted in multiple media and by multiple (and multiply-situated) actors (Derrida 1998; Anderson 2004). This has been ongoing, intercultural work over almost three decades and across several generations of digital technologies: to build infrastructures that reflect and facilitate Indigenous ways of knowing, being, and doing things (Martin & Miraboopa 2003), and to accommodate the specific material conditions and cultural requirements of remote-living Aboriginal people.

In Australia's central Western Desert, these conditions include pervasive sand and dust, intense heat, persistent pests, limited infrastructure in and between small communities across vast distances, and inconsistent and/or unreliable internet services. There is little personal ownership of computers; desktops and laptops tend to be held in schools, libraries, community offices, art centres, and other communal spaces, and used in small groups. This is starting to shift, as the last several years have seen a rapid proliferation of smartphones and tablets, and the rollout of 4G mobile coverage to APY communities in early 2018.[4] Yet challenges to access remain, as mobile data becomes a significant personal expense, so that WiFi passwords or locations of unsecured WiFi networks are eagerly sought. Those who can afford to maintain a phone line and internet (ADSL) service also face high demand from relatives (in a way not dissimilar to demand for transport).

Aṟa Irititja has been available on mobile devices since 2015. There is also a downloadable app called Aṟa Winki (launched in 2017), which contains a selection of archive content that can be accessed offline, and serves as a gateway through which users might enter the full archive if they wish to know more about a particular archive item.

While Aṉangu are often fluent in multiple languages, they might not be literate in English or comfortable sitting in front of a computer screen, typing on a keyboard, or manipulating a mouse. Eye health remains a major concern (Kaplan-Myrth 2004). The built-from-scratch home for 'returned' photographs had to overcome what Michael Christie (2004: 6) has called the "tyranny of text" and the linearity of search and retrieval of conventional databases. The Aṟa Irititja founders sought a different structure and approach for preserving and activating things with such cultural importance.

The 'returns' upon which Aṟa Irititja was founded have never been simply about the relocation of physical objects from elsewhere back to their sites of origin. The archival drive

---

4   The Aṉangu Pitjantjatjara Yankunytjatjara (or APY) Lands are a semi-autonomous region, as delineated in the *Aṉangu Pitjantjatjara Yankunytjatjara Land Rights Act* (1981). The Aṟa Irititja project began in these Lands in the far northwest corner of the state of South Australia, with the network growing to neighbouring communities in Western Australia and the Northern Territory, including predominantly Ngaanyatjarra speakers. Quite apart from modern administrative boundaries, the region has always been united as a speech community of mutually intelligible dialects of the Western Desert languages; Ngaanyatjarra, Pitjantjatjara, and Yankunytjatjara (NPY) speakers also share many cultural ties.

(Derrida 1998) here has also been motivated by a political commitment to expanding what an archive could be and could do. Archives tend to be premised on the preservation of knowledge, usually objectified in the form of text-based media (such as letters, documents, files, or books), in the interest of extending the power of a centralised authority, usually the state. This authority is intertwined with notions of a definitive history, and the everyday work of an archive is propelled by the value invested in comprehensiveness and finitude. In contrast, the founders of Ara Irititja wanted to enable ways for Anangu to transmit knowledge, pushing the 'archive' to allow for multiple coexisting voices and perspectives, to be always revisable, and therefore infinite. Photographs had to be connected to the stories they inspired.

Anthropologist Fred Myers writes of "the fundamental condition that Indigenous people in Australia, as in other places, have been compelled to live through the representations of others ... this [is a] defining problem of Indigenous life" (Myers 2006: 252). The existence and persistence of Ara Irititja are reflexive, recursive responses to this condition – that Aboriginal people have had to live their lives through the representations of others. This archive was forged to preserve and activate Indigenous ways of knowing, as an alternative to the archive as an instrument of colonial power relations. At the same time as it extends the striving for more Anangu control and autonomy into a new medium, Ara Irititja is also a profoundly intercultural production (Myers 2004), an ongoing process of collaboration with non-Indigenous co-producers. This is a paradox exemplified in our writing together.

Returning photographs

In the early 1990s, as Dallwitz and others searched for and discovered photographic collections relevant to Anangu interests, it was quickly decided that the return of the analogue media was impractical. The climate and lack of infrastructure in the Central Australian desert are not conducive to conventional archival preservation in the form of the temperature- and humidity-control standards of galleries, libraries, museums, and other kinds of archives. More importantly, too many people had claims to the photographs. Photographs are not objects in the conventional sense of property, a tangible thing with a singular owner that can be alienated from that person.[5] Instead, photographs inspire stories, extend rights to self-determination, and affirm connections between people, kin, and their significant places.[6]

Why and how have photographs come to enjoy this special status? Before Ara Irititja, Anangu had little or no visual access to representations of themselves. Viewing brings people joy. Digitisation was a strategy to allow visual access to photographs to be as expansive as possible, enabling people to see and feel connected to kin, country, and the practices of the past (rituals, songs, dances, stories) that are repeated in the present to maintain cultural life.

As Haidy Geismar asserts, digitising inherently involves multiple levels of translation: images, words, sounds, and objects are translated into binary code, and code is in turn (re)

---

5   Our argument is here inspired by Myers (1989), a powerful account of how, for Central Australian Aboriginal people, land is inalienable.

6   Our thinking is grounded in the efforts to rigorously rethink how objects are understood, especially with the advent and proliferation of digital technologies; see Myers (2004); Edwards, Gosden & Phillips (2006); Salmond (2012); Bell, Christen & Turin (2013).

translated into representational effects and outputs (Geismar 2013: 256). Translation is itself an anthropological metaphor, as Sue Gal chronicles, including a family of productive processes in which text (or object, or practice) changes form but is also imagined to, somehow, simultaneously, stay the same (Gal 2015: 226). In the case of Ara Irititja, digitising photographs (and making them accessible via a network of computer workstations) allows them to be reincorporated into Anangu cultural lives and political aims. Women sing along with digital video (tapping their feet and moving their hands in time with their filmic selves); and when the Ara Irititja archive is in use, laughter and shout-outs to anyone in earshot abound: *Come, see your sister! Ha ha, look how young you were!*

The digital object is not equal to the analogue object, nor is the former a surrogate or replacement for the latter. Jim Enote, former director of the A:shiwi A:wan Museum and Heritage Center at Zuni (New Mexico), is critical of digital repatriation initiatives, provocatively asking, "If digital surrogates were so good ... why didn't the institutions, researchers, and scholars keep them, and return the original, non-digitised, analog object to the community themselves?" (Bell, Christen & Turin 2013: 7–8). Enote insists on acknowledging the responsibility embedded in transmitting Indigenous knowledge: "when information comes back ... whether images, songs or materials come back to a museum or library in a native community ... it becomes a beacon, a catalyst for communities for revising, for cultural change, for social change" (Bell, Christen & Turin 2013: 8). Digitised photographs in Ara Irititja allow for and inspire new kinds of activities, new utterances, and new social relations that are part of contemporary culture-making. The archive is generative.

In the case of Ara Irititja, the return of photographs has been inextricable from larger political claims to Indigenous peoples' right to represent themselves, to control their own knowledge and lives, and to have the autonomy and freedom to continue to transmit knowledge in media that are culturally appropriate. As an increasingly rich literature is demonstrating, return is only the beginning of a shift in power relations between Indigenous peoples and the institutions holding their cultural materials.[7] Further, we must all reckon with ontologies in which objects are not inanimate. As Aaron Glass argues, objects both represent the past and "become expressions of revitalized cultural identity" (Glass 2004: 126). Photographs, in Central Australia, are being mobilised in this way, incorporated into vibrant and ongoing cultural work.

From its inception, Ara Irititja has accommodated annotations to photographs in text (typing into predefined database fields) and audiovisual recording features in which stories become part of the archive in real time. Photographs inspire storytelling (see Thorner & Dallwitz 2015). Photographs and the stories they inspire are valued as Indigenous knowledge, and therefore are in need of preservation for the future. Also, knowledge is treated holistically; photographs and stories are presumed to belong together, and much archival labour is invested in shaping digital tools to approximate, replicate, extend, and honour this. Haidy Geismar, mobilising classical anthropological theory (Mauss 1990; Strathern 1988) to "define

---

7   See Bell, Christen & Turin (2013), the introductory article to a special issue of *Museum Anthropology Review*, which includes many wonderful examples. See also Peers & Brown (2003); Glass (2004); Kramer (2004); Brown & Peers (2006); Krmpotich & Peers (2014).

the digital," suggests that the "blurring nature of persons and things … in which objects and voices, information, experience, knowledge, images, and sounds become part of the same 'thing'" (Geismar 2013: 258) long preceded the advent of digital technologies. In her fieldwork in Vanuatu, a relational database to manage museum objects fitted into "a preexisting understanding of how materiality and sociality are mutually constitutive" (Geismar 2013: 258).

For Aṉangu, who has access to what knowledge is strictly controlled by gender, seniority, initiation status, and kinship group. The maintenance of men's-only and women's-only archives and the treatment of photographs of the deceased are two ways in which Aṛa Irititja has worked to enact and replicate Indigenous protocols in digital form (Thorner 2010, 2013). 'Protocols' are guidelines for culturally correct, ethically good behavior that are not necessarily confined to or constrained by Western legal regimes (see Anderson 2008, 2011; Anderson & Younging 2015; also Morphy 2015). As with culture itself, protocols are dynamic and negotiated in ongoing culture-making processes.

The next section focuses on an example of one senior law woman's words about what to do with her photographs after her death.[8] As a reflection upon the mission explored in this volume, this example provides one glimpse into what archival returns look like in Central Australia. We use an extended quote to draw out the stakes of this work – the repatriation, reactivation, and re-narrativisation of photographs – and to illustrate why it's so urgent and important for contemporary Aṉangu. Aaron Glass has noted that:

> [t]here is a huge diversity of terms used in the discourses of object return, all of which address the undoing of some past deed through use of the common prefix 're': repatriation, restitution, reparation, restoration, recovery, reinstatement, re-emplacement, reunification, reconstitution, revitalization, recapture, rejuvenation, revival, remuneration, rehabilitation, relief. All have different inflections and legal ramifications. (Glass 2004: 118)

In implicitly invoking the undoing of the harms of the colonial past (and often-interventionist present), these action words also imply re-doing, that is, doing again, differently. These terms suggest the possibility that in the re-doing is some restorative justice. As we elaborate below, critically reflecting on Aṛa Irititja and how it is being used in remote communities is an opportunity to consider the challenges of an archive preserving 'culture' yet also reflecting, accommodating, and inspiring change in social lives.

Shifting protocols

As noted briefly above, the Aṛa Irititja Aṉangu Community Archive accommodates cultural restrictions on 'sorrow' through protocols for handling media (photographs, video/audio recordings, and metadata about them) of those recently deceased. These norms have been adapted from linguistic taboos against pronouncing such people's names. When someone dies, his or her name is avoided, in favour of epithets like 'the old bushranger', or descriptive phrases such as 'that one's father', coupled with facial gestures towards the deceased's

---

8　'Senior law woman' is the English term used to denote a respected female elder holding much cultural knowledge; such a person is also considered responsible for transmitting knowledge to younger generations.

relative. People with the same or similar-sounding names to the deceased person are called by the substitution word *Kunmaṉara* 'one whose name cannot be mentioned'. It is the sound of the name that creates the greatest sadness and, in fact, there are many linguistic strategies to obliquely talk about the deceased. Things with similar-sounding names might be called *kunmaṉu*; for example, 'key' became *kunmaṉu* after Keith died. There are other creative substitutions: after Jack died, car-jacks became *katulpai* 'thing to lift/raise up'; following the death of a person called Dan, 'ten' was called 'blue one' after the colour of the 10-dollar note in Australian currency.

Aṉangu grieving practices also include avoiding seeing or coming into contact with other traces of the deceased: the burning of his/her possessions and camp, moving away from the site of the death, and avoiding hunting grounds frequented together. These practices are both to avoid the spirit of the dead person making mischief on the living and to manage the pain of being reminded of a loss.

In the archive, the treatment of photographs of the recently deceased emerged from these linguistic taboos and cultural practices. When an Aboriginal person dies, print photographs are usually tucked away, out of sight, for a period of time. In Aṟa Irititja, when someone begins to access the online archive, a warning appears (with the option to also click on an audio file stating the same warning) in Pitjantjatjara and in English: "Be careful! Aṟa Irititja contains pictures and voices of Pitjantjatjara and Yankunytjatjara people who have passed away." People are advised to proceed with caution, a convention designed to help users avoid deep offence or sadness. Many books, films, and television programs with Indigenous content now often begin with a page or a screen with similar kinds of warnings, and in museums and cultural centres, photographs of people who have recently died are often physically covered.

When someone in the Aṟa Irititja network is known to have died, archivists in Adelaide reclassify the person within the database: the person is 'hidden' (in Pitjantjatjara, *pati* 'shut', as opposed to *uti* 'open') in a 'sorrow' category that requires an extra layer of security to enter. The metadata and the media in which the person is 'tagged' become visually inaccessible to everyday users of the archive, and users with administrative access can elect to show or hide 'restricted content'. In this context, digital photographs become like the deceased's personal effects, effaced from the unrestricted or daily-use space of the archive. Yet the analogy is not complete; such images are brought back into the open-access archive after a period of mourning has ended.[9] In this context, digital photographs are less like objects (permanently destroyed or abandoned after a death) and more like names that eventually come back into social life. They are hybrid things with a status that is continuously negotiated: durable like analogue artifacts, yet infinitely replicable (more like spoken utterances).

Indeed, as noted above, for Aṉangu, photographs must not be thought of as inanimate; rather they wield a fundamental essence of the person(s) pictured. Elizabeth Edwards eloquently argues that photographs – because they are often of people – tend to blur "the distinction between person and thing, subject and object" (Edwards 2012: 222). This blurriness between

---

9   The period of restriction is indefinite and unpredictable, depending on the family's preferences, and often on the circumstances of the death. For example, if a person led a significant, full life that the family feels should be celebrated, the sorrow restriction might apply for several months. However, in the case of a sudden or traumatic death of a young person, the sorrow restriction might be as long as 15 years.

subject and object has been considered in depth in accounts of Indigenous Australia (e.g. Munn 1970; Myers 1986). Social persons come into being via their relationships to 'country', and the named places for which they bear responsibility are themselves "objectification[s] of ancestral action and potency" (Myers 2001: 23–24) (See Figure 1). How, then, to think about photographs in this context? They are too painful to encounter in the first stages of grief, and yet too important (to individual memory-work, social constitutions of relatedness, political activism) to be permanently destroyed. This remains true even as the medium has shifted from print to pixels, in the transition from analogue to digital. Photographs extend claims to justice via land rights; photographs also inspire contemporary cultural and language revitalisation work. Yet they are not just "vehicles of meaning" (Keane 2003: 411). In the example below we are most interested in how meaning is negotiated, especially as the materialities of digital media offer new affordances.

Practices are always changing. Rather than avoiding photographs because of the pain that seeing them might cause, some people now seek them out as a source of comfort – as Jennifer Deger has written, "to remember, to feel him close" (Deger 2006: 122). Aṉangu have also come to rely on the easy replicability of prints from the digital archive: as project coordinator John Dallwitz wrote in 2018, "Ara Irititja always supplies photographs for the funeral booklets, and digital images for memorial services. This is normal practice now" (Dallwitz, Dallwitz & Rive 2018: 4). Photographs from the archive have become a resource for both private grieving and public remembering, incorporated into contemporary rituals of making sense of a death.

Figure 1. Young women crossing a flooded creek near Amata, Janet Inyika's home community, c. 1964–1966. From left: Yanyi Bandicha, Tjimpayi Presley, Mayana Burton, Wanatjura Lewis, and Janet Inyika (photo: collection of Margaret and David Hewitt. Reproduced courtesy of Ara Irititja AI-0000198)

'Mrs Never-Give-Up'

In the last few years, there have been several advance directives, in which people choose the photographs for their own funeral services and/or instruct others on how to use their photos after their deaths. On 23 November 2011, elder Janet Inyika recorded a living will in an interview with Aṟa Irititja oral historian Linda Rive. Linda explains Janet's significance:

> Janet was an important person to the NPY [Ngaanyatjarra Pitjantjatjara Yankunytjatjara] Women's Council,[10] and to Aṟa Irititja, because of her ability to understand where she stood in history, and because she had a strong drive to make the world a better place. She was a tireless activist, campaigning to stop drug and alcohol abuse. She earned the fond nickname Mrs Never-Give-Up (see Figures 2, 3, and 4).

Figure 2. An adult education class held at Pukatja (Ernabella), November 1952. Oral historian Linda Rive speaks with affection for this photograph, taken the year Janet Inyika was born: "It seems like Janet has been attending women's meetings her whole life!" The baby on the left is Janet. (photo: collection of Hamilton Aikin. Reproduced courtesy of Aṟa Irititja AI-0051360)

---

10   NPY Women's Council (NPYWC) was founded in 1980 because Aṉangu women felt excluded from important land rights discussions being handled by the Pitjantjatjara Council (an organisation established in 1976 to fight for Aṉangu rights to land and to provide much-needed services to remote-living people and their communities in Central Australia). A group of senior women established their own administrative structure to oversee the protection of sacred sites important to them. Women were a strong force in the establishment of Aṟa Irititja during the 1990s, and, in 2001, a dedicated Aṟa Irititja stand-alone computer was installed in the NPYWC office in Alice Springs. Over the following years, NPYWC assumed a leading role in the Aṟa Irititja *Minymaku Kutju* (Women's Only) project, and policies and future directions were formally endorsed at an NPYWC Executive Meeting in 2006.

Figure 3. Ngaanyatjarra Pitjantjatjara Yankunytjatjara Women's Council meeting at Mimili, May 1998. Janet Inyika is pictured reading something on NPYWC letterhead. Swags and tarps for camping are visible behind the women (photo: Liza Balmer, collection of NPY Women's Council. Reproduced courtesy of Aṟa Irititja AI-0021898)

Figure 4. Janet Inyika's last NPY Women's Council meeting, at Ngururrpila, September 2016 (photo: Angela Lynch. Reproduced courtesy of Aṟa Irititja AI-0184159)

In 2016, Janet herself explained her nickname:

> I was given the name Mrs Never-Give-Up because I am *tungunpungkupai*.[11] This means I am determined and perseverant against all odds to reach the goals that we women desire, which is for our families to live a happy, peaceful, and prosperous life. I never give up any

---

11   Translation note: *tungunpunganyi* is a verb that means 'to stand firm against pressure'. See Goddard (2006) for further discussion of Pitjantjatjara/Yankunytjatjara words.

Figure 5. Janet Inyika, with interpreter Linda Rive, launching the new Opal unleaded petrol at the BP Terminal in Largs Bay, South Australia, February 2005, together with the then Federal Minister for Health, Tony Abbott (not in the photo). Janet was proud that petrol-sniffing declined greatly following the introduction of this fuel (photo: Mark Brake. Reproduced courtesy of Ara Irititja AI-0147593)

of my campaigns, be it fighting to close down bottle shops and alcohol outlets, opening remote area renal dialysis units, or demanding a total roll out of low-octane petrol, in order to combat the scourge of petrol-sniffing (see Figure 5).

Janet's insistence, persistence, and resistance, her reflexive awareness of herself as an important figure, and her faith in Ara Irititja as crucial to her causes make her living will an exemplary text and, in featuring Janet, her words and her work here, we honour and acknowledge her advocacy. Janet Inyika's living will was spoken, in conversation with Linda Rive in Alice Springs, while Janet was still healthy. She died five years later, on 30 December 2016.[12]

I have my own ideas about what will happen after my death. This is what I have been thinking about – when I have my funeral, I do not want images of me deleted [from Ara Irititja]. *Ngayuku kurantja wiyangku wantintjaku. Munu paintja.*[13]

---

12 This extended quote is an extract from Ara Irititja, and is reproduced here with permission from archive manager John Dallwitz and oral historian Linda Rive.

13 Translation notes: *Ngayuku* 'anything pertaining to me'. *Kura*, the root of *kurantja*, means 'bad/not good' and has been adapted by Anangu users of Ara Irititja to mean 'delete, erase, or reject'. *Wiyangku wantintjaku* is a commanding statement akin to 'never do!' The sentence might be translated as an imperative: 'Never delete representations of me.' Linda explains that Janet is asking for permanent non-deletion – permanent visibility – of material pertaining to her. *Munu paintja wiya* is another way of saying 'and do not demand that I be banished', which is what would have traditionally happened. *Paini* is what one does when shouting at dogs to go away: '*Pai!*' It is quite a strong statement.

I am saying this for my daughters and my grandsons and granddaughters, for them to see and hear. You see, I have done a lot of things, and I have been thinking about that.

I am addressing my family here. These words are directed towards my family now.

Listen, in the future, when I pass away, I do not want any of you to destroy or delete any images of me on television, nor destroy any photographs you may have of me.

Other family members of mine, when you get together, I want you to continue listening to my voice and hear what I have to say and please do not delete those sounds or anything about me.

I started working a long time ago ... working for Women's Council *warka palyakatinyi, wangkakatinyi,*[14] working on projects and speaking up about certain subjects on a regular basis, to assist in the lives of *ngaltutjara tjutaku*.[15] It is because of this that I have been thinking a lot about what might happen in the future.

In the future, when the time comes ... when the plane lands at Amata airstrip with me in my coffin, I want the Women's Council to film it with a camera, starting from the airstrip and going into Amata, to the ceremony. I want my coffin to be filmed as it takes that final journey to the songs that will be sung. But all of you, sometime in the future, you may hear my voice again, even after I have long passed away ... I want you to remember that those recordings were made a long time ago. Perhaps other people will have photographs of trips that I have been on, for instance when I went to Adelaide with my friend here [Linda Rive, see Figure 5], when I spoke up for the benefit of all, and photographs were taken of me – I do not want any of you, my family members, to destroy those images. Please do not do that.

I am saying these words particularly for my daughter[s] ... my niece ... and my son ... and any Anangu, for that matter, who may be my kin.[16] You are my kin and I want you to honour my words and do not banish images or sounds of mine, please.

I want my picture to remain, which I want you to show people. Pictures of me, when, say, I went to Sydney [for the opening ceremony of the 2000 Olympic Games], and all good pictures of me, I want you to keep looking at those pictures.

If you want to see pictures of me, well please go right ahead, and do not grieve or be sad for me. Don't say that you don't like it, because this is what I want. I have made this plan for my own children. *Palya*? 'Okay'?

In this extended quote, Janet externalises her desires for what should happen to representations of her after her death. Her words communicate a deep understanding of what the archive is and how it works: recording her wishes within Ara Irititja will ensure that her immediate kin will access them. Janet was the first, but since then others (Yanyi Bandicha, Anyupa Yuminiya

---

14 *Warka* is derived from English 'work'; *palyakatinyi* can be translated as 'creating, working, making things happen over a period of time', and *wangkakatinyi*, similarly, 'working hard over (or talking about for) a long period of time'.

15 *Ngaltutjara* 'ones deserving of sympathy, compassion, and/or assistance'. *Tjutaku* 'on behalf of all of those'. Here Janet is referring to clients of the NPY Women's Council, specifically women who have sought support and/or help with mental health problems and drug addictions, and those suffering domestic violence and poverty.

16 Names have been omitted here, at the suggestion of Linda Rive and John Dallwitz.

Figure 6. Janet Inyika (far right) and Ilawanti Ken (far left) teaching children *inma* for the 25th anniversary celebration of Pitjantjatjara Land Rights in 2006 (Photo: collection of the Pitjantjatjara Council [no photographer recorded]. Reproduced courtesy of Aṟa Irititja AI-0096630)

Ken) have asked oral historian Linda Rive to record their wills into the archive.[17] John Dallwitz states that "This is one of the many functions that Aṉangu have found for Aṟa Irititja that were never imagined when we first started in 1994" (Dallwitz, Dallwitz & Rive 2018: 3–4). Through these utterances, respected elders, the managing archivist, and the translator/interpreter all acknowledge and create the archive as dynamic and flexible, able to change over time. Moreover, these women are putting the archive to work for them in unanticipated ways, incorporating the medium into their own drives for change in their communities. Aṟa Irititja also becomes a holding place for each woman's struggle against her own mortality, the finitude of their capacity to fight, the fragility of their knowledge, and the precarity of their wisdom, experience, and achievements. The archive becomes an instrument that they imagine will keep their work going after they're gone (for example, see Figure 6).

Janet "was a great supporter and valued adviser to Aṟa Irititja ... Her cultural and historical knowledge was often sought" (Aṟa Irititja 2017: 7). Janet herself said "*Nyangatja Aṟa Irititja tjukurpa mulapa. Aṟa Irititja is the main one for Aṉangu. It holds our true record*" (Dallwitz, Dallwitz & Rive 2018: 12).[18] Linda interprets this as Janet saying that there is nothing more

---

17 Yanyi was the first to respond to Janet's living will and recorded a brief statement on 2 March 2012, and further extended it just after Janet's funeral, on 2 February 2017. On the same day in February 2017, Janet's good friend Anyupa lodged her own wishes for her death and burial, including instructions regarding photographs of herself and her work. These are held in their profiles in Aṟa Irititja. At the time of writing, both Yanyi and Anyupa are alive and well, living at Ernabella.

18 Translation notes: *Nyangatja* 'this that is before you' reinforces the emphasis in the phrase. *Tjukurpa* 'law, stories, and Dreaming' simultaneously invokes Aṉangu cosmologies (the Dreaming), a modality of cultural transmission (stories), and the accepted rules for appropriate social behaviour (law). *Mulapa* 'true' has two different possible valences: 'real and/or genuine', in the sense of 'not false', and also 'really/very', in the sense of 'emphasising for the sake of persuading'. Linda explains that "Janet ... was saying this was her true word. Aṉangu say 'my word is my truth'."

weighty than this: the archive is a custodian of histories and a resource for contemporary cultural work in Central Australia.

Janet mobilises the archive as a vehicle of direct and multimodal communication to her kin: "I am saying this for my daughters and my grandsons and granddaughters, for them to see and hear ... I am addressing my family here, these words are directed towards my family now" and later "you are my kin and I want you to honour my words." This repetitive demand carries a kind of warning that listeners should pay attention; indeed it is consistent with a genre of public speaking, *alpiri*, which involves warnings, directives, and harangues. A style of oratory used by old people, it is used to put pressure on people who are behaving incorrectly, and to voice grievances. Janet confidently presumes that her recorded words will urge her family to act in specific ways.

Janet's invocation of two senses (sight and hearing) emphasises multiple pathways of knowledge transmission (and implicitly communicates her understanding that the archive holds both the audio of her original voice recording, and its transcription and translation into text). The archive is linguistically effaced in Janet's words; she implicitly constructs it as an unmediated and ongoing pathway of communication between a deeply respected, knowledgeable old woman and her descendants. In other words, she is mobilising the affordances of the digital archive to connect her words with those who are not co-present (and even beyond her lifetime). Simultaneously, Janet also imagined the archive as having agency: Linda notes that Janet trusted Ara Irititja to "continue her fight for her."

For Janet, the archive is a technology that preserves her ongoing presence, a way for her to live on after her physical death. She is directive: do not destroy photographs, continue listening to my voice, film the final journey of my coffin and the songs that will be sung, honour my words. She is also repetitive: do not banish images or sounds of mine, I want my picture to remain, I want you to keep looking at those pictures. The repetition coupled with the penultimate phrase, "Don't say that you don't like it, because this is what I want," implies that Janet anticipates some resistance, that she knew she was suggesting – and hoping to usher in – a change in protocols. Janet insists that showing and looking at pictures after her death are good things to do; these are actions that honour her and allow the work she's done to continue.

Indeed, Janet is proud of her work, and much of the motivation behind her living will is to insist that her work live on.[19] Her persistence and repetition, insisting that any representations of her remain visible, audible, and unrestricted, communicate a tension between existing cultural protocols and personal choice: can the archive accommodate both? Is it up to her to decide what happens to photos (and videos and other representations) of her after her death? Who wields what responsibility here: the deceased person, the archive, the surviving kin? 'The archive' and 'Anangu' culture and identity are not equal, and must not be conflated, as tempting as it may be to imagine complete transformation of the digital according to a cultural vernacular.[20]

---

19   See Bell (1981) and Dussart (2000) for more on the labour and creativity involved in asserting the value of women's work in Central Australia.

20   See Thorner (2010) on Ara Irititja 'Indigenising' digital technologies. The phrase "cultural vernacular" comes from Coleman (2010). Thorner has stepped away from 'Indigenising' as a frame for her scholarship, dissatisfied with its implication that Indigenous cultures and digital technologies are, *a priori*, separate and/ or incompatible. Instead, she prefers to think in terms of 'interface' and 'intercultural production' as framing devices and helpful metaphors.

Never giving up: On negotiations

With Janet as an instigator, the archive becomes a vehicle for change in cultural practices. Yet Janet's words also forecast that such change may be hard and/or slow. Linda recounts:

> After her death, some of her closest family members came into Alice Springs to see me to prepare for her funeral and memorial booklet. As instructed by Janet, I played the voice recording to them. "Brace yourselves. Are you ready?" They said yes, they were ready. I played it to them. Wide-eyed, they stood to attention and listened to it right through to the end, nodded and said, "Yes, we will obey her wishes."
>
> I played it to a number of other women, including Yanyi and Anyupa, and this is why Anyupa was so forthright in giving her instructions. When she saw how well Janet's instructions were received and obeyed, it gave her more authority to make her own demands.

All of the media and metadata in which Janet is tagged are *uti* 'open' and visible, not restricted, *pati* 'closed'. This is a great shift from the practices of the recent past, preceding the advent of the archive, in which photographs were torn out of the pages of books, or prints were burned,[21] actions that people have come to regret.[22] Kinyin McKenzie says:

> In the past, people would never look at photos of deceased people. Even now, people are very sensitive about it. We may make a funeral booklet and a funeral slideshow and everyone may watch it. But after that, we do not look at those pictures. We stop looking after the funeral.
>
> Having said that, we still want the photos kept on Ara Irititja, kept hidden, so we can look at them in the future. But pictures of deceased people must be closed. The decision to reopen the pictures must be made by more than one family member – younger siblings or parents, for instance.
>
> *Kumpilpa kanyinytjaku* – keep them, but keep them hidden.[23]

When photographs or other media go into 'sorrow', those with administrative logins can choose to view or hide the restricted content; all other users proceed into archive contents without visual access.[24] 'Sorrow' restricts images and media but doesn't restrict the written

---

21 Maria Stewart, pers. comm. to Linda Rive, 27 September 2011. See Michaels (1994: 1–18) and Peterson (2003) for more on the development of protocols in the 1970s–1980s to regulate the unfettered circulation of images of Central Australian Indigenous people.

22 Both Dallwitz and Stewart mention retrospective sadness – contemporary feelings of regret – among Anangu over photographs that were permanently destroyed in the past (John Dallwitz, pers. comm. to Sabra Thorner, 21 January 2019; Maria Stewart, pers. comm. to Linda Rive, 27 September 2011).

23 Pers. comm. to Linda Rive, 26 September 2012.

24 If a user doesn't have access but wishes to see, hear, or visit with these archive items (see Thorner 2016 for more on 'visiting with' photographs; this a vernacular shorthand that animates viewing into a process involving dynamic emotional and social work), usually it is easy enough to ask someone with administrative access to change the settings for the one session of use. This is a system that protects those who might be hurt by viewing such media, and simultaneously allows pathways for viewing for those who wish, instead, to see. This flexibility is one of Ara Irititja's most remarkable and innovative features as a database.

word; if a person is 'in sorrow', you can still search and find that person by name. John Dallwitz notes that "it's the voice, the saying of the name that's painful, so this is what's limited by sorrow, and less so the name in print."

Janet's living will remains exceptional, unprecedented, in the context of Ara Irititja. Her instructions, and her family's decision to follow them, offer a new possibility for the role of photographs in mourning practices, yet do not indicate a wholesale rejection of, or departure from, 'sorrow' as a category through which photographs move. A counter-example will illustrate. Nganyinytja was another senior law woman who didn't want herself put into sorrow after her death, and yet, in 2007, when she died, as John states:

> [I]t was a massive loss. We all agreed: we didn't care what she asked. Just over a month, while the funeral was going on, out of respect for the whole process, she was put into sorrow ... then at the end, you know, she'd always wanted us to keep her open [and so her records were 'opened' again] ... The processes of Ara Irititja and the decision-making of the families overruled Nganyinytja for a short time. (Pers. comm., 21 January 2019)

In discussing both Janet and Nganyinytja's wishes together, John further clarifies:

> Janet's not saying there should be no such thing as 'sorrow'. She's saying: I want my story to keep going, and I don't want you to destroy it because of a tradition. I want you to do this for me. What I have to say now is still going to be important into the future, I want you to keep this in front of you into the future. She's using Ara Irititja to keep her message alive.

Cultural protocols are continuously negotiated, these negotiations are crucial to culture (not detrimental to it),[25] and photographs, via the digital archive, are the media through which this is occurring. The archive can hold Janet's photographs and Nganyinytja's, and treat them differently; the platform has been designed with the infrastructural flexibility to withstand and sustain different desires. Moreover, Ara Irititja has become an impetus for ongoing discussions about correct behaviour after the death of significant people; it is this that keeps culture alive, dynamic, present. The flexibility of this archive – the fact that negotiation is productive and not destabilising – makes Ara Irititja quite different from conventional archives.

Janet may have been wishing to usher in an enduring change in how photographs are handled when Anangu die, to be celebrated as enduring objectifications of a person's good work(s), instead of hidden away as tangible reminders of the deceased that are too painful to bear. Perhaps more importantly, her living will has inspired ongoing conversation about what good or right behaviour is. Other women followed Janet's lead, imagining photographs as affirmations of their knowledge, experience, and status as elders. Janet's never-giving-up hasn't ended with her death; rather, her significance lives on via the conversations and processes she set in motion (see Figure 7). The photograph – once an interface between Indigenous cultural practices and Western colonial imagining, collecting, archiving, and viewing practices, an object to be recontextualised – becomes, too, the medium through which protocols are

---

25 Negotiation over who is responsible for stories, objects, and rituals is crucial in Central Australian Indigenous claims (and counterclaims) to country, autonomy, and relatedness; see Myers (1989); Dussart (2000).

Figure 7. Linda carried out Janet Inyika's instructions and filmed the arrival of Janet's coffin at Amata airstrip, January 2017 (photo: Linda Rive, collection of NPY Women's Council. Reproduced courtesy of Aṟa Irititja AI-0190944)

negotiated. The legacy Janet leaves, then, is best understood not by (potentially) changing the status of the object, but by (implicitly) insisting that negotiating the status of the object reinforces Aṉangu values (such as autonomy over such objects and collections, collective decision-making, and appropriate remembering and honouring of a person upon her death).

Forms of translation

There is a multiplicity in the knowledge the archive holds. In order to (re)present the quote above, we have copied and pasted the English text from Janet's profile in Aṟa Irititja.[26] Linda translated and transcribed this text from an original audio recording of the conversation between her and Janet, also held in Aṟa Irititja (classified under the category 'NPY Language').[27] Of course, the text transcription and the audio file are not the same thing. In the audio version, Linda speaks mostly in English, though also a bit in Pitjantjatjara; Janet speaks mostly in Pitjantjatjara and a bit in English. In addition to the voices, the audio includes a dog barking in the distance and other ambient sounds. Listening affords a fuller sense of being there than the text on screen (or printed on these pages).

The one-time event of the recorded conversation between Janet and Linda is accessible, in an archival sense, in multiple ways. The audio recording is a more Aṉangu way of transmitting knowledge and also preserves spoken language, whereas the text makes the utterance more accessible to people who don't speak Pitjantjatjara as a first language, and/or who are more comfortable with text as a form of knowledge transmission. Different pathways of using the archive lead users to arrive at these different records, the audio recording and the translated

26 Profiles in Aṟa Irititja are 'entity records' in IT jargon; these are the foundational units of data in Aṟa Irititja's 'Keeping Culture' software. They contain information about people (additional names, language group(s), places of birth and death) written in text, and with the possibility of video and audio annotations.

27 The sound recording is item # AI-0108322.

transcription, though all are interconnected to photographs of Janet, newspaper articles about her and her work, her funeral booklet, and many other materials. The archive provides a sense of the full and important life Janet lived, and how she imagined herself, her work, and her legacy. It offers a glimpse of how she wanted to be remembered. There is also a sense of the ontological shifts she sought to usher in: to change the way people who are gone might be remembered, and to change how media get archived: preserved, accessed, taken up in new ways. The archive is always incomplete, and the labour of archiving, infinite.

We have called Janet's words above a 'living will', and it is that, in the sense of a set of formalised instructions about the kind of death a person wants, an instrument that allows a dying person to have some control over his/her end of life care. It is also suggestive of a conventional will, a legal document that delineates what should happen to a person's assets after death. In imagining her death, Janet sets forth funerary and grieving practices, kinship responsibilities for remembering and honouring the deceased person, and the correct treatment of representations of that person. Photographs, here, are both like and unlike property. Discussing her recorded words as a will implicitly constructs photographs (and other media featuring Janet) as a kind of legacy. Discussing her recorded words as a *living* will implies that Janet's wishes should hold the weight of biomedical choices at the end of life. Both of these terms emphasise honouring the final wishes of a dying person and imply that following her instructions is a pathway to preserving the dignity of someone grappling with her own mortality. Linda poignantly suggests that Janet, perhaps, "saw her life's work as her estate. She had little else to leave behind, apart from her artworks."

Concluding thoughts

In this chapter, we strive to write in a way that is multivocal – including Thorner's arguments as developed through, with and alongside the words of archive co-creator John Dallwitz, oral historian Linda Rive, and Anangu senior law woman Janet Inyika. This is a narrative strategy we have forged to reflect the work of Ara Irititja, an ongoing and dynamic intercultural production (Myers 2004), and especially to honour Janet's work and extend it into the future. The archive, here, is a site of negotiation, an infrastructure that holds culturally significant materials and enables and inspires the collaborative work of culture-making.

As Fred Myers argues (1986: 127–158), negotiation is a form of cultural production, and a culturally appropriate pathway of initiating change and incorporating it into social lives. Negotiating is productive, not threatening. Janet's words, quoted at length in this chapter, are directive, repetitive, even corrective in tone; they seem to be both anticipating and initiating the negotiations over what might happen to photographs (and other media) of her after her death. They may also be an expression of new assertions and new domains of individual authority, and evidence of a desire to inscribe that authority into the archive. In this sense, Janet's living will forges a new genre of metadata, and the archive is increasingly driven by the purposeful desire to produce new records that define correct conduct in more individuated terms.

That the status of photographs ('open', or 'closed' in sorrow) can be changed, and that different people's photographs (and other media) can be handled differently are important ways in which Ara Irititja responds to and objectifies the desires of Anangu. This is an archive dedicated to continuing and recursive innovation and reinvention. The ongoing negotiations over what to do with photographs are significant and signal one way in which photographs are being continuously integrated into Aboriginal storytelling. In other words, what is done with photographs – whether and how they are 'returned' from elsewhere; how access to them can be customised and dynamic in using a digital tool – must be considered on a case-by-case basis, and always alongside the discussions and decision-making over how or if they should be circulated.

The return of Indigenous cultural records, thus, is neither an ending nor a resolution. Instead, via the archive, return is a beginning, an opening-up. The work of archiving – in the sense of ongoing negotiation, and negotiation as culture-making – doesn't end, isn't supposed to end; rather, it remains ongoing. As the examples presented and analysed here indicate, this is a field that includes Indigenous people and non-Indigenous allies, colonial institutions, and decolonising ambitions. Ara Irititja provides an infrastructure for more Indigenous control and autonomy – the longstanding goal of land rights activism in Central Australia – yet also inspires the debate that keeps culture alive, vibrant, contemporary, and transmitted to the next generations. Writing together, we suggest that these processes of collaborating and negotiating are producing the contemporary archive, keeping it dynamic and instrumental in Aṉangu imaginings of their selves, socialities, and futures.

References

Anderson, Jane. 2004. *Authors, owners and archives: A working paper.* AIATSIS Seminar Series. Canberra: AIATSIS.

Anderson, Jane. 2008. *Framework for Indigenous community protocols.* Canberra: AIATSIS.

Anderson, Jane. 2011. *Protocols and guidelines for ethical engagement with Indigenous and local communities: WIPO briefing for Estée Lauder.* New York.

Anderson, Jane & Gregory Younging. 2015. Renegotiated relationships and new understandings: Indigenous protocols. In Patricia W Elliott and Daryl H Hepting (eds.), *Free knowledge: Confronting the commodification of human discovery*, 180–198. Regina: University of Regina Press.

Ara Irititja. 2017. *Janet Inyika funeral booklet, 'In loving memory of Janet Inyika'.* Ara Irititja Archive No.: AI-0187343, Collection: NPY Women's Council.

Bell, Diane. 1981. Women's business is hard work: Central Australian Aboriginal women's love rituals. *Signs: Journal of Women in Culture and Society* 7(2). 314–337.

Bell, Joshua A, Kimberly Christen & Mark Turin. 2013. Introduction: After the return. *Museum Anthropology Review* 7. 1–21.

Brown, Alison K, Laura Peers & members of the Kainai Nation. 2006. *Pictures bring us messages / Sinaakssiiksi aohtsimaahpihkookiyaawa: Photographs and histories from the Kainai Nation.* Toronto: University of Toronto Press.

Christie, Michael. 2004. Computer databases and Aboriginal knowledge. *Learning Communities: International Journal of Learning in Social Contexts* 1. 4–12.

Coleman, E Gabriella. 2010. Ethnographic approaches to digital media. *Annual Review of Anthropology* 39. 487–505.

Dallwitz, John, Dora Dallwitz & Linda Rive. 2018. *Ara Irititja: An Anangu project / Nganampa warka, Report for 2017 and to May 2018.* Adelaide: Ara Irititja Anangu Community Archive.

Deger, Jennifer. 2006. *Shimmering screens: Making media in an Aboriginal community.* Minneapolis: University of Minnesota Press.

Derrida, Jacques. 1998. *Archive fever: A Freudian impression.* Translated by Eric Prenowitz. Chicago: University of Chicago Press.

Donaldson, Ian & Tamsin Donaldson (eds.). 1985. *Seeing the First Australians.* Sydney: George Allen & Unwin.

Dussart, Françoise. 2000. The politics of ritual in an Aboriginal settlement: Kinship, gender, and the currency of knowledge. Washington, DC: Smithsonian Institution Press.

Edwards, Elizabeth. 2001. *Raw histories: Photographs, anthropology, and museums.* Oxford: Berg.

Edwards, Elizabeth. 2012. Objects of affect: Photography beyond the image. *Annual Review of Anthropology* 41. 221–234.

Edwards, Elizabeth, Chris Gosden & Ruth B Phillips. 2006. *Sensible objects: Colonialism, museums and material culture.* Oxford: Berg.

Gal, Susan. 2015. Politics of translation. *Annual Review of Anthropology* 44. 225–240.

Geismar, Haidy. 2013. Defining the digital. *Museum Anthropology Review* 7. 254–263.

Glass, Aaron. 2004. Return to sender: On the politics of cultural property and the proper address of art. *Journal of Material Culture* 9(2). 115–139.

Goddard, Cliff. 2006. *Pitjantjatjara/Yankunytjatjara to English dictionary.* 2nd edn. Alice Springs: IAD Press.

Lydon, Jane. 2005. *Eye contact: Photographing Indigenous Australians.* Durham, NC: Duke University Press.

Kaplan-Myrth, Nili. 2004. *Political visions: Blindness prevention policy as a case study of community-government relations in Aboriginal health.* Discussion Paper No. 10. Melbourne: VicHealth Koori Health Research and Community Development Unit.

Keane, Webb. 2003. Semiotics and the social analysis of material things. *Language & Communication* 23. 409–425.

Kramer, Jennifer. 2004. Figurative repatriation: First Nations 'Artist-Warriors' recover, reclaim, and return cultural property through self-definition. *Journal of Material Culture* 9(2). 161–182.

Krmpotich, Cara & Laura Peers. 2014. *This is our life: Haida material heritage and changing museum practice.* Vancouver: UBC Press.

Martin, Karen & Booran Mirraboopa. 2003. Ways of knowing, being and doing: A theoretical framework and methods for Indigenous research and Indigenist research. *Journal of Australian Studies* 76. 203–214.

Mauss, Marcel. 1990. *The gift: The form and reason for exchange in archaic societies.* Translated by WD Halls. London: Routledge.

Michaels, Eric. 1994. *Bad Aboriginal art: Tradition, media, and technological horizons.* Minneapolis: University of Minnesota Press.

Morphy, Howard. 2015. Open access versus the culture of protocols. In Raymond Silverman (ed.), *Museum as process: Translating local and global knowledges,* 90–104. Abingdon, Oxon, UK: Routledge.

Munn, Nancy. 1970. The transformation of subjects into objects in Walbiri and Pitjantjatjara myth. In Ronald Berndt (ed.), *Australian Aboriginal anthropology,* 141–163. Nedlands: UWA Press.

Myers, Fred R. 1986. *Pintupi country, Pintupi self: Sentiment, place, and politics among Western Desert Aborigines.* Washington, DC: Smithsonian Institution Press.

Myers, Fred R. 1989. Burning the truck and holding the country: Pintupi forms of property and identity politics of Aboriginal land tenure. In Edwin N Wilmsen (ed.), *We are here: Politics of Aboriginal land tenure,* 15–42. Berkeley: University of California Press.

Myers, Fred R. 1994. Culture-making: Performing Aboriginality at the Asia Society Gallery. *American Ethnologist* 21(4). 679–699.

Myers, Fred R. 2001. Introduction: The empire of things. In Fred R Myers (ed.), *The empire of things: Regimes of value and material culture,* 3–61. Santa Fe, NM: School of American Research Press.

Myers, Fred. 2004. Ontologies of the image and economies of exchange. *American Ethnologist* 31(1). 5–20.

Myers, Fred. 2006. We are not alone: Anthropology in a world of others. *Ethnos* 71(2). 233–264.

Peers, Laura & Alison K Brown. 2003. *Museums and source communities: A Routledge reader.* London: Routledge.

Peterson, Nicolas. 2003. The changing photographic contract: Aborigines and image ethics. In Christopher Pinney & Nicolas Peterson (eds.), *Photography's other histories,* 119–145. Durham, NC: Duke University Press.

Pinney, Christopher and Nicolas Peterson (eds.). 2003. *Photography's other histories.* Durham, NC: Duke University Press.

Salmond, Amiria. 2012. Digital subjects, cultural objects: Special issue. *Journal of Material Culture* 17(3). 211–228.

Smith, Bernard. 1988 [1985]. *European vision and the South Pacific.* 2nd edition. New Haven, CT: Yale University Press.

Stoler, Ann Laura. 2009. *Along the archival grain: Epistemic anxieties and colonial common sense.* Princeton, NJ: Princeton University Press.

Strathern, Marilyn. 1988. *The gender of the gift: Problems with women and problems with society in Melanesia.* Berkeley: University of California Press.

Thorner, Sabra. 2010. Imagining an Indigital interface: Ara Irititja Indigenizes the technologies of knowledge management. *Collections: A Journal for Museum and Archives Professionals* 6(3). 125–146.

Thorner, Sabra. 2013. *Indigenizing photography: Archives, activism, and new visual media in contemporary Australia.* New York: New York University. (PhD dissertation.)

Thorner, Sabra. 2016. Visual economies and digital materialities of Koorie kinship and community: Photographs as currency and substance. *Anthropology & Photography* 6. London: Royal Anthropological Institute.

Thorner, Sabra & John Dallwitz. 2015. Storytelling photographs, animating Anangu: How
    Ara Irititja – an Indigenous digital archive in Central Australia – facilitates cultural
    reproduction. In Juilee Decker (ed.), *Technology and digital initiatives: Innovative
    approaches for museums*, 53–60. London: Rowman & Littlefield.

Language Documentation & Conservation Special Publication No. 18
Archival returns: Central Australia and beyond
ed. by Linda Barwick, Jennifer Green & Petronella Vaarzon-Morel, pp. 285–301
http://nflrc.hawaii.edu/ldc/sp18
http://hdl.handle.net/10125/24888

Nura's vision: Nura's voice

Suzanne Bryce
Ngaanyatjarra Pitjantjatjara Yankunytjatjara Women's Council
(Aboriginal Corporation)

Julia Burke
Central Land Council

Linda Rive
Aṟa Irititja Aboriginal Corporation

Abstract

For Nura Nungalka Ward (1942–2013) the art of teaching was a lifelong passion, culminating in *Ninu grandmothers' law*, published by Magabala Books (2018). This autobiography is an extensive ethnography of daily life for Pitjantjatjara and Yankunytjatjara families still living on their traditional lands amid the profound changes brought by the arrival of white settlers, doggers, missionaries and atomic bomb tests. Nura's achievement – compiling her life history illustrated with striking photographs into an English language autobiography – seems like a natural progression. Until you consider that Nura spoke and taught in Pitjantjatjara, her *Aṉangu* (Aboriginal) language from the remote northwest corner of South Australia, and the fact that she possessed no family photograph albums. How did she make that leap, way beyond her life experience in an oral storytelling tradition, to embrace the idea of a book? How did the return of archival records to Nura's kin via a digital repository in the early 2000s help shape Nura's memories?

This chapter details Nura's process: her compelling drive to teach and her willingness to embrace new technologies, such as the digital archive Aṟa Irititja, which she first used to record her knowledge and then drew on to achieve her ambitions. We discuss the complexities that occur when accessing the digital content and Nura's vigilance in ensuring that she broke no cultural rules in the process. We also share Nura's decade-long journey as she collaborated with three non-Aboriginal friends to move her spoken word story through the digital archive and into the printed form, in what is the most significant publication to date to be sourced through the Aṟa Irititja Project.

Keywords: supported memoir, Indigenous languages, oral history, archives

Introduction[1]

This is the story of Nura Nungalka Ward, the making of her autobiography, and her enthusiasm for digital archival technology as a means to share knowledge and ensure the longevity of cultural practice.

Nura Ward was a Pitjantjatjara woman from the Western Desert of Central Australia. She was born, at her own reckoning, somewhere between 1939 and 1943 at a time when *Anangu*, the name that Pitjantjatjara people[2] call themselves, were modifying their traditional way of life and entering a society they did not know. Nura, who passed away in 2013, was a great teacher, storyteller, matriarch, strong Law woman and consummate instructor of dance. Nura wrote about her life because she wanted the world to know how she had grown up in the northwest corner of South Australia – learning cultural etiquette through traditional living and relying on the land to supply all her needs. She felt this knowledge would bring happiness to the lives of all those who were willing to listen and learn, in particular her descendants.

Nura was clear that her knowledge was important. Firstly she believed in herself and was convinced of her story's intrinsic value; secondly she wanted to make a record that her grandchildren's grandchildren could access. Her tools included the digital archive Aṟa Iṟititja,[3] which she engaged with to seek, add to and preserve knowledge. Nura knew that the lives of her descendants would be very different to her own and in her autobiography, *Ninu grandmothers' law*, she made for them a kind of map, a way home and, potentially, a way into their future (Ward 2018).

Strong in both worlds

Nura's storytelling was grounded in her childhood love of *milpatjunkunytja*, 'a ritualised form of storytelling in the sand'. The social meaning behind young girls' use of telling story in the sand intrigues researchers in Central Australia (Eickelkamp 2008; Green 2014). Sitting cross-legged, a girl smooths the ground with her hand, draws a scene using symbols, taps for emphasis with a stick or her story wire and, like turning the page of a book, she wipes the symbols clean in the sand and continues. She uses gesture and makes a sound in her mouth that signals her body to relax and engage in the unfolding story. *Milpatjunkunytja* can be a lifelong pleasure as well as a useful tool; for Nura, and women like her, it became one of many ways of teaching and describing for as long as she was able to get herself down to sit on the ground.

As a child, many experiences, traditional and new, informed Nura's curiosity and intelligence. She absorbed knowledge as she experienced life on country, on outback cattle

---

1   The authors would like to thank Ann Davis for assistance with this chapter.

2   *Anangu* is the name that Ngaanyatjarra, Pitjantjatjara and Yankunytjatjara people living throughout Australia call themselves; it is used throughout this chapter without further translation.

3   *Anangu* translate *Aṟa Iṟititja* as 'stories from the past'; Aṟa Iṟititja is used throughout this chapter without further translation. Aṟa Iṟititja is a digital knowledge management project and archive for Ngaanyatjarra, Pitjantjatjara and Yankunytjatjara people. This multifaceted project returns and collectively documents *Anangu* historical material and preserves it for the future.

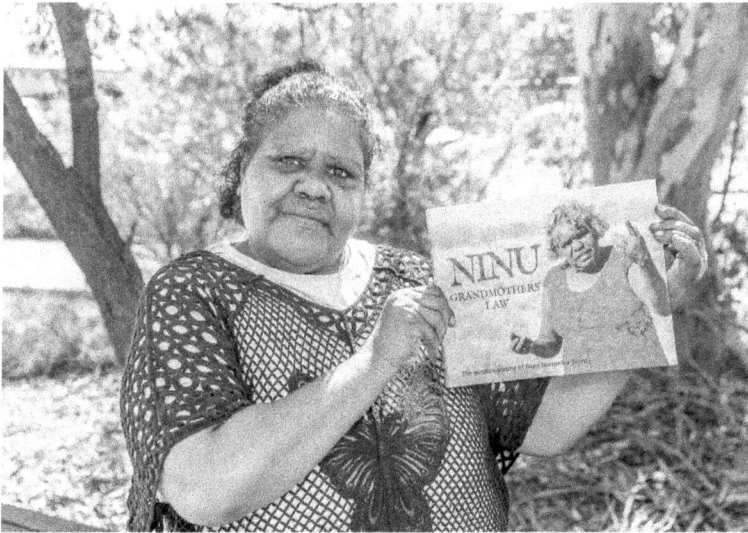

Figure 1. Nura's niece Melissa Thompson displays *Ninu grandmothers' law* at its launch, 16 August 2018 (photo: Emma Murray / Collection NPY Women's Council)

stations when her parents were working, and at the Ernabella Presbyterian Mission school in the Musgrave Ranges of northwest South Australia, where she learnt to read and write in Pitjantjatjara. It must have been a rare and extraordinary time when the richness of *Aṉangu* traditional life met with the 20th century. Many exceptional people with abundant talents and gifts emerged in this time of cultural collision and Nura was one of them.

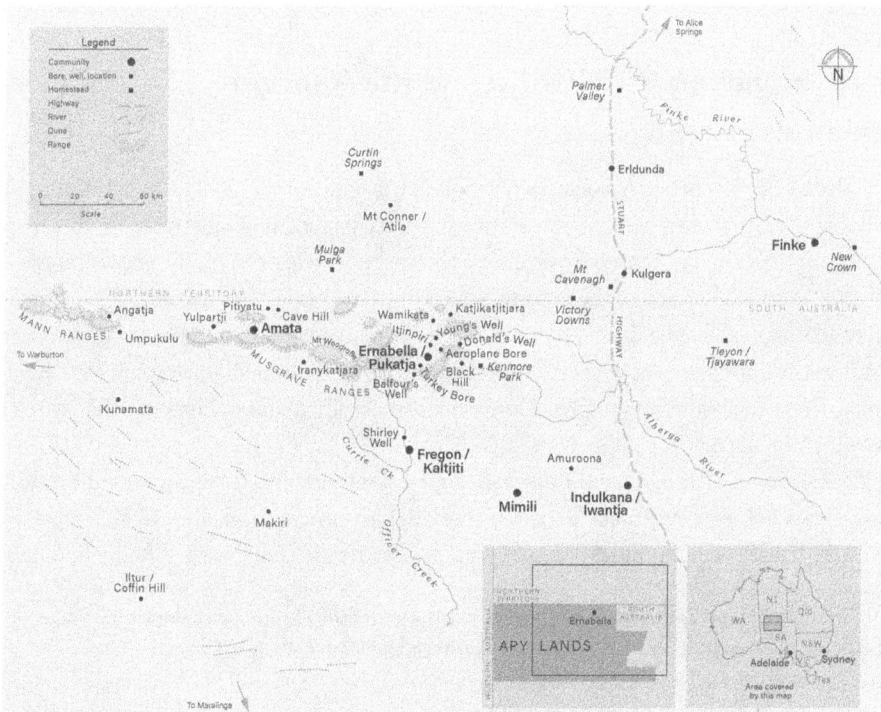

Figure 2. Locations in Nura's story (map: Brenda Thornley. Original map published in Ward 2018: xvi)

Nura possessed a remarkable creativity – and energy to match. Working at various jobs, she learnt to see the world through different lenses and she put her knowledge together in new ways. When describing bush medicines, for instance, she would liken them to medicines she had learnt to use at the clinic as a primary health care worker in order to teach about both. As such, *wanka* 'itchy processionary caterpillar nest' (*Ochrogaster lunifer*), which provides a treatment for burned skin, was like Vaseline gauze and *papawitilpa* 'medicinal creeper vine' (*Mukia maderaspatana*) was like penicillin (Ward 2018: 22).

In fact, bringing different domains together was her specialty. She was passionate about learning and applying her knowledge of bush medicine. She also wanted to rekindle other people's interest at a time when clinics were increasingly being accessed for medicines and western medical approaches. She was watching the development of a new phenomenon in Ernabella, television and video, produced locally. Not surprisingly, Nura was the first *Aṉangu* to approach the newly formed media organisation Ernabella Video and Television (EVTV) to make a film about bush medicine. She did it the proper way, drawing in the senior women, the experts. In this film, Nura was the younger assistant and her young daughters were alongside her as the older women expounded on preparations and treatments.

Many years later, in her autobiography, Nura remained consistent in her thinking about preserving culture:

> Our children's own grandchildren and great grandchildren are the ones who will benefit most from my history. I carry all that information and knowledge in my head, but they are going to need to have it written down for them. (Ward 2018: xv)

Digital archiving: Aṟa Irititja and the Aṉangu Community Archive

The 'Welcome' screen of the Aṟa Irititja Aboriginal Corporation's (AIAC) Aṉangu Community Archive invites the user inside, the entrance portal beautifully illustrated with an ever-changing dramatic image chosen from among the vast collection of 174,928 photographic item numbers.[4] Admission access to the archive is password protected. Once inside, the user takes a journey among multimedia drawn from 524 collection holders. Individuals, organisations and cultural institutions have shared their collections to bring multimedia materials back home to *Aṉangu*. These include photographs, films, sound recordings and documents that date from 1884 to the present day.[5]

Prior to the era of mobile phones and digital photography, most *Aṉangu* did not have personal cameras or convenient access to facilities to process film due to the remoteness of Western Desert communities from towns. *Aṉangu* relied on being gifted photographic

---

4   Aṟa Irititja Aboriginal Corporation incorporated in 2016; previously Aṟa Irititja was under the banner of the Pitjantjatjara Council Inc. Aṟa Irititja photographic items totalled 174,928 at 22 December 2018.

5   Some collection holders have chosen to donate to AIAC their hard copy pre-digital collections containing, for example, transparencies, negatives and prints. AIAC keeps these materials in archival conditions at the South Australian Museum. The museum has a collaborative partnership with AIAC.

prints from visitors to their community. While outsiders visiting the Aṉangu Pitjantjatjara Yankunytjatjara (APY)[6] Lands often took photos and made audiovisual recordings but did not return them, some were archived at public institutions such as the Australian Institute of Aboriginal and Torres Strait Islander Studies (AIATSIS)[7] and the Presbyterian Church, Victoria, while others were stored in personal photo albums as memories of their visits to the outback.

Aṟa Irititja was officially established in 1994 to repatriate multimedia of interest to *Aṉangu* that was sourced from within private collections and public institutions. Multimedia are shared as 'born digital' or recreated in a digital format. Originally written in FileMaker Pro, the software has undergone several developments since the project's inception. The original instructions to the software engineer were complex: develop a database that handles different media, incorporates cultural restrictions, and is easy to use for an audience with limited literacy and, often, failing eyesight.

Prior to the internet *Aṉangu* audiences used Aṟa Irititja on a stand-alone computer located at a community venue such as a school, arts centre, or office. Scales et al. (2013: 151–170) point out that Aṟa Irititja's functionality has been re-engineered at times in response to Pitjantjatjara community feedback. Today Aṟa Irititja is both a digital knowledge management project and an archive that uses interactive browser-based multimedia software known as Keeping Culture KMS (knowledge management system).[8] The move to a browser-based software may increase access for *Aṉangu* when there is simultaneously internet connectivity, possession of a screen (mobile, tablet, or computer) and knowledge of the access login/password. Aṟa Irititja analytics show that additional metadata is added by trained community operators; this is verifiable by viewing live activity reports, which also show that *Aṉangu* users are mostly logging in from an art or education centre via a generic password.

Aṉangu often use the archive collectively, with several generations crowded around a screen sharing the navigation and storytelling. The archival records mirror an album of family photographs with the add-on capacity for interactive storytelling. *Aṉangu* can annotate or record stories through text, audio, or video formats directly onto an image or a page. This profiling applies to any entity in the archive, be it concrete or abstract, a person or an activity. Navigation is multilayered through several profile groups including *Aṉangu* 'people's names', *Ngura* 'places and locations', *Puṉu* 'plants' and Animals. Searches can be further refined using a combination of profiles plus the inclusion of dates and keywords.

Aṟa Irititja has prioritised the recording, transcribing and translating of oral histories in Pitjantjatjara and Yankunytjatjara languages, in particular with senior *Aṉangu*. Use of the live recording annotation function enables *Aṉangu* elders to record their own knowledge in their own words, bypassing literacy challenges and making text redundant in favour of audio and video annotation. Active engagement with their own history and material "affirm[s], enlivens and consolidates their own history" (Dallwitz et al. 2017: 255).

---

6   APY, standing for Aṉangu Pitjantjatjara Yankunytjatjara, refers to the 12 *Aṉangu* communities on the Pitjantjatjara and Yankunytjatjara lands of the northwest corner of South Australia.

7   Housed in Canberra, ACT.

8   The KMS software has been designed and built by Douglas Mann, founder and lead developer of Rightside Response.

Figure 3. Screenshot from Aṟa Irititja, Aṉangu Community Archive, Cynthia Shannon Photo /
Cynthia Shannon Collection AI-0076239: Nura Ward teaches *inma* – traditional dance – to little
girls at Amata in 1985. Note the interaction in the 'stories' entries that record both a contribution
from Nura Ward as well as Tineale Colson, one of the dancers

Nura has contributed to Aṟa Irititja through both oral history recording and annotations.
Her movie annotations are of vital importance. She was virtually the last person alive who
could identify the elderly people that Charles Mountford photographed in 1940, elucidating
their family connection and traditional names.[9] Her movie annotations, averaging three to
five minutes long, were recorded with Nura facing the built-in camera and speaking to the
image in her own language. Not all *Aṉangu* are comfortable with the live annotation recording
process but Nura embraced the technology with ease. With a fluent language speaker beside
her operating the computer, there was no need for any interruptions to clarify information,
which added to this ease.

Aṉangu these days provide Aṟa Irititja with personal multimedia or will suggest someone
who holds sought-after material. People who have worked with *Aṉangu* contact Aṟa Irititja
to seek guidance for depositing their multimedia collection. The Aṉangu Community Archive
provides a rich source for picture researchers either for *Aṉangu* publications, such as local
celebratory events and funeral booklets, and other non-*Aṉangu* publications. *Aṉangu* students,
both school- and tertiary-level, rely on the archive as a primary research tool.

As entry to the Aṉangu Community Archive is password protected, it is a private collection for *Aṉangu* and not available to the general public. AIAC is not obliged to provide
non-*Aṉangu* researchers with access to its collections. However, research that is instigated or
supported by *Aṉangu* with evidence of community consultation is considered.

> I've worked with Aṟa Irititja for ten years ... The most worthwhile moments are to
> experience the enjoyment that *Aṉangu* feel when they look at family from the past and
> the present, and their security in knowing that their heritage is private, safe and accessible

---

9   The State Library of South Australia has shared 648 images from the 1940s Mountford Sheard Collection with
     Aṟa Irititja.

inside Aṟa Irititja. Aṟa Irititja gives *Aṉangu* the power to create their own history rather than being the subject of a stranger's historical analysis. (Burke 2013)

Aṟa Irititja was designed to acknowledge and accommodate cultural practices and has enjoyed a great deal of success as a result. It was developed at a time when *Aṉangu* held fast to strong traditional beliefs about how the living relate to their dead. As recently as 20 years ago, images of a newly deceased person were destroyed, as were any personal belongings such as clothes or blankets. A bereaved family would exchange houses and motor cars as a way to divert memory. It was greatly distressing for *Aṉangu* to come across images or the voice of deceased family members in books, sound recordings, or films.

The design of Aṟa Irititja had to meet this and other cultural requirements so that the archive could store images that are managed in 'sorrow' and 'sensitive' categories. These are out of direct sight and have to be deliberately selected to be viewed. Families rely on Aṟa Irititja to keep abreast of deaths and manage the archive accordingly. After a suitable time, a bereaved family can let the archive managers know that they are ready to have the images, audio and video of their deceased relative visible again.

The last decade has seen much loosening of the rules governing such images. The archive managers are finding that *Aṉangu*, as they ready themselves for their passing, have begun to say they don't want their own images suppressed. The families still tend to put the images away for a period of time for their own sakes and sense of propriety but have also come to appreciate a memorial service that features a 'slide' show of the deceased person as part of a celebration of their life. Aṟa Irititja is responsive to this change; it has not been an instigator, however, and acts with caution. Due to its flexible design, Aṟa Irititja administrators can respond as individuals and families indicate their needs and preferences.

Finding family on Aṟa Irititja

In 2001, the first Aṟa Irititja computers loaded with the Aṉangu Community Archive arrived on the APY Lands and at the Ngaanyatjarra Pitjantjatjara Yankunytjatjara (NPY) Women's Council office in Alice Springs. The opportunity to find photographs of ancestors was exciting and new for *Aṉangu*. Julia and Nura, working for NPY Women's Council, explored the archive together, with Julia as the computer operator and Nura the navigator.

Starting in the category 'Collections', Nura would scan the names of those individuals or organisations that had donated multimedia. Photographs shared from institutions such as the South Australia Museum feature her ancestors, while the Richard Seeger Collection from Museums Victoria shows Nura and her childhood friends at play in 1949.[10] Nura appears in many guises in more contemporary photos, such as the Suzanne Bryce Collection, where she addresses a women's meeting to teach about women's health. Jumping into a collection, Nura would scrutinise the face of every person. Some people were easy to recognise, while others were only identified by the shape of their nose, and even earlier ancestors, likely long deceased by the time of Nura's birth, were identified by common family facial characteristics. She would announce their name, location and activity to add as metadata.

---

10   See, for example, the Richard Seeger Collection from Museums Victoria, RS ER 1949/99 & RE ER 1949/359.

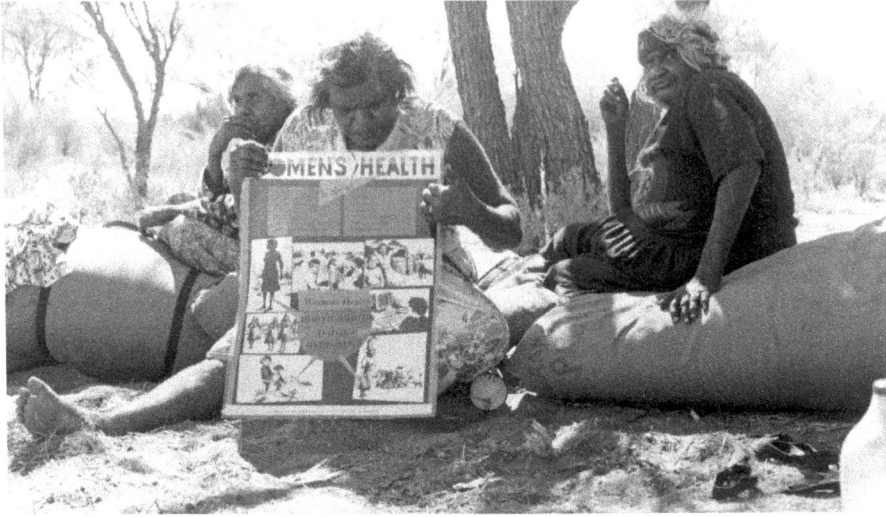

Figure 4. Nura addresses a women's meeting to teach about women's health (photo: Suzanne Bryce / Suzanne Bryce Collection)

She said:

> This is my history. I am talking about the early days of my life to put onto Ara Irititja, for all the younger generations to read and hear. I want them to be able to look at the photographs of us, and for them to read the stories about how our predecessors lived. (Ward 2018: xiii)

Julia joined Ara Irititja in 2002 as the women's project officer. She travelled from her base in Alice Springs to train community operators to use the newly installed Anangu Community Archive computers across the APY communities and several in Pitjantjatjara communities of the Northern Territory. In a rush of excitement, people would crowd around and compete to control navigation via the computer mouse on a journey through the collection straight towards their family and country. The need for annotation in order to expand the available metadata to assist later search functionality was often at odds with the desire to enjoy the archive for its pure entertainment value. We would refer to the addition of metadata as 'growing the archive'.

Towards a book

Although the deciding moment to make a book has been forgotten, Nura's insistence to begin formal oral history recording in mid-2005 brought her family to stay at Julia's home for recording sessions in the garden. Even a hospital admission later in 2006 could not deter Nura from her task. She filled a journal with stories in Pitjantjatjara accompanied by her illustrations. One page recalls her childish delight at running and jumping into a whirlwind in play with other children (Ward 2006: 4).

Nura's ability to plan for her book and begin writing it in Pitjantjatjara was compelling to her friends. In the beginning she may not have envisaged publication of a proper book to be sold in bookshops. Her book-making might have stayed at the level others had achieved

Figure 5. *Aṉangu* at Utju, NT looking at the Aṉangu Community Archive computer (photo: Linda Rive / Aṟa Irititja [Linda Rive] Collection)

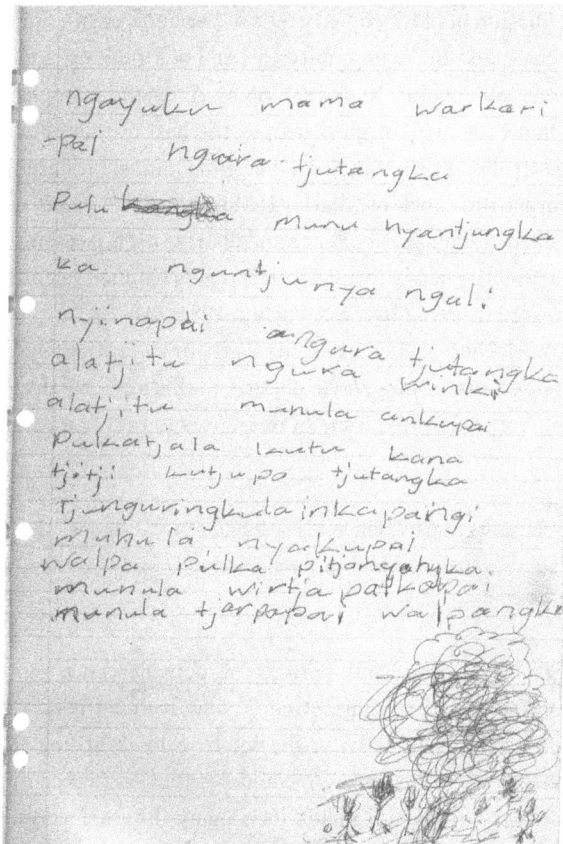

Figure 6. A page from Nura Ward's journal in 2006, where she outlines some of the stories that she plans to record and which features the whirlwind illustration (Nura Ward Collection)

before her with a mission school printing press and grade readers written and illustrated in Pitjantjatjara by the *Aṉangu* teachers of the 1960s. However, she was moving with the times; she had the support of both Aṟa Irititja and NPY Women's Council, where she had been staff and was still an important advocate. She also had charismatic ways that drew people to her and invited them to assist her. She began with Julia, and then Linda Rive and later Suzanne Bryce joined the 'book-making' team. These three women were Nura's friends. They became 'the compilers', a committee of three, combining their skills in interview, translation and knowledge of publishing. They committed to making the book happen, hopefully in Nura's lifetime.

As fast as Linda and Julia could make draft copies of the manuscript, Nura would love to give them out – sell them, in fact. They were spiral bound and photocopied with a few black and white photographs.

> The first copies of my history book were made in 2009 and everyone went crazy for it! All the white people, the teachers, the sisters, the policemen, everyone went mad for it! Aṟa Irititja makes me copies of my book and I give them out to all the people. I want to publish the book properly with beautiful photographs. (Ward 2018: xv)

We compilers believe that Nura's distribution of photocopied drafts of her book over a number of years was a clever strategy. It accustomed her community to her book-making and her family could see that it generated a welcome income. Book-making by Aboriginal people was not common. Many books had been made about Aboriginal people, the best of them done in close consultation, but nevertheless control was firmly in non-Aboriginal hands. Pitjantjatjara people, adults in the 1970s, did not forget the shock of Charles P Mountford's *Nomads of the Australian desert* (1976), which had spelled danger, great offence and distress for the ceremonial secrets the book revealed – so much so that the newly formed Pitjantjatjara Council negotiated an injunction to have the book suppressed in 1976 (Toyne & Vachon 1984: 51).

Interestingly it was often at memorial services before funerals that new attitudes to the use of images of the deceased were being tested. Nura spoke directly to this after the death of her brother Punch Thompson in 2013. Nura raised the issue of references to him as a recently deceased person:

> I am writing a genuine history book, so we must include his story and say his name. The government came to his funeral, so we must keep him in the book. I'm so proud of him. (N. Ward, pers. comm. to Linda Rive, 16 October 2013)

Nura too was unwell after a series of strokes, and periods of convalescence became opportunities. Julia's garden continued as Nura's writing retreat. Away from her community responsibilities and any criticism for her unusual activity, she sat by a low-burning fire, a voice recorder in hand and an exercise book in her lap. We could see that Nura was driven by the force of her own will and intent. She has articulated it in many different ways. She was determined that her history, and that of her brother and all the people of her generation, would not be forgotten and buried under the immensity of changed circumstances.

Without Aṟa Irititja, Nura would not have been able to make the type of book she did, with images that first prompted so many memories and now serve to enthrall the reader. Furthermore, publication would not have been possible without the gradual relaxing of attitudes to the use of images. *Ninu grandmothers' law* is full of people and places from the past and the book can be read by anyone, picture by picture. Nura had her impeccable memory, her immense storytelling capacity and her own drawings. But without Aṟa Irititja she would have made a different book.

She was completely clear about her readership: her family in all the generations to come. She said:

> This is my history. I am talking about the early days of my life to put onto Aṟa Irititja, for all
> the younger generations to read and hear. I want them to be able to look at the photographs
> of us, and for them to read the stories about how our predecessors lived. (Ward 2018: xiii)

She knew that the people she called 'staff' – the service providers – were going to read it too. She made a clear request to have the book in all the clinics of the APY Lands. Nura would not be surprised to learn that other people are now wanting to tell their story and that their perceived readership is family. She would be pleased that she did it 'first'. Many other *Aṉangu* have her facility as a storyteller, but Nura stands out among her peers for her determination and agility in making technology work for her vision.

As it happened, the compilers had 701 exceptional archival images stored under Nura's name from Aṟa Irititja including many that Nura had treasured. They approached families for permission when they felt an image was sensitive due to a more recent passing, and there are many images of deceased family members, with only a warning at the front of the book. Photos from cultural institutions required reprint permissions and others needed their donation contracts checked for reproduction conditions. All individuals and organisations that were approached gave their permission. It is sad to note that Nura did not see her book published and resplendent with all its final images.

Career woman

During her career Nura made significant contributions to NPY Women's Council, Nganampa Health, Congress Alukura and Bangarra Dance Theatre, and as a senior woman at home in her community, she was called upon by the police and many other agencies. Interviews with Nura about her work are sketchy compared to her recollection of the early history. They lack the detail, the powerful recall, the humour and the vitality of the subjects that she chose. When she is telling her history she is invoking a sense of place and people so that we almost hear the bird calls or feel the temperature of the day.

Nura agreed this part of her life should go in the book but appeared detached from her 'whitefella' work and the need to be recognised or remembered for it. The compilers were curious about this modesty because Nura was never halfhearted. She believed deeply in the work she engaged in and she gave herself to it with energy, enthusiasm and great intelligence. When she was working with her co-worker (in Pitjantjatjara this relationship is coined as *malparara* 'with a colleague') – training her counterpart, tutoring her in working slowly, in allowing Nura to lead, in seeing the depth at which Nura could work and she could not – she burned with her own fierceness and determination to get the job done.[11] The job always involved some improvement in the lives of other *Aṉangu* and it was always important.

Did she live long enough and have sufficient health and vitality to reflect on all of her achievements? The simple answer is 'no'. For Nura, recording her story was greater than an autobiography and more a gift of wisdom for her descendants. Her 'work' life therefore sits outside of this genre. The compilers and publisher, however, were aware of the importance of Nura's professional life and of the audience who would want to know about her entire life. As the press release from publisher Magabala Books describes:

> Part biography, part customs manual and food guide, part traditional social history and women's customs and governance, *Ninu Grandmothers' Law* is a rare testament to one woman's advocacy for her family, people and culture. (Magabala Books, press release, *Ninu Grandmothers' Law*, 24 April 2018)

Nura speaks for herself, reflecting on her desire to be more productive:

> I have been thinking about the life I have lived. I have been a hard worker all my life, and I want to write more and still have more stories to tell. I want to write a midwife book. (Ward 2018: 135)

With better health and a longer life, Nura might well have been on her second book.

Nura's voice

Throughout the book Nura's presence is steady. Her repetitions and meanderings are reassuringly familiar. As is her railing about the things that troubled her:

> I feel so sorry for the children of today. They are so deprived compared to us … our lives and the lives of our children growing up have been impoverished and deprived. But if the younger generations can read about our earlier lives, perhaps it may help them to turn things around. That's the idea, anyway. (Ward 2018: xv)

We feel confident that the book is true to Nura's voice. The three compilers had sat with her for more than a decade. We knew her well: her kindnesses, her bubbling sense of humour, her family problems, her old mother, her interest in all kinds of people. We saw her pack her tucker box with vegetables for stir-fry, learn Shiatsu, keep her grandchildren close, and travel all over the place in her role as an NPY stateswoman. And, above all, treasure her family and tell stories.

---

11 *Malparara* 'with a *malpa*' means two people – usually one of them *Aṉangu* – collaborating and working together in partnership and mutual respect, recognising and valuing different skills and knowledge of each person.

Early drafts were laid out chronologically under topic headings not yet formed into chapters, such as 'Early Life' and 'Marriage Customs'. The seventh draft, submitted for consideration to Magabala Books in 2011, includes 71,000 words recorded by Nura, entirely transcribed and translated from Pitjantjatjara into English by Linda Rive. Magabala Books encouraged the compilers to edit the manuscript further in order to be considered for publication. Funds secured from the Australian Government's Your Community Heritage program (2011), in addition to support from Ara Irititja, enabled work to continue.

As the years passed and her health declined, so did her vocal abilities, but her storytelling remained passionate and filled with humour. By 2012, Nura was becoming increasingly unwell, and it reflected in her voice, yet she still recorded dozens of short stories, even from her hospital bed. Throughout all stages of her life her enunciation and diction were a joy for the transcriber and translator to work with. She was thoughtful in her delivery and skillful in making the point of her story clear. Knowing that her material was destined for Ara Irititja, she made sure she reiterated facts, especially names of people and their relationship to others. Anangu users of the archive will find Nura's body of work rewarding, as she has contributed greatly to Anangu genealogies and information about traditional lands.

With Nura the interview process was a simple matter. She gave herself with enthusiasm – her own fascination, enjoyment, or amusement for her subject immediate in her voice, her composure, and her focus. Her intention was to inform, to educate and to draw in the listener and future listeners.

As Linda said at the launch of *Ninu grandmothers' law*:

> Nura was incredibly strategic in writing her book because she had a big grand plan in her mind and she knew what she wanted. She always knew which stories she had told and which stories she still had to tell. We were always chasing her, sometimes she was in hospital and we would be running to the hospital to get stories. I remember once in the car park, with the wind blowing, and she was sitting in the car and the car needed to go and she still wanted to tell another story. She was always willing to tell more and more and more with all of our questions. But in the end it was her grand plan, her story and the stories she wanted to tell and it was always directed to her daughters, nieces, granddaughters and to the family. (L Rive, speech at the launch of *Ninu grandmothers' law*, 16 August 2018)

The compilers, too, were strategic as they followed certain threads and worked on edits. Unlike with Julia and Linda, Suzanne and Nura did not view Ara Irititja together, so topics for interview arose from their years of working together. At the Red House, Suzanne was intent on collecting Nura's stories, previously heard out bush, about healers and healing, using plants and animals. As a child, Nura fell ill several times and was close to death. Her accounts of these illnesses and her healing through traditional means within her family were especially powerful.

Our editing process further refined the voice and challenged or examined interpretations of Pitjantjatjara words or phrases that did not ring true. This process was rigorous and continued right through to the final wrangling of the captions for images included in the book. In assessment of the manuscript, the editor of Magabala Books commented:

Creating a written narrative from oral transcriptions is a complex task. Barring section repetitions that can be addressed, overall I think Mrs Ward and her team have come up with a balance that allows Mrs Ward's spoken voice to come through on the page. (Magabala Books, email to Julia Burke, 7 March 2012)

Family voices

While the book was taking shape, the compilers felt anxious that Nura's solitary voice might not reach her family. The younger generations of Nura's family are hardly in the text, only occasionally mentioned or referenced by her, except to say that the work was for them, for their children's children and for a long time to come. How would young people brought up on communities, in houses, who travelled in cars and went away to high school relate to this book? Would they value it? Make a connection to it as a powerful representation of Nura's life and times? Would they recognise the gift?

As compilers we took a decision to include more of the contemporary family, inviting more people to claim the book as their own. We had strictly adhered to an agreement that it was to be Nura's voice alone, and indeed she did not need help in filling her pages. However, with a Magabala Books' editor asking for a foreword and an afterword, there was an opportunity to include other family members.

Suzanne had tried some interviews with young family members and settled on Nura's niece Melissa Thompson, hoping to revisit a conversation held with Melissa at the Women's Law and Culture event at Kiwirrkurra. Melissa had performed alone, dancing as Nura had taught her. The experience had prompted deep and poignant feelings towards her Aunty Nura, who was no longer able to travel. Nura did not see Melissa's pride as, her body painted, she invoked *tjukurpa* 'the Dreaming ancestors'.

Melissa was shy to speak with a recorder visible. Nura gently urged and prompted, feeding her lines such as "I grew you up." Melissa progressed to remembering how Nura introduced her to women's Law through *inma* 'the sacred dance and song'. As they both revisited the *inma*, Nura sang the verse, adding in detail and context as Melissa recalled the occasion. Such was the rich and textured layering of conversation with Nura. This lively exchange between them was trimmed down to become the foreword. This means the book begins with the life experience of the younger generation and the flavour of Nura's influence. It profiles Melissa. Nura grew Melissa up in many essential ways. Melissa claims Nura and the book; in doing so she anchors all that follows. At the book's launch Melissa said:

I'm Nura's niece, Nura's brother's daughter. I'm so happy, so happy for the book ... I know, when I grew up she used to teach me and I've written it in the book, all my stories are in the book, I'm on the front page. (M Thompson, speech at the launch of *Ninu grandmothers' law*, 16 August 2018)

Later, discussing how the book made her feel, she said:

Thank you for the book. It connects me to my land, my spirit and my *walytjapiti* 'relations'. Because of my ancestors I've got knowledge and it makes me strong. I feel sad for my country today when I see the olden days' pictures. (M Thompson, pers. comm. to Julia Burke, 18 November 2018)

At the other end of the book, Nura's daughter Anne steps in for the afterword. She spoke of sitting down at the family's homeland as a source of strength, how eating from the land brings her back to what is true for her and what has always been true. In her speech at the launch of *Ninu grandmothers' law* Anne said:

I'm the daughter and I'm thanking everyone. My mother made this *tjukurpa* 'story' and it has something to teach all of us, and we pass it on to our children, the young ones. (A Ward, speech at the launch of *Ninu grandmothers' law*, 16 August 2018)

Feedback

With no funds to launch *Ninu grandmothers' law* officially or to bring the family to the launch in Alice Springs from the APY Lands, Adelaide and Port Pirie, we asked friends and supporters of Nura's to contribute. They did this with great generosity, which was an expression of their esteem for Nura and their belief in her book. For the family the launch was a reunion that lasted a few happy days. They watched people arriving and greeted old friends, and they saw the book selling. We all signed each other's books to remember the day. Nura would have been utterly delighted and busy signing her name.

Nura's relative Donald Fraser told Suzanne proudly, "We have the book at home" (pers. comm. 17 August 2018). This is a new phenomenon. Few *Anangu* families have books in their homes, with bibles and hymn books as the exception. There have been very few books like *Ninu grandmothers' law* produced in the Pitjantjatjara Yankunytjatjara Ngaanyatjarra language domain, apart from autobiographies by Yami Lester (Lester 2000) and Lizzie Ellis (Ellis 2016) among a few others.

Andrea Mason, CEO of NPY Women's Council, spoke at the launch of *Ninu grandmothers' law*. She described Nura's book as not only a life story but also a manual for leaders, both *Anangu* and non-Aboriginal people (A Mason, speech to launch *Ninu grandmothers' law*, 16 August 2018). A teacher from the APY Lands described *Ninu grandmothers' law* as a guide for teachers to deliver 'more culturally responsive' programming:

So, for instance, I was introduced to the concept of *alpiri* 'broadcast speech style' in the book.[12] I hadn't come across that before. If *Anangu* are saying they want their children to be strong in both worlds and they need to be strong in culture, then perhaps concepts like that we could be teaching them again. And perhaps with the PA system in the morning, something as simple as getting an *Anangu* person to speak on it to tell the kids what's happening during the day. (J Norton, pers. comm. to Suzanne Bryce, 18 September 2018)

---

12 *Alpiri* was a feature of daily life, an early morning briefing on the movement and hunting strategies for the day.

The compilers have taken *Ninu grandmothers' law* on many bush trips to share with *Aṉangu*, handing it around and sitting back to watch as people view it: they peruse it slowly, going from image to image. The photographs tell part of everyone's story, right across the APY Lands. People look carefully, they study the page, they name the 'early days people' and discuss the family connections, the place and the activity, the foods, birds, or plants. There is much touching and pointing and remembering. The adults viewing the book remember walking as children on journeys just like those Nura and her family undertook, some even remembering particular journeys they shared with Nura, their families travelling together. *Aṉangu* readers search the photos for the story that they tell about their own families, whereas non-Aboriginal readers follow the details of Nura's stories in a search for knowledge about an era that is little documented in the public realm.

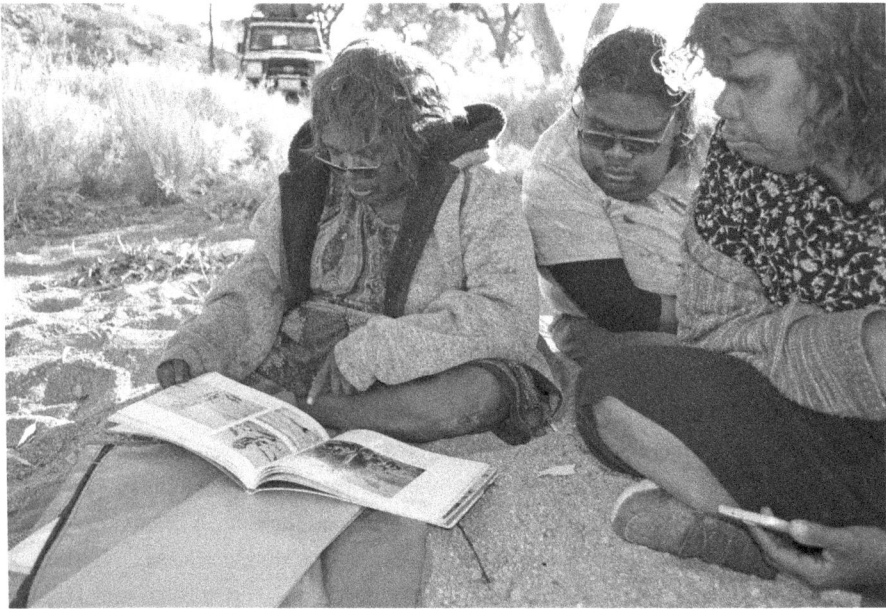

Figure 7. *Aṉangu* look at *Ninu grandmothers' law* (photo: Suzanne Bryce / Suzanne Bryce Collection)

Future makers

Just a generation before Nura's, a wise Pitjantjatjara woman, Nganyinytja (OAM), spoke of her country with its intersecting *tjukurpa* 'Dreaming' lines and sacred places as being "like an open book" (James & Tregenza 2014: 17). For many years she practised cultural tourism to teach people to "read her book." All her family became involved in the hosting and teaching process and by this means she hoped to preserve and pass on her knowledge to them. However, in Nura's lifetime *Aṉangu* moved from an oral culture to one that embraces digital technologies, the preservation of images and the production of books. Nura was a forerunner in this process.

Aṟa Irititja preserves knowledge about the past. It is a vault held safe against future loss, the death of elders and cultural shifts. It may also influence storytelling in the future. We have seen that *Ninu grandmothers' law* provides a new means of making archival returns, putting generations of stories into the hands of the children of the future. Nura's vision and voice have created a precedent for change. Many *Aṉangu* now say with great enthusiasm that they want to tell their story "just like Nura" and, like Nura, they have a strong belief in the intrinsic value of their lives. A young woman flipping through *Ninu* said she wanted to do her story and patted the pocket where she carries her hard drive. She said with a grin, "I have all the photos already" (K Connelly, pers. comm. to S Bryce, 28 October 2018).

Sources

Aṟa Irititja Aṉangu Community Archive

References

Burke, Julia. 2013. https://www.irititja.com/challenges/volunteers.html/ (Accessed 19 October 2019.)

Dallwitz, John, Janet Inyika, Susan Lowish & Linda Rive. 2017. Our art, our way: Towards an Aṉangu art history with Aṟa Irititja. In Darren Jorgensen & Ian McLean (eds.), *Indigenous archives: The making and unmaking of Aboriginal Art*, 250–268. Perth: UWA Publishing.

Eickelkamp, Ute. 2008. 'I don't talk story like that': On the social meaning of children's sand stories at Ernabella. In Jane Simpson & Gillian Wigglesworth (eds.), *Children's language and multilingualism: Indigenous language use at home and school*, 79–99. London: Continuum International.

Ellis, Elizabeth Marrkilyi. 2016. *Pictures from my memory: My story as a Ngaatjatjarra woman.* Canberra: Aboriginal Studies Press.

Green, Jennifer. 2014. *Drawn from the ground: Sound, sign and inscription in Central Australian sand stories.* (Language Culture and Cognition). Cambridge: Cambridge University Press.

James, Diana & Elizabeth Tregenza. 2014. *Ngintaka.* Adelaide: Wakefield Press.

Lester, Yami. 2000. *Yami.* Alice Springs: Institute for Aboriginal Development Press.

Mountford, Charles. 1976. *Nomads of the Australian desert.* Adelaide: Rigby.

Scales, Sally Anga, Julia Burke, John Dallwitz, Susan Lowish & Douglas Mann. 2013. The Aṟa Irititja project: Past, present, future. In Lyndon Ormond-Parker, Aaron Corn, Kazuko Obata & Sandy O'Sullivan (eds.), *Information technology and Indigenous communities*, 151–170. Canberra: AIATSIS Research Publications.

Toyne, Phillip & Daniel Vachon. 1984. *Growing up the country.* Melbourne: McPhee Gribble/ Penguin.

Ward, Nura. 2018. *Ninu grandmothers' law.* Broome, WA: Magabala Books.

Ward, Nura. 2006. *Kupi Kupi* 'Whirlwind'. Unpublished.

15

Language Documentation & Conservation Special Publication No. 18
Archival returns: Central Australia and beyond
ed. by Linda Barwick, Jennifer Green & Petronella Vaarzon-Morel, pp. 303–323
http://nflrc.hawaii.edu/ldc/spl18
http://hdl.handle.net/10125/24889

i-*Tjuma*: The journey of a collection – from documentation to delivery

Elizabeth Marrkilyi Ellis
Australian National University

Jennifer Green
The University of Melbourne, ARC Centre of Excellence for the Dynamics of Language

Inge Kral
Australian National University

Abstract

In 2018, a collection of some 60 edited and subtitled films, resulting from a documentation project (2012–2018) in the Ngaanyatjarra Lands on verbal arts of the Western Desert, was ready to be returned to the Ngaanyatjarra community. In this case study, we describe the journey of this return and the cultural, ethical, and technological issues that we negotiated in the process. From the archived collection lodged with PARADISEC (Pacific and Regional Archive for Digital Sources in Endangered Cultures), we developed a workflow that harvested selected media and their associated metadata and transferred them to LibraryBox, a portable digital file distribution tool designed to enable local delivery of media via the LibraryBox wi-fi hotspot. We detail here the return of the curated collection in a series of community film festivals in the Ngaanyatjarra communities and via the delivery of media from LibraryBox to individual mobile phones. We also discuss the return of a digital collection of historical photographs of Ngaanyatjarra people and strategies to re-inscribe such old records for new purposes. These endeavours are motivated by the imperative to 'mobilise' our collection of Western Desert Verbal Arts by making the recordings available to the Ngaanyatjarra community. We anticipate that the lessons we learnt in the process will contribute to better design for local solutions in the iterative cycle of documentation, archiving, and return.

Keywords: archiving, verbal arts, Ngaanyatjarra language, endangered languages, archival access, Indigenous Australia

Introduction[1]

This chapter is in part an exploration of a collaborative journey, from documentation to delivery, of the Western Desert Verbal Arts (WDVA) audiovisual collection in the Ngaanyatjarra Lands region of Western Australia. At the same time, it is a critical reflection on the 'practice' (Bell et al. 2013) of obtaining and disseminating digital collections, the practice of digital returns, and our own practices as researchers. As anthropologist Fred Myers discussed in his deliberations on the complex issue of returning archival film to a Pintupi community (Myers 2017), we wanted to 'mobilise' our collection of Western Desert Verbal Arts by making the recordings available to the Ngaanyatjarra. The journey was premised on a desire to "engage ethically and properly with people" (Myers 2017: 186) in the process of returning digital material derived from linguistic, ethnographic, and anthropological research (see also Haviland 2016). We also aimed to explore ways of "moving forward with people in tandem with their desires and aspirations" rather than simply "looking back over times past" (Ingold & Gatt 2013: 141). Our interpretation of this challenge was to find a way for Ngaanyatjarra people to gain sustainable access to the films made in the WDVA project, preferably in their homelands. To this end we pursued a number of strategies. In the short term we held a community film festival in October 2018 in the Ngaanyatjarra Lands, targeted primarily for a Ngaanyatjarra audience, and we distributed the films on USB bracelets. These were branded with the term 'i-*Tjuma*' (Figure 4). The Ngaanyatjarra word '*tjuma*' means 'story, narrative', and in this context the 'i' signifies the migration of these traditional storytelling practices into the digital domain via our experiment with their narration on iPads. As part of what we hoped would be a long-term solution, we tested the delivery of media via the LibraryBox data dissemination device, which we envisaged being housed in appropriate community facilities. Coupled with this, we were mindful of our obligation to archive this valuable collection *tjitji marlangkatja marlangkatja pirniku* 'for future generations' and for future research pursuits.

A further element in the journey involved consulting with Ngaanyatjarra people regarding a collection of historical photographs to seek consents for these images to be included in a forthcoming publication about changing communication and social interaction in the Western Desert (Kral & Ellis forthcoming). This photographic collection was variously sourced from institutional archives (the Australian Institute of Aboriginal and Torres Strait Islander Studies, the Berndt Museum, the State Library of Western Australia and the South Australian Museum), as well as community access platforms such as Ara Irititja, a digital archive and

1   Firstly we thank all those in the Ngaanyatjarra community who participated in this research over many years. We thank Julia Miller, Nick Thieberger, and Marco LaRosa, who assisted with the workflow from PARADISEC to LibraryBox, Claudia Rowe, and Bergen O'Brien who helped with film editing, Gary Proctor from Warburton Arts Project, and Franco Saliba, Warakurna Community youth worker who assisted with the film screenings, and Christine Bruderlin who assisted with the design and production of the small 2018 limited edition book and postcards. Ellis has been supported by an ELDP (Endangered Languages Documentation Programme) (SG0187) and an ARC (Australian Research Council) Discovery Indigenous Award (IN150100018); Green by ARC Fellowships (DP110102767, DE160100873); and Kral by an ARC DECRA Award (DE120100720). We thank Jane Simpson, Co-CI (IN150100018) and the ARC Centre of Excellence for the Dynamics of Language (CE140100041). We also thank two anonymous reviewers for their constructive feedback on an earlier version of this chapter.

social history project of the Pitjantjatjara Council, and Tjumalampatju, the digital archive of the Ngaanyatjarra Council.[2] We wanted to return these legacy materials to family members and the community, but also to enrich the archival collections by amassing 'genealogical fragments' (Haviland 2016) and adding new dimensions to the metadata for the images. We anticipated that the lessons learnt in the process of 're-animating' these precious collections (Anderson 2018) would inform our current and ongoing practice and give us a much-needed diachronic perspective on the many complex issues involved in the iterative cycle of documentation, archiving, and return. Not the least of these challenges is the dynamic nature of cultural practices, what Myers has termed "circumstances of cultural flow" (Myers 2017: 187), and the difficulty of envisaging future uses of materials enabled by developments in technology that we are yet to imagine. In this respect, this analysis is an attempt to envisage, with the benefit of hindsight, what the future might hold in terms of attitudes to archiving, and digital possibilities.

The WDVA project fieldwork 'team' consists of an Indigenous researcher (Ngaatjatjarra linguist Elizabeth Marrkilyi Ellis), who is also a Ngaanyatjarra Lands community member, and two non-Indigenous researchers (Green and Kral). Between us we have many decades of shared history, forged since the late 1970s in intercultural projects including language documentation, interpreting, translating, and teaching. Ellis facilitated our collecting processes and gave the non-Indigenous team an intimate proximity to the community. Nevertheless, the multiple layering of interactions with historical and contemporary images of Ngaanyatjarra people brought to the surface myriad complexities and dilemmas associated with consent, copyright, ownership, and ultimately Ngaanyatjarra peoples' relationships with photographic and filmed images of themselves.

Our desire to enable Ngaanyatjarra community control over the direction and dissemination of Ngaanyatjarra cultural collections was set against the emerging contradictory reality of the digital world. As Christen outlines:

> The digital terrain poses both possibilities and problems for indigenous peoples as they seek to manage, revive, circulate, and create new cultural heritage within overlapping colonial/postcolonial histories and oftentimes binary public debates about access in a digital age. (Christen 2011: 185)

It is widely recognised that digital technologies allow for new ways of knowing about cultural heritage, offering opportunities for education, regeneration, and community empowerment (see Were 2014: 133). In Australia, so Barwick and Thieberger state:

> ... the importance of providing Indigenous cultural heritage stakeholders with access to the research and documents that record their cultural heritage is widely acknowledged and features prominently in the policies and programs of numerous collecting and educational

---

2   Tjumalampatju (Our Stories): https://tj.keepingculture.com/welcome; Aṟa Irititja (Stories from the Past): https://www.irititja.com/. Both archives return materials of cultural and historical significance to Aboriginal people by way of the interactive multimedia software known as the Aṟa Irititja Knowledge Management System.

institutions, as well as in the research aims and methods of researchers. (Barwick & Thieberger 2005: 133)

These factors notwithstanding, the digital world has also unleashed an expectation that digital items will be easy to download and circulate widely, and this is often at odds with the parameters determined at the outset of language documentation projects in remote Indigenous communities. This alerts us to what Myers describes as the potentially fraught environment of "shifting protocols and introduced media forms" (Myers 2017: 172).

The Ngaanyatjarra Lands

The Ngaanyatjarra Lands lie within the Western Desert, fanning out into Western Australia from the tri-state border with South Australia and the Northern Territory (see Figure 1). Approximately 2000 people live in the Ngaanyatjarra Lands communities. Residents are predominantly Ngaanyatjarra speakers, but the speech community also comprises speakers of other mutually intelligible Western Desert languages (including Ngaatjatjarra and Pitjantjatjara). English is also widely spoken (Kral 2012). The 'Lands' population includes descendants of the last nomadic groups of the Western Desert (the first wave came into Warburton Ranges Mission in the 1930s, and the last in the 1960s). As a group, the Ngaanyatjarra have never left their traditional lands, nor has this region been annexed or occupied by outsiders (Brooks 2002, 2011).

Figure 1. Map showing Western Desert languages and some of the communities where they are spoken (map: Jennifer Green)

Early Ngaanyatjarra encounters with photographic images

Our audiovisual documentation of verbal arts in the Western Desert is located within a trajectory of developments in photographic and film recording technologies, altered sensibilities in regard to research and archiving practices, and changing community attitudes to recordings, to images of the 'self', and to archived heritage collections. In order to place the WDVA collection in an historical context, we firstly give a brief outline of the relatively recent dynamic, yet at times fraught, encounter with photographic images and film in the Ngaanyatjarra region.[3]

In the initial encounters with cameras in the mission era, Ngaanyatjarra agency was all but negated, images were seldom returned to Ngaanyatjarra people, and the camera remained in the hands of the outsider, whether missionary or anthropologist (McGrath 2010). Additionally, many of the early images were circulated entirely independently of their Aboriginal subjects and had the effect of projecting a certain view of desert society to the outside world, one predominantly controlled by Anglo-Australians.

Cameras were among the first objects the missionaries brought with them after the United Aborigines Mission (UAM) established a permanent settlement in the Warburton Ranges in 1934. From the 1950s onwards audio recording for Bible translation work also became commonplace (Glass 2019). Anthropologist Pamela McGrath suggests that the images taken reveal an intimacy in the nature of the relationship between the missionaries and the Aboriginal people who were in the vicinity of the mission (McGrath 2010: 91).[4] Nevertheless, the content of the images was determined by the missionaries and often used as propaganda in publications, such as the UAM newsletter the *United Aborigines Messenger*, to illuminate the transformative goal of the mission's evangelising endeavour.

In 1935, anthropologist Norman Tindale and his team from the Board for Anthropological Research at the University of Adelaide (Tindale 1936), including photographer Cecil John Hackett (Jones 2011: 100), cinematographer EO Stocker and anthropologist CP Mountford (Mountford 1938, 1939), set up a camp in the Warburton Ranges.[5] For the Ngaanyatjarra this was the first time that they were the subject of long-term ethnographic investigation by outsiders, and "the first time film recordings were taken of their lives" (McGrath 2010: 80; see also McGrath 2015), although at times the cameras did not work, and some early recordings were ruined (Mountford 1976: 63).

In 1953, William Grayden made a journey from Perth to the Rawlinson Range via Warburton Ranges Mission and recorded some of the earliest images of families living around the Rawlinson Range, near what is now the Warakurna Community. In Grayden's later account (Grayden 2002) are numerous images of Rawlinson Range people, mostly unnamed. Grayden returned to the region in the late 1950s, this time as a member of a West Australian Government Select Committee inquiring into perceived bureaucratic neglect of Aboriginal people. In time, his film and photographic images became embroiled in the 'Warburton Range controversy' – a

---

3   For Australia-wide perspectives on Indigenous encounters with photographic images see Lydon (2014).

4   Collections include photographs taken by Harrie and Marion Green in the 1930s–1950s and held at the South Australian Museum, Adelaide and at the State Library of Western Australia, Perth. Also included are photographs taken by Dawn and Toby Metcalfe held at Aṟa Irititja and the Berndt Museum.

5   Images from this expedition are archived at the South Australian Museum.

fierce national public debate about the health and welfare of desert Aboriginal people. The debate pivoted around the recruitment of images of people in situations of physical distress to illustrate arguments about political neglect and it sparked accusations of propaganda and also disagreement about the norms of Aboriginal wellbeing. Significantly no Ngaanyatjarra people are named in the film, *Their Darkest Hour*, nor in Grayden's ensuing account (Grayden 1957) and no biographical details are included (McGrath & Brooks 2010).[6] Moreover, the perspectives and voices of the Aboriginal people who appear in these images are noticeably absent. The images were not seen in the Ngaanyatjarra Lands until some 50 years later when McGrath embarked on a 're-documentation' project in 2008 and 2009 (McGrath 2010). In another event, a decade after Grayden's encounter, anthropologist Richard Gould and his wife Betty visited Warburton Ranges Mission. Image-making was also central to their ethnographic pursuits. Gould's publication (Gould 1969) of a number of images of men's ceremonies caused a furore in the community. This led to the Ngaanyatjarra community resisting the presence of researchers over subsequent decades.

In retrospect, some Ngaanyatjarra have described how unnerved they were by these early photographic encounters. Belle Davidson (b. 1944), a Pitjantjatjara media worker at Ngaanyatjarra Media, stated in 2013:

> People taking a picture with a camera, that first picture. And we always frightened for that camera. We don't want to be in the camera early days. Nervous I think. Don't like looking at it, it was a strange one. *Ngurrpangkatja*. Don't know nothing.[7]

A shift towards a more collaborative and sympathetic approach to image-making took place in the late 1960s when Ian Dunlop and the Commonwealth Film Unit recorded the 'People of the Western Desert' film series in the vicinity of what is now the community of Patjarr with families who had only recently come out of the desert. Dunlop was to capture some of the last images of desert living (Brooks 2012).[8] His documentation marked a shift in attitude – most noticeably the 'subjects' are all named. Ultimately we need to appreciate the fact that early ethnographers were people of their time. While some of their actions and the mistakes they made would be unthinkable today, the role and power of the ethnographer-photographer, their relationships with Indigenous 'others' and the role of images at large have changed over time.[9]

It was not until the 1970s, with the advent of Indigenous community-controlled media organisations and cheaper cameras, that cameras became more readily available for people in remote Australia. This was a turning point where Indigenous people in remote locations

---

6   William Grayden's film, *Their darkest hour*, sometimes referred to as Manslaughter, was shown at public meetings in churches, town halls and activist conferences across the nation for years afterwards (McGrath & Brooks 2010: 116).

7   WDVA project file name: DECRA20130702_BD_BLK_02.

8   Between 1965 and 1967 Ian Dunlop of the Commonwealth Film Unit undertook several months of filming in the Western Desert and produced 'People of the Western Desert' (Parts 1–10 and Parts 11–19). See Brooks (2012); Deveson & Dunlop (2012); Myers (2017); Turner (2018).

9   This is not to claim, however, that the current benefit of hindsight will futureproof current ethnographers from critiques some time down the track.

shifted from being "the object of other people's image-making practices" (Ginsburg 2008: 139) to controlling new forms of media cultural production.[10] In 1992, Irrunytju Media (now Ngaanyatjarra Media) was established in the Ngaanyatjarra Lands and has since been responsible for promoting language, culture, music, and stories through analogue (and now digital) media production and broadcasting. It is only since the arrival of digital photography and mobile phones in the 2000s, which did away with the time-consuming and expensive film development process, that Aboriginal people in the Western Desert have started to gain control over capturing and disseminating photographic images for their own sociocultural purposes (as seen most notably on Facebook). Anthropologists Daniel Miller and Heather Horst suggest that world-wide the most astonishing aspect of the digital technologies is not the speed of technological innovation, but rather "the speed by which society takes all of these for granted and creates normative conditions for their use" (Miller & Horst 2012: 28).

The rapid take-up of digital technologies and practices in the Ngaanyatjarra Lands is nothing short of breathtaking. It has taken place in a context where photography only recently enabled a form of cultural remembering that was previously unknown. Prior to this, when an individual had passed away personal items belonging to them would be burned because it was considered that a person's *kuurti* 'spirit' still remained in the objects. Until recently images and sound recordings of the deceased were destroyed, printed images were covered over and the term *kunmanarra* was temporarily used as a substitute personal name. These days, however, older people are confronted with the fact that younger people not only retain and display photographs of the recently deceased, but also post condolence messages accompanied by these images on Facebook. Such changes are challenging previous orthodoxies regarding images of the deceased, yet Western Desert people are accommodating these transformations as taken for granted practice.

With the passing of time, the existence of the images taken by outsiders has given Ngaanyatjarra people access to photographic records of family members who have since passed – a source of delight to most. Moves to repatriate the images have led to them being available to a local audience, often through local digital archives and art exhibitions. This is enabling the Ngaanyatjarra to re-engage with images of their forebears, often for the first time.

Revisiting the photographic archive

As mentioned above, many of the historical photographic and film collections have been archived in museums, national institutions such as AIATSIS, or local community access databases such as Aṟa Irititja and Tjumalampatju. The latter community access databases have for some time been repatriating historical images of Western Desert people and recording contemporary images for the future. As researchers, we negotiated access to relevant images and compiled a set of these that would eventually be included in the published volume on changing communication and social interaction in the Western Desert (Kral & Ellis forthcoming).

---

10 Internationally, by the 1960s, visual anthropologists (Worth & Adair 1972; Turner 1992) had begun to facilitate the provision of cameras for Indigenous peoples to record themselves. In remote Australia, this turn took place in the mid-1980s when film and analogue video production and broadcasting commenced at Yuendumu with the Warlpiri Media Association (Michaels 1986).

Prior to doing this we needed to gain consent from Ngaanyatjarra people for the inclusion of individual images and, in consultation with them, amass information regarding the content of the images, as best we could.

Led by Ellis, interactions with elders were facilitated in the Ngaanyatjarra language, either by viewing digital images on a large computer screen that we take with us on field trips for this purpose or in other cases on paper printouts. Photos from the early mission days were viewed by the very few elders who are able to attribute names to the faces from the past. With failing eyesight themselves, they peered and squinted at images from the 1930s, 40s, or 50s, often only able to approximate the identity of the unnamed people in the photos. At other times people like Norma Giles, whose own parents and siblings were the main subjects in a series of images Ian Dunlop took in the 1960s, could illuminate precise details and contribute anecdotal memories that were triggered in the process of viewing the images (Figure 2). McGrath (2010) also discusses how information recorded in these processes of 're-documentation' can "provide considerable insights into historical sociality and significance beyond the original moment in which the image was taken" (McGrath 2010: ix).

While for Ngaanyatjarra people these photographic images certainly provided a unique window into their past, our project was also concerned with enabling access to more recent recordings made as part of our Western Desert Verbal Arts project. The final phase of the WDVA project focused on how to best return this large corpus of audiovisual documentation of verbal arts to the Ngaanyatjarra community. It is to this process that we now turn.

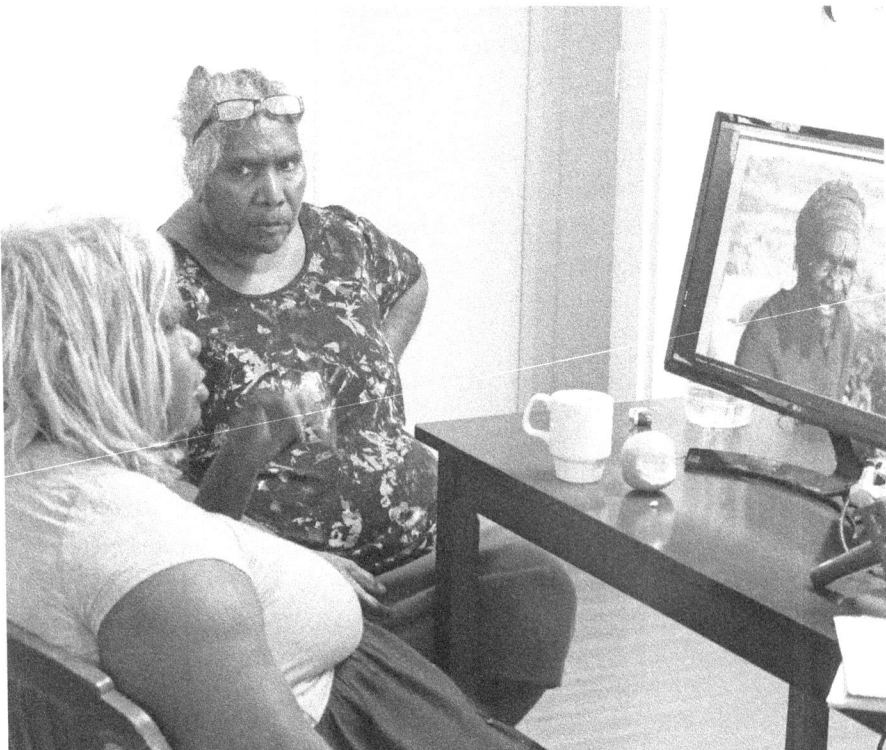

Figure 2. Norma Giles and Lizzie Ellis discuss an archival image from the Ian Dunlop Collection (AIATSIS: DUNLOP_113_CS-000137776) taken in 1965 (photo: Jennifer Green)

The Western Desert Verbal Arts collection: 2012–2018

Across the Western Desert, oral traditions are central to cultural practice and social interaction. The rich and diverse repertoires of the verbal arts are evident in stories, song, and dance, and embrace respectful ways of speaking, sign language, and the use of graphic symbols to accompany sand story narratives. These multimodal speech arts are a valued part of the traditions of Western Desert people, yet at the same time they are highly endangered.

Between 2012 and 2013 we began to document the verbal arts of the Western Desert, supported by an ELDP (Endangered Languages Documentation Programme) Small Grant (SG0187).[11] Recordings were made with 20 narrators spanning three generations. These included male and female storytellers telling *tjuma* (oral narratives linked to the *tjukurrpa* 'Dreaming', and personal narratives); and women and adolescent girls telling *mirlpa* (sand stories), along with five adolescent girls and young women who transferred this drawing practice to iPads.[12] Also included in the collection are recordings of children's songs and games (Ellis, Green & Kral 2017), and an additional collection of speech styles and respect registers. In recognition of the multimodal nature of these verbal art forms and communicative styles, the majority of the recordings were made with video. In many instances we used multiple cameras to capture different perspectives simultaneously. The success of this project led to Ellis being awarded an ARC Discovery Indigenous Fellowship (2015–2019) and as a team we continued our documentation of Western Desert Verbal Arts. In 2016, a further 23 iPad stories were recorded with 10 young women, as well as more children's songs and games.[13]

Returning the WDVA collection

The WDVA collection designated for return to the Ngaanyatjarra community in October 2018 included a collection of 60 edited films (with English subtitles, and oftentimes both English and Ngaanyatjarra) that were clearly in the public domain. Other films from the final set of 80 films were not distributed, as the storytellers had passed away – emphasising the importance of endangered language documentation work and the critical time frames that much of this work operates within. After consultation, these particular films were given to close family members. The journey to return the collection was not taken lightly and involved a significant amount of planning and coordination. The researchers travelled from Canberra and Melbourne and drove together many thousands of kilometres to the various communities in the Ngaanyatjarra Lands.

---

11 Preliminary documentation of respect registers was undertaken by Kral and Ellis 2010–2011 for a Language Recording and Archiving Project for Ngaanyatjarra Media supported by a Maintenance of Indigenous Languages and Recordings (MILR) Program grant.

12 Introducing new media to Indigenous artists in parts of remote Australia has precedents stretching back at least to the 1930s when anthropologists supplied people with pencils, crayons and paper and encouraged them to draw in order to get a perspective, through the lens of graphic media, on how Indigenous people 'viewed the world' (see Hinkson 2014: 30–35).

13 The full collection will be archived at AIATSIS at the conclusion of the project. The public collection will be available through ELAR (The Endangered Languages Archive), PARADISEC, Tjumalampatju, and Aṟa Irititja.

The i-*Tjuma* Film Festival

The public events for the i-*Tjuma* returns centred on two locations – the first the immaculately curated Tjulyuru Gallery space at Warburton, where the projected films vied for attention with an exhibition of some of the crown jewels of the unique collection of Ngaanyatjarra acrylic paintings, and the second at the Warakurna community hall (Figure 3), a large, airy space used for youth activities such as basketball and film nights. At Warakurna our attempts to screen the i-*Tjuma* collection were thwarted on the first night by a power outage. A group of senior women and a gang of children had already gathered outside the community hall as the late afternoon light faded. The youth worker, who was coordinating the event – setting up the screen and projector, laying out chairs and overseeing the sausage sizzle – informed us that the technician would have to travel from a community a few hundred kilometres away to fix the problem. Reluctantly we re-scheduled the event for the following evening. The next evening an enormous rain storm meant that it would be unwise to show the films, as few people would venture out in the downpour, and the rain on the iron roof of the hall would all but drown out the sound of the audiovisual recordings. Finally, on the third night, we showed the films to an audience of Ngaanyatjarra people, arts workers, and school teachers.

On both film nights, we augmented the program of films with a short introductory talk about the verbal arts documentation project. We also distributed i-*Tjuma*–branded USB bracelets containing the 60 films for home viewing on TVs and play stations; a small book of two transcribed and translated iPad stories with embedded QR codes linked to the edited online films; and postcards depicting images from the iPad stories from each of the 10 younger storytellers (Figure 4). A barbecue meal after showing the film gave us time to demonstrate how to download films from LibraryBox onto individual mobile phones via wi-fi.

Figure 3. Film night in the Warakurna community hall, October 2018 (photo: Jennifer Green)

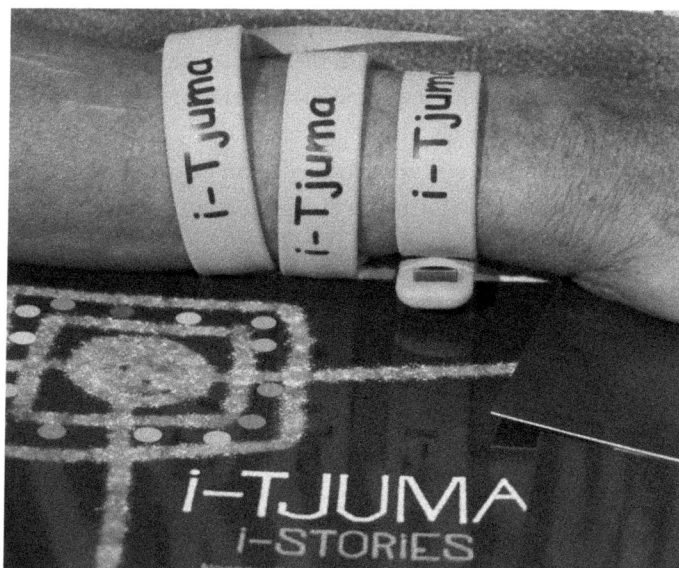

Figure 4. i-*Tjuma*–branded USB bracelets and the book of iPad stories with embedded QR codes linked to the edited online films (photo: Jennifer Green)

Responses to films

Responses to the films were positive. At Warburton one of the older women affirmed that it was "all good, good to bring it back like this, bringing it back to the people that did it" and that she was "not worried" to see herself in the films. At Warakurna a younger woman said she liked the goanna hunting story the best because it was a story about older women hunting at Pangkupirri near Tjukurla Community.[14] She elaborated further, "My aunty taught me to hunt for goannas ... watching the film reminded me of my own goanna hunting experience with my aunties." Moreover, she noted that these films are important because future generations will see them and learn traditions like how to hunt for goannas.[15] These endorsements were reiterated by school staff:

> It had a lovely feeling that night and it really felt like people had ownership of the project and they were really proud of the stories and the filming ... Coming back to the community in an appropriate way ... Handing back to the people is so important ... (Deputy Principal, Warburton School, interview, 3 November 2018)

> To hear the story of the project resonated with me around protocols for language and the whole event highlighted cultural change and how people are dealing with that. Really interesting to see the generational change in the material and practices as well as the content and format of the stories. Revealing so much about what is important to people at that time. To me it is an important bank of material to have. (Principal, Warburton School, interview 3 November 2018)

---

14   WDVA project-Hunting story *Pangkupirri 1*. PARADISEC: WDVA1-MIR_02.

15   WDVA project-Interviews: Norma Giles-20181022 and Selina Shepherd-20181026.

These responses affirmed that the documentation project was of value to the community and that Ngaanyatjarra people and those who work with them could see the importance of this collection for future generations. The next step would have been simply to archive the collection either at AIATSIS or in a more locally accessible community access database (Aṟa Iṟititja or Tjumalampatju). Our aim, however, was to explore an interim step that would ensure that the collection was more directly placed in the hands of Ngaanyatjarra people.

Distribution and ownership

In a tangible sense, individual 'ownership' of the materials rested on the distribution of the 60 films on the USB bracelets, coupled with a small book of two of the iPad films and a set of colourful postcards, in tandem with the film festival. This solution, however, was a short-term one. We hoped that a more long-term solution for the ongoing delivery of the media would be via the LibraryBox data dissemination device. We envisaged this device being housed in an appropriate community access site. We teamed up with PARADISEC to trial the development of a model for repatriating audiovisual language recordings in endangered language communities via wi-fi.

The workflow – from documentation to LibraryBox

At the time LibraryBox was a commercially available 'digital distribution tool' – a combination of a router, a USB drive and open-source software that provided a small, low-powered webserver that is off-line and self-contained. The webserver acted like a captive portal and delivered files that were stored on the USB drive. To use LibraryBox, the user connected to the wi-fi and launched the browser on their mobile phone. Attempting to visit any webpage would push the user to the LibraryBox homepage on the device, thereby linking to the menu for viewing or downloads.[16]

The potential advantages of such devices are that they do not require an internet account or password, they enable users to bypass potentially complicated website interfaces, and downloading media from the device is free. This makes media available to users on their private mobile phones, in a context where access to computers is limited. A potential constraint, however, is the limited storage capacity of the mobile devices themselves. As mentioned earlier, we were confident that all the films destined for delivery via LibraryBox were in the public domain. The self-contained edited films included attributions to storytellers, filmmakers, editors and funding sources as well as links to archival reference numbers for the original media that is archived elsewhere.

Our workflow is illustrated in Figure 5. The edited films were transcribed in Ngaanyatjarra and translated into English using ELAN.[17] From ELAN an .srt file (a captioning file format) of the transcribed/translated text was exported and then imported into the FinalCut (FCPro) film

---

16   http://librarybox.us/whatis.php (Accessed 12 December 2018.) Note: The LibraryBox device is no longer available for purchase.

17   ELAN is one of a suite of tools that has been developed by The Language Archive at the Max Planck Institute for Psycholinguistics in Nijmegen, The Netherlands (Wittenburg et al. 2006).

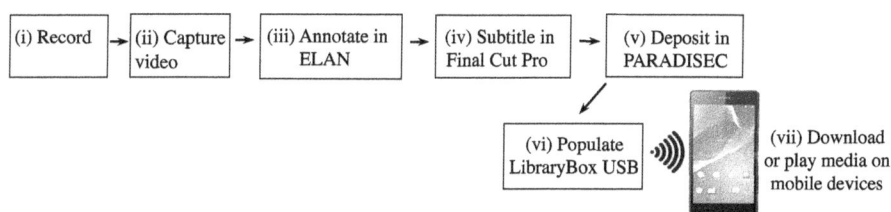

Figure 5. Workflow, from recording to delivery via LibraryBox to mobile devices

editing program to speed up the time-consuming process of subtitling each film. The media and metadata were then deposited in PARADISEC as part of a broader workflow of archiving the high-quality files in safe and secure repositories for the future.[18]

The existing architecture from PARADISEC was used to populate the LibraryBox USBs with our deposited collection of media. A file browser was generated in PARADISEC, based on the WDVA collection metadata in the PARADISEC catalogue.[19] File types/genres, such as sand stories or iPad stories, were grouped together and a link created for users to access media from the file browser. A customised interface was created that allowed organised viewing of the files based on the grouped file types from PARADISEC. In all there were 60 files in .mp4 format. The file sizes were initially too large for the capacity of the USBs so they were compressed to make easily streamable versions. This created a duplicate lower resolution set of the media collection. Once the USB was populated and plugged into the LibraryBox, an offline url was activated. After connecting to the wi-fi 'PARADISEC Catalog' the user would be nudged toward the offline url: catalog.paradisec.offline/static (Figure 6). Films could then be played or downloaded. Although the off-line delivery can be accessed by both Apple and Android devices, we found that downloading the media only worked on Android phones. In the circumstances, this was not a problem, as the overwhelming preference in communities where we work appears to be for Android phones (Carew et al. 2015: 310).

We had high expectations of LibraryBox as a file-sharing device. Its implementation promised to go at least some way toward addressing the problem of how to repatriate a curated set of audiovisual language recordings to the community via wi-fi. However, after purchasing two LibraryBox devices we found that one was defective. When we tried to have it replaced we discovered that LibraryBox devices were no longer available, in itself a lesson in just how short the shelf life of some technical solutions can be. Undeterred, we continued with the trial of the device, in the hope of being able to provide some practical advice for the development and implementation of similar devices in the future.

When we demonstrated the LibraryBox device to Ngaanyatjarra people during our travelling film festival there was initial interest, but this soon led to frustration. What we discovered was that a number of improvements could be made to the delivery of media via devices of this type. In many respects, the PARADISEC architecture was too structured and rigid for our needs. For instance, the file names needed to tally with the PARADISEC standardised format for file names (for example, WDVA1-TJU_01.mp4). Three-part file names are

---

18   http://www.paradisec.org.au (Accessed 19 December 2018.)

19   The collection can be found at PARADISEC under WDVA1 – Western Desert Verbal Arts Project Collection: http://catalog.paradisec.org.au/collections/WDVA1

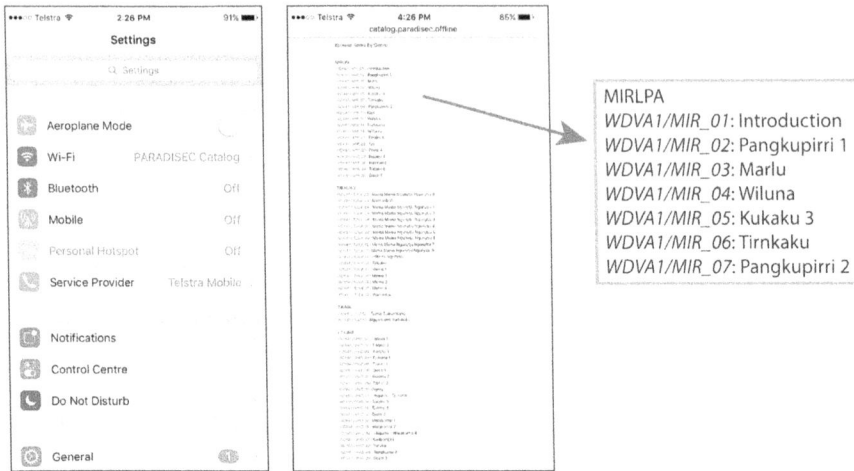

Figure 6. Screenshots showing the 'PARADISEC Catalog' interface and menu on a mobile phone

a PARADISEC requirement, and when combined with our own film titles this rendered overly long file names in the touch screen menu list (Figure 6). The resulting interface was unwieldy, counterintuitive, and not optimal for a stand-alone community delivery device. It required significant literacy skills on the part of the user in order to navigate to target items for download. Given the low-level literacy context, an icon-based interface would be more appropriate, especially when considering the small size of the touch screen buttons on many mobile phone screens. The capacity to browse content by genre would also greatly improve functionality. In addition, we had not anticipated other technological difficulties arising from a context where the models and types of phones most in use were in various states of degradation (with broken screens, insufficient memory, poor volume, etc.). Ultimately, we only succeeded in fully downloading media from our LibraryBox to one iPad mini owned by a community member at the Warakurna film showing.

The LibraryBox was later placed in the art centre at Warakurna, where we did eventually connect the device to several mobile phones. We had hoped that this would generate further interest. We concluded, however, that the LibraryBox device, populated via PARADISEC, was not the best pathway for a stand-alone community repatriation system. This was partly because of constraints in the creation of the interface via PARADISEC. This pathway may work well where heritage materials stored on the device are delivered back to individuals by a researcher who then oversees the wi-fi delivery. However, for stand-alone devices for use in non/semi-literate communities a different approach is needed. It may be that further developments by the PARADISEC team using 'Raspberry Pi' will build on what has been learnt in this trial.[20] After archiving, a less sophisticated repatriation approach may bypass PARADISEC, entailing a simplified workflow from the wi-fi device to mobile phones in tandem with the development of an accessible icon-based interface. A local hard drive repository of the lower-quality .mp4 files could also be left as a backup in the event of the device failing.

---

20   See http://www.language-archives.services/about/pi (Accessed 23 January 2019.)

Figure 7. Inge Kral and Phillipa Butler experiment with downloading media from the LibraryBox device to a mobile phone, Warburton, October 2018 (photo: Jennifer Green)

This trial reveals much about the volatility of digital technologies and reminds us of the necessity to ensure that high-quality, secure archiving processes are prioritised. This is particularly the case in situations where local archiving solutions are not sufficient, as technologies rapidly become redundant, hard drives fail, and access to and oversight of collections housed in community facilities can be sporadic.

Layered consent

Another issue that has become apparent in our ongoing engagement with the WDVA collection and with its communities of origin is what we term the problem of 'layered consent'. Easy access to media that is enabled by digital technologies is often at odds with the parameters determined in the initial negotiations about consent for uses of research materials derived from language documentation projects in remote Indigenous communities. Roughly speaking, the longer the time frame in the cycle of documentation, archiving, and return, the more acute the problem. In the case study presented here, wide circulation of the WDVA project films led to new opportunities as well as new dilemmas. The popularity of the films following the public display of these aesthetically engaging audiovisual materials catalysed requests for the films to be broadcast on Indigenous Community Television (ICTV), published in a collected volume of iPad stories (Ellis, Green & Kral forthcoming), and potentially displayed in the new Western Australian Museum.[21] While the narrators and authors of these materials were overwhelmingly positive about these new possibilities for their voices and visual artworks to reach wider audiences, such uses of the materials had not been foreseen in the original consent

---

21   Several of these films can be seen by accessing the Ngaanyatjarra portal through the ICTV language website (https://ictv.com.au/languages) (Accessed 25 January 2019.)

form that was signed as a necessary component in the process of ethical research. This meant more work for the research team, and a proliferation of layered consents that in the long term will always struggle to keep up with developments in technology, and with dynamic and changing community sensibilities and attitudes to recordings, to images of people, and to archived heritage collections. As recognised by others, the process of negotiating ongoing consent, or 're-consenting' research materials,[22] is both necessary and time-consuming (Janke & Iacovino 2012).[23] We also recognise the need to have processes that enable such updated and reinvigorated documents of consent to be fed back into the archives where the original media are lodged, so that the archives can in turn engage ethically and in an informed way with ongoing requests for the materials they safeguard. Clearly one critical issue outlined in such consent forms is the question of access. Our project also enabled us to confirm, in a safe environment, that the open access conditions originally placed on a selection of the WDVA films by the narrators held true when they actually saw the films (of themselves) on the big screen in a public location. However, the issue of future access to other types of materials, for example the special speech register recordings, is not so straightforward.

Conclusions

Developments towards participatory models for archiving attempt to break down traditional boundaries between depositors, users and archivists and expand the audiences and uses for archives. They try to address the significant problem of what Anderson has termed 'information colonialism' found not only in the legacies of past research practices, but also in the present day where, she suggests, the 'logics of extraction' still prevail (Anderson 2018).[24] One strategy may entail devolution away from the large archival institutions and the formation of smaller, locally based derivative archives. Such models may enable more direct interactions between archives and communities of origin. This reflects an increasing desire to empower communities and allow them a greater role in the direction and management of their cultural collections. As Christen (2011: 185) notes, "In the last twenty years, many collecting institutions have heeded the calls by indigenous activists to integrate indigenous models and knowledge into mainstream practices."

Nowadays there are various options to access materials online, and these bring great opportunities as well as new challenges. Across Australia the advent of digital technologies has introduced a capacity for the storage of memory evident in community cultural archives or content management systems such as Ara Irititja (Hughes & Dallwitz 2007; Thorner 2010), Our Story (Gibson 2009), Mukurtu (Christen 2008), and Storylines (Webb 2015), and, in the Ngaanyatjarra Lands, Tjumalampatju. The importance of involving speaker communities in archival processes has gained increasing recognition (Henke & Berez-Kroeker 2016: 428) and this heightened sensibility to 'do the right thing' (see Campbell 2014: 102) does seem to be trickling down, or up as the case may be, and informing the ethical processes of new generations of students, researchers, and all those engaged at the language documentation

---

22   Diana James pers. comm. to Jennifer Green, June 2019.

23   See also the National Statement on Ethical Conduct in Human Research (2007 [2018]: 17).

24   https://creativecommons.org/2019/01/30/jane-anderson/ (Accessed 21 May 2019.)

interface. Such endeavours are driven by "concerns for social responsibility and cultural equity, community demand and aspirations, efforts to apply research to the task of reviving and sustaining traditions, and safeguarding endangered intangible cultural heritages" (Treloyn & Emberly 2013: 160). In this intercultural domain, balances of power and agency are shifting, but these changes must also contend with the proliferation of digital materials that are being generated. As Christen continues:

> While digital technologies allow for items to be repatriated quickly, circulated widely, and annotated endlessly, these same technologies pose challenges to some indigenous communities who wish to add their expert voices to public collections and also maintain some traditional cultural protocols for the viewing, circulation, and reproduction of some materials. (Christen 2011: 185)

This study has demonstrated clearly that delivery solutions need to be tailored to the technological capacities of particular communities. We have shown how some interactions with digital objects have the potential to empower but just as well to frustrate. However, understanding the fine-grained detail of these interactions and the sources of frustration can assist with envisaging and designing better solutions. What is sorely lacking are metrics and methods to test the efficacy and sustainability of these solutions. In this context, we advocate for a multi-dimensional approach, making paper-based resources that can be held in the hand, distributed to various audiences in art galleries, schools and museums as well as creating modern digital objects that may be disseminated by mobile phones and other devices in ways that appeal and are accessible to a new tech-savvy generation. There are, however, many questions that we do not have answers for. We do not know what the impact of archived heritage materials is on the circulation of verbal arts as dynamic and socially embedded cultural practices, instantiated in the day-to-day interactions of those to whom these elements of intangible cultural heritage belong (see Ahearn 2017; Bialostocka 2017; Kral, Green & Ellis, 2019). Although safeguarding these verbal arts could arguably be perceived as an end in itself, the key to the vitality of these traditions lies in their transmission to future generations. Access to collections, beyond the time frame of research projects such as described in this chapter, is a key issue. We do not know how low-tech recordings made on mobile phones and shared on Facebook are being circulated within communities, and whether or not those who create these records see them as being on a par with high-end recordings of verbal arts practices made by funded research teams. Should such records be archived, or are they properly regarded as ephemera of living language in practice? What our project has provided, however, is a space for the "expert voices" of the Ngaanyatjarra to be heard, and for the sensibilities of changing cultural practices to be considered with respect and attention. What is needed are the means to ensure that this kind of long-term engagement between research teams and the communities they work with is neither a one-off, nor an exception to the rule.

References

Ahearn, Laura M. 2017 [2012]. *Living language: An introduction to linguistic anthropology.* 2nd edn. Chichester, West Sussex, England: Wiley Blackwell.

Anderson, Jane. 2018. Negotiating who 'owns' Penobscot culture. *Anthropological Quarterly* 91(1). 267–305. (https://doi.org/10.1353/anq.2018.0008)

Barwick, Linda & Nicholas Thieberger. 2005. Cybraries in paradise: New technologies and ethnographic repositories. In Cushla Kapitzke & Bertram C Bruce (eds.), *New libraries and knowledge spaces: Critical perspectives on information and education,* 133–149. Mahwah, NJ: Lawrence Erlbaum Associates.

Bell, Joshua A, Kimberly Christen & Mark Turin. 2013. Introduction: After the return. *Museum Anthropology Review* 7(1–2). 1–21.

Bialostocka, Olga. 2017. Inhabiting a language: Linguistic interactions as a living repository for intangible cultural heritage. *International Journal of Intangible Heritage* 12. 18–27.

Brooks, David. 2002. History of the Ngaanyatjarra lands. In Overview of Ngaanyatjarra people and culture: Cultural awareness course booklet. Unpublished manuscript, 2–11. Warburton, WA: Ngaanyatjarra Community College.

Brooks, David. 2011. Organization within disorder: The present and future of young people in the Ngaanyatjarra lands. In Ute Eickelkamp (ed.), *Growing up in Central Australia: New anthropological studies of Aboriginal childhood and adolescence,* 183–212. Oxford: Berghahn Books.

Brooks, David. 2012. Disruption vs continuity in the desert: The case of the respectful film-maker. Canberra: Unpublished manuscript, November 2012.

Campbell, Genevieve. 2014. Song as artefact: The reclaiming of song recordings empowering Indigenous stakeholders – and the recordings themselves. In Amanda Harris (ed.), *Circulating cultures: Exchanges of Australian Indigenous music, dance and media,* 101–127. Canberra: ANU Press.

Carew, Margaret, Jennifer Green, Inge Kral, Rachel Nordlinger & Ruth Singer. 2015. Getting in touch: Language and digital inclusion in Australian Indigenous communities. *Language Documentation & Conservation* 9. 307–323.

Christen, Kimberly. 2008. Archival challenges and digital solutions in Aboriginal Australia. *The SAA Archaeological Record* 8. 21–24.

Christen, Kimberly. 2011. Opening archives: Respectful repatriation. *American Archivist* 74(1). 185–210. (https://doi.org/10.17723/aarc.74.1.4233nv6nv6428521)

Deveson, Pip & Ian Dunlop. 2012. The ethnographic filmmaking of Ian Dunlop in a decade of change. *Humanities Research* 18(1). 2–36.

Ellis, Elizabeth Marrkilyi, Jennifer Green & Inge Kral. 2017. Family in mind: Socio-spatial knowledge in a Ngaatjatjarra/Ngaanyatjarra children's game. *Research on Children and Social Interaction* 1(2). 164–198. (https://doi.org/10.1558/rcsi.28442)

Ellis, Elizabeth Marrkilyi, Jennifer Green & Inge Kral (eds.) (forthcoming). *i-Tjuma i-Stories: Ngaanyatjarra 'iPad' stories from the Western Desert of Central Australia.* Perth: UWA Publishers.

Gibson, Jason. 2009. *Managing Indigenous digital data: An exploration of the Our Story database in Indigenous libraries and knowledge centres of the Northern Territory.* UTS ePress. (Retrieved from https://opus.lib.uts.edu.au/handle/10453/19485.)

Ginsburg, Fay. 2008. Rethinking the digital age. In Pamela Wilson & Michelle Stewart (eds.), *Global Indigenous media: Cultures, poetics and politics,* 287–305. Durham, NC and London: Duke University Press.

Gould, Richard A. 1969. *Yiwara: Foragers of the Australian desert.* New York: Charles Scribner's Sons.

Glass, Amee. 2019. *Taking the Word to the desert people.* Kangaroo Ground, Victoria: Wycliffe Australia.

Grayden, William L. 1957. *Adam and atoms: The story of the Warburton Aborigines.* Perth: Frank Daniels Pty Ltd.

Grayden, William L. 2002. *A nomad was our guide: The story through the land of the Wongi – the Central Desert of Australia – 1953.* Perth: NH Holdings Publications.

Haviland, John B. 2016. Making *gambarr*: It belongs to me, I belong to it. In Jean-Christophe Verstraete & Diane Hafner (eds.), *Land and language in Cape York Peninsula and the Gulf Country,* 455–480. Amsterdam and Philadelphia: John Benjamins. (https://doi.org/10.1075/clu.18)

Henke, Ryan & Andrea L Berez-Kroeker. 2016. A brief history of archiving in language documentation, with an annotated bibliography. In Michael Alvarez Shepard, Gary Holton & Ryan Henke (eds.), *Language Documentation & Conservation* 10. 411–457. (Retrieved from https://scholarspace.manoa.hawaii.edu/handle/10125/24714.)

Hinkson, Melinda. 2014. *Remembering the future: Warlpiri life through the prism of drawing.* Canberra: Aboriginal Studies Press.

Hughes, Martin & John Dallwitz. 2007. Aṟa Irititja: Towards culturally appropriate IT best practice in remote Indigenous Australia. In Laurel E Dyson, Max Hendriks & Stephen Grant (eds.), *Information technologies and Indigenous people,* 146–158. London and Melbourne: Information Science Publishing.

Ingold, Tim & Caroline Gatt. 2013. From description to correspondence: Anthropology in real time. In Wendy Gunn, Ton Otto & Rachel C Smith (eds.), *Design anthropology: Theory and practice,* 139–158. London and New York: Bloomsbury.

Janke, Terri & Livia Iacovino. 2012. Keeping cultures alive: Archives and Indigenous cultural and intellectual property rights. *Archival Science* 12(2). 151–171. (https://doi.org/10.1007/s10502-011-9163-0)

Jones, Philip. 2011. *Images of the interior: Seven Central Australian photographers.* Adelaide: Wakefield Press and South Australian Museum.

Kral, Inge. 2012. *Talk, text & technology: Literacy and social practice in a remote Indigenous community.* Bristol, UK: Multilingual Matters.

Kral, Inge, Jennifer Green & Elizabeth Marrkilyi Ellis. 2019. Wangkarra: Verbal Arts of Australia's Western Desert. *International Journal of Intangible Heritage* 14. 33–47.

Kral, Inge & Elizabeth Marrkilyi Ellis. (forthcoming). *In the time of their lives: Wangka kutjupa-kutjuparringu: How talk has changed in the Western Desert.* Perth: UWA Publishers.

Lydon, Jane. 2014. *Calling the shots: Aboriginal photographies.* Canberra: Aboriginal Studies Press.

McGrath, Pamela F. 2010. Hard looking: A historical ethnography of photographic encounters with Aboriginal families in the Ngaanyatjarra lands, Western Australia, vol. 1. Unpublished PhD (Anthropology): The Australian National University.

McGrath, Pamela F. 2015. Three weeks with strangers: Photography and the production of social identity during the 1935 Board of Anthropological Research expedition to the Warburton Range, Western Australia. *The Australian Journal of Anthropology* 26. 74–93.

McGrath, Pamela F & David Brooks. 2010. Their darkest hour: The films and photographs of William Grayden and the history of the 'Warburton Ranges controversy' of 1957. *Aboriginal History* 34. 115–140.

Michaels, Eric. 1986. *The Aboriginal invention of television: Central Australia 1982–1986.* Canberra: AIAS.

Miller, Daniel & Heather A Horst. 2012. The digital and the human: A prospectus for digital anthropology. In Heather A Horst & Daniel Miller (eds.), *Digital anthropology*, 3–35. London and New York: Berg.

Mountford, Charles P. 1938. Gesture language of the Ngada tribe of the Warburton Ranges, Western Australia. *Oceania* 9(2). 152–155.

Mountford, Charles P. 1939. Aboriginal crayon drawings, Warburton Ranges, Western Australia. *Oceania* 10(1). 72–79.

Mountford, Charles P. 1976. *Nomads of the Australian desert.* Adelaide: Rigby Limited.

Myers, Fred R. 2017. Whose story is this? Complexities and complicities of using archival footage. In Jane Anderson & Haidy Geismar (eds.), *The Routledge companion to cultural property*, 168–193. Routledge Handbooks Online: Routledge. (https://doi.org/10.4324/9781315641034.ch9)

National Statement on Ethical Conduct in Human Research 2007 (Updated 2018). The National Health and Medical Research Council, the Australian Research Council and Universities Australia. Canberra: Commonwealth of Australia. https://www.nhmrc.gov.au/about-us/publications/australian-code-responsible-conduct-research-2018 (Accessed 19 October 2019.)

Thorner, Sabra. 2010. Imagining an Indigital interface: Aṟa Iritij̄a Indigenizes the technologies of knowledge management. *Collections: A Journal for Museum and Archives Professionals* 6(3). 125–146.

Tindale, Norman B. 1936. Legend of the wati kutjara, Warburton Range, Western Australia. *Oceania* 7(2). 481–485.

Treloyn, Sally & Andrea Emberly. 2013. Sustaining traditions: Ethnomusicological collections, access and sustainability in Australia. *Musicology Australia* 35(2). 159–177.

Turner, Jan. 2018. The view from below: A selected history of contact experiences, Patjarr, Gibson Desert, Western Australia. *Journal of the Anthropological Association of South Australia* 42. 13–47.

Turner, Terence. 1992. Defiant images: The Kayapo appropriation of video. *Anthropology Today* 8(6). 5–16.

Webb, Damien. 2015. Curating with community. Conference paper. Cape Town: IFLA
 WLIC 2015. (Retrieved from: http://library.ifla.org/1143/1/168-webb-en.pdf.) (Accessed
 19 October 2019.)

Were, Graeme. 2014. Digital heritage, knowledge networks, and source communities:
 Understanding digital objects in a Melanesian society. *Museum Anthropology* 37(2).
 133–143.

Wittenburg, Peter, Hennie Brugman, Albert Russel, Alex Klassmann & Han Sloetjes. 2006.
 Elan: A professional framework for multimodality research. In *Proceedings of LREC,
 Fifth International Conference on Language Resources and Evaluation* (vol. 2006).

Worth, Sol & John Adair. 1972. *Through Navajo eyes*. Bloomington: Indiana University Press.

16

Language Documentation & Conservation Special Publication No. 18
Archival returns: Central Australia and beyond
ed. by Linda Barwick, Jennifer Green & Petronella Vaarzon-Morel, pp. 325–338
http://nflrc.hawaii.edu/ldc/sp18
http://hdl.handle.net/10125/24890

Ever-widening circles: Consolidating and enhancing Wirlomin Noongar archival material in the community

Clint Bracknell
Edith Cowan University

Kim Scott
Curtin University

Abstract

Returning archival documentation of endangered Indigenous languages to their community of origin can provide empowering opportunities for Indigenous people to control, consolidate, enhance, and share their cultural heritage with ever-widening, concentric circles of people, while also allowing time and space for communities to recover from disempowerment and dislocation. This process aligns with an affirming narrative of Indigenous persistence that, despite the context of colonial dispossession, can lead to a positive, self-determined future. In 2007, senior Noongar of the Wirlomin clan in the south coast region of Western Australia initiated Wirlomin Noongar Language and Stories Inc., an organisation set up to facilitate cultural and linguistic revitalisation by combining community-held knowledge with documentation and recordings repatriated from the archives. Fieldnotes created in 1931 from discussions with local Aboriginal people at Albany, Western Australia have inspired the collaborative production of six illustrated bilingual books. Working with archival research material has presented challenges due to issues of orthography and legibility in written records, the poor quality of audio recordings, and the incomplete documentation of elicitation sessions. As the archive is so fragmentary, community knowledge is vital in making sense of its contents.

Keywords: archival repatriation, Noongar, Aboriginal, language revitalisation, music revival

Introduction

Although colonisation has decimated Aboriginal languages and song traditions in Australia, many Aboriginal communities are working with both senior knowledge-holders and archival documents to, as Aboriginal linguist Jeanie Bell (2002: 47) puts it, resist being "victims of a system that set out to destroy us." This chapter will discuss processes developed by an Aboriginal cultural organisation based in both an urban and rural region of Australia to consolidate, enhance, and share the group's endangered language, song tradition, and cultural heritage. In 2007, senior Aboriginal people belonging to the Wirlomin family clan from the south coast of Western Australia (WA) organised as Wirlomin Noongar Language and Stories Inc. (Wirlomin) in order to formalise longstanding efforts to maintain local Noongar culture and work on repatriated archival cultural material with the Noongar community. The six published bilingual stories Wirlomin have developed and illustrated so far – *Noongar mambara bakitj* (2011), *Maamang* (2011), *Dwoort baal kaat* (2013), *Yira boornak nyininy* (2013), *Noorn* (2017) and *Ngaawily nop* (2017) – originate from both archives and community knowledge. Today, more than a hundred people including the authors of this chapter are registered Wirlomin members.

Many of us formally gather a few times each year to share and build Noongar language, stories, and song, reconnecting fragmented elements of intangible cultural heritage and re-uniting them with Country. Our intention was, and is, to claim, control and enhance our heritage. We choose to do this by starting with a small community of descendants and pro-gressively sharing with ever-widening circles, employing the following staged process:

1. Connecting archival material with its home community of origin;
2. Interpreting and making decisions about this material as a dynamic group including the descendants of archival informants and contemporary language custodians;
3. Reconnecting story, language, and song to Country via visits to relevant sites; and
4. Sharing with the broader local community, visiting schools, and publishing books.

Although we have only applied this process in our south coast Noongar context, as will be described in more detail below, we feel it could be a useful model for groups working with similarly endangered Indigenous languages.

The status of Noongar language

In Australia, 669,900 Aboriginal and Torres Strait Islander people account for approximately 3 per cent of the nation's total population (Australian Bureau of Statistics 2017). The most recent National Indigenous Languages Survey indicates that only "around 120" of more than 200 Aboriginal languages are still spoken and that "about 13 can be considered strong" (Marmion, Obata & Troy 2014: xii). More than 30,000 Aboriginal people in the predominantly urban/rural southwest corner of WA identify as *Noongar* – also sometimes spelled *Nyungar* – a word meaning 'person', 'man', 'ally' or even 'mankind/humanity' in the local Aboriginal language and used today to refer to the Aboriginal people, country, language, and culture of the region (Douglas 1968). This constitutes one of the largest Aboriginal cultural blocs in Australia in terms of geography and population (SWALSC 2009; see Figure 1). Although the Noongar language remains critically endangered, consecutive Australian Bureau of Statistics census surveys recorded Noongar as a language spoken at home by 167 people in 1996 (McConvell & Thieberger 2001: 44); 196 people in 2001 (AIATSIS 2005: 75); 240 people in 2006; and 369 people in 2011 (Australian Bureau of Statistics 2017). It appears that language revitalisation movements since the 1980s have resulted in a slowly growing community of speakers, or at least a growing identification with the Noongar language.

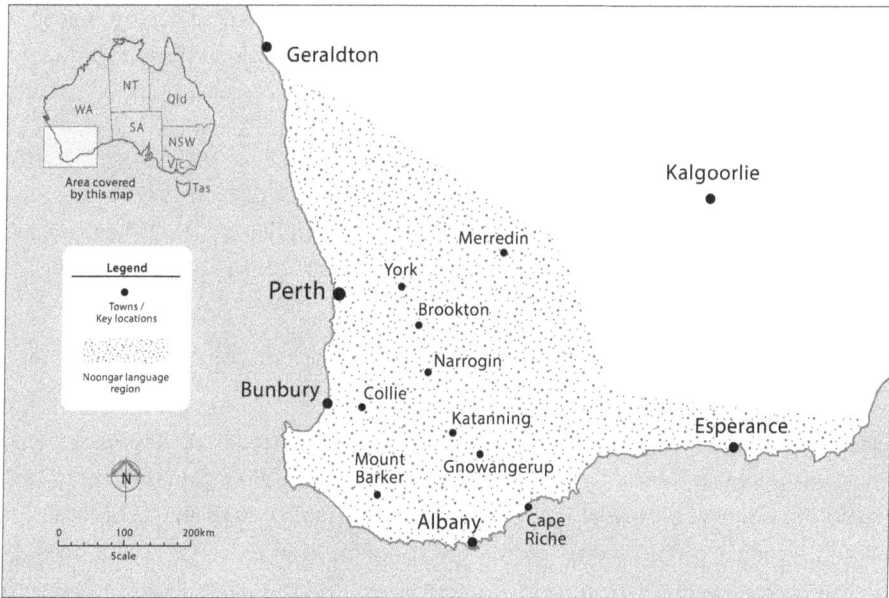

Figure 1. The Noongar language region of Western Australia and key locations mentioned in this chapter (map: Brenda Thornley)

A 1985 Noongar language conference at Marribank – also known as Carrolup – near the town of Katanning in the south of WA brought Noongar people interested in sustaining the language together with linguists such as Wilf Douglas, Alan Dench, and Nicholas Thieberger. At that time, there was a "a clear interest among members of the Noongar community to record what was still known among the older people and to pass that knowledge to younger people" (Thieberger 2004: 7). At a subsequent meeting in 1990 at Wellington Mills Recreation Camp, located in between the towns of Bunbury and Collie in southern WA, participants including the late language custodians Cliff Humphries, Ned Mippy, Kathy Yarran, Hazel Winmar, and Peter Farmer Snr worked together to create a Noongar language resource replete with sentences and songs, while officially recognising Noongar as a single language with three mutually intelligible dialects (Bunbury Noongar Aboriginal Progress Association 1990).

Two years later, a large-scale meeting was held with many of the same senior participants and the broader Noongar community at Narrogin, WA to reach agreement on a spelling system (Whitehurst 1992). Then a reporter for Golden West Network (GWN), Gina Williams recalls more than a dozen different possible spellings for the word *Noongar* being proposed during the meeting and remembers that "the bulk of the time was spent on deciding how best to spell that single word" (pers. comm., 19 October 2018). After hiding the Noongar language from authorities for so long, it must have been a difficult process for language custodians and their families to openly speak about it and reach consensus on its finer details. Although tensions were high, the group agreed upon a standard orthography, as "everyone in the room realised this was really important" (Gina Williams, pers. comm., 19 October 2018). Speaking about the senior language custodians involved, Williams states:

This was a time when everyone else thought Noongar language was dead. These people are still here – their voices resonate in this language and it is a privilege. These magnificent people were so generous with their knowledge. (Pers. comm., 19 October 2018)

These meetings informed the production of resources including the *Noongar dictionary* (Whitehurst 1992) and the *Noongar our way kit* (Wooltorton & Collard 1992) to support the introduction of Noongar language as a Language Other Than English (LOTE) subject in WA schools and a variety of other language education initiatives in ensuing years.

Wordlists and recordings

Many collections of transcribed Noongar words exist. British naturalist Robert Brown collected the first in 1801 at Albany (1800–1855) and Protector of Aborigines Charles Symmons authored a published grammatical description of the Noongar language in 1842. In the early 20th century (1904–1912), journalist and ethnographer Daisy Bates surveyed a large number of Noongar people across the southwest region to compile a series of diverse and detailed vocabularies, all of which are now accessible online (Thieberger 2016, 2017). American graduate student Gerhardt Laves became the first trained linguist to study Noongar when he visited Albany in 1931 as part of a broader study of Aboriginal languages. Laves (1929–1932) used the International Phonetic Alphabet (IPA) to transcribe stories told by speakers of the southeastern Noongar dialect – Kurin. His work languished in obscurity for more than half a century but has since been returned to Australia and undergone processes of community repatriation and digitisation (Henderson et al. 2006; Henderson 2008, 2013), and partially inspired the official establishment of Wirlomin Noongar Language and Stories Inc.

Linguist Ken Hale's (1960) interview with Tom Cowan and Tom Kickett at York, WA is possibly the first audio recording of Noongar language elicitation. Subsequently, Douglas (1964–1967) and CG von Brandenstein (1967–1970) made audio field recordings as part of their Noongar language research. All of this material is held at the Australian Institute of Aboriginal and Torres Strait Islander Studies (AIATSIS) archives today and together comprises less than five hours of Noongar speech. Douglas's significant 1960s fieldwork at Mount Barker, Gnowangerup, Narrogin, Brookton and Merredin – along with his continued collaboration with the community – underpinned a series of published Noongar vocabularies (1968, 1976, 1996), and Carl George von Brandenstein's time in Esperance, WA with Charlie Dabb and other Noongar speakers informed his published 're-created' vocabulary *Nyungar anew* (1988).

More recent recordings of Noongar conducted as part of language revitalisation projects are held at the AIATSIS archives with conditional access available (Thieberger 1986; Bunbujee 1989–1990). Additionally, 83 audiocassettes and 15 videocassettes featuring Noongar language custodian Cliff Humphries recorded and transcribed by Tim McCabe (1997) are held at the State Library of Western Australia, although access is presently restricted. Early this century, historian Bob Howard made a range of Noongar wordlists available online. He and Tim McCabe also produced audio recordings with Noongar speaker Alma Woods which are currently held at the Albany Public Library (Thieberger 2007: 62). Additional audio recordings of language elicitation with speakers including Lomas Roberts (McCabe & Miniter 2001), Hazel Brown

(Scott 2002) and Albert Knapp (Bracknell 2015) are held in our project archive and serve as documented evidence of the persistent presence of Noongar language.

Noongar language revival

Wirlomin is certainly not alone in its efforts to sustain Noongar as a spoken language. Noongar Boodjar Language Cultural Aboriginal Corporation operates out of Bunbury, WA and a small number of committed LOTE teachers provide Noongar language education at WA primary schools including Moorditj Noongar Community College. Noongar language classes are also offered by community organisations including the Langford Aboriginal Association and – due to the continued efforts of Tim McCabe to share the knowledge of the late Cliff Humphries – at least one prison. Community radio station Noongar Radio 110.9fm features Noongar language segments and the children's television program *Waabiny Time* on the National Indigenous Television Network showcases the language for a national audience, albeit at an early childhood level. Furthermore, actors from Yira Yaakin Theatre Company performed Shakespearean sonnets translated into Noongar at the Globe Theatre, London, UK in 2012, serving as a forerunner for a variety of youth education programs.

The Noongar language is still emerging from the devastation of an unjust recent colonial history. Many Noongar people literally had the language "flogged out of them" (Della Rae Morrison, pers. comm., 19 October 2018) and past government policies of assimilation implicitly denied basic human rights to Aboriginal people who spoke their languages in public (Haebich 2000). Recently there has been a rapid movement from denigration and wilful damage to something more like public interest, if not celebration, of the Noongar language, particularly in terms of its importance to all people in southwest Australia – not just the Noongar community – for identity and belonging. Within this context, it is reasonable to demand that Noongar stories and songs first be consolidated among, and shared from, the Noongar community. This belief guides the beginning of the Wirlomin process – returning archival material to its home community and providing empowering opportunities for language revitalisation.

Who are Wirlomin?

The Noongar word for bush stone curlew, *Burhinus grallarius,* is *wirlo* and -*min* is a suffix used to describe a collective of people associated with or similar to something. *Wirlomin* is used as a proper noun to name our clan, group and family. The *wirlo* is a predominantly nocturnal, skinny, long-legged and large-eyed bird that relies on camouflage for survival. When we visit schools, Hazel Brown sings out its eerie call to groups of children and delights in telling them how scared she was when she first heard its voice. As she says, *wirlo* can disguise itself so well you might never see it. Partly because of its blood-curdling call, some Noongar groups regard *wirlo* as a messenger of death. For us Wirlomin, it is a spiritual companion and, often being invisible, its defining characteristic is its voice. This vulnerable bird speaks from the realm of spirit to remind us of our place and of who we are. Noongar language can also function in that way.

Wirlomin is a communal identity used to refer to a particular Noongar community that is now stretched across a wide area of southern WA. Hazel Brown and Helen Hall are among the last of a generation of senior Noongar people who have ensured the survival of the term. Hazel Brown explains:

> Old great-great-grandmother's old father used to shout like a curlew, and disguise himself to look like a curlew. And that's why that family called themselves Wirlomin. *Wirlo*, that means curlew, see? And actually they're a very shy bird. You'll hear them, but you'll very seldom see 'em. Unless you're very quiet, very quiet ... (Scott & Brown 2005: 22)

She refers to a specific Wirlomin site and ritual:

> We got right in the swamp, freshwater, got right up there close, and just before we get towards where the old camps were, Daddy said, "You gotta stop here now and make a fire. You gotta make smoke and let 'em know that you're coming."
>
> So he cleared the ground and he got a little bit of dry grass and he dug a hole and he lit a fire. He had to be very careful 'cause it was summertime and we didn't have any water.
>
> The fire burned up and he chucked some green bushes on; and then the smoke, see. Soon as the smoke went up ... well, you shoulda heard the curlews, boy. Hear them singing out. They singing out over there, and then on this side. All around us ...
>
> Daddy sang out: "Wirlo wii wii wii ..."
>
> He said, "That's it, you're right now. That's the Wirlomin people letting us know. We're right now." And he just hit the two sticks together like that, and no more.
>
> We heard 'em, but we didn't see one. (Scott & Brown 2005: 24)

The *wirlo* may be hidden from view but heard by those who go through certain processes, wait and listen out. One might benefit from working with endangered Indigenous languages in a similar fashion.

The network of Noongar people connected to Wirlomin heritage covers a large area of ancestral country, ranging from approximately Cape Riche along a quite narrow strip of land reaching beyond Esperance. This area intersects with territory specified in the Tindale map (1974) as: *Koreng* – after the southeastern dialect *Kurin* (Laves 1929–1932); *Wudjari* – a term from the neighbouring Ngatju language, according to von Brandenstein (1988: 131); and *Njunga* – presumably one of the many alternate spellings of Noongar. The southeastern Noongar region is also referred to as *Ngokgurring* – 'shell' people (Taylor in Curr 1886: 392) and *Kwetjman* – 'boney' people (Douglas 1976: 6). More than anything, these names suggest a multiplicity of relationships between people and place.

Archives and the home community

Along with material collected from our senior people over the past 10 years or more, Laves' Noongar language fieldnotes have been crucial to Wirlomin language revitalisation activities. His notes were neglected until the 1980s when his family sent them to Australia to be placed under the guardianship of AIATSIS. In 2006, AIATSIS, John Henderson at the University of Western Australia and a reference group of Noongar people including descendants of Laves' informants and key stakeholders set in place an initial protocol for the return of the Laves material to its community of origin. Some of those in the reference group worried that it is one thing to suggest rules for who should control the access to those materials, but another thing altogether to find a way to genuinely return that material to a community of people descended from the informants, let alone consolidate it in ways that bring that community together.

As Wirlomin people, many of the individuals involved in the Laves reference group chose to band together and develop relevant material over a series of workshops under the guidance of elders descended from Laves' informants. Wirlomin committee member Iris Woods explains:

> We're very proud that our old people did come down to Albany and talk about their language. They sang in song, they talked about the history, but mainly stories. So everything was written down and recorded by this Laves. When I first laid eyes on the paperwork and saw that written material and Kim said this is what the story's about, it actually brought tears to my eyes because I was proud ... it's a treasure to me. (Pers. comm., 12 September 2015)

In 1931, Bob and Malcolm Roberts, Fred Winmer, Simon Williams, and George Nelly told Laves stories that would inspire many of the Wirlomin books.[1] Hazel Brown was only a child in 1931, and Bob Roberts was a young man. She and her siblings Lomas Roberts and Audrey Brown called all the informants 'uncle', and their father was brother to two of them (Bob Roberts and Malcolm Roberts) and brother-in-law to another two (George Nelly and Simon Williams). Gerald Williams was the son of Simon Williams. George Nelly had died when his children – Helen Hall and Russell Nelly – were still very young. Since we began this process, a number of Wirlomin people important to the return, consolidation and development of material have passed away, including Lomas Roberts, Audrey Brown, Gerald Williams Sr, Edward Brown Sr, Geoffrey Woods, Gerald Williams Jnr, and Russell Nelly. The aging of our senior people and the turbulence in our community means that there is no doubt we will lose more key people.

Wirlomin was incorporated in 2010 as an organisation with a cultural elders reference group (CERG) and committee. As a voluntary organisation, Wirlomin has relied on a diverse range of small federal and state government grants, plus support from two separate Australian Research Council projects, to continue its work. Longstanding Wirlomin committee members include senior Noongar language teachers Yibiyung Roma Winmar and Iris Woods, and Noongar cultural ambassador Ezzard Flowers, who had previously overseen the repatriation of the 1940s Carrolup paintings by Noongar children from Colgate University in the USA. Wirlomin is also indebted to the tireless efforts of non-Indigenous committee secretaries Mary Gimondo and Lefki Kaillis as generous collaborators in the cross-cultural team so important to an organisation like this.

In recent years, the Wirlomin CERG has expanded from its initial focus on representing the senior descendants of Laves' informants in order to facilitate work with archival audio recordings. CG von Brandenstein's (1967–1970) field recordings at Esperance feature captivating – although poorly recorded – performances of Noongar song by brothers Charlie and Sam Dabb (Bracknell 2017). As the children of Sam Dabb and nephew and niece of Charlie Dabb,

---

1   *Noorn* (2017) is based on a story Tinjel Fred Roberts told to his great-grandson Ryan Brown.

Henry and Annie Dabb guide the process of working with this material. Albert Knapp is also now a member of the CERG after graciously sharing two old Noongar songs – and one of his own composition – with Wirlomin members at a number of meetings and workshops. Every year, Wirlomin members review the CERG members group and nominate new members in order to ensure solid cultural governance for working with heritage material.

Making decisions

The Wirlomin CERG provides archival material with a grounding in cultural context and kin. Wirlomin committee member Yibiyung Roma Winmar describes the process of workshopping the Laves material with the elders:

> Well, everyone came down here to Albany to return the stories back to the descendants. All the families that were involved and the family groups came together. We sat down and went through the manuscripts word by word actually. And people'd say, "Yeah, I remember that, and this is the way it's said," and it was, well, people cried and cried some more, you know with happiness and, well, relief, because there was a time when our language was suppressed and now here we have it back from somebody else. Gifted back more or less overseas to come back to West Australia. It was unexpected. And then I think you sort of realise how much you had valued it and how much you'd missed out on. (Pers. comm., 12 September 2015)

Guided by the CERG, Wirlomin workshops involve the gradual interpretation of archival heritage material and the group working together to reach consensus on orthographic and semantic issues. For example, Laves wrote the surname of his 1931 informant Fred Winmer as *Windmill*, *Williams*, and *Winmer*. Sometimes it has been written elsewhere as *Winmar*. Elders of our group preferred the spelling *Winmer* to reflect their sense of how it should be pronounced. This was only one of many discussions about how we might best match the spelling and sound of a particular word.

The IPA Laves employed in his notes is hard to read, and rather idiosyncratic. His notes have no punctuation, and often no translations. We studied the current standards for IPA and, after applying it to transcriptions of recordings of Lomas Roberts, Cedric Roberts, Audrey Brown, and Hazel Brown speaking Noongar language, went through parts of Laves' transcriptions with some of the elders identified as being related to the informants. Lomas Roberts had heard parts of some of the stories before, recognising words and phrases, although he was befuddled by some of the text and said some of the language did not sound right.

There seemed to have been changes in Noongar language in the 70 plus years since Laves had made his notes. When pronouncing a particular word in the way indicated by Laves' script, Lomas Roberts' elder sister Hazel Brown said, "Yes," with a look of surprise, "we used to say it like that" (pers. comm., 15 January 2007). Occasionally, the elders pointed out mistakes that Laves appeared to have made in translation. Often, they were reminded of stories and anecdotes, or encouraged the group to talk about things that may otherwise have been neglected. Even in the early stages of this process, it was easy to see the value-adding quality of bringing together archives and elders.

Linguist John Henderson (2008) had digitised and converted Laves' manuscript to search-able typescript, making the material far easier to read and work with. However, in a Noongar community workshop setting, using digital files projected up onto a screen at the front of the room imposed a counterproductive classroom-like structure on proceedings. Alternatively, transcribing the material in Laves' notes onto butcher paper facilitated a more dynamic and flexible workshop environment. The butcher paper could be put on the floor in the centre of an inner circle of elders, with others gathering outside, coming in and moving away. The elders would pick up pens and scribble over the paper, making corrections.

Some of our most recent workshops focused on interpreting Charlie Dabb's songs recorded by CG von Brandenstein (1967–1970). The small group involved included Henry and Annie Dabb, Gaye Roberts, Roma Winmar, Iris Woods, Justin Miniter, and the authors. Before the workshops, we edited the songs and relevant metadata out of the long, digitised field recordings. As a group, we spent whole days meticulously listening to each lyric on repeat and at various different speeds using Transcribe! software. We would make annotations and corrections on lyric sheets, often using our own personal orthographic conventions.

At one point, we were puzzled. It seemed as if Charlie Dabb was singing the English word *white* at the beginning of a song. The original tape recordings sounded sped up, dubbed at a higher speed, so we reduced the speed and pitch of the audio back to something sounding more like what the original performance would have sounded. After this modification, we heard more nuanced vowel sounds and a few consonants that had not previously been noticeable. Henry Dabb asked for confirmation of where the song had been recorded (Pink Lake, near Esperance, WA). Then he suggested that his uncle Charlie Dabb was not singing *white* but *waalitj*, a Noongar word for the wedge-tailed eagle. This discovery opened up an understanding of the rest of the lyrics, which had once seemed obscure but were suddenly revealed to be describing an eagle hanging in the sky.

Contextualising in Country

As longstanding Wirlomin member Olivia Roberts explains, "Every story that we share actually has got a place so we're mapping back to where we and where our rellies [relatives] used to go" (pers. comm., 12 September 2015). During the first cycle of the process to claim, control and enhance our heritage – culminating with the publication of *Maamang* (2011) and *Noongar mambara bakitj* (2011) – we filmed Hazel Brown and Lomas Roberts taking us to places that connected with the stories we had developed, and to old camping and dancing grounds and other sites along the south coast of Western Australia that were important to them. Fifty copies of an edited version of that film were distributed at the start of our second cycle of workshops. In late 2012, we visited one of the sites where the core version of *Dwert baal kaat* (2013) belongs, and retold it with its text of rocks, earth, and water as our witness. Some of us visited some of the more remote sites associated with this story in 2015 and 2018 with support from South Coast Natural Resource Management, a government organisation.

Yibiyung Roma Winmar played a major role in putting *Ngaawily nop* (2017) together, helping with the text and also, with her daughter, Alta, doing the illustrations. Yibiyung came with us when we took the story to its origin landscape, and although it is part of her ancestral country she had never been there before:

> It's very emotional. I feel full. I feel full of tears, I feel full of joy. It's hard to explain, like when somebody's been away for a very long time and they've returned on a journey and you rush out to meet them and there's all these hugs and tears and ... The project now has enabled me to come to these places ... It's a spiritual journey, to be walking this way again, reinforcing that bond to Country. (Wirlomin Noongar Language and Stories Inc. 2010)

In an Aboriginal context, the term 'Country', written with a capital letter, signifies land, sea, and sky as "nourishing terrain" (Rose 1996: 1): alive, multidimensional, and intertwined with local Aboriginal people and culture. Embedded with aspects of an ancient worldview associated with its place of origin, an Aboriginal language is one of the most powerful manifestations of the spirit of Country.

Sharing with the broader Noongar community

Before the publication of each Wirlomin book, we have held an event at the Noongar Centre in Albany, WA, featuring an exhibition of the book illustrations as artwork, photographs from all the workshops so far, and a reading of each of the stories. We have also ceremoniously handed out advance copies of the books, sometimes including a CD of the stories being read aloud in Noongar language to the Cultural Elders Reference Group and other individuals who represented key families in the Albany Noongar community. Our intention was to celebrate the stories, as well as to create a sense of community ownership and a situation where individuals might find employment in schools and other places because of their knowledge of both the stories and the process of their creation. More than this, we wanted to use these stories to bind a community together rather than allow rivalry over our collective heritage to exacerbate other community tensions and tear us apart, as sometimes happens in oppressed communities. We hoped the people who received the stories would share them with their family and friends.

As part of the process of returning stories to their home community and sharing them from there, we have also given presentations at local schools. These sessions usually begin with an introduction of ourselves as Wirlomin Noongar, an illustrated explanation of our process, then the sharing of some of the published stories and one or two songs. The team of presenters has varied slightly as individuals felt ready to take on greater roles, and has always included elders. These presentations placed some of us in a novel position: non-Indigenous people were listening avidly to what we had to say, and grateful for what we were sharing. Judging by the enthusiasm with which Noongar students introduced themselves to our group, and the extent to which they wished to share stories told in their own families, many other Noongar people also felt proud.

Although some among our group of presenters have teaching experience, most of those involved had little prior experience of presenting like this, certainly not as a group. At the end of a string of visits to south coast schools in 2012, Wirlomin member Connie Moses said, "I'm just so proud to be part of the journey. We are a team ... we're growing together. I just can't wait to get up and dance and sing. It's just so wonderful to hear everyone speak" (Scott & Nelly 2013: 35). Iris Woods noticed increased group cohesion as the week progressed, stating: "It was deadly because we did it all and we were a group, one and all. You could feel the power among us" (Scott & Nelly 2013: 35). Ezzard Flowers acknowledged the highly charged and visceral nature of the presentations, observing the need to "acknowledge where each of us are at emotionally, spiritually and socially, because that can affect your performance too" (Scott & Nelly 2013: 35). Russell Nelly stressed the personal significance of Wirlomin Noongar Language and Stories Inc. as part of his journey of connecting to heritage and family:

> All you people here, you're my family whether you realise it or not. I wanna tell you it's a privilege to share what we feel with the kids ... I get emotional at times, but when I get emotional I'm listening to the old fellas. Because they're talking to me, along with them talking to you guys ... Wirlomin is not just a name. Prior to this I was lost. I had circumnavigated Australia three times looking for my identity and it brought me all the way back to Katanning. I heard of the Wirlomin mob. I thought, no they don't want me. That's all changed now. We've got something tangible. What we've lost, we are resurrecting it. So, my people, we go with our heads up high, proudly. (Scott & Nelly 2013: 35)

Evidence of community development via developing and sharing stories and language is implicit in these observations. Decolonisation is a word some might also apply to this work (Araluen 2017): shaking off some of the legacy of oppression, and reconnecting with cultural heritage so as to heal and strengthen ourselves today. Neither 'community development' nor 'decolonisation' are commonly used in our community, but their conceptual heft is recognised.

Conclusion

A small minority of the original Noongar population survived the first 50 years of colonisation (from 1829) (Aboriginal Legal Service 1995). Western Australia was then home to an apartheid-like regime until deep into the 20th century (Haebich 2000). Noongar language, and the Noongar community itself, is still recovering from that. This is the fundamental basis for the kind of work described here. Australia is a stolen country. Noongar language was nearly taken from us. The circumstances in which Noongar cultural heritage was decimated demand that language revitalisation be undertaken as part of a process to empower Noongar people. This is possible by starting with a small 'home community' and progressively sharing with ever-widening circles. The fragmented and incomplete nature of archival records relating to the Noongar language emphasises the need for those within its home community of origin to make corrections, add missing metadata and make informed decisions about their cultural heritage material. In revitalising language by running it through living Wirlomin Noongar bodies, we make ourselves instruments for this deep, spiritual heritage that thousands of generations have entrusted to us in this part of the world.

References

Aboriginal Legal Service of Western Australia. 1995. *Telling our story: A report by the Aboriginal Legal Service of Western Australia (Inc.) on the removal of Aboriginal children from their families in Western Australia*. Perth: Aboriginal Legal Service of Western Australia.

Araluen, Evelyn. 2017. Resisting the institution. *Overland* 227. 3–10.

Australian Bureau of Statistics. 2017. *Statistics*. (http://www.abs.gov.au) (Accessed 4 March 2019.)

Australian Institute of Aboriginal and Torres Strait Islander Studies (AIATSIS). 2005. *National Indigenous languages survey report*. Canberra: Department of Communications, Information Technology and the Arts.

Bates, Daisy. 1904–1912. Papers of Daisy Bates in the south-west of Western Australia. MS/365, Series XII Language: Grammar and vocabularies. Canberra: National Library of Australia.

Bell, Jeanie. 2002. Linguistic continuity in colonised Country. In John Henderson & David Nash (eds.), *Language in Native Title*, 43–52. Canberra: Aboriginal Studies Press.

Bracknell, Clint. 2015. Unpublished digital audio recording of a Wirlomin reference group meeting at Yardup, WA, April 2015. Albany: Wirlomin Noongar Language and Stories Inc. Collection.

Bracknell, Clint. 2017. *Maaya waab* (play with sound): Song language and spoken language in the south-west of Western Australia. In Jim Wafer & Myfany Turpin (eds.), *Recirculating songs: Revitalising the singing practices of Indigenous Australia*, 45–57. Canberra: Asia Pacific Linguistics.

Brown, Robert. 1800–1855. Papers and correspondence of Robert Brown [microform], M1193, M2494–2496. Canberra: National Library of Australia.

Bunbujee, Kelly. 1989–1990. Interviews for Nyungar Language Project, stories, oral history, songs, language elicitation, recorded in Bunbury and Collie. BUNBURY_01 (011413–011419). Canberra: AIATSIS Audiovisual Archive.

Bunbury Noongar Aboriginal Progress Association. 1990. *Nyungar nyinalanginy wangkininy: Nyungar language conference*. Bunbury: Bunbury Noongar Aboriginal Progress Association.

Curr, Edward. 1886. *The Australian race: Its origin, languages, customs, place of landing in Australia, and the routes by which it spread itself over that continent*. Melbourne, Vic: Government Printer.

Douglas, Wilfred. 1964–1967. Language elicitation, narratives and songs from south-west Western Australia. DOUGLAS_W01 (A001322–A001324). Canberra: AIATSIS Audiovisual Archive.

Douglas, Wilfred. 1968. *The Aboriginal languages of the south-west of Australia: Speech forms in current use, and a technical description of Njunar*. Canberra: Australian Institute of Aboriginal Studies.

Douglas, Wilfred. 1976. *The Aboriginal languages of the south-west of Australia*. Canberra: Australian Institute of Aboriginal Studies.

Douglas, Wilfred. 1996. *Illustrated dictionary of the south-west Aboriginal language.* Claremont, WA: Edith Cowan University.

Haebich, Anna. 2000. *Broken circles: Fragmenting Indigenous families 1800–2000.* Fremantle: Fremantle Arts Centre Press.

Hale, Ken. 1960. Balardung and Mirning language elicitation. OGRADY-HALE_01 (014053–014055). Canberra: AIATSIS Archive.

Henderson, John. 2008. Capturing chaos: Rendering handwritten language documents. *Language Documentation & Conservation* 2(2). 212–243.

Henderson, John. 2013. Language documentation and community interests. In Mari Jones & Sarah Ogilvie (eds.), *Keeping languages alive: Documentation, pedagogy, and revitalization*, 56–68. Cambridge: Cambridge University Press.

Henderson, John, Hannah McGlade, Kim Scott & Denise Smith-Ali. 2006. *A protocol for Laves' 1931 Noongar field notes.* Perth: UWA and AIATSIS.

Laves, Gerhardt. 1929–1932. Papers of Gerhardt Laves. MS/2189, Items 2.18–2.27. Canberra: AIATSIS Archive.

Marmion, Doug, Kazuko Obata & Jakelin Troy. 2014. *Community, identity, wellbeing: The report of the second national Indigenous languages survey.* Canberra: AIATSIS.

McCabe, Tim. 1997. Cliff Humphries' recorded archives of Noongar traditional songs, stories and words. OH4151. Perth: State Library of Western Australia.

McCabe, Tim & Jason Miniter. 2001. Unpublished cassette tape recording with Lomas Roberts. Albany, WA: Wirlomin Noongar Language and Stories Inc. Collection.

McConvell, Patrick & Nick Thieberger. 2001. *State of Indigenous languages in Australia 2001.* Canberra: Department of the Environment and Heritage.

Rose, Deborah Bird. 1996. *Nourishing terrains: Australian Aboriginal views of landscape and wilderness.* Canberra: Australian Heritage Commission.

Scott, Kim. 2002. Unpublished cassette recording with Hazel Brown. Albany, WA: Wirlomin Noongar Language and Stories Inc. Collection.

Scott, Kim & Hazel Brown. 2005. *Kayang and me.* Fremantle, WA: Fremantle Arts Press.

Scott, Kim & Ryan Brown. 2018. *Noorn.* Crawley: UWA Publishing.

Scott, Kim & Russell Nelly. 2013. *Dwoort baal kaat.* Crawley: UWA Publishing.

Scott, Kim & Lomas Roberts. 2011. *Noongar mambara bakitj.* Crawley: UWA Publishing.

Scott, Kim & Iris Woods. 2011. *Mamang.* Crawley: UWA Publishing.

Scott, Kim, Hazel Brown & Roma Winmar. 2013. *Yira boornak nyininy.* Crawley: UWA Publishing.

Scott, Kim, Roma Winmar & Joyce Cockles. 2018. *Ngaawily nop.* Crawley: UWA Publishing.

South West Aboriginal Land and Sea Council (SWALSC). 2009. *Settlement agreement.* (http://www.noongar.org.au) (Accessed 4 March 2019.)

Symmons, Charles. 1842. *Grammatical introduction to the study of the Aboriginal language of Western Australia.* Perth: Western Australia Almanack.

Thieberger, Nick. 2004. *Linguistic report on the single Noongar Native Title claim.* Perth: SWALSC.

Thieberger, Nick. 2016. Daisy Bates in the digital world. In Peter K Austin, Harold Koch & Jane Simpson (eds.), *Language, land and song: Studies in honour of Luise Hercus*, 102–114. London: EL Publishing.

Thieberger, Nick. 2017. *Digital Daisy Bates.* (http://bates.org.au)

Tindale, Norman. 1974. *Aboriginal tribes of Australia: Their terrain, environmental controls, distribution, limits, and proper names.* Berkeley: University of California Press.

von Brandenstein, Carl Georg. 1967–1970. Songs, messages, texts and language elicitation from south-eastern Western Australia, 1967–1970. VON-BRANDENSTEIN_C04 (A002150–A002159), Tape 35 (002158B 002159A) and Tape 37 (002159A). Canberra: AIATSIS Audiovisual Archive.

von Brandenstein, Carl Georg. 1988. *Nyungar anew: Phonology, text samples and etymological and historical 1500-word vocabulary of an artificially recreated Aboriginal language in the south-west of Australia.* Canberra: Pacific Linguistics.

Whitehurst, Rose. 1992. *Noongar dictionary: Noongar to English and English to Noongar.* Bunbury, WA: Noongar Language and Cultural Centre.

Wirlomin Noongar Language and Stories. Inc. 2010. Unpublished DVD video of fieldtrip to Doubtful Island Bay. Albany, WA: Wirlomin Noongar Language and Stories Inc. Collection.

Wooltorton, Sandra & Glenda Collard. 1992. *Noongar our way.* Bunbury, WA: Noongar Language and Culture Centre.

Index

www.ingramcontent.com/pod-product-compliance
Lightning Source LLC
Chambersburg PA
CBHW081048280326
41928CB00054B/3167